Parties under Pressure

Parties under Pressure

The Politics of Factions and Party Adaptation

MATTHIAS DILLING

The University of Chicago Press
Chicago and London

The University of Chicago Press, Chicago 60637
The University of Chicago Press, Ltd., London
© 2024 by The University of Chicago
Published 2024

33 32 31 30 29 28 27 26 25 24   1 2 3 4 5

ISBN-13: 978-0-226-83023-0 (cloth)
ISBN-13: 978-0-226-83025-4 (paper)
ISBN-13: 978-0-226-83024-7 (e-book)
DOI: https://doi.org/10.7208/chicago/9780226830247.001.0001

Library of Congress Cataloging-in-Publication Data

Names: Dilling, Matthias, 1987– author.
Title: Parties under pressure : the politics of factions and party adaptation /
    Matthias Dilling.
Description: Chicago : The University of Chicago Press, 2024. |
    Includes bibliographical references and index.
Identifiers: LCCN 2023050821 | ISBN 9780226830230 (cloth) |
    ISBN 9780226830254 (paperback) | ISBN 9780226830247 (ebook)
Subjects: LCSH: Partito della democrazia cristiana. | Österreichische Volkspartei. |
    Christlich-Demokratische Union Deutschlands. | Political parties. | Political party
    organization. | Political parties—Europe—Case studies. | Christian democracy—
    Europe. | Comparative government.
Classification: LCC JF2051 .D56 2024 | DDC 324.2094—DC23/eng/20231228
LC record available at https://lccn.loc.gov/2023050821

Contents

Illustrations

Figures

Tables

Abbreviations

ACLI Associazioni Cristiane dei Lavoratori Italiani (Christian Association of
Italian Workers)

ADR Alternativ Demokratesch Reformpartei (Alternative Democratic Reform
Party)

AFD Alternative für Deutschland (Alternative for Germany)

ARP Anti-Revolutionaire Partij (Anti-Revolutionary Party)

BHE Bund Heimatvertriebener und Entrechteter (League of Expellees and
Deprived of Rights)

CCD Centro Cristiano Democratico (Christian Democratic Center)

CDA Christen-Democratisch Appèl (Christian Democratic Appeal)

CDS-PP Centro Democrático e Social–Partito Popular (Democratic and Social
Center–People's Party, initially founded as CDS)

CDU Christlich Demokratische Union Deutschlands (Christian Democratic Union
of Germany)

CHU Christelijk-Historische Unie (Christian Historical Union)

CISL Confederazione Italiana Sindacati Lavoratori (Italian Confederation of
Workers' Unions)

CSU Christlich Soziale Union in Bayern (Christian Social Union in Bavaria)

CSV Chrëschtlech Sozial Vollekspartei (Christian Social People's Party)

DC Democrazia Cristiana (Christian Democracy)

DP Deutsche Partei (German Party)

EAK Evangelischer Arbeitskreis (Protestant Working Group), a faction in
Germany's CDU

EXIL-CDU Christlich Demokratische Union im Exil (Christian Democratic
Union in Exile), an association in the early CDU recognized as representing the
Christian Democrats escaped or expelled from the Soviet occupation zone or
German Democratic Republic

FDP Freie Demokratische Partei (Free Democratic Party, Germany)

FPÖ Freiheitliche Partei Österreichs (Freedom Party of Austria)

GVP Gesamtdeutsche Volkspartei (All-German People's Party)

KVP Katholieke Volkspartij (Catholic People's Party)

LDP Jiyū-Minshutō (Liberal Democratic Party)

MIT Mittelstands- und Wirtschaftsunion (Union for Small and Medium-Sized Businesses and the Economy); initially named Bundesarbeitskreis Mittelstand (Federal Working Group for Small and Medium-Sized Businesses), a faction in Germany's CDU

MP Member of Parliament

MRP Mouvement Républicain Populaire (Popular Republican Movement)

ÖAAB Österreichischer Arbeiter- und Angestelltenbund (Austrian League of Blue- and White-Collar Workers); later renamed Österreichische Arbeitnehmerinnen- und Arbeitnehmerbund (Austrian League of Employees), an auxiliary organization in Austria's People's Party

ÖBB Österreichischer Bauernbund (Austrian Farmers' League), an auxiliary organization in Austria's People's Party

ÖVP Österreichische Volkspartei (Austrian People's Party)

ÖWB Österreichischer Wirtschaftsbund (Austrian Business League), an auxiliary organization in Austria's People's Party

PCI Partito Comunista Italiano (Italian Communist Party)

PDP Parti Démocrate Populaire (Popular Democratic Party)

PDR Rietspartei (Party of the Right)

PDS Partito Democratico della Sinistra (Democratic Party of the Left)

PLI Partito Liberale Italiano (Italian Liberal Party)

PPI Partito Popolare Italiano (Italian People's Party)

PRD Partido de la Revolución Democrática (Party of the Democratic Revolution)

PRI Partito Repubblicano Italiano (Italian Republican Party)

PSDI Partito Socialista Democratica Italiano (Italian Democratic Socialist Party)

PSI Partito Socialista Italiano (Italian Socialist Party)

RPF Rassemblement du Peuple Français (Rally of the French People)

SFIO Section française de l'Internationale ouvrière (French Section of the Workers' International)

SPD Sozialdemokratische Partei Deutschlands (Social Democratic Party of Germany)

SPÖ Sozialdemokratische Partei Österreichs (Social Democratic Party of Austria); 1945–1991: Sozialistische Partei Österreichs (Socialist Party of Austria)

VVD Volkspartij voor Vrijheid en Democratie (People's Party for Freedom and Democracy)

PART I

Problem and Theory

1

The Puzzle: The Varying Substance and Speed of Party Adaptation

I believe that dangers await only those who do not react to life.
MIKHAIL GORBACHEV (1989)

Around the world established political parties face mounting pressures. The rise of populism and radicalism, changes in countries' class structures and people's religious practices, and new policy concerns around mass migration, public health crises, and climate change have eroded many parties' traditional strongholds and challenged them to find new ways of mobilizing support. The rise and diversification of social media have reinforced those pressures, calling for new formats to communicate political messages and facilitate participation. The very fact that many established parties from the left to the right have responded to these changes by passing at times far-reaching programmatic and organizational reforms underlines Peter Mair's (1997) seminal verdict that political parties can be incredibly adaptable organizations.[1] However, party adaptation is far from being uniform. From Austria to Japan, parties have varied in the extent to which they have been able to reform their platform or organization in response to environmental changes. While Austria's People's Party (ÖVP) struggled for nearly fifty years to reform its corporatist organization and agrarian platform when facing diversifying societal interests, Germany's Christian Democratic Union (CDU) abandoned many traditional positions and shifted some power over candidate selection to party members after national reunification transformed the country's demographic structure. Unlike Italy's similarly dominant and corrupt Christian Democratic Party (DC), Japan's Liberal Democrats adapted to an economic crisis and corruption scandal by centralizing the party's organization and passing public-sector reforms. In Latin America, Argentina's Peronists and Brazil's Workers' Party shifted toward market-liberal positions and expanded clientelist practices (Hunter 2010; Levitsky 2003), whereas many other labor parties failed to adapt to their shrinking trade-union base (Morgan 2011; Seawright 2012).

Why do some parties adapt meaningfully to social, economic, and political transformations while others struggle to do so? This question is of paramount importance for the quality (and perhaps even survival) of democracy. Of course, party adaptation is not automatically good for democracy. Programmatic or organizational reforms might reflect the views of fringe or radical elements, as recently seen in Rachel Blum's (2020) study of the Tea Party's capture of the GOP in the early 2010s in the United States. However, the absence of party adaptation almost certainly weakens democracy. E. E. Schattschneider's (1942) argument still holds that political parties are a cornerstone of modern democracies. They exist to aggregate people's interests and translate them into political decisions. Over time, they provide democracies with an element of predictability and stability by creating expectations about the preferences they represent. They thus facilitate voters' decision-making and the interaction among politicians. Parties that do not pass meaningful reforms, or that do so only with a significant delay, risk fueling people's dissatisfaction and face a heightened risk of declining or disappearing. Italy's DC, Austria's ÖVP, Venezuela's Democratic Action Party—all these parties either disappeared or shrunk significantly when failing to adapt to their new environment, and radical and populist parties seized the space that opened up (e.g., Bufacchi and Burgess 1998; Morgan 2011; Müller et al. 2004). Their rise has allowed nativist and illiberal language and positions to enter the political mainstream and has entailed a global wave of democratic backsliding (Haggard and Kaufman 2021). When several parties in the same system face pressure to adapt, the aggregation of their responses (or lack thereof) tend to transform the entire party system (Morgan 2011; Seawright 2012). Explaining why established parties vary in their ability to adapt is thus of crucial importance for the resilience of democracy at large and the topic of this book.

To approach this question, the book proposes redeeming a concept that has historically held a bad reputation in party politics—*party factions*, defined as organized internal groups with no formal ties to the central party. Party factions have predominantly had a poor reputation since Madison's ([1787] 1961) essay on the evil of factionalism.[2] Treated as synonymous for internal divisions, factions have been associated with weakening a party's ability to avoid fragmentation and respond to grievances (e.g., Ceron 2012, 2015; Coppedge 1994, 47; Katz 1980, 3, 6; Kitschelt et al. 1999, 136–37; Van Kersbergen 1995, 29). However, all parties are collective actors in that, as Giovanni Sartori (1976, 72) explained, they are "an aggregate of individuals forming constellations of rival groups." Party adaptation is fundamentally about parties' ability to mediate between these groups and aggregate their preferences into a single set of choices. What does the party stand for? Which voters should

the party try to mobilize? How should those voters be mobilized? Agreeing
on answers to these questions is challenging for any party. Party factions importantly influence how well parties are equipped to do so. Factions differ
from other types of groups within political parties, like territorial branches or
youth organizations, in that they organizationally span across party branches
and are free to form, rearrange, and disappear without the party's approval.
This organizational pervasiveness and flexibility matter for adaptation in two
ways. Factions can help integrate different views by connecting actors across
different branches of the party. They can also support innovation by enabling
new groups to rise and new ideas to circulate. A proliferation of competing
factions, however, risks paralyzing parties' internal decision-making. In other
words, not only an extremely low level but also an extremely high level of
factionalism weakens a party's ability to adapt, whereas a moderate level of
factionalism supports it. This book aims to show why and how.

What Is Party Adaptation?

Party adaptation refers to the intentional changes a party makes to its offering to voters in response to changed environmental conditions in order to
meet its primary goals (Levitsky 2003, 9; see also Gauja 2016, 19; Harmel and
Janda 1994, 265; Levy and Bruhn 2006, 98). When Angela Merkel took the
podium on 2 December 2003, the delegates to the party congress of her Christian Democratic Union had just passed far-reaching reforms. In response to
the 1998 election defeat the party had suffered for its handling of Germany's
economic downturn in the 1990s, the CDU abandoned its long-held support
for a welfare state with high levels of social spending and embraced market-
liberal positions. Its new program called for, among other things, replacing
the linear-progressive income tax with a simple three-stage rate and a raise in
the retirement age. Organizationally, the CDU shifted some power over selecting candidates for party and public office from party functionaries toward its
members. When the new platform was less popular than expected, the party
moderated its economic positions and instead embraced a socially progressive course. This was not the first time the CDU had reinvented itself. Initially including a notably left-wing orientation after World War II, the party's
platform moved to the right to fight off rising challengers in the 1950s. In the
1960s and 1970s, the CDU responded to the shrinking of its traditional base of
churchgoing Catholics by formulating its first comprehensive party program,
professionalizing its organization, and stimulating membership recruitment.
    Party adaptation is not the same as success, survival, or vote share. Clas-
sifying a party as having adapted because it was successful while suggesting

that it was successful because it had adapted would be circular reasoning. Instead, this book captures variation in party adaptation by drawing on Anika Gauja's (2016) distinction between the subject, substance, and the speed of reform. The *subject of reform* refers to areas that members of the party's decision-making bodies have identified as requiring changes in response to environmental transformations. Although what constitutes pressure for reform varies across parties depending on their history and context (Cyr 2017, 65; Levitsky 2003, 9; Morgan 2011, 51), party elites often have a good idea of the challenges that require adaptation. For instance, parties might have to change the type (e.g., from clientelist to programmatic) or content (e.g., from redistribution to market liberalism) of their offers to voters or adjust their organization to incorporate new social groups. Unlike the party's rank and file, party elites, including the party leader, other members of the party's leadership board, and the delegates to national decision-making bodies, usually have the power to introduce reforms (Gauja 2016, 14–16).[3]

The changes party elites introduce are the *substance of reform*. Elites with divergent preferences and support bases are usually involved in parties' discussions over what and how to adapt (Seawright 2012, 23). These discussions often entail conflict, leading to the watering down of proposals or even gridlock. As a result, parties might fall short of fully addressing the areas they identified as requiring reform. For instance, to stop their party's dependence on clientelism and corruption, Italy's Christian Democrats discussed changing the rules for selecting party congress delegates to reduce factions' incentives to pay local brokers, downsizing the leadership board to facilitate decision-making, and empowering the DC's regional branches over national factions. Internal conflicts, however, resulted in only a fraction of the proposals being introduced. The *speed of reform* reflects how swiftly the proposed changes are introduced. Some time lag is likely. Most political parties are complex organizations, and deliberations take time. Still, while Germany's Christian Democrats managed to introduce the aforementioned reforms within five years of their crushing 1998 defeat, Austria's Christian Democrats required nearly twenty years after their 1990 defeat to introduce meaningful parts of the proposed reforms, many of which the party had been discussing since the 1960s. Such proposals often emerge around catalytic events, like election defeats or scandal, and this book traces how long it took parties to introduce (parts of) them following such events.

The substance and speed of "adaptive reforms" are thus the indicators of party adaptation that this book relies on. This conceptualization allows for "reading history forward" (Capoccia and Ziblatt 2010, 943). Although party elites often know what they need to adapt to, they cannot know with certainty whether particular reforms will pay off electorally. Defining adaptation in electoral terms thus not only would risk introducing an element of circularity but also would rule out the potential of actors miscalculating reforms' effects. They might overestimate their popularity among voters or, as Lupu (2016) demonstrated, be punished for diluting the party's traditional branch and subsequently performing poorly in office. It is consequently possible for parties to adapt (i.e., introduce the reforms identified as needed and do so relatively quickly) but still lose votes. Moreover, politics is a lot about people and human agency, but there might be situations when the party simply does not have the "right" hand. The magnitude of the *mani pulite* (clean hands) corruption scandal in Italy played an important role in the Italian Christian Democrats' demise. At that stage, it would have been difficult for any party to adapt. However, this book evidences that the corruption scandal was largely endogenous to the DC's very high level of factionalism and that the party's low ability to adapt had already become obvious well before the scandal erupted. Simply looking at (the number of) reforms would also not capture adaptation. Many organizational changes in political parties have been the result of path-dependent reinforcement of early organizational choices (e.g., Bentancur, Rodríguez, and Rosenblatt 2020; Krauss and Pekkanen 2011). In contrast, adaptive reforms relate to changes made in response to external events like scandals, election defeats, or dramatic shifts in public opinion and often require parties to break with previous practices.

Explaining Party Adaptation

Analytically, the variation in party adaptation points toward an important puzzle around political parties and modern democracies more broadly. The populism and backsliding literature typically paints the picture of established parties that struggle to adjust to environmental changes and are pushed aside by new organizations and movements (e.g., Haggard and Kaufman 2021; Mudde 2007, 2019; Zielonka 2018). Studies of party change, in contrast, have shown that political parties can adapt to strategic reform incentives (e.g., Mair 1997; Harmel et al. 1995; Harmel and Janda 1994). Parties as diverse as the UK Conservatives, the Liberal Party of Australia, and the French Socialists have passed far-reaching reforms to their platforms and organizations in response to election defeats, changes in rival parties, and scandals—especially when they were free from the constraints of government (e.g., Bale 2012; Gauja 2016). The mere presence of strategic motivators, however, is not sufficient to explain party adaptation, which leaves underexplored why some parties, like Germany's CDU, changed relatively quickly after a defeat, whereas others, like

Austria's People's Party, required four or more consecutive election defeats to do so or, like Italy's DC, did not pass any meaningful reform. Although Sartori (1966, 1976) suggested that the presence of strong antisystem parties to the left and right might restrict centrist parties to pursuing very similar positions and coalitions, his work is more about the vulnerability of democracy than of political parties. Even when facing bipolar opposition, parties can decide—and in fact have decided—to realign their platform (Capoccia 2005).

Why do some parties fail to adapt or do so only with a significant delay even when facing strategic incentives for reform? A prominent approach has focused on the institutional constraints on *party leaders' autonomy*. There are good reasons to expect party leaders to be among the most reform-friendly actors within political parties as they face the immediate pressure to perform well at the next election or be replaced (Lupu 2016, 32). In contrast, conventional wisdom dating back to John May's (1973) "special law of curvilinear disparity" suggests that giving too much power to lower-rank party elites and members would hinder reform because they tend to be more committed to the party's traditional positions.[4] Wiliarty (2010, 2) has thus rightly outlined that party adaptation is usually associated with an organization that disempowers members and empowers party leaders. Centralizing power in the hands of leaders or preventing the routinization and entrenchment of vertical accountability mechanisms to begin with has thus often been seen as essential for adaptive reforms (Kirchheimer 1966; Kitschelt 1994; Levitsky 2003; Ziblatt 2017).

The leadership autonomy argument focuses on party adaptation against party activists, but Sarah Wiliarty (2010) and others have emphasized a path toward adapting with party activists, which serves as the starting point for this book's argument. This line of argument stresses political parties' collective nature, as parties typically bring together people with different political preferences. The individuals coming together in the same party often form, join, or are sorted into *groups within their party* because they live in the same part of the country, come from the same sociodemographic background, or uphold similar political views.[5] Such intraparty groups, like local party branches (Bentancur, Rodríguez, and Rosenblatt 2020; Ellinas 2020), women's associations (Wiliarty 2010), and legislative caucuses and factions (Bloch Rubin 2017; DiSalvo 2012), have played a key role in party adaptation by helping parties identify and aggregate important preferences. However, not all internal organizations are equally useful for party adaptation. Although forming special groups for particular target constituencies, like women or particular professions, and incorporating them in the party's decision-making bodies can facilitate incorporating particular interests, Morgan (2011) has warned that formally incorporating special interests into the party's organizational structure often backfired. Such formally incorporated groups often refuse to let go of their privileged position when their electoral relevance declines. This book shows that party factions, by lacking such formal ties to the central party, provide parties with greater flexibility in incorporating special interests than other types of intraparty groups.

The emergence, development, and persistence of intraparty groups points toward a broader puzzle around the development of political institutions. Integrating different preferences has been a core challenge for virtually all political parties (Aldrich 1995; Levitsky 2003, 12; Seawright 2012, 23), and parties usually set up specific rules, often referred to as institutions, for this purpose (Panebianco 1988). Initial rules regulating the incorporation of special interests often become deeply entrenched as a result of learning and coordination effects and adaptive expectations, guiding subsequent institutional choices and making setting up new rules increasingly costly (Anria 2019; Bentancur, Rodríguez, and Rosenblatt 2020; compare Pierson 2000a, 253–54). Actors who refuse to play by these rules risk being gradually marginalized even in initially unrelated aspects of intraparty politics (Krauss and Pekkanen 2011; compare Page 2006). Adaptive reforms, especially when concerning the privileges of intraparty groups, have been difficult (Hunter 2010), and we should thus see path-reversing change attempts to dissipate over time as actors increasingly endorse the existing rules. This expectation, however, clashes with the frequent pushes for substantive reforms and the changes we observe in many parties (e.g., Faucher 2015; Gauja 2016; Wauters 2014; compare Mahoney and Thelen 2010). While the same territorially based and occupational groups have dominated in Austria's People's Party and Venezuela's Democratic Action Party for decades, Italy's DC saw the rise and fall of numerous intraparty groups over the fifty years of its existence. In contrast, some intraparty organizations persisted in the CDU, whereas others rose and subsequently declined, and Japan's Liberal Democrats saw a shift in the internal balance of power from factions to its prefectural branches in the mid- to late 1990s. Institutional approaches can thus be improved by specifying which conditions favor change over stability in the way parties incorporate societal interests and how that influences party adaptation.

This Book's Argument and Main Contributions

To make such a contribution, this book combines recent work on factionalism with a historical-institutionalist analysis of party organizations to explain the extent to which and how quickly parties adopt adaptive reforms. Its main argument advances in three steps.

First, factions, while sometimes vilified, differ from other types of intraparty organizations in important ways that can enhance party adaptation by providing the flexibility for old interests to decline and new interests to rise within political parties. Parties' organizations are composed of vertical and horizontal levels, which include their membership associations, national headquarters, and representation in public office (Eldersveld 1964; Katz and Mair 1993). Factions facilitate connecting party elites and members across party levels, in contrast to parties' territorial branches (e.g., in specific regions or provinces) or legislative camps or caucuses, which are, by design, much more limited in this regard. Their *organizational pervasiveness* supports the integration of social and political groups by connecting actors across different branches of the party. Moreover, unlike the auxiliary organizations that parties often include for young people, women, or different occupational or ethnic groups, factions are neither set up nor sanctioned by the party but depend only on the alliances party elites are able and willing to forge. Their flexibility supports innovation by giving a platform to new or previously minor groups. They can thus facilitate adaptation by supporting elite renewal, incorporating new grievances, and building coalitions around new policy positions.[6] However, a proliferation of factions is likely to undermine the party's internal gatekeeping mechanisms and lead to more and more groups seeking to influence decisions.[7] The relationship between the level of factionalism and party adaptation is thus likely to be inverted U-shaped. Very high and very low levels of factionalism hinder party adaptation, whereas a moderate level of factionalism supports adaptation. The level of factionalism refers to the extent to which factions rather than other types of groups, like local party branches or auxiliary organizations, dominate the party's internal decision-making. The number of factions and the share of members of party assemblies, the cabinet, and the legislature who belong to a faction allow capturing this.

Second, parties' early organizational choices importantly shape their subsequent level of factionalism. The literature on the causes of differences in factionalism has been notoriously fragmented and often focused on country-level factors like the electoral system (see chapter 2). By formulating observable expectations for different institutional, structural, and cultural variables and carefully tracing at which stage in the causal process they play a role, the book highlights the fact that a party's initial internal institutions have a notable effect on party elites' decision to form and join factions rather than relying on other types of intraparty organizations. Among the many choices party elites make when forming their organization, a party's initial set of rules to select its national leaders is likely to be particularly important for its subsequent level of factionalism because those rules affect which type of internal groups party elites are likely to rely on to assume leadership positions. This book shows that this logic goes beyond the selection of the individual party leader. The more leadership positions, including the party secretary and other members of its leadership board, are elected by a central assembly that brings together delegates from different organizational branches of the party, the more important alliances between elites from different party branches and the higher the level of factionalism will be.

Third, changing a party's level of factionalism is often difficult because it can leave key decision-makers in a dilemma. Failing to adapt to a changed environment often entails electoral decline or even collapse and thus threatens party elites' political career. We would therefore expect that party elites, in order to protect their career, seek changes within the party that moderate levels of factionalism. However, actors with the power to promote such reforms are likely to have benefited from the party's level of factionalism. That level of factionalism is likely to become deeply entrenched within the party as party elites try to strengthen their own internal networks through campaigning, clientelism, and changes to the party's organization. Parties with very high and very low levels of factionalism thus provide their elites with conflicting incentives. Factionalism's effects on party adaptation is negative, but its effect on the elites' holding party leadership positions has been positive. In such cases, changing the level of factionalism will not be impossible but difficult. In contrast, party elites in moderately factionalized parties do not face this dilemma because the effects of moderate factionalism on both their prospects of holding leadership positions and party adaptation are positive. Chapter 2 provides the microfoundations for the origins, development, and effects of different levels of factionalism on party adaptation and contrasts the argument with competing explanations. This three-step argument is based on two scope conditions. Political parties need to allow for internal competition and have formal rules that regulate the selection of the party leadership. Personalistic parties in which the party leader can simply bypass internal rules as well as communist, sectarian, and other parties that suppress intraparty pluralism are therefore not part of my universe of cases.

By analyzing how factionalism can create incentives for both organizational change and stability and how that affects party adaptation, this book makes a novel contribution to the study of political parties and institutional development. It is the first systematic look at the development and effects of different levels of factionalism on parties' ability to adapt to a transformed environment. It integrates insights into party change, organization, and factionalism with recent advances in the study of political institutions. This book shows that variation in factionalism explains why election defeats, public scandals, and changes in a party's dominant internal coalition do not unequivocally propel reform. It contributes to the party change and party organization literature by highlighting the effect of factions, in contrast to other types of intraparty groups, on parties' ability to integrate special interests and innovate traditional positions and structures. By demonstrating a relationship between the level of factionalism and party adaptation that has an inverted U shape, the book mediates between DiSalvo's (2012) view of factions as important "engines of change" and Boucek's (2012) and Ceron's (2019) findings that factions can block change.

The book also contributes to insights into the value of resources for party adaptation. Cyr (2017) has shown how parties can use their organizational and ideational resources to cope with environmental transformations. By focusing on the varying trajectory of parties with a well-developed ideological brand and organization, the book shows that a party's level of factionalism crucially influences its ability to capitalize on available resources to adapt to a changing environment. It also plays an important role in explaining whether a party is able to transform its ideological brand, something Lupu (2016) has shown to be highly relevant for a party's trajectory.

Moreover, this book seeks to contribute to overcoming the strange fragmentation of the study of party politics. Research on party change and organization has traditionally been divided into studies on so-called advanced industrial democracies (e.g., Bale 2012; Gauja 2016; Kitschelt 1994), on the one hand, and so-called developing democracies, on the other hand (e.g., Bentancur, Rodríguez, and Rosenblatt 2020; Cyr 2017; Hunter 2010; Morgan 2011). Differences in party competition in different parts of the world certainly continue to exist. However, several parties in, for example, Latin America, have shown to be highly adaptable (e.g., Bentancur, Rodríguez, and Rosenblatt 2020; Hunter 2010; Levitsky 2003), whereas the more recent decline of many old parties has reinforced doubts over European parties' adaptability (e.g., Przeworski 2019; Zielonka 2018). Dividing the field along geographical lines has thus become highly debatable, and the book shows how drawing on insights developed in the study of Latin American politics importantly enhances our understanding of the varying adaptation of parties in Europe.

Finally, the book integrates recent advances in the study of institutional development with the literature on party organization to address a theoretical paradox. Previous books have drawn on path dependence, positive feedback effects, and negative externalities to explain why the same type of intraparty groups have often persisted within political parties (Anria 2019; Bentancur, Rodríguez, and Rosenblatt 2020; Krauss and Pekkanen 2011). If positive feedback effects or negative externalities explained why factions persisted in some parties and were absent in others, we would expect attempts to change the level of factionalism to dissipate over time as more and more actors adapt to the practices in place. This view, however, does not account for the frequent reform attempts and some parties' departures from traditionally dominant internal groups (e.g., Faucher 2015; Wauters 2014). In contrast, the scholarship on incremental institutional change would expect actors to pass reforms that would change the incentives to form or join factions if the current level of factionalism does not correspond to contextual demands (Greif 2006; Mahoney and Thelen 2010). This book bridges the party organization literature's focus on path dependence and the literature on incremental institutional change to account for political parties' organizational stability and change when under pressure to adapt.

Cases and Methodology

Empirically, a key challenge in evaluating different explanations for party adaptation is that the changes to which parties need to adapt are highly context dependent (e.g., Cyr 2017, 65; Gauja 2016, 16; Levitsky 2003, 9; Morgan 2011, 51). For instance, differences across party families influence what constitutes pressure for parties to adapt and the range of options available to them. The decline of religion as a driver of political behavior in Europe has been a key challenge to Christian democratic parties, while representing an opportunity for center-left and radical-right parties to infringe upon Christian Democracy's labor and national-conservative constituencies. In turn, Christian democratic parties' cross-class catch-all appeal has typically provided various potential directions for reform (Frey 2009), whereas left-wing parties' working-class history has usually limited them in the extent to which they could, for instance, introduce austerity measures in response to economic crises.[8] Consequently, identifying and tracing the changes to which parties need to respond, their varying reform proposals in response to these changes, and their internal dynamics around which, when, and how much of these proposed reforms were eventually implemented require in-depth knowledge of individual parties. Studies of party adaptation have thus often come in the form of in-depth single case studies (e.g., Anria 2019; Bale 2012; Bentancur, Rodríguez, and Rosenblatt 2020; Hunter 2010; Krauss and Pekkanen 2011).

At the same time, this book contends that it is possible to show why and how particular factors, and not others, explain the variation in the substance and speed of adaptation across a well-defined set of parties. This variation is particularly well illustrated by short periods of profound political change, like the COVID-19 pandemic, the 2008 financial crisis, or the rapidly unfolding collapse of Europe's Communist regimes, as they entail immediate pressure for parties to get their act together. The 1990s and early 2000s were a series of short episodes of such profound change for an entire party family: Western European Christian Democracy. These parties were one of the dominant political forces in European politics after World War II. While their roots in political Catholicism usually made them socially conservative, transnationalist, and antimaterialist, their religiously inspired views provided them with an inherently cross-class appeal (Accetti 2019; Van Kersbergen 1994, 35–42). Their catch-all character has led many scholars to consider these parties to be particularly well equipped to adapt to different demands (Van Kersbergen 1995, 29; 1999, 354; Conway 2001, 306–7; Frey 2009). Yet many of them could not cope when the fall of European communism suddenly required them to respond to increasing migration following the Balkan wars, the loss of anticommunism as a mobilizing issue, and economic and political challenges resulting from European integration (fig. 1.1).

Focusing on the varying adaptation of Christian democratic parties allows for studying the trajectory of parties that have experienced very similar moments of profound environmental transformations. This facilitates within-case analysis by ensuring that actors were operating under similar contextual conditions, that key concepts travel across cases, and that the argument's scope conditions are met. It also redresses a lacuna in the study of European politics because Christian Democracy has been substantially understudied compared to other party families. Since Kalyvas's (1996) seminal book on the origins of Christian Democracy, we find very few book-length studies at all.[9] This gap is consequential because Christian Democracy is essential to understand European politics. Alongside Social Democracy, Christian democratic parties were the pivotal governmental parties in Western Europe after 1945 and had a significant influence on establishing and consolidating constitutional democracies, a moderate version of market economy, and European integration (Conway 2022; Kaiser 2007; Müller 2011, chap. 4; Van Kemseke 2006). Finally, their varying level of adaptation and factionalism is surprising given what we might expect from these parties' cross-class, catch-all character. This book shows that in several alternative explanations, we would expect cases to adapt that did not and cases to fail to adapt that adapted. Christian democratic parties thus nicely echo the broader puzzle around party adaptation that motivates this book.

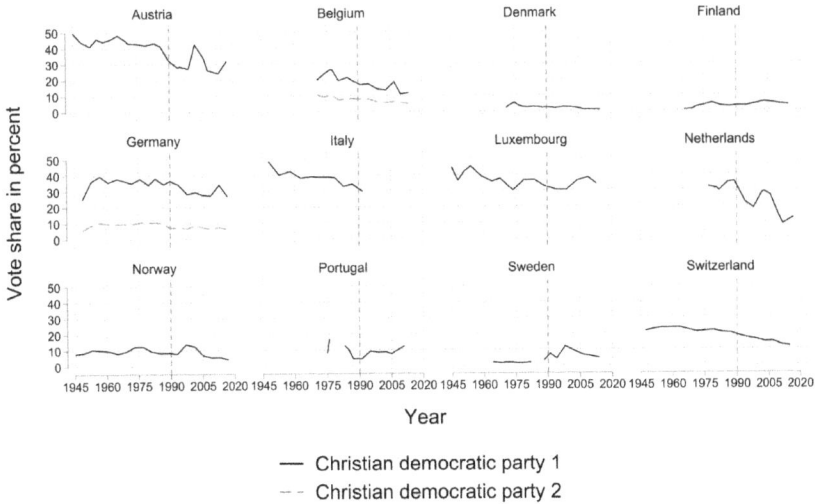

FIGURE 1.1. Christian democratic parties' vote share before and after 1990

Source: Armingeon et al. (2022) and Nordsieck (2021) for results under 2 percent. Austria: Austrian People's Party (ÖVP). Belgium: Christian People's Party (CVP, called Christian Democratic and Flemish since 2001), Social-Christian Party (PSC, called Humanist Democratic Center after 2002). Denmark: Christian People's Party (KRF). Finland: Finnish Christian League (SKL, called Christian Democrats since 2001). Germany: Christian Democratic Union (CDU), Christian Social Union (CSU). Italy: Christian Democracy (DC). Luxembourg: Christian Social People's Party (CSV). Netherlands: Christian Democratic Appeal (CDA). Norway: Christian People's Party (KRF). Portugal: Democratic and Social Center (CDS, People's Party added in 1993). Sweden: Christian Democratic Unity (KDS, called Christian Democrats since 1996). Switzerland: Swiss Conservative People's Party (CVP, called Christian Democratic People's Party of Switzerland since 1970).

The book uses crises as important focal points to frame the puzzle and identify key episodes because variation in party adaptation becomes particularly visible during such times, but its argument also sheds light on the causes of party adaptation in a more continuous perspective. Political parties almost continuously face the challenge to adapt. For instance, we must not assume postwar Christian Democracy's catch-all appeal to be a given. When most of these parties emerged as new organizations after World War II, one of the core challenges they faced was integrating social-Catholic, liberal, and national-conservative interests while keeping left- and right-wing competitors in check. Already at that stage, as well as in their response to the gradual erosion of their rural-religious constituencies in the 1960s and 1970s, these parties displayed notable variation in their ability to adapt, and this book's argument also helps explain that variation in their history. This book thus follows a comparative-historical approach that focuses on the trajectory of a single party family over time. It traces the trajectory of individual parties while keeping an eye on any pattern that links a cause to the variation in party adaptation across these cases. It combines the comparative and country-specific literature in political science and history with a rich record of archival material, including minutes of party meetings, party statutes, manifestos, campaign and press material, and key politicians' personal notes and correspondence collected in eight archives in four European countries. This allows for the use of solid historical evidence when assessing the observable expectations of the book's framework against alternative explanations.

Because the concept of party adaptation does not easily lend itself to quantitative measures, this book takes inspiration from Kitschelt (1994, 3–4) to probe the plausibility of its argument for the Christian democratic parties that competed elections before and after 1990. To measure how well social democratic parties adapted to changes in European societies, Kitschelt used the difference between their average electoral performance in the 1970s and the 1980s. The rationale is that, although party adaptation is not a sufficient condition for party success, a party that fails or requires several electoral cycles to pass reforms when facing environmental pressure to do so is likely to lose votes over time. I compare the change in Christian democratic parties' vote share in legislative elections before 1990 (i.e., 1945 to 1989) and after 1990, taking 2017 as the end point for studying their adaptation to the transformations of the early 1990s.[10] I use the relative rather than absolute change in parties' average vote share to account for parties' different baselines and plot that together with the level of centralization of the parties' initial leadership selection process as the factor that is expected to drive their level of factionalism.

Even though the small number of cases prohibits statistical significance tests, figure 1.2 provides a strong graphic representation of the book's argument and encourages an in-depth investigation of selected parties. Twelve of thirteen parties for which data are available support the predicted curvilinear relationship.[11] Among the parties close to the fitted line, Italy's DC, Austria's ÖVP, and Germany's CDU provide the best conditions for an in-depth comparison. They emerged in the aftermath of World War II and in countries where prewar democracy had been replaced by a right-wing authoritarian system. All three parties brought together actors from the social-Catholic working class, the liberal middle class, and the discredited conservative right. They followed strong Catholic predecessor parties, could build on support of the Catholic Church, and quickly assumed a dominant position in their respective party systems, which gave them access to offices, public contracts, and funds to reward supporters. They were also all in government when the key transformations of the 1990s occurred. Tracing these parties' history since their inceptions in the 1940s shows that their varying levels of adaptation depended on their level of factionalism and the initial rules to select their leaders rather than, for example, party institutionalization or centralization as factors shaping leadership autonomy.

This book assesses these findings' portability beyond the three main cases in two steps. First, it evaluates the argument for additional cases that have been close to the line in figure 1.2 and that provide fruitful conditions for a structured comparison. Second, it expands the focus to a different period and region by investigating France's Popular Republican Movement (MRP) and Japan's LDP. The French MRP was one of the major Christian democratic parties in the first years after World War II but dissolved in 1967 after failing to adapt its platform and organization to the escalating Algerian crisis and major changes in the political system. The case provides good conditions to test my theory in a different context while still sharing many party-family-related characteristics. The LDP is particularly insightful because its history can be divided into two very different parts: a long period of struggle to adapt to the changes in Japanese society and several corruption scandals, and the post-1994 period of successful adaptation. Whether facing similar or quite different contextual conditions, these cases display remarkable similarities to the book's main cases regarding the link between early organizational choices, factionalism, and party adaptation.

Chapter Overview

The following chapter prepares the empirical analysis by presenting a new theory that integrates recent research on factionalism with insights from historical institutionalism to explain variation in party adaptation. The chapter formulates observable expectations for each step of the book's three-step argument linking early organizational choices to different levels of factionalism and party adaptation. It also formulates testable expectations for the book's main competing account—the level of leadership autonomy—and other alternative expectations relevant at different stages of the causal chain.

Part 2 focuses on the main cases. Chapter 3 explains why Italy's DC failed to pass significant reforms when facing profound transformations in Italian politics in the early 1990s despite the party leadership's notable autonomy from lower-level party bodies. It shows that the DC's lack of adaptation is not unequivocally explained by the magnitude of the "clean hands" corruption scandal. The latter was endogenous to the DC's high level of factionalism and poor adaptation before 1992, which originated in the politics behind the

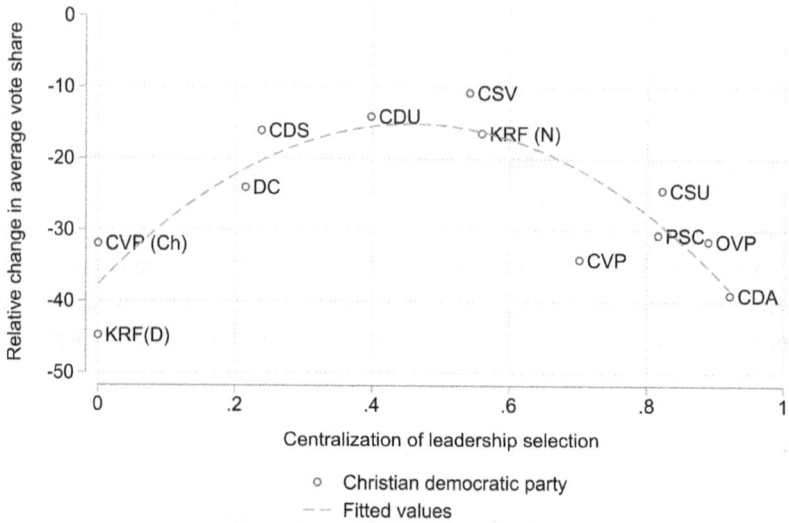

FIGURE 1.2. Initial leadership selection and relative change in vote share

Electoral performance: Relative change in average vote share between 1945 to 1989 and 1990 to 2017. For example, the Dutch CDA lost almost 40 percent when comparing its average vote share before and after 1990. The DC did much worse than losing 24.1 percent of its pre-1990 average vote. It competed in only one election after 1990, when its vote share dropped below 30 percent for the first time in its history. Because the DC was so deeply divided over questions of party reform, it split several times, massively declined in the 1993 local elections, and ultimately dissolved in 1994. Centralization of the initial leadership selection process: I use data from the parties' first statutes and Rae's (1967, 53–58, 62) fractionalization index. The degree of centralization equals $F = 1 - \Sigma(S_i)^2$, where S_i refers to the proportion of seats each party branch is entitled to fill on the party's leadership board. It ranges from 0 to 1. Higher values express a higher degree of decentralization of the selection process.

choice of a centralized leadership selection in 1946. While Italy's DC demonstrates why and how too much factionalism hinders party adaptation, chapter 4 shows that giving no room to factions also weakens a party's ability to adapt. Austria's People's Party experienced extended periods in opposition and electoral decline, for which its static neo-corporatist platform and organization was blamed. And yet it took the party decades to implement meaningful reforms. While the ÖVP was the most rigidly institutionalized party among the book's main cases, the chapter shows that an exclusive focus on the institutional constraints party leaders faced leaves important questions open about the causal process leading to a relatively poor record of adaptation—questions the book's factionalism argument helps address. Chapter 5 evidences why and how a moderate level of factionalism supported adaptation within Germany's CDU. The chapter shows how party leaders enjoyed much lower autonomy than previously suggested even for the party's most successful period in the 1950s and how and why the party's moderate level of factionalism enabled adaptation at several key moments before and since 1990.

Part 3 evaluates the portability of the book's insights beyond the Christian Democrats in Italy, Austria, and Germany. Chapter 6 tests the book's argument for three additional cases from the same party family and time period. Chapter 7 applies the book's argument to two parties that have been challenged to adapt under quite different contextual conditions. By increasing cross-case variation on the type of environmental transformations alongside institutional and structural conditions, this chapter probes the argument's scope. The trajectory of France's MRP reveals important similarities to the development of Austria's ÖVP. Japan's LDP echoes many insights that chapter 3 outlines for Italy's DC but also allows for identifying the conditions under which parties can escape the fate of high levels of factionalism and, post-1994, shows similarities to Germany's CDU.

The theoretical and empirical parts of the book generate important lessons for the comparative study of party change, party organization, factionalism, and institutional development. The conclusion discusses these implications. They suggest a perspective on party adaptation that combines a focus on the specific challenges to which parties need to adapt with their level of factionalism and the conflicting incentives the latter can create for parties' key decision-makers. It is by disaggregating these incentives and analyzing the effects different levels of factionalism create that we can better understand what guides parties' ability to adapt to profound societal and political transformations.

2

The Theory: Factionalism, Party Adaptation, and Multilevel Path Dependence

At any given moment, politics is situated on multiple "paths," each of which contributes
to the array of the choices available to actors.

LIEBERMAN (2002, 704)

Why do some political parties manage to reform in response to a new societal or political context, whereas other parties fail to make adaptive reforms, introduce only minor changes, or take significantly longer to introduce them? Answering this question requires considering the politics *within* political parties. Party leaders and activists often hold different political views (Enos and Hersh 2015; Kitschelt 1989a; Lupu 2016, 30–34; May 1973). A prominent argument in the literature therefore expects adaptation to be easier the more autonomy from activists party leaders enjoy to introduce reforms. Scholars of European party competition have typically associated this view of party adaptation *against* activists with the centralization of decision-making powers in the hands of party leaders (Kirchheimer 1966; Ziblatt 2017, 41–44), whereas Steven Levitsky (2003) and other Latin Americanists have associated leadership autonomy with weakly institutionalized accountability mechanisms within parties.[1]

In contrast, this chapter presents an alternative theory that emphasizes party adaptation *with* activists. It builds on recent studies that have shown how the internal groups that party leaders and activists often form can support parties in responding to environmental changes by identifying and aggregating important societal signals and facilitating internal reform coalitions (e.g., Bentancur, Rodríguez, and Rosenblatt 2020; Bloch Rubin 2017; DiSalvo 2012; Ellinas 2020; Wiliarty 2010). The theory presented in this chapter expands on the existing approach in four ways. First, it shows that factions differ from other types of intraparty groups in important ways for party adaptation. While historically having a bad reputation, their organizational flexibility and pervasiveness make factions more suitable to respond to

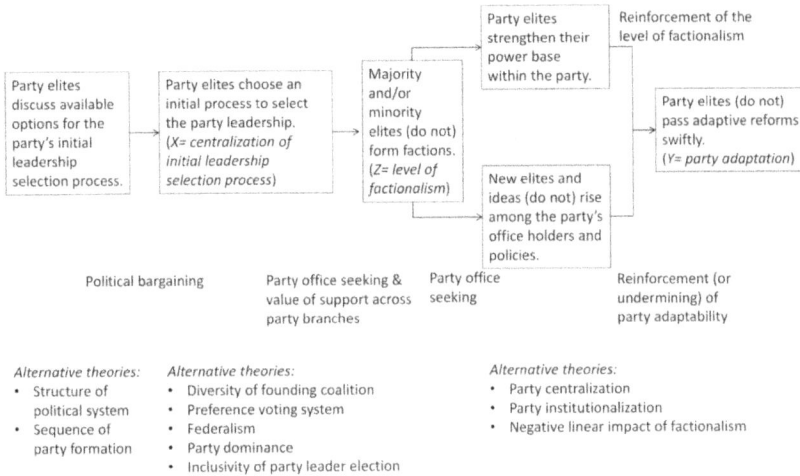

FIGURE 2.1. Causal chain and alternative explanations

changing societal conflict lines and facilitate the rise of new leaders and ideas than parties' territorially based branches or special organizations for socio-demographic groups. Within limits, factions thus importantly support party adaptation. Second, the chapter draws on historical-institutionalist approaches to explain the extent to which, why, and how factions, compared to other in-traparty groups, emerge, develop, and persist within political parties. Third, by drawing on historical-institutionalist insights prominent in the study of Latin American politics to shed light on the varying adaptation of parties in other parts of the world, the theory contributes to overcoming the strange fragmentation of the study of party politics along geographical lines. Fourth, although several recent accounts have highlighted parties' organizational and ideational resources as important for coping with environmental transforma-tions (e.g., Anria 2019; Bentancur, Rodríguez, and Rosenblatt 2020; Cyr 2017), this chapter explains why and how a party's level of factionalism crucially influences parties' ability to capitalize on their available resources to adapt to a changing environment.

The remainder of this chapter outlines why and how the focus on the ori-gins, development, and effects of different levels of factionalism is important for enhancing our understanding of the causes of varying party adaptation. Preparing the process analysis in the book's subsequent chapters, the chapter engages with different alternative explanations as they arise along the causal process (fig. 2.1).

Factions and the Politics of Leadership Selection

Factions differ from other types of intraparty groups in important ways for party adaptation.[2] The individuals coming together in the same political party often form, join, or are classified into groups because they live in the same part of the country, share particular sociodemographic characteristics, or uphold similar political views. Factions are one example of such groups. Other examples include parties' territorial or administrative branches; their special auxiliary organizations for women, young people, or particular professions; or less organizationally pervasive groups like tendencies, legislative caucuses, or local cliques. Such intraparty groups are essential for the operation of modern political parties because, similar to the party itself, they help resolve various collective action and coordination problems (e.g., Aldrich 1995; Bloch Rubin 2017; Sartori 1976, 72). In contrast to parties' administrative branches and auxiliary organizations, factions but also tendencies, caucuses, and cliques typically emerge without the approval or even knowledge of the party leadership or headquarters (Bloch Rubin 2017, 3; Skocpol and Williamson 2012, 89; Leonardi and Wertman 1989, 98).[3] Unlike tendencies, caucuses, or cliques, factions have a more formal organization that connects members and facilitates collective action across different parts of the party (table 2.1). A party is characterized by a higher level of factionalism the greater the number of factions within that party and the higher the seat share factions rather than other types of intraparty groups control on different party bodies.

Why do factions become the predominant type of internal groups within some parties but not in others? Bloch Rubin (2017, 16) has rightly highlighted that setting up their own dissident organizations, rather than relying on those with central party support or sponsorship, "requires a considerable outlay of time, creative energy, and material resources." We thus require an explanation for why the incentives to invest in developing factions outweigh the incentives to rely on other types of intraparty groups. If factions were the legacy of preexisting groups (e.g., Panebianco 1988; Capperucci 2010), we would expect factions to form along previous group lines and factional structures to spread across party levels as party formation progresses. Because federalism provides party elites with career paths outside of national-level politics (Carty 2010, 143), we might expect a lower level of factionalism in federal than in unitary polities as party elites focus more on building subnational camps rather than factions. We would also expect to see a similar level of factionalism in parties operating under similar political systems. Relatedly, if the level of subnational autonomy drove the level of factionalism, we would expect to see fewer factions with more decentralized power across subnational units

TABLE 2.1. Factions in contrast to other intraparty groups

		Organizational pervasiveness	
		Yes	No
Organizational flexibility	**Yes**	Factions	Camps (including caucuses, cliques, and tendencies)
	No	Auxiliary organizations	Party branches

Source: Dilling (2023).

in federal states. If factions emerged in dominant parties as a substitute for interparty competition (e.g., Arian and Barnes 1974; Boucek 2012; Key 1949), we would expect factionalism to emerge once a party's dominant position in government has been established and to observe a similar number of factions across dominant parties. If high factionalism was endogenous to the availability of clientelist resources (e.g., Chalmers 1972; Zuckerman 1979), we would expect a similar number of factions across cases where such means are available, especially when combined with a preferential voting system (Ames, 1995; Carey and Shugart 1995). If factions developed out of preexisting local clientelist networks, factions should emerge from the bottom up rather than the top down. If a preferential voting system triggered the emergence of factions (e.g., Pasquino 1972), we would expect constituency candidates to support their campaigns for preference votes by forming factions. Alternatively, if factions emerged because national party elites wanted their supporters to get elected to the legislature, we would expect factions to emerge in the run-up to legislative elections. In contrast, a closed-list proportional representation system should discourage factions (Carey 2007; Carey and Shugart 1995).

A diverse founding coalition, a preferential voting system, federalism, and party dominance explain incentives for competition between members of the same party, but party disunity does not equal factionalism. Apart from federalism, which might dampen conflicts at the national level, these factors do not explain why political actors would rely on factions rather than on other types of intraparty groups. To explain this, other studies have looked at political parties' internal rules but with mixed results. Several studies suggested that a smaller selectorate when choosing the party leader would lead to a higher level of factionalism by requiring winning over fewer people to produce a majority and thus decreasing the costs of faction building (Ceron 2019; Krauss and Pekkanen 2011; Thayer 1969). However, drawing on Olson's (1965) theory of collective action, Bloch Rubin (2017) showed that smaller groups are more likely to collaborate informally rather than building formally organized groups, and Ceron's (2019, 77) comparative analysis has also found little support for this argument. Similarly, we might expect fewer factions the more centralized control the party leader has over making policies, allocating funds, and selecting candidates because she could threaten to expel or deselect candidates who are active in (rival) factions (Carey 2007). However, Carty's (2010) work suggests that building and sustaining factions is less costly in centralized than in decentralized parties, thus making us expect to see higher factionalism under centralization. Finally, proportional internal electoral rules plausibly stimulate factionalism (Sartori 1971, 1976; Ceron 2019), but factions have often emerged already before such rules have been introduced (Leonardi and Wertman 1989, 109–10).

My argument is that the more centralized a party's initial process to select its leadership board, the higher its initial level of factionalism is likely to be because the centralization of the party's leadership selection process affects where party elites are likely to look for support in their struggle for power.[4] Focusing on the election of the party leader is too narrow to explain different levels of factionalism, because the pie that party elites compete for is often larger than only the position of the party leader (e.g., Bentancur, Rodríguez, and Rosenblatt 2020, 8, 12). The leadership in most parties is a collective rather than a single actor, including a range of offices alongside the individual party leader (e.g., Poguntke 1998, 2000). Together, they form the party's leadership board, or national executive, which is the supreme governing body and often holds the effective decision-making authority within the party (Poguntke 2000, 105–10, 126).[5] Although party elites are surely reluctant to follow rules that do not suit their interests (Duverger 1951, 76; Sartori 1976, 84; Panebianco 1988, 35), the rules and procedures organizing the selection of the party leadership can hardly be ignored completely—especially because party elites have an incentive to detect rivals who are not playing by the rules (Bentancur, Rodríguez, and Rosenblatt 2020, 18; Katz and Mair 1992, 6). Party elites may informally agree on the allocation of posts before formal meetings (Kriechbaumer 1995a, 34; Bösch 2001, 266–67), but the way the leadership board is selected likely influences who will be included in such informal networks.[6]

When studying the selection of parties' leadership board, we need to remember that parties are complex systems that comprise a set of organizational party branches (Katz 2002, 87). *Party branches* refer to a party's organization in different territorial and political arenas. Katz and Mair (1992, 4–6) have traditionally distinguished three arenas: First, the "party as a membership organization," which includes subnational party branches, like the CDU's organization in the different German Länder, and auxiliary party branches, such

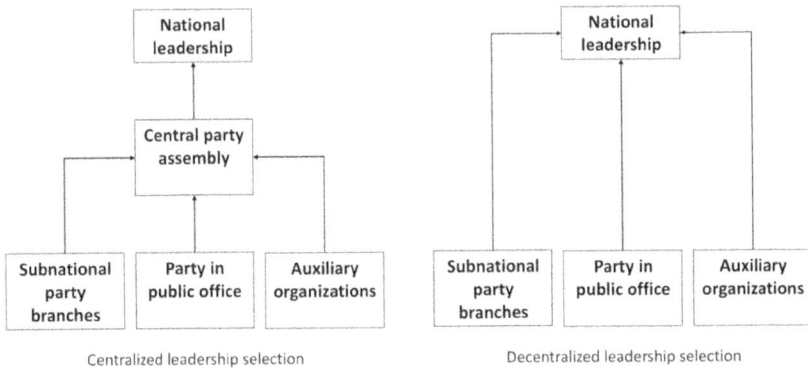

FIGURE 2.2. A centralized and decentralized leadership selection process

as the party's youth or women's movement. Second, the "party as a governing organization," which covers the party's groups in the national legislature and government (i.e., the party in public office). Third, the "party as a central or bureaucratic organization," which includes the staff or secretariat at the party's national headquarters (see also Katz 2002, 98). In each of these branches, the party includes leaders of particular social or political groups, to whom I refer as party elites.

A prominent way of conceptualizing how parties integrate their different organizational branches when selecting their national leadership board is to look at how centralized the selection process is (e.g., Fabre 2011; Poguntke et al. 2016).[7] Under a centralized process, different branches of the party come together in a single central assembly to elect the party leadership, meaning that the selection process is centralized in a single election in which delegates from different party branches participate. In contrast, this intermediate, centralized step is absent under a decentralized selection process. Instead, the different party branches send their delegates directly to the national executive (fig. 2.2). To identify the same unit of analysis across parties, I rely on party statutes and follow Poguntke (1998, 161–64). He has defined a party's national leadership board as having the formal function to lead the party in everyday politics. It is smaller (i.e., fewer than seventy-five members) and meets more often (i.e., usually once per month) than deliberative bodies like the national congress or party council. Some parties have an additional, smaller leadership board that meets between the national executive meetings and is often called executive committee or presidium. I focus on the larger national executive because the executive committee is usually a subcommittee of the national executive and I want to focus on where the formal decision-making power is. Moreover, as the executive committee is usually chosen from the midst of the national executive, it is at the level of the latter that I expect sub-stantive variation in terms of the selection process. Finally, many parties do not have an executive committee (Poguntke 2000, 107–10).

To ensure that the level of centralization a party initially adopts to select its leaders indeed shapes its level of factionalism, it should be the starting point of the causal process. A competing argument would be that the party's initial leadership selection process was endogenous to something else, thus making it an intervening rather than independent variable causing the out-come. Country-level variables often correlate with parties' organizational for-mat (Webb, Poguntke, and Scarrow 2017). Germany's 1967 party law required parties to pursue a largely centralized leadership selection process. Federal-ism could incentivize party elites to build strong provincial or regional party branches and introduce a decentralized leadership selection process (Filippov, Ordeshook, and Shvetsova 2004, chap. 6). If the political system determined a party's initial leadership selection process, I would expect to see a speedy decision-making process that results in the party's leadership selection pro-cess mapping onto the requirements of the political system. Relatedly, the se-quence of party formation can shape parties' organization (Panebianco 1988). When a party is the merger of preexisting autonomous groups, either refer-ring to geographically dispersed subnational groups like in Germany's CDU (Bösch 2001) or previously independent parties like in Uruguay's Broad Front (Bentancur, Rodríguez, and Rosenblatt 2020), we might expect it to adopt a decentralized leadership selection process. In contrast, we would expect par-ties whose formation is controlled by a national center to adopt a centralized selection process. Similarly, parties' first statute typically specifies a bundle of rules. Parties that decentralize candidate selection and decision-making over the party platform might also decentralize their leadership selection process (Von dem Berge and Poguntke 2017, 141–46). If such compound selection explained a party's leadership selection process, the latter should map onto the level of (de)centralization in other relevant areas of intraparty decision-making and either emerge at the same time as or after party elites have de-cided the level of (de)centralization in those other fields.

To evaluate whether parties' initial leadership selection process is the ade-quate starting point of the causal process or driven by any of the factors men-tioned thus far, an understanding of critical junctures that emphasizes con-tingency and agency provides a powerful tool kit for analysis (Capoccia and Kelemen 2007; Capoccia 2015, 165–69). If an institutional selection process is a critical juncture, I expect to observe an uncertain institutional outcome, the availability of different options, the translation of actors' ultimate choice into the institutional outcome, and the initiation of a relatively long-lasting process of institutional path dependence (Capoccia and Kelemen 2007, 349; Capoccia 2015, 148). The key question for institutional selection during critical junctures is this: Do actors have a choice when discussing their party's organizational format? The competing view is that structural antecedents either closed off alternative options or determined actors' preferences in a way that one, and only one, option was the way to go (Capoccia 2015, 167–69; Collier and Collier 1991, 27). To determine whether agency or structure drives institutional selection, it is not sufficient to look at preexisting conditions and the institutional outcome because, for agency to matter, the outcome does not need to diverge from what we would expect given the structural context. After all, it may be one of the options actors can choose from.

I therefore trace the decision-making process leading to a party's initial leadership selection process (Capoccia and Kelemen 2007, 352; Capoccia 2015, 165–66). The process usually starts when actors, often elites representing particular social or political groups, begin negotiating about coming together in a political party. It ends with the ratification of the first national party statute. The party statute establishes "formalized structures, rules and procedures[. They] constitute one of the principal ways in which the internal struggles of parties are channeled, constrained, and even pre-empted" (Katz and Mair 1992, 6). Such a set of rules, also called institutions, is important to create behavioral expectations and thus facilitate collective action (North 1990, 33). These rules are often accompanied by informal extensions and elaborations, including socially sanctioned norms of behavior and internally enforced standards of conduct (North 1990, 4, 40, 46). Actors may have different preferences regarding the leadership selection process. Some may prefer a decentralized selection process, whereas others may advocate a centralized selection process. Many attempts to form a party have failed because of disagreement over organizational questions. For instance, French Catholics negotiated merging into a single Christian democratic party in the 1940s. Disagreement over the leadership selection process played an important role in the negotiations' failure and the initial emergence of three separate parties (Bazin 1981, 158–238). Yet many negotiations have come to an agreement (as in the parties discussed in this book).

Factions are more likely under a centralized than under a decentralized leadership selection process because cooperation between actors coming from different organizational branches of the party is more beneficial to assume leadership positions. To see why this is the case, let us assume that we have two parties, P1 and P2. Both parties are led by a national executive (NE), use the NE as the key decision-making party body, and have N branches (A, B, C, D, . . . N). These branches can be, among other things,

Party I: Centralized   Party II: Decentralized

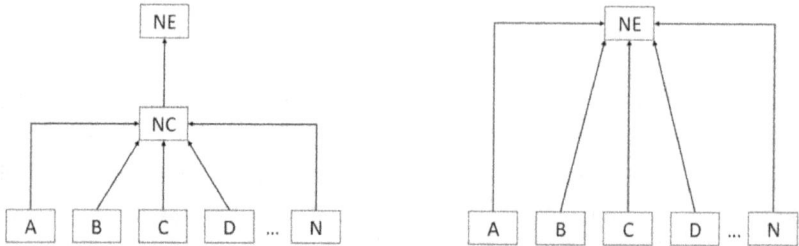

FIGURE 2.3. A centralized and decentralized leadership selection process in practice

the party's organizational branches in regions, *Länder*, or states; the party's parliamentary group at the national level; or auxiliary organizations like the youth and women's movement. Although P1 and P2 are similar in these three points, they differ in how they select the national executive. P1 has a centralized selection process. A, B, C, D, . . . N send their delegates to a central deliberative assembly (NC, for "national congress" or "national council"), which then elects the members of the party's leadership board (NE, for "national executive") out of all delegates. In contrast, P2 has a decentralized selection process. A, B, C, D, . . . N send their delegates directly to the national executive (fig. 2.3).

Let us now assess whether cooperation between members of A, B, C, D, . . . N (i.e., cross-branch cooperation) would be beneficial for gaining seats in the national executive. For this, it is important to identify who the members are. I focus on the strategic interaction between party elites. This is a more beneficial approach to study parties that have a collective leadership than focusing on the interaction between a single party leader and second-rank elites. Parties include different territorial, political, and social groups, each of which has its own leaders. They aggregate and represent the preferences of different parts of the party membership. Their interaction is thus important and complements studies that have focused on the interaction between party members and elites (e.g., Michels [1911] 1959; Kitschelt 1994).

I distinguish between two groups of party elites: *Majority elites* are defined as holding power in their party branch. I understand holding power as being supported, at least at the time of the previous branch leadership election, by a majority within their party branch. This group thus includes the party branch leader and her allies. For example, in the early years of the CDU's Land branch in Rhineland, majority elites included branch leader Konrad Adenauer and his supporters like Robert Pferdmenges. I use M+ to refer to majority elites in all branches. I refer to majority elites in a certain branch by indexing the branch (e.g., $M+_A$, $M+_B$, ... $M+_N$). When referring to majority elites within an unspecified party branch, I use the index i (i.e., $M+_i$). *Minority elites* are defined as not holding power within their respective party branch. They thus do not include the branch leader or her allies.[8] I use M− to refer to minority elites in all branches, $M-_A$, ... $M-_N$ to refer to minority elites in a specific party branch, and $M-_i$ to refer to minority elites within an unspecified party branch. While M+'s and M−'s individual motivation may be diverse (Strøm 1990), I assume that they seek leadership positions within the party, as they are beneficial for both office- and policy-related goals (Schlesinger 1984, 381–89). They will therefore choose the behavior they expect to be the most promising to access these positions given the playing field imposed by the party statute.

Let us now turn to the benefits of cross-branch cooperation (between, for example, $M+_A$, $M-_B$, $M-_C$ and $M-_D$ or between $M+_B$ and $M+_C$). The total number of delegates sent to the national congress and national executive differs. This has to do with the way political parties are often formally structured. The number of seats at central party assemblies or committees decreases the more one approaches the top level of the party hierarchy (e.g., the number of seats decreases when moving from the national congress to the national executive; Poguntke 1998). Thus, while the few delegates a branch (N) may directly send to the NE usually represent the majority elites of the respective branch ($M+_N$), the delegates whom party branches send to the NC are more numerous and usually include $M+_i$ and $M-_i$.

If the selection process of the national leadership (NE) is centralized (P1), cross-branch cooperation is beneficial for both majority ($M+_i$) and minority ($M-_i$) elites. We can easily see why. $M+_i$ and $M-_i$ would need support from beyond their own party branch to win a majority at the NC and thus proceed to the NE. Thinking about the delegates from party branch N, it is obvious that $M+_N$ need support from the delegates coming from other branches to win a majority in order to gain NE seats.[9] Minority elites ($M-_N$) can compensate for the lack of support in N by cooperating with delegates from other branches. Both $M+_N$ and $M-_N$ can engage in backroom deals or horse-trading with $M+_{non-N}$ and $M-_{non-N}$ to organize the required number of votes or present a joint candidate slate at the NC. Thus, cross-branch cooperation is highly beneficial for both $M+_N$ and $M-_N$. This also applies to $M+_{non-N}$ and $M-_{non-N}$. We can thus say that cross-branch cooperation is highly beneficial for $M+_i$ and $M-_i$. In fact, it is a sine qua non for obtaining seats in the national executive.

By contrast, if the selection process of the NE is fully decentralized (P2), cross-branch cooperation is beneficial neither for $M+_i$ nor $M-_i$. As the selection process of NE happens within A, B, C, D . . . N (and not at the NC), $M+_N$'s access to the NE is guaranteed as they are backed by the majority of their respective party branch. Thus, they do not need cross-branch cooperation to proceed to the NE. In turn, while $M-_N$ are in a minority position in their party branch, they would not gain from cooperating with actors from other party branches. For instance, support from $M+_B$ or $M-_C$ does not help $M-_A$ in the selection process taking place within A. In other words, and in contrast to a centralized selection process, the location of support within a particular party branch rather than its overall amount within the party is essential under a decentralized selection process.

Under a centralized selection process, majority and minority elites thus benefit more from building networks across party branches than under a decentralized process. In parties with a centralized leadership selection process, it is likely that actors who are concerned about not having enough support from delegates from other party branches when the central assembly (NC) is electing the NE start building and sustaining networks across party branches. This can be the case for majority elites ($M+_i$) who have a territorially concentrated power base but do not enjoy much support beyond that territory. It can also describe the situation of minority elites ($M-_i$) who seek to become a force at the NC by joining forces with minority elites from other party branches. Their networks are likely to solidify as factions. By contrast, majority elites who have played an important role during the party formation process are likely to hold important positions (e.g., in public office, the preparing steering committee of the party), be well known across party branches, and enjoy widespread support within the party. They are thus less incentivized to initiate the factional game as their election to the NE is likely, and they may even oppose factionalism as the latter risks weakening their dominant position. Yet as their rivals risk gaining in influence as a result of their factions, even those actors who were initially reluctant to form factions start doing so to avoid falling behind in the competition for leadership positions. The (reluctant) acceptance of factions by the DC's initial leader Alcide De Gasperi illustrates this. De Gasperi did not need to form a faction to ascend to the DC's leadership board. His popularity as prime minister and among many Catholics made him the DC's undisputed leader. However, chapter 3 shows that when minority elites from the party's internal left and right formed factions and threatened his power, De Gasperi eventually gathered his supporters in his *centristi* faction. I therefore expect factions to be a valuable way of building support across party branches and consequently expect the number

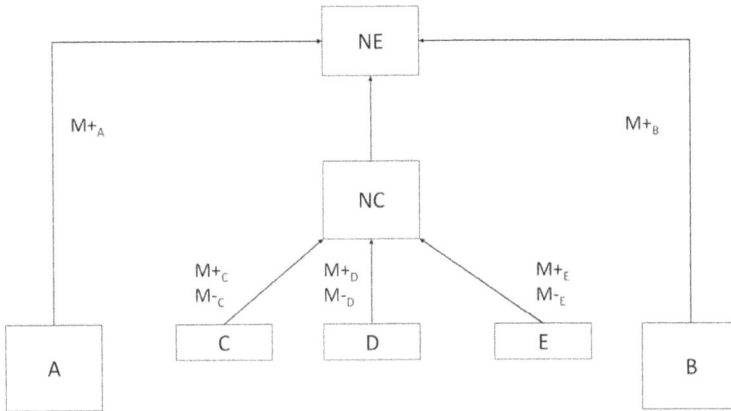

FIGURE 2.4. A party with a mixed leadership selection process

of factions to be higher in parties with a centralized leadership selection process than in parties with a decentralized one.

In contrast, in parties with a decentralized procedure to select the NE, support within rather than across party branches is the dominant resource. As their support base has allowed majority elites ($M+_i$) to access the national party leadership, they have little incentive to provide room for the emergence of factions. Instead, they are likely to try to suppress any attempts by minority elites ($M-_i$) to form factions. Such attempts are unlikely anyway given factions' low benefits. Competition thus tends to unfold mainly within the organizational branches of the party and between branches. In France's MRP, for example, the party's branches in France's *départements* and its parliamentary group in the National Assembly were the groups that put forward policy proposals and candidate slates at meetings of the party congress or party council (chapter 7). Attempts to establish factions connecting party elites across branches were rare, and the party's only notable faction (Rénovation Démocratique, or Democratic Renovation) was short lived.

Let us now consider the case of a party with a mixed leadership selection process. The example presented in figure 2.4 includes elements of a centralized and decentralized selection procedure. Some party branches (i.e., A and B) send delegates directly to the NE, whereas other party branches (i.e., C, D, and E) send delegates to the NC, which also selects some NE positions. We thus have some majority elites whose party branch directly sends delegates to the NE (i.e., $M+_A$ and $M+_B$) while other majority elites (i.e., $M+_C$, $M+_D$ and $M+_E$) need to compete for NE seats at the NC.

We can easily see how this creates an incentive structure that combines aspects of the centralized and decentralized selection process described earlier.

As under a decentralized selection process, $M+_A$ and $M+_B$ hardly benefit from engaging in collective action across party branches. Their access to the NE is ensured as long as they maintain their power base within their party branch. In turn, in their efforts to get elected to the NE, $M-_A$ and $M-_B$ would not benefit from support by majority or minority elites from other party branches (i.e., $M+_{non-A}$, $M+_{non-B}$, $M-_{non-A}$, $M-_{non-B}$). Thus, $M+_A$ and $M+_B$ as well as $M-_A$ and $M-_B$ are not expected to be involved in the formation of factions but to focus on their network within their own party branch. In contrast, minority elites and majority elites from party branches that do not directly send delegates to the NE benefit from cross-branch cooperation to pick up the seats elected at the NC (i.e., $M+_C$, $M-_C$, $M+_D$, $M-_D$, $M+_E$, $M-_E$). Hence, I expect them to form networks across party branches, which are likely to develop into factions.

If factions are entities organized across party branches, how can they form within a mixed selection procedure if some party branches are not part of the negotiation process? We need to remember that the four types of intraparty groups (i.e., factions, camps, auxiliary organizations, party branches) are best understood as ideal types, with groups moving from "camps" to "factions" as they are being organized across more and more levels of the party. As we move from parties with a decentralized process to parties with a centralized leadership selection process, party elites are more and more incentivized to mobilize support across party branches and the more likely local camps are to develop into factions. Similarly, the three scenarios of leadership selection procedures (i.e., centralized, decentralized, and mixed) can also be seen as ideal types. In practice, party branches that select their representatives for the party leadership autonomously may still send delegates to the party congress. However, because the access of majority elites from those branches to the party leadership is guaranteed as long as they maintain their power base within their branch, they have less of an incentive to join or invest in factions than do the majority elites from branches that do not send delegates directly to the party leadership. This creates an incentive structure that combines elements of the incentives created by a very centralized and decentralized leadership selection process and consequently results in a moderate level of factionalism. It reflects what happened within Germany's CDU (chapter 5). Although factions like the Protestant Working Group and the left-wing Social Committees emerged, factions never became the sole dominant organizational unit of intraparty politics because the leaders of the CDU's large Land branches did not have an incentive to form factions.

For a moderate level of factionalism to emerge, the share of NE seats autonomously filled by party branches relative to those elected by the NC needs to be sufficient to counteract the incentives to form factions. If, to give a numerical example, only one NE position was filled by a party branch autonomously while all other party branches sent their delegates to the NC, which then elected twenty-nine NE positions, the incentives to form factions would prevail. In other words, for parties with a mixed leadership selection process, my model predicts a dual logic for $M+_i$ and $M-_i$ to get elected to the NE. For this dual logic to influence a party's initial level of factionalism, a similar share of NE seats needs to be filled by party branches autonomously and by the NC.

What would happen if a party adopted a leadership selection process that discourages the formation of factions while other institutional or organizational factors encourage it (or vice versa)? The book's comparative-historical approach helps disentangle such causal complexity by clarifying at which stage of the causal process those factors matter. For example, Germany's Social Democratic Party, with its initially centralized leadership selection process, has been more factionalized than the country's CDU with its initially mixed leadership selection process (Ceron 2019, 37). Yet Germany's Social Democrats have never reached the extreme levels of factionalism observed in Italy's late Socialist Party (PSI) (Barnes 1967; Zariski 1962). It is plausible, and in line with the theoretical reasoning outlined next, that the presence of a preferential voting system and a tradition of clientelist party-voter linkages in Italy but not in Germany account for this variation in the development of factionalism.[10]

Reinforcing Factionalism

If a party's initial leadership selection process is likely to shape its level of factionalism, would this imply that changes to the rules would lead to changes in the level of factionalism? Given the growing inclusiveness of many parties' internal election rules,[11] we might expect growing uniformity in parties' level of factionalism. However, despite organizational reforms in the past decades, we have seen remarkably stable differences in parties' respective levels of factionalism. Institutional choices made early in parties' history have often set party organizations on a specific path of development, especially with regard to the distribution of power between key actors (e.g., Anria 2019; Bentancur, Rodríguez, and Rosenblatt 2020; Hunter 2010; Krauss and Pekkanen 2011). They established veto players, who typically objected to changes that would jeopardize their power, and inspired complementary institutions that gradually crowded out opponents to the institutional arrangements (Bentancur, Rodríguez, and Rosenblatt 2020; Krauss and Pekkanen 2011; see also North 1990, 95, 104; Pierson 2000a, 255; Page 2006, 110–13).

To theorize the development of party organizations and factionalism over time, I build on Greif's (2006) concepts of self-enforcing, self-reinforcing,[12] and self-undermining processes in institutional development. Self-enforcement refers to the confirmation or reproduction of an institution. Actors are endogenously motivated to keep behaving according to the institution in place because they have observed other actors behaving according to the existing institution and they expect them to maintain this behavior. Their behavior, in turn, contributes to motivating other actors to behave in the manner associated with the institution to begin with (Greif 2006, 15–16, 161–62). The self-reinforcement of an institution enforces the behavior associated with it in more situations (e.g., factions becoming the party's key organizational unit at the national and subnational level) and for more actors (e.g., new party elites being socialized into the level of factionalism). In contrast, self-undermining enforces the behavior associated with it in fewer situations and for fewer actors (Greif 2006, 17). Consequently, when an institution is reinforced or undermined, the behavior associated with it does not change. But the institution becomes more (in the case of reinforcement) or less (in the case of undermining) robust to exogenous shocks (Greif 2006, 168). I am thus talking about an incentive-based feedback process that drives the development of the initial level of factionalism.

I expect the reinforcement of a party's initial level of factionalism to unfold in two ways. First, party elites use available resources to build the networks valuable under the initial level of factionalism, for instance, through campaigning, ideological appeals, or clientelism. The initial level of factionalism guides toward whom (e.g., majority and minority elites in party elites' own or other party branches) these efforts are likely to be directed. Second, Ahmed (2013) has outlined how political parties try to manipulate political institutions, like the electoral system, to contain rivals and protect their influence. Similarly, party elites modify the party organization in a way that is likely to increase their influence given the networks they have. This might include changes in the electoral system used for internal elections or the formalization of previously informal institutions.

THE RESOURCE FEEDBACK EFFECT

In highly factionalized parties, minority elites and those majority elites with weak cross-branch support need to increase their vote share at the central party assembly (NC) to become an option for a change in the majority coalition. They thus need to create incentives for delegates at the NC to support their (minority) factions. Nonmaterial incentives include aspects like charismatic or ideological appeals and social pressure. Material incentives include bribes and patronage. Clientelism has been primarily theorized in terms of voter-party linkages (e.g., Kitschelt and Wilkinson 2007), but there is no reason the material reward of individuals in exchange for their vote cannot take place at elections within parties (e.g., Zuckerman 1979). Minority factions can incentivize national congress delegates to support their candidate slate by offering them financial rewards or party positions if they win. Clientelism, a preferential voting system, and the availability of resources through government participation all provide existing factions with strategic opportunities to enlarge their share of supporters. Majority factions are likely to respond to minority factions' efforts by offering similar incentives to the NC delegates. By trying to expand support for their factions, minority and majority factions confirm and reinforce factions' importance in internal elections because they create incentives for further NC delegates to endorse a specific faction. This makes it increasingly unlikely that candidate slates that are not endorsed by a faction stand a chance in these elections. Over time, this leads to an increasing share of NC delegates being split into different factional blocs, and delegates coming to the NC for the first time would be socialized into that logic of high factional competition.

In weakly factionalized parties, the location rather than the overall support within the party is the decisive resource. Majority elites need to ensure the loyalty of the majority within their own party branch. I therefore expect majority elites to create incentives for those members who are involved in the leadership election in their respective branches to continue to support them. This may include strengthening their personal links to these members by, for instance, participating in branch-specific events, building a public image that is ideologically or personally appealing to these members or providing pork (Filippov, Ordeshook, and Shvetsova 2004, 203–6). These are also likely strategies for minority elites to enhance their chances at the branch leadership elections, yet they are at a competitive disadvantage. Majority elites have access to both the national executive and the leadership committee of their specific party branch. They are likely to be present in the media, which provides them with a tool to simultaneously address many members of their branch. Moreover, their leadership position is likely to entail the chance to take part in important decisions regarding the allocation of funds, which makes them more likely than minority elites to gain benefits for their party branch. The resource feedback effect can thus contribute to the long-term survival of majority elites in office. Similar to the reinforcement of highly factionalized parties, the more and the longer that majority and minority elites invest in building such networks within their party branches, the more entrenched the existing low level of factionalism becomes, and the more likely newly emerging party elites are to be socialized into a weakly factionalized party.

Finally, I expect a combination of both resource feedback processes described here to be present in moderately factionalized parties. On the one hand, majority and minority elites from branches that directly send delegates to the national executive are incentivized to follow similar strategies as described for weakly factionalized parties. On the other hand, majority and minority elites from branches with no direct representation in the national party leadership depend on support at the central party assembly, which entails strategies similar to those described for highly factionalized parties. As both (i.e., within-branch and across-branch) resource feedback effects exist, neither becomes predominant.

THE ORGANIZATIONAL FEEDBACK EFFECT

Beyond reinforcing the key resources needed to gain seats in the national party leadership, party elites also reinforce the initial level of factionalism in their attempt to increase the value of their existing resources by modifying the party's organization. In parties with an initially high level of factionalism, minority factions try to increase their power and by doing so reinforce the importance of factions in intraparty politics. As outlined above, $M+_i$ and $M-_i$ are likely to form factions to increase their vote share at central party assemblies (NC). Yet despite factional activities, they might still fall short in comparison to popular majority elites. The minority factions are therefore likely to seek changes that alter the party's internal playing field. This can include the shift from a majority system to a system of proportional representation for internal elections to help minority factions translate their votes at the NC into seats in the party leadership (NE) (Issar and Dilling 2022, 208–11). Another example is the introduction of quotas that ensure minority factions' representation in the NE (Morgan 2011, 40).

Minority factions represent only a minority at the NC, but changes in the party statutes usually require a simple majority (and often more) of the NC delegates. Minority factions are therefore likely to try to shift the majority coalition in their favor.[13] As minority elites face majority elites who have benefited from the party's organizational structure, the former have better chances of splitting the majority coalition if they compromise (Greif 2006, 200). Minority elites thus propose modifications that largely confirm the behavior associated with the initial institutions that have allowed majority elites to assume power while including deals that promise to increase their influence. To be even considered as a potential partner for majority elites, minority factions need to strengthen their factional networks to make a strong showing at the NC (compare Pierson 1993, 603, 607). By becoming a potential option for a minimum-winning coalition, minority factions can hope to split the existing majority coalition and become part of a new coalition. They could then include their organizational preferences into any deal or agreement on which this coalition would be based. An alternative strategy for minority factions is to shift the majority coalition by applying pressure in a different organizational branch of the party, such as threatening to sabotage votes in parliament if the party leadership does not accept specific statutory modifications. Minority elites' networks across party branches are therefore likely to be reproduced within the party's parliamentary group. This contributes to factions being organizationally waved into all levels of the party organization and to the party's parliamentary group becoming an arena of factional conflict (McAllister 1991, 206).

Once minority elites have managed to gain influence within the party to realize the two strategies outlined here, they have increased the strength of their factions and their organizational proposals are thus unlikely to seek factions' elimination. In other words, successful minority elites, who have assumed leadership positions, are likely to reinforce the initial path of institutional development (Greif 2006, 195, 197, 204–5). Similarly, as majority elites are likely to counter the emergence of minority factions by forming their own factions, they also are unlikely to prefer the complete elimination of factionalism. Instead, I expect them to prefer organizational change that reduces small factions' influence without jeopardizing the influence of their own factions. Ahmed (2013, chap. 3) has shown how majority actors can use electoral reform as a defensive move to protect their influence. Within political parties, such changes may include the introduction of a majority bonus for the strongest faction or an electoral threshold that factions need to overcome. Both majority and minority factions thereby make the party organization increasingly accommodating for factional activities. Such changes are unlikely to be restricted to the national level. The introduction of thresholds or the organization of internal elections based on factions' candidate slates can also be introduced at the subnational or even local level.

In parties with an initially low level of factionalism, majority elites (M+) have few incentives to shift the election of the national executive (NE) from the different organizational branches to a central assembly (NC). Although minority elites might prefer this, their opportunities to influence institutional development are restricted. Similar to minority factions in highly factionalized parties, minority elites can try to shift the majority coalition. They are more likely to succeed in doing so if they propose compromises that confirm the basic logic of the selection process in place while improving their own chances of gaining representation in the NE. As a result, statutory modifications are likely to continue to give little room for factional activities and mainly address the seat shares to which party branches are entitled in the NE. This reinforces low levels of factionalism.[14] This confirms that the majority coalition that minority elites would need to split exists within minority elites' own party branch rather than at the NC. They therefore focus their efforts on gaining influence within their own branch. Once they have assumed power within their respective branch, thereby becoming majority elites ($M+_i$), they have successfully adapted to the system in place and are unlikely to push for a fundamental reorganization of the party.

Finally, factions alongside parties' territorial branches and auxiliary organizations characterize the decision-making process within moderately factionalized parties. Majority elites whose party branch directly sends delegates to the national executive are likely to oppose a more centralized selection process of the party leadership, as that would risk undermining their power base. In contrast, minority elites refuse a complete decentralization of the leadership selection, whereas the leaders of party branches that do not send delegates directly to the national executive would be likely to accept a further decentralization only if it would guarantee their representation in the national executive. This, however, might risk reducing the influence of majority elites whose representation in the party leadership has already been secured. Statutory modifications are thus likely to reinforce the existing strategies to gain influence, and a moderate level of factionalism prevails.

This discussion suggests that many variables highlighted by previous studies of the origins of factionalism might be better theorized as reinforcing factors rather than causal ones. Once an initial level of factionalism has emerged, party elites use the resources resulting from, for example, their parties' position in government or push for proportional electoral rules for internal elections to strengthen their respective groups. By being reinforced over time, the level of factionalism becomes more robust (Greif 2006, 168). An event that might have initiated a different level of factionalism, if it had occurred at an earlier point in time, is therefore unlikely to have the same effect if it occurs at a later moment in the institutional development (Pierson 2000a, 263). This means that a dramatic change in the party's organization, which could, for instance, be imposed by a change in the country's legal infrastructure, becomes increasingly unlikely to alter fundamentally the level of factionalism the later it occurs in the reinforcing process. Years, potentially decades, of internal practices, norms, and networks are not gone overnight simply because party elites have been forced to alter their party's organization. They are likely to have the incentives and resources to maintain the level of factionalism.

Party-Level Effects: Reinforcing or Undermining Adaptation

FACTIONALISM AND PARTY ADAPTATION

To show how factionalism affects party adaptation, we need to move beyond the focus on path dependence on a single level. An initial level of factionalism initiates two potentially divergent feedback effects on two different units. The first feedback effect affects factions and factionalism and has just been described in the previous section. The second feedback effect helps describe how different levels of factionalism may reinforce or undermine parties' ability to adapt to societal and political changes.

The changes to which parties need to adapt have been a common starting point to study party adaptation (e.g., Gauja 2016, 19; Harmel and Janda 1994, 265; Levitsky 2003, 9), but on their own, they are not sufficient to explain variation in party adaptation (Levitsky 2003, 10–11; Przeworski and Sprague 1986, 183–85). Although parties often pursue various policy-, vote-, and office-seeking goals, contextual changes can emphasize trade-offs between them, urge parties to rethink their priorities, or require them to adjust the strategies they have employed to achieve their primary goal (Strøm and Müller 1999, 9–10). Election defeats, damages to the party's legitimacy or reputation, and changes in other parties, often following broader constitutional changes or shifts in public opinion and society's composition, signal to parties that reforms are needed (Gauja 2016, 13; Barnea and Rahat 2007, 378; see also Dalton 2006; Katz and Mair 1995; Kreuzer 2001; Morgan 2011, 8). Gauja (2016, 13) has called this the "Swiss cheese" model, whereby incentives for party reform are particularly pronounced when drivers for change are simultaneously present at the level of the political system, party system, and the party itself. However, facing the hyperinflation in Latin America, Europe's various crises since 2008, and a general decline in party membership, parties have varied enormously in the extent to which they adopted new policies or organizational formats like open primaries (Gauja 2016, 2020; Kriesi and Hutter 2019; Morgan 2011, 51).

To account for such variation, we need to take seriously the politics *within* political parties and, in particular, the choices made by party leaders and elites (e.g., Corrales 2002). Party adaptation requires innovation and integration (Kreuzer 2001; Seawright 2012). Allowing new elites to rise supports innovation because it increases the chances of new ideas being introduced and circulated within the party (Gauja 2016, 32; Harmel and Janda 1994; Levitsky 2003, 11; Panebianco 1988, 242–44). Yet political parties typically include a wide range of politicians who rely on different groups of activists and voters for support (Seawright 2012, 23). They tend to uphold and represent a broad spectrum of political views—albeit often painting a more complex picture than initially proposed by May (1973) (see, e.g., Enos and Hersh 2015; Kitschelt 1989a; Lupu 2016, 30–44; McCloskey, Hoffmann, and O'Hara 1960). Within the same party, we are thus likely to find actors who have very different ideas about which direction the party should go or whether the party should abandon any traditional positions and practices at all (Gauja 2016, 39; May 1973; Przeworski and Sprague 1986). When parties cannot resolve such divisions and integrate different views, they typically fail to adapt (Tanaka 2005).

The leadership autonomy argument has focused on ways for party leaders to bypass or suppress internal opposition. The conventional wisdom suggests that party leaders have a particular interest in introducing reforms to enhance their electoral prospects (Lupu 2016, 31–32; Seawright 2012, 23). Indeed, the election of new leaders has often (albeit not always) coincided with policy and organizational innovations (Bale 2012, chap. 8; Panebianco 1988, 242–44). Centralizing power over policy making, candidate selection, and party finances in the hands of the national party leadership can empower leaders to introduce adaptive reforms (Kirchheimer 1966; Ziblatt 2017). However, centralization does not equal autonomy. Party elites depend on support within the party to become and remain leaders, which can dramatically limit their room for reform (Koelble 1992; Müller and Steininger 1994b). In fact, parties' internal recruitment and selection procedures have shaped whether reform-minded leaders are likely to emerge to begin with (Grzymala-Busse 2002; Krauss and Pekkanen 2011). Other studies, particularly on Latin American parties, have highlighted that party leaders tend to have more autonomy when parties never fully institutionalize such internal accountability mechanisms (Levitsky 2001, 2003; also Burgess and Levitsky 2003; Kitschelt 1994; Morgan 2011; Roberts 1998; Seawright 2012). It allows new leaders to rise quickly thanks to the absence of predictable career paths and delay party meetings or ignore their decisions to pursue reforms (Crisp 1996, 2000; Levitsky 2003, 3–4, 20; Roberts 1998, 47). It also empowers lower party levels to diverge from the national leadership's course and experiment with new strategies (Levitsky 2003, 21; see also Wills-Otero 2016). However, weak institutionalization also comes at a cost. Party institutionalization provides valuable organizational resources to implement reforms (Bolleyer 2013; Cyr 2017; Kreuzer 2001, 62–63; Ziblatt 2017). The lack of routinized procedures also tends to encourage intense infightings, particularly when parties are in opposition (Levitsky 2005), which is when we would expect them to face particular pressure to adapt (Gauja 2016).

This book proposes an alternative account that considers parties' diversity of internal groups as a potential asset rather than foil of party adaptation. Adapting their platform or organization to a new environment requires parties to identify interests associated with this new environment and facilitate the rise of leaders associated with these interests within the party (Levitsky 2003, 13; Seawright 2012, 25–26, 167–71). Intraparty groups, including parties' territorial branches, auxiliary organizations for women, youth, or other sociodemographic groups, and factions, have played an important role in identifying and aggregating the preferences of important constituencies, recruiting and mobilizing support for new party elites, and implementing leadership decisions (e.g., Allern and Verge 2017; Bentancur, Rodríguez, and Rosenblatt 2020; Blum 2020; Ellinas 2020; Poguntke 2002, 2006; Wiliarty 2010). Among the different intraparty groups, factions' flexibility and pervasiveness make them particularly relevant for party adaptation. Factions provide parties with flexibility that helps them keep up with voters' demands by giving a voice to grievances that would risk remaining undetected or marginalized by parties' territorial branches and auxiliary organizations (Bloch Rubin 2017, 4, 14–15; DiSalvo 2012, 58–59). The latter are built along territorial or functional lines sanctioned by the party, which may or may not reflect salient conflict lines (Morgan 2011, 59), whereas factions are able to form, split, and rearrange in response to salient societal interests and political positions. Moreover, factions' organizational pervasiveness helps connect like-minded party elites across party levels, unlike more localized caucuses or camps. This facilitates deliberation and coordination and the spread of new ideas and positions within the party (Blum 2020, chap. 2; McAllister 1991, 209). Factions can thus serve as flexible coalition partners for parties' more stable territorial branches and auxiliary organizations. This supports leadership renewal, which typically requires changing a party's internal dominant coalition rather than merely replacing its leader (Harmel and Janda 1994, 274, 278–80; Panebianco 1988, 38).

However, a proliferation of factions risks resulting in notoriously unstable internal coalitions, the dependence on a class of factional brokers, and the failure to integrate people not affiliated with a faction (e.g., Boucek 2012; Krauss and Pekkanen 2011). In highly factionalized parties, large and small factions rather than party branches or auxiliary organizations are the main actors of intraparty politics. Delegates at national, subnational, and local party meetings can be classified according to their factional affiliation. This has implications for parties' ability to integrate changing societal interests and facilitate leadership renewal. When discussing the development of Mexico's highly factionalized PRD, Greene (2007, 190) has highlighted that factions, while being highly fluid in their alliances and composition, were ever-present. Efforts to join the party and rise to positions of influence without affiliating with a faction frequently failed (see also Krauss and Pekkanen 2011, 127–28 on Japan's LDP). Factional membership thus functions as barriers to innovation (Greene 2007, 190, 205–6), and new party leaders can emerge only if they have factional support. Building this support within highly factionalized parties is complicated and likely comes at the cost of reform proposals.

At internal elections, there is, in principle, a nearly infinite number of factional alliances to win power because there is almost no limit to divide and rearrange delegates into different factional blocks. The institutional constraints keeping factions together are weaker than for parties' territorial branches and auxiliary organizations. Small and large factions, and the party elites affiliated with them, can play off competing coalition offers against each other and simply split and rearrange as soon as disagreement emerges or better offers (e.g., in terms of funds, positions, policies) become available. I consequently expect the number of factions but also the level of fractionalization (i.e., the number of factions and their seat share in party committees) to increase over time. This flexibility undermines innovation and integration. Negotiations are likely to be tedious or fail to generate any agreement. The need for multifaction coalitions also risks weakening the integrative role ideology can play because factions can always try to go for a better offer. Policies simply become part of the usual horse-trading. Over time, the difference between trading policies, offices, and funds likely becomes blurry. Highly factionalized parties are thus better described as systems of competing factions rather than as a single party (Belloni 1978, 88). This entails all the problems we know from negotiations between political parties: divisions over who should lead, who gets which portfolio, with whom to form a coalition—divisions over practically everything related to politics. While the individual party leader might change, leadership renewal is thus quite unlikely, as new leaders are likely to depend on a wide range of factional leaders. I therefore expect to see fewer and more slowly realized adaptive reforms in highly factionalized parties, with reform-oriented factions likely to break away eventually.

Although too much factionalism thus undermines parties' internal coalition building and change (Boucek 2012; Ceron 2019), party adaptability does not linearly improve as factionalism declines. In weakly factionalized parties, the party's territorial and public office branches and auxiliary organizations rather than factions are the key organizational unit. Territorial party branches support vertical integration. They help parties build local roots and aggregate interests from the local to any intermediary and eventually the national level

(Bentancur, Rodríguez, and Rosenblatt 2020, 13; Poguntke 2002, 50). In turn, auxiliary organizations for young people, women, or specific sociodemographic groups, by virtue of being reproduced across party levels, facilitate horizontal and vertical integration of particular target constituencies (Allern and Verge 2017; Levy and Bruhn 2006, 73–83; Morgan 2011, 82–84). Both parties' territorial branches and auxiliary organizations have provided important stimuli for party reform (Bentancur, Rodríguez, and Rosenblatt 2020; Neumann 2012; Schmid 1990; Wiliarty 2010). However, they privilege predefined interests. Because they are less flexible than factions, they are likely to struggle to integrate interests that do not map onto the existing group structures. For example, the auxiliary organizations in Venezuela's Democratic Action Party were built to integrate specific employment sectors and were consequently ill suited to integrate the growing share of voters in unregulated employment relations (Morgan 2011, chap. 6). Overall, declining levels of party membership seems to indicate auxiliary organizations' limitations when political parties need to integrate a diversifying electorate (Poguntke 2002, 59). In turn, territorial branches risk compartmentalizing and marginalizing minorities in the party as a whole if they only represent a minority within most territorial branches.

The organizational rigidity of weakly factionalized parties is likely to undermine party adaptation. It is likely to weaken the prospects of elite renewal by closing off the way to the party leadership for actors who do not have a power base within one of the existing territorial or auxiliary party branches (Crisp 1996, 43; Barr 2005, 77–79; Kitschelt and Kselman 2010, 12; Lawson 1988; Morgan 2011, 43). Minority elites may succeed in replacing their branch's leadership. Yet they would need to succeed in doing this across the majority of branches to replace the party's dominant coalition. I thus expect leadership renewal to happen very slowly and to see the long-term dominance of a relatively well-defined group of majority elites. Because their influence depends primarily on the support of their respective party branches, the interests of traditionally privileged groups are likely to dominate (Seawright 2012, 169). Given the lack of flexible horizontal ties between party elites, which factions would help create, internal mediation is likely to be cumbersome. Reform proposals are likely to be watered down to appease relevant majority elites, resulting in only partial and slow adjustments to the party's platform and organization and driving reform-oriented elites out of the party.

A moderate level of factionalism might therefore facilitate the integration of changing interests and the rise of new elites and ideas without unleashing the centrifugal forces that characterize highly factionalized parties. By creating horizontal links between minority elites, factions help overcome the regional dispersion of political interests (Greene 2007, 190; Levy and Bruhn 2006, 52). This helps integrate previously diffuse interests, allowing minority or emergent interests to "get on party leaders' map" and indicate the number of potential supporters (Morgan 2011, 59). Moreover, unlike auxiliary organizations, factions are not set up or sanctioned by the party but crystallize around people and positions (Blum 2020; Boucek 2012). They are more flexible to respond to changing public opinion because their boundaries evolve as new conflict lines supersede old divisions (Krauss and Pekkanen 2011). Once the factional leader has lost a contest or an issue has lost in relevance, factions often rearrange (e.g., Bell and Criddle 2014, 60; Boucek 2012, 151–63).

Factions therefore support innovation by making old groups decline and helping new groups and ideas to rise (DiSalvo 2012). In practice, this supports the alternation between different leadership coalitions (Levy and Bruhn 2006, 49–52). While maybe not occurring as regularly as the "thermostatic model" might lead one to expect (Wlezien 1995), the alternation between leadership coalitions is likely to facilitate programmatic and organizational changes (Greene 2007, 73; Langston 2006, 144). By reducing the risk of permanently marginalizing specific views, factions also help keep parties together and attract new elites (Greene 2007, 77), which is important because a party's ability to renew its leadership depends on having access to a pool of such new elites (Seawright 2012, 169–71, 198–9). At the same time, because majority elites whose respective party branches are directly represented in the national leadership are not incentivized to form their own faction, we are likely to observe a relatively constant number of factions over time. This reduces the risk of moderately factionalized parties suffering from the gridlocks that result from the flexible rearrangements of multifaction coalitions in highly factionalized parties. Moderately factionalized parties are thus more likely to pass crucial reforms of the party's platform and organization and to do so more swiftly than weakly and highly factionalized parties.[15]

Does the effect of different levels of factionalism depend on the type of changes to which a party needs to adapt? Some localized challenges do not require a national party response, thus arguably making the flexible horizontal ties factions create between party elites less valuable. Yet parties need to avoid being torn apart by conflicting subnational demands. The struggle of Austria's ÖVP to integrate different subnational interests resulted in high disunity and contradictory policy positions (chapter 4). In contrast, the CDU's moderate level of factionalism helped generate reforms amid various subnational demands (chapter 5). Thus, the outlined effects of different levels of factionalism likely remain relevant.

MULTILEVEL PATH DEPENDENCE AND
CHANGING THE LEVEL OF FACTIONALISM

Why do party elites not abandon a very high or very low level of factional-ism once they realize its negative effects? To answer this question, we need to look at the interplay between the two feedback effects an initial level of factionalism initiates. To recap, the first feedback effect affected the develop-ment of factions and factionalism over time. The second feedback effect has been outlined in the previous section and describes how different levels of factionalism reinforce or undermine parties' ability to adapt to environmen-tal changes. When studying their interplay, we need to remember that some things are easier to change for parties than others, as Hunter (2010, chap. 2) famously outlined when studying Brazil's Workers' Party. Changes that do not affect the power relations among party elites are likely to happen even in weakly and highly factionalized parties. For example, they might introduce membership consultations or primaries to boost their image as long as party elites maintain control over their implementation. In contrast, parties are likely to proceed much more slowly with reforms that challenge entrenched internal dynamics (Panebianco 1988, 243; also Greif and Laitin 2004, 633–34).

Changing the level of factionalism entails uncertain gains for party elites that are also relatively far in time compared to the imminent losses such changes likely entail. They may help the party resolve gridlocks, integrate reform-oriented elites, and implement programmatic and organizational re-forms. Yet it remains uncertain when and to what extent these reforms will pay off (e.g., in terms of election results, access to offices, or the realization of poli-cies). Instead, moving power away from factions (in highly factionalized par-ties) or making space for factions (in weakly factionalized parties) would be a likely and imminent blow to the power base of party elites who have benefited from the existing level of factionalism (Müller and Steininger 1994b, 24–25). These actors are majority elites in weakly factionalized parties and factions that are relevant for a minimum-winning coalition in highly factionalized parties. Apart from eroding their own power, such changes might also help their rivals to gain influence. Because party elites who have benefited from the level of factionalism are likely to have veto power over organizational changes (Gauja 2016, 138–39), they can block reforms that jeopardize their influence (Levitsky 2003, 20–21). The immediate gain of keeping intraparty power is likely preferred over reforms that would undermine their influence and may or may not end up helping the party achieve its goal. We would thus expect to see very highly and weakly factionalized parties to make changes that leave the party's internal distribution of power largely untouched (Gauja 2016, 139).

Under what conditions would we expect path-reversing change? Parties like the British Labour Party, the French Socialists, and the Flemish Christian Democrats have changed their internal distribution of power (Faucher 2015; Gauja 2016; Wauters 2014). Labour's and the French Socialists' introduction of primaries, for instance, moved the power over the selection of the party leader from party congress delegates to the party members, which weakened the long-term dominance of the trade unions and factions in both parties respectively (Faucher 2015). Consecutive electoral defeats might eventually convince party elites to accept changes that weaken their power base (e.g., Faucher 2015). Numerous gradual changes might culminate in significant transformations (*layering*; Hunter 2010, 8; Mahoney and Thelen 2010). Yet why did parties, like Japan's LDP, reform relatively quickly, while others, like Italy's DC, did not despite many institutional similarities across both cases (e.g., Bettcher 2005)? While a skillful leader, like Junichiro Koizumi in Japan's LDP, might increase the chances of swift adaptation (e.g., Köllner 2006), organizational reforms are often a necessary precondition for transformative leaders to rise in the first place (Faucher 2015, 806; Krauss and Pekkanen 2011, 238).

To understand when party elites are willing to move away from very high or very low levels of factionalism, it helps to take into account the multi-leveled nature of party organizations and look at the interaction between factionalism's effects at different party levels. Institutions with conflicting effects across political levels can broaden the scope for change (e.g., Lieberman 2002; Orren and Skowronek 1996). They often incentivize actors to devise new rules, repeal existing ones, or change their enactment in order to increase institutional coherence (Boas 2007, 35; Jacobs and Weaver 2015, 454; Béland, Rocco, and Waddan 2019, 396–97, 404). However, when frictions between levels are due to the same institution rather than different institutions, they complicate rather than facilitate institutional change. A moderate level of factionalism is self-reinforcing with regard to both party elites' leadership ambitions and party adaptation. If self-reinforcing effects predominate, more and more actors should endorse the rules in place, and transformative change attempts should thus dissipate (Anria 2019; Bentancur, Rodríguez, and Rosenblatt 2020). In highly and weakly factionalized parties, however, factionalism is self-reinforcing at one level but self-undermining at another. This leaves party elites with dueling incentives. Tedious reform attempts are likely to follow, as actors are trying to reconcile both by passing changes to treat the problems entailed by the level of factionalism without abandoning it. Yet as negative and positive feedback effects originate in the same institution, such attempts are likely to be ineffective.

Institutional change becomes more likely as the coalition for sustaining the level of factionalism erodes. Factionalism's spillover from the intraparty to the parliamentary and electoral arena increased the number of people with a vested interest in maintaining the level of factionalism but also connected factionalism to an increasing number of other institutions. Changes in these adjacent institutions can weaken the coalition of those who want to keep the level of factionalism. Chapter 7 outlines how factional elites in Japan's LDP benefited from the competition between LDP candidates that the country's single nontransferable vote (SNTV) electoral system encouraged. By providing money and policy expertise, they incentivized constituency candidates to join their faction, thereby recruiting new supporters and expanding their influence to the local level. Candidates who refused to join a faction were increasingly unlikely to win against the candidates backed by factions and thus gradually crowded out (Krauss and Pekkanen 2011, chap. 4). When a corruption scandal forced the LDP into opposition, the new government replaced SNTV with a mixed electoral system that did not reward competition between candidates from the same party. As a result, numerous constituency candidates, parliamentarians, and local brokers had little reason to continue supporting factions, especially because the latter had been blamed for the LDP's scandals, lack of reforms, and electoral losses. This tipped the balance of power in favor of change, and within five years of the electoral reform, the LDP changed its leadership selection and saw a decrease in factionalism.

Conclusion

This chapter has presented a new theory that outlines why giving factions no room or too much room, in contrast to a moderate level of factionalism, is likely to undermine a party's ability to get its act together and pass adaptive reforms when facing environmental transformations. A party's level of factionalism is influenced to a large extent by how it initially chooses its national leaders. The more leadership positions are initially elected by a central party assembly, the more party elites will be incentivized to form factions. While the resulting level of factionalism is likely to be reinforced through party elites' efforts to assume leadership positions, party elites face incentives to abandon very low or very high levels of factionalism when needing to adapt their party to a transformed environment. The interplay between these incentives helps understand why parties struggle so much to change their level of factionalism even when electorally encouraged to do so.

The chapter has formulated observable implications that would support this theory and those that would support alternative arguments. Analyzing a few cases in considerable depth allows for evaluating whether and at which stage of the causal process evidence supports the expectations. My argument is supported only if it accounts for all steps in the causal process in all cases while alternative theories do not (Waldner 2014, 128). The case studies that follow will unfold along the steps that structured this chapter. By focusing on meaningful steps in terms of my own and alternative theories, the book's empirical part evaluates whether my framework or the discussed alternative theories provide a more convincing explanation for the selected parties' initial leadership selection process, level and development of factionalism, and party adaptation.

Analyzing parties' organizational development, factionalism, and adaptation covering a long period of time requires uncovering groups within political parties, party elites' motivation behind relying on some groups rather than others, and the reform proposals these groups put forward and their motives for doing so. To uncover these often hidden aspects of parties' internal politics, my analysis draws on primary research in eight archives in four countries.[16] I analyzed party statutes and manifestos, the motions and amendments associated with them, and the accounts of their implementation. I uncovered party elites' networks and motivation by analyzing party elites' notes and letters, interventions and proposals at party meetings, and publications in party- or faction-specific outlets. While party elites often disguised any motives in public that would damage their reputation, they were more forthcoming in their personal notes and correspondence with allies. Minutes of party meetings provided evidence on the specific challenges party elites identified for the party, on the steps taken to adapt, and the obstacles encountered. This primary material is combined with the comparative and country-specific literature in political science and history and statistical data. Language constraints did not allow also conducting archival research on Japan's LDP and the three cases close to the fitted line in figure 1.2. For these cases, I relied on a rich survey of published studies. The empirical part of the book starts in the next chapter with an analysis of Italy's DC.

PART II

The Main Cases

Italy's DC: Centralized Leadership Selection, High Factionalism, and Centrifugal Pressure

> If it must break apart, the DC will not do so in two but in a thousand pieces, like a crystal.
>
> GIULIO ANDREOTTI, qtd. in Damato (1979, 5)

When election results started coming in on 27 March 1994, it became clear that this was the end of an era. People later described it as "the Great Transformation" (Bardi and Morlino 1994) and the beginning of a "New Italian Republic" (Gundle and Parker 1996). Forty-six years of Christian democratic dominance had come to an end. In fact, Italy's previously strongest party, Democrazia Cristiana (Christian Democracy, DC), had not even competed in the election. It had disintegrated over the direction and extent of reform in the face of profound transformations in Italian politics. Many people might argue that the DC's collapse was inevitable when the *mani pulite*, or "clean hands," scandal revealed the extent to which corruption had pervaded Italian politics. It implicated leading party elites like former prime ministers Giulio Andreotti and Arnaldo Forlani and led to the arrest of over five hundred Christian Democrats in the mid-1990s (Wertman 1995, 136; Smith 1997, 483–85).

This chapter will show that *mani pulite* is crucial for understanding the end of the DC but not sufficient to explain the party's lack of adaptation and that existing accounts of party adaptation would have expected the DC to have initially good chances of adapting. Its frequent changes in party leadership positions and the largest internal factions alongside growing electoral pressure especially in the early 1990s created incentives commonly associated with adaptive reforms. The party leadership initially enjoyed notable formal powers over the allocation of funds and candidate selection, and their flexibility to postpone repeatedly important party meetings, especially during periods of intense pressure, provided them with substantive autonomy from the DC's party congress and council. However, and in line with this book's argument, they were unable to use this autonomy to make urgent changes to the party's platform and organization because of the DC's high level of factionalism. High factionalism already prevented programmatic and organizational reforms in response to the changes in party competition following the end of the Cold War and the gradual shrinking of the party's religious-rural constituency before 1990. Unable to agree on any updates to its traditional appeal, the party increasingly turned to clientelism and corruption as a way to ensure its ongoing success, which endogenously set the stage for the *mani pulite* scandal commonly associated with the party's downfall.

The chapter begins by showing that the eventual choice of a centralized leadership selection process in 1946 incentivized party elites to form factions. It then traces the development of factionalism, showing that clientelism and Italy's electoral system, while not causing the DC's high level of factionalism, were important reinforcing factors by making factional ties valuable for a growing number of actors within and outside the party. High factionalism also drove party elites' incentives to adjust the DC's organization in line with factions' interests, thereby further entrenching factions' prominence within the party. The DC's high level of factionalism already impaired party adaptation before 1990 by blocking the rise of anybody who did not join a faction and rendering internal coalitions highly unstable. The Christian Democrats were thus ill equipped to adapt in the face of changing political rivals, a severe economic recession, and the *mani pulite* scandal. Italy's DC thus shows how a single institutional choice (i.e., centralized leadership selection) can initiate both a self-reinforcing (i.e., high factionalism ensuring a growing set of actors' careers) and self-undermining (i.e., high factionalism threatening these careers by obstructing party adaptation) process of institutional development. The interplay of both processes is key to understand the paralysis of the party's reform process.

The Origins and Consequences of a Centralized Leadership Selection

FROM THE END OF FASCISM TO PARTY LEADERSHIP ELECTIONS

From the beginning of party formation in October 1942, the DC faced the challenge to integrate an array of different social and political groups. From the ranks of the prewar Italian People's Party (PPI) came centrist members around Alcide De Gasperi and Catholic trade unionists, like Giovanni Gronchi and Achille Grandi. They were joined by predominantly southern conservatives and monarchists, such as Carlo Petrone, Stefano Reggio D'Aci, and Stefano Jacini. An antimonarchist group around Domenico Ravaioli came from Rome. The final group that shaped the DC's early years came from northern Italy and brought together young Catholic academics, like Giuseppe Dossetti and Amintore Fanfani, who emphasized left-leaning economic policies, democratic pluralism, and institutional transparency.[1] Toward the end of fascism, they faced a well-organized and popular political left and liberal elites who sought to recover their prewar dominance (Galli and Facchi 1962, 38; Scoppola 1991, 85–90, 108; Smith 1997, 118). Together with De Gasperi's close ties with the Vatican and his integrationist maneuvering, this helped prevent a fragmented political Catholicism (Scoppola 1991, 104, 107).

The context of party formation pointed the DC toward selecting its national leadership by formally dividing the available seats between the northern, central, and southern groups. The Allied landing in continental Italy in September 1943 separated party formation in the liberated south from that in the still Fascist north (Galli and Facchi 1962, 35). Although the northern group still needed to act clandestinely, De Gasperi and the Christian Democrats in southern and central Italy used the regained freedom in June 1944 to advance party formation (Chassériaud 1965, 27–28; Leonardi and Wertman 1989, 35, 125–26). By July 1944, they had elected a party council (Consiglio Nazionale) and executive (Direzione Nazionale) (Capperucci 2010, 59–61).[2] When the northern Christian Democrats could finally act freely after the liberation in late April 1945, their compliance with the programmatic and organizational decisions taken by the central and southern groups was far from obvious. Even though Mussolini's Fascist state had been highly centralized, regionalist identities had traditionally been strong on the Italian peninsula (Smith 1997, 1–10). In addition, the prolonged period of armed resistance had inspired a spirit of solidarity and popular participation in the north (Scoppola 1991, 81–82). It emphasized the ideological differences between this new generation of social reformists and the ex-PPI moderates and trade unionists in central Italy and the conservatives in the south (Capperucci 2010, 61–62). While being cut off from the rest of Italy, the northern group had developed its own leadership structure (i.e., Consiglio Direttivo per l'Italia settentrionale).[3] This "Christian democratic federalism" continued at the first meetings after the liberation when the northern delegates organized as a distinct group (Comitato DC Alta Italia) (Capperucci 2010, 69) and the southerners also repeatedly emphasized their distinct identity (Scoppola 1991, 82).[4]

Alternatively, the cross-class nature of the DC's founding groups could make us expect to see a neo-corporatist organization, similar to the Austrian ÖVP's, which ensured the representation of different occupational and social groups in the party leadership. Corporatism had been less entrenched in Italy than in Austria before fascism, and Mussolini had made little effort

TABLE 3.1. Centralization of the party council and party executive selection process

Time	Executive	Council	Comments
January 1919 (PPI)	0.00	0.58	Four of the 20 party council seats elected by the national congress reserved for minority slate.
July 1944	0.00	0.29	Used at the interregional congress on 30 July and at the party council on 31 July
April 1946	0.00	0.17	Decided by party executive on 17 April and proposed at first national congress on 24 April; 10 of the 60 party council seats elected by the national congress reserved for minority slate
April 1946	0.715	0.275	Competing statutory proposal presented at the first national congress by Ravaioli's group
April 1946	0.33	0.17	Election of national party executive by party council on 29 April
September 1946	0.22	0.69	Ratified by party council; 32 out of 59 party council seats elected by the national congress in a single election

Source: *PPI Statuto*, 18.01.1919; *Lo Statuto*, 1945; *Progetto di Statuto*, 1946; *Statuto*, 1947, ASILS-DC Statuti; *Il progretto di statuto e le mozioni sulla riforma costituzionale, sulla riforma agraria, e sui problem sindacali presentate da "Tendenza" e "Politica d'oggi"*, 1946, HAEU-ADG-78; *Consiglio Nazionale eletto dal I Congresso Nazionale; Consiglio Nazionale della D.C.*, 29.04.1946, both Salvi (1959, 215–18).

to link his brand of state corporatism to Catholic teaching. However, many Catholics initially understood Pope Pius XI's encyclical *Quadragesimo anno* (1931) as endorsing it to ensure class cooperation (Misner 2004, 651, 666–67, 670). While the DC officially spoke out against corporatism and built its organization along territorial rather than class lines, proposals to ensure the representation of different sociodemographic groups within the DC emerged repeatedly during the years of party formation.[5]

Despite these structural conditions, the Christian Democrats debated for two years how to integrate the different groups in the party leadership. The church, which only gradually endorsed the DC, did not intervene in those discussions (Galli and Facchi 1962, 33–35; Warner 2000, 105–10). The debate was between those in favor of a centralized process to select the party leadership and those advocating a more decentralized process (table 3.1). To recap, the level of centralization of the leadership selection process refers to the number of party bodies sending full members (i.e., those with voting rights) to the national party executive and their respective seat share in this leadership committee. Adapting Rae's (1967, 53–58, 62) fractionalization index allows measuring the degree of centralization: $F = 1 - \Sigma(S_i)^2$, where S_i refers to the proportion of seats each party branch is entitled to fill in the national executive. It ranges from 0 to 1, with higher values expressing a higher degree of decentralization (Rae 1967, 58).

For the DC's first interregional congress in July 1944, De Gasperi proposed a centralized leadership selection process. The DC's organizational branches in Italy's provinces should send delegates to the national party congress, which would elect nearly all members of the party council (fractionalization index: 0.29), and the party council would then elect the party leadership (fractionalization index: 0.00) (Webster 1961, 173–75; Capperucci 2010, 66–67, 113). Although this proposal resembled the basic structure of the prewar PPI, it differed from the latter by suggesting an even more centralized structure.[6] This and the political bargaining process that followed illustrate that the DC's rules to select its leaders were not a mere legacy of the PPI (cf. Chassériaud 1965, 37–38, 46).

De Gasperi's suggested leadership selection process did not guarantee the representation of any specific group, like trade unionists or northerners. Instead, it advantaged actors with widespread support among the national congress and party council delegates. De Gasperi surely enjoyed such a support as his opposition to fascism had made him widely popular among many Catholics. Initially imprisoned by Mussolini before spending most of World War II in exile in the Vatican, he became the leading voice in the formation of the DC (Galli 1978, 73; Capperucci 2009, 443). He represented the Christian Democrats in the transitional government and eventually became prime minister in December 1945 (Smith 1997, 418). De Gasperi's influence therefore did not depend on any guaranteed representation in the party leadership. In contrast, the other four main groups involved in party formation, like Dossetti's northern Christian Democrats, would have benefited from a selection process that would have guaranteed the representation of particular provinces or regions. De Gasperi managed to convince the delegates that the party council would be carefully balanced along regional lines without relying on formal quota, with eight seats each accorded to the southern and central provinces and the at that time still occupied north (Capperucci 2010, 81).[7] As northern representatives were immediately integrated in the party executive after the liberation in late April 1945, they had little reason to oppose De Gasperi's proposal.[8]

When the provisory party executive, led by De Gasperi, proposed an even more centralized selection process in 1946, they faced opposition at the first national party congress.[9] The Roman group around Domenico Ravaioli criticized the centralized leadership selection process for excluding minority groups from the party leadership.[10] They proposed to build auxiliary organizations for, among others, trade unionists, business owners, craftsmen, and nonmanagerial employees and to include their leaders in the party leadership together with delegates from other party branches.[11] If this proposal had been adopted, the leadership selection process would have been much more decentralized (fractionalization index: 0.751). Yet De Gasperi succeeded in negotiating the merger of the eight competing slates for the party council into a single list, informally ensuring the representation of all relevant groups (Galli 1978, 82; Capperucci 2010, 110, 113). A centralized leadership selection process thus prevailed. Thirteen of sixteen executive seats were elected by the party council, which was nearly entirely elected by the national congress.[12]

The party council ultimately ratified the DC's first national statute in September 1946.[13] Fearing that they may lose further ground relative to De Gasperi, the other regional groups tried to change the proposed statute to guarantee the representation of minority slates. Their attempt, however, was foiled by De Gasperi and his supporters, who had a majority at that meeting (Galli and Facchi 1962, 39).[14] Italy's Christian Democrats thus established a centralized selection process of the party leadership with two main consecutive arenas of intraparty competition: The national party congress elected the majority of the party council (54.2 percent).[15] The party council then elected fifteen of the seventeen members of the national party leadership (fractionalization index: 0.22).[16] Involving at times vivid discussions and negotiations over competing options, the period of institutional uncertainty had lasted for only around two years, but the eventual outcome proved momentous for the DC's level of factionalism and adaptability in the decades to come.

FROM A CENTRALIZED LEADERSHIP SELECTION TO FACTIONALISM

The divisions between the groups that came together in the DC may seem to make factionalism inevitable, especially given Italy's long tradition of political fragmentation. For centuries, the mistrust and competition between different regions, provinces, and even towns and families had been an important reason for the delay in the creation of an Italian state (Smith 1997, 6–24). Such internal fragmentation had also characterized political Catholicism before and during the interwar period (Scoppola 1963, 28–32, 62–68, 137, 146–9). It started reemerging after the war when the Christian Democrats clashed over tax reform, land distribution, economic planning, and freedom of consciences (Smith 1997, 425). Aware of their internal divisions, they initially tried to delay difficult decisions, but conflicts eventually erupted forcefully.[17]

However, the other parties discussed in this book were similarly divided along territorial and class lines without becoming as factionalized as the DC. The puzzle is not about the existence of internal divisions but about the varying organizational formats parties developed in response to these divisions. When DC minority elites promoted recognizing the regional and ideological divisions within the party's organization during the two years of negotiating the DC's first statute (Capperucci 2010, 84–86), this mainly referred to regionally concentrated groups (e.g., Ravaioli's group from Rome). Surely, factions in the mature DC also had a regional stronghold, and the prewar network of the Catholic trade unions helped Gronchi to reconnect with allies across Italy (Galli and Facchi 1962, 33–35). Yet neither these divisions nor the legacy of informal and clientelist networks within political movements, known as *trasformismo* (Smith 1997, 103–7), explain why and when party elites began expanding their networks across regions and waving them into all levels of the party organization (McAllister 1991, 209).

Analyzing the emergence of the DC's first factions shows that the organizational characteristics structuring the selection of the party leadership, rather than the DC's internal diversity, eventually dominant position in government, or Italy's preferential voting system, drove party elites' incentives to form factions. As the national congress brought together delegates from different organizational branches of the party, the support of a single branch did not suffice to get elected to the party council and subsequently to the national executive. It was thus vital for party elites to expand their power base beyond particular provinces, and chapter 2 has expected party elites who lacked such a network to build one by forming factions. This expectation is supported by the evidence around the formation of the DC's first faction, called Politica Sociale (Social Politics), in early March 1946 (Galli and Facchi 1962, 46). Although its formation preceded the ultimate decision regarding the DC's first statute, it was, nevertheless, driven by the institutional constraints structuring the access to the party leadership. Gronchi and other trade unionists had experienced the negative consequences of the provisional centralized selection procedure adopted at the interregional congress in July 1944. It had left the trade unionists with only one seat in the provisory party leadership.[18] Moreover, they had not received any of the two newly created vice secretary positions in August 1945.[19] Although Gronchi served in the transitional government, the trade unionists had to fear that their influence within the DC would decrease if they were unable to make a strong showing at the first national party congress in April 1946 (Galli and Facchi 1962, 34–46). They most likely knew that De Gasperi did not plan on substantially changing the centralized selection process after participating at several meetings to discuss the DC's organization in the run-up to the national congress.[20] Consequently, they started organizing the trade-unionist base, put forward their own motion at the party congress (Gronchi 1962, 173–74), and tried to mobilize support from left-leaning congress delegates.[21] Only three days before the national congress, Politica Sociale addressed the delegates via its own newspaper:

> The leaders and friends of Politica Sociale . . . are greeting the national congress delegates who are coming from all parts of Italy . . . Politica Sociale wants to be a . . . voice for all those friends who share the same religious, political, and social beliefs within the DC but also within the Italian General Confederation of Labor and for the leaders of all united trade unionist movements in Italy. Those who have followed our first issues and the new members we have been admitting bear witness that we neither lack loyalty nor clarity . . . Today, we inform the leaders of the Democrazia Cristiana and the upcoming party congress about the positions presented in our motion Politica Sociale.[22]

The centralized selection of the DC's leadership board, in combination with party elites' ambition to gain intraparty power, drove these factional activities. Concentrating on the election of the individual party leader would not fully explain Gronchi's move (cf. Ceron 2019; Krauss and Pekkanen 2011). Gronchi was not a candidate to lead the party. It was beyond doubt that this position was reserved for De Gasperi. Only by broadening our understanding of the figurative pie party elites were competing for, we can fully grasp the origins of factionalism in the DC. Other party elites whose influence did not go beyond some few provincial party branches followed Gronchi's example. As the influence of the DC's conservative right hardly reached beyond the Italian south, they had failed to prevent the national congress from endorsing the abolition of Italy's monarchy and to secure more than a single seat in the new party leadership (Galli and Facchi 1962, 44; Galli 1978, 82). After the new leadership had led the party into another coalition with the Communists and Socialists in June 1946 and to painful losses in the local elections in November, Jacini formed the right-wing faction Parola Nuova (New Word) (Capperucci 2010, 119–26).[23] In turn, despite growing disagreements with De Gasperi, Dossetti had refrained from seeking the open confrontation at the national congress. A deeply religious man, he often felt uneasy with the strategizing and maneuvering of politics (Pombeni 1979, 204–9). Yet only controlling a minority of the seats in the party leadership, he and his northern Christian Democrats lacked the power to realize their Keynesian and participatory democratic views. In several letters to De Gasperi, Dossetti criticized that they were practically excluded from all important decisions, and he resigned from the party leadership twice in protest.[24] When De Gasperi led the

DC into a coalition without the Communists and Socialists, Dossetti and his supporters ultimately formed the Cronache Sociali (Social Chronicles) faction (Pombeni 1979, 225, 374–75, 388, 391). While Cronache Sociali remained less well-organized than other factions in the DC's history (Pombeni 1976, 152–58), its purpose was to connect those who were "geographically distant but spiritually close" (Chassériaud 1965, 280). At party congresses, like in 1949, it would install booths to distribute the faction's newspaper, connect sympathizing delegates, and try to recruit new supporters (Galli 1978, 126).[25]

To translate their support at national congresses more adequately into seats at the party council and, subsequently, the party leadership, minority factions tried to replace the majority system used for party council elections with a system of proportional representation (PR). PR had already been used to select the delegates to the party congress in April 1946 to reduce the tensions between monarchists and republicans that divided the local and provincial party branches.[26] This did not cause factions to emerge at the national level. If anything, the majority system that was in place to elect the party council and the party leadership dampened factionalism by incentivizing some minority elites to align with De Gasperi (Sartori 1971, 638–39). Already the statutory proposal put forward by Ravaioli's Roman group sought to expand the use of PR for internal elections.[27] Dossetti and his supporters attempted to introduce it for party council elections but were blocked by the majority around De Gasperi in September 1946 (Capperucci 2010, 119–21).[28] Jacini's Parola Nuova picked up the proposal in the run-up to the 1947 congress. Jacini confirmed the dominant role the DC's leadership selection played in the formation of factions by demanding via his faction's newspaper: "To win the battle in the country, it is essential that PR will be applied within the party and that all internal groups find representation within its leadership and parliamentary life" (qtd. in Capperucci 2010, 139). His initiative failed as the upcoming general election convinced most delegates to comply with De Gasperi's appeal to demonstrate unity (Capperucci 2010, 177–79).[29] Yet it evidences that the use of PR for internal elections, ultimately adopted in 1964, was not the cause but the result of factionalism (Leonardi and Wertman 1989; cf. Sartori 1971; Zariski 1978).

As expected, while minority factions quickly started forming coalitions to increase their influence at party congresses (Capperucci 2010, 308–10; Boucek 2012, 147), De Gasperi, whose election as party leader had shown his widespread support across the DC's organizational branches, only reluctantly but eventually invested into forming a faction. Initially, he sought to suppress minority elites' factional activities by accusing them of violating the party statutes, which implied the threat of party expulsion.[30] However, although the national leadership had the final say over the party's electoral lists and the party's finances (Chassériaud 1965, 78–83), the formal centralization of power proved ineffective to prevent factionalism (cf. Carey 2007).[31] Networks across party branches were simply crucial for party elites to gain power. The threat of party expulsion ultimately lost its credibility when Gronchi's Politica Sociale organized the first publicly noticed factional rally in November 1948 and the party leadership decided against enforcing any sanctions as they feared party fissions.[32] Eventually, Attilio Piccioni, a close ally of De Gasperi, acknowledged the need to build a faction to avoid losing control of the party (Galli 1978, 123). By mobilizing for his positions, De Gasperi's supporters became known as *centristi* within the DC, which pointed toward this group's developing organizational structure (Magri 1954, 358, 366; Boucek 2012, 145–46).

Reinforcing High Factionalism

INTRAPARTY POWER, CLIENTELISM, AND THE ELECTORAL SYSTEM

The DC's initial system of factions had emerged even before a preferential voting system was introduced for Lower Chamber elections in January 1948, which demonstrates that neither the electoral system nor clientelism initiated factionalism within the DC (cf. Pasquino 1972). Gronchi's Politica Sociale faction even predated all postwar elections in Italy, including the local elections in mid- and late March and the Constituent Assembly election in June 1946. While Gronchi probably knew that a preferential vote mechanism had been adopted for the 1946 elections, I have found evidence that the electoral system was used only to advance factional interests in the run-up to the 1948 general election.[33] The uncertainty regarding the electoral outcome appeared to have actually tempered Gronchi's factional activities before the elections in 1946 (Smith 1997, 423).[34] The fact that factionalism in the DC predated Italy's PR system, which allowed voters to express three to four preference votes depending on district magnitude, also helps understand why clientelism did not cause factionalism in the DC. Clientelism on its own would not explain why party elites started moving beyond their local networks to build networks that operated at all party levels. The link between clientelism and factionalism depends on specific institutional settings, such as an electoral system that allows for competition between candidates of the same party (Ames 1995; Carey and Shugart 1995; Golden and Chang 2001). Yet factionalism preceded such a system in postwar Italy.

However, the electoral system and clientelism were important reinforcing factors of factional competition—together with party elites' drive to gain
power within the party and the incentives generated by the initially adopted
centralized leadership selection. Clientelism and patronage, in addition to
campaigning and ideological appeals, helped factions to incentivize delegates
to support them at the party congress. This contributed to factionalism spilling over from the national to the local party level because the number of
congress delegates ultimately depended on the number of party members in
each local branch of the DC (Godechot 1964, 118–26). Factions built strong local roots and cooperated with local party cadres who offered factional leaders
to increase their supporters at the subnational and national party congresses
in return for some payoffs (Pridham 1979, 78; Hine 1993, 118; Donovan 1994,
77).[35] As a result, factional competition started structuring internal competition at more levels of the party and involving a growing set of actors.

Clientelism and patronage in combination with Italy's open-list electoral
system were also useful for minority factions to make their voice heard after
performing poorly at party leadership elections, as theorized in chapter 2. By
threatening to defect in parliament, on whose support the DC-led government
depended, minority factions could increase pressure on the party leadership
(Boucek 2012, 133). They could increase their blackmail potential by increasing
their parliamentary seat share through the accumulation of preference votes
(Chassériaud 1965, 81–83). For this purpose, factional elites cooperated with
local actors who provided votes in exchange for money, public contracts, or
other benefits. Such corrupt networks also included criminal organizations,
like the Mafia (Bufacchi and Burgess 1998, 119). Consequently, factionalism
spilled over from competition within the DC to competition between different DC candidates in general elections and members in both houses of parliament. Yet the pursuit of preference votes did not only enhance minority
factions' influence within the DC's parliamentary group but also emphasized
the value of factional networks within the party hierarchy. The most available source of preference votes was party members along with their families
and friends. This increased the importance for factional leaders to control the
party membership (Hine 1993, 131). Moreover, districts varied in the extent to
which voters expressed preference votes in addition to their party vote, which
made the place on the party list crucial for a candidate's success (Hine 1993, 131;
Boucek 2012, 125). Factions' attempts to increase their seat share in parliament
therefore fed back into reinforcing factionalism at the intraparty level.

While factions had started emerging before the DC's victory in the 1946
election and before the 1948 election made it Italy's dominant party, factional

leaders benefited from the party's position in office to reward supporters (Zuckerman 1979, 158; Hine 1993, 131). Factional leaders built strong ties with state and civil society organizations and exploited public resources. This did not only help to make the factional system persist over time but also prepared the way for the corruption scandal threatening the DC many years later. Benefiting from its permanent position in office, the DC built close links with the Christian Association of Italian Workers (ACLI), the Italian Confederation of Workers' Unions (CISL), Catholic Action, the National Confederation of Direct Cultivators (Coldiretti) and other organizations (Zariski 1965, 26; Belloni 1978, 80–82; Katz 1980, 109–10, 112).[36] They provided factional leaders with funds and facilitated the penetration in social milieus, which helped factional elites to build a set of local clients (Zuckerman 1979, 123–25; Parisella 1997, 202–3). Amintore Fanfani consolidated these ties by developing the so-called *sottogoverno* (literally "under-government" or "underground government"), which referred to the patronage system controlled by factional leaders and their allies (Boucek 2012, 29, 125). They organized the exchange of private goods for votes and of public contracts for money that went directly into the accounts of particular factions (Zuckerman 1979, 120; Della Porta and Vannucci 1994, 236; Golden and Chang 2001, 596). Portfolios, like Post and Telecommunications and the Fund for the South (Cassa per il Mezzogiorno), that controlled numerous public projects were highly popular among factional leaders and usually held by the DC (Leonardi and Wertman 1989, 94). This reinforced actors' incentives to engage in factional activities because they became useful not only to increase intraparty influence but also to make money (Zuckerman 1979, 108).

Although factions thus ended up competing for more than party leadership positions, this does not change the fact that the competition for these positions initiated the factional game. It is crucial to understand why party elites relied on factions to mobilize support. Later chapters show that party elites in other parties also competed for portfolios and public resources but did so without relying on factions. Similarly, clientelism and an electoral system that allows for competition between candidates from the same party supported a high level of factionalism. The latter, however, was endogenous to the choice in favor of a centralized leadership selection in 1946. This decision had led to a system of competing factions, which was reinforced over time as factions' interests affected the recruitment of party members, the parliamentary decision-making, and the allocation of funds (Boucek 2012, 135).

The development of the number of factions illustrates factionalism's reinforcement (fig. 3.1). Brief moments in which the number of factions decreased, like in 1964, 1973, and 1989 must not be misinterpreted as a decrease

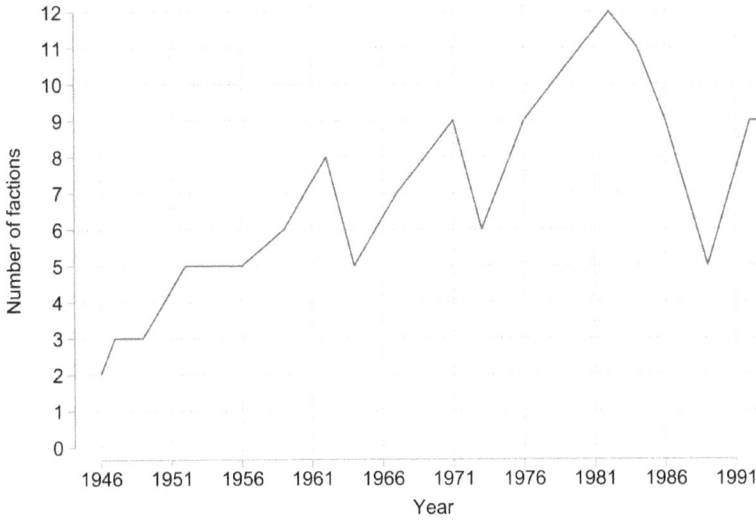

FIGURE 3.1. Factionalism in the DC, 1947–1993
Source: Boucek (2012, 148–71).

TABLE 3.2. Strength of factional lists, 1964, 1973, and 1989

1964		1973		1989	
List	%	List	%	List	%
Impegno Democratico*	46.5	Iniziativa Popolare*	34.2	Azione Popolare*	37
Nuove Cronache	21.3	Nuove Cronache*	19.8	Area del Confronto*	35
Forze Nuove and Base*	20.7	Impegno Democratico*	16.5	Andreotti	17.8
Centrismo Popolare	11.5	Base	10.8	Forze Nuove	7.0
		Forze Nuove	10.0	Fanfani	3.2
		Morotei	8,7		
SUM	100	SUM	100	SUM	100

Source: Boucek (2012, 154, 159, 171). Multifaction coalitions marked with an asterisk.

in factional competition. Small factions had, as expected in chapter 2, formed coalitions to increase their chances at elections taking place at the national congress. These coalitions were often very similar in strength. They also encompassed nearly all delegates at the national congress, which is illustrated by the fact that the reported results in table 3.2 add up to 100 percent. Factionalism remained high.

If the book's argument is correct, we should see high levels of factionalism in parties with an initially centralized leadership selection process beyond the DC. Italy's other main parties during that period support this. Except for the Neo-Fascists and Communists, which fall outside of the book's scope by

heavily restricting internal competition, the remaining parties initially adopted a generally centralized leadership selection process and became highly
factionalized (Belloni 1978, 73, 88; Ceron 2019, 28–29; Katz 1986, 102).[37] The
Socialist Party (PSI), as the party with the highest level of centralization, became the most factionalized party among them (Ceron 2012, 284–93).

Three points emerge from this brief within-country comparison. First,
although observing such similar rules may point toward the impact of
country-level factors on parties' leadership selection process, this analysis
has evidenced that, at least for the DC, such factors did not predetermine its
leadership selection. Second, these cases underline that a party's number of
factions per year provides a good initial but in itself incomplete measure of
factionalism. While the PSI included only an average of three factions until
the late 1960s (Ceron 2012, 292–93), the party was still highly factionalized
as these three factions controlled nearly 100 percent of party congress votes
and seats on the party's leadership board (e.g., Zariski 1962, 376, 378–79).
Zariski's (1962) analysis reveals intense factional conflicts over control of the
party's leadership board, the growing dominance of national factions over
provincial party branches, and repeated gridlocks. This intense factionalism
was only temporarily interrupted by the party's return to Marxist-Leninist
internal rules, which led to a temporary decrease in factionalism, with the
latter resurging when these undemocratic constraints were eased. Third, Italian parties illustrate the value of the book's comparative-historical design.
In many ways, their high levels of factionalism seem overdetermined, with
many factors associated with high factionalism coinciding within Italy's most
highly factionalized parties (e.g., centralized leadership selection, preferential voting and a history of local clientelism, access to government funds and
resources). The book's design helps disentangle this complexity by distinguishing between reinforcing and initiating factors of the DC's high levels of
factionalism.

FACTIONS AND ORGANIZATIONAL CHANGE

While the clientelist activities described in the previous section helped factional elites to gain the resources that were valuable for assuming intraparty
power given the playing field established by the first party statute, they also
tried to modify this playing field in their favor. They thereby reinforced the
incentives to form factions as the dominant strategy to gain influence within
the party. These institutional change attempts not only confirmed and reinforced the importance of factional competition at the national level but
also reproduced it at the regional, provincial, and local party levels. I analyze

such attempts as important episodes in the DC's organizational development (Capoccia and Ziblatt 2010). We can clearly identify when actors made a formal attempt to change the institutions in place, which usually took place at the party council, which prepared the national congress, and at the national congress itself. The latter was empowered to change the party statute, unless it outsourced power to the party council. The key episodes are summarized in table 3.3. Analyzing them allows tracing the path-dependent development of the DC's organization over the long run without getting lost in historical details. Episodes are analyzed together when they encompass the same actors and are close in time.

After defeating minority factions' previous attempts to introduce PR, De Gasperi wanted to encourage small factions to join his majority group by introducing a seat bonus for the faction with the largest vote share at party council elections. The plurality slate at the national congress would gain four-fifths of the party council seats, and the remaining one-fifths were split among the minority candidates.[38] The proposal passed after De Gasperi had given the different factions virtually proportional representation on his own candidate slate for the party council election.[39] Against De Gasperi's intentions, however, the adjustment encouraged party elites to strengthen their factional ties because a faction needed to win only a narrow plurality at the national congress to gain a substantial seat share at the party council. This improved its prospects for the election of the national leadership. Several party elites subsequently sought power through their own factions (e.g., Pastore's Forze Sociali, or Social Forces; Andreotti's Primavera, or Spring). When Fanfani eventually succeeded in uniting most of the party's center-left in his faction Iniziativa Democratica (Democratic Initiative) (Boucek 2012, 147), investing in factional ties, for the first time, led to an internal change in power.

As the internal electoral system adopted in 1952 further undercut the extent to which the party leadership reflected the diversity of groups in the DC, minority factions' campaign for PR gained legitimacy. A coalition of minority factions failed only narrowly to get their motion in favor of PR moved to a vote at the 1954 party congress (Capperucci 2010, 632–42).[40] While another attempt failed in 1956, minority factions obtained the first concession from Fanfani's majority faction, who wanted to finally settle the conflict around the electoral system (Leonardi and Wertman 1989, 110–12).[41] The plurality faction's seat share in the party council was reduced from four-fifths to two-thirds, meaning that the minority slates would henceforth hold twenty of the sixty party council seats elected by the national congress.[42]

The reform episodes discussed so far confirm two points in line with the theoretical framework in chapter 2. First, factions had become the dominant

TABLE 3.3. Main statutory modifications

Year	Modifications	Attempt	Proposal backed by	Effects
1946, 1946, 1949	Introducing PR	Failed	Left- and right-wing minority factions	The debate on PR was framed. Minority factions advocated it for representing intraparty diversity, while majority factions rejected it for encouraging disunity.
1952	Plurality slate at party council elections awarded four-fifths of the seats; remaining one-fifths split among minority candidates	Successful	De Gasperi wanted to increase intraparty cooperation.	Actors were incentivized to develop factions. Winning a plurality at the national congress provided de facto a majority at the party council.
1954, 1956	Introducing PR	Failed	Left-wing minority factions	As the changes in 1952 had further weakened the representation of intraparty diversity, the campaign for PR gained legitimacy.
1956	Decrease in majority seat bonus from four-fifths to two-thirds	Successful	Concession by party leader Fanfani	Minority factions had reached the first concession from majority elites.
1962	Ex-officio membership in the party leadership for former party leaders and DC prime ministers	Successful	Leaders of large factions	Leaders of large factions gained guaranteed membership in the party leadership.
1964	Introduction of PR based on vote share of factions' manifesto motion at the provincial and national congresses	Successful	Small factions hoped to increase their influence while large factions wanted to contain factional defections in parliament.	Factional competition expanded to the local level. New factions emerged which made factional coalitions necessary.
1965	Increase in the number of deputy party leader positions from one to four	Successful	Factional leaders	It facilitated multifaction coalitions.
1967	Allocating party and governmental positions proportional to factional strength	Successful	Massimiliano Cencelli and his *pontieri* faction	Distribution of offices completely depended on factional strength.
	Abolishing factional manifesto motions	Successful	Large factions wanted to encourage coalitions to reduce fragmentation.	The reforms passed between 1967 and 1973 failed to reduce factional fragmentation.

Year	Reform	Outcome	Intention	Effect
1969	Introducing a preference vote component within the bounds of a single faction slate	Successful	Large factions hoped the preference vote mechanism would trigger tensions between small factions.	
1970	3% threshold for representation at the national congress	Successful	Large factions sought to reduce the influence of small factions.	
1972	15% threshold for the party council	Successful		
1973	Any faction gaining 54% at the party congress was awarded 64% of the party council seats; remaining 36% distributed proportionally among minority lists; reduction of electoral threshold to 3%; introduction of factional lists at the local level	Successful		
1976	National congress directly elects party leader	Successful	Party leader Zaccagnini tried to democratize the DC.	No effect on the factional system.
1978	Reintroduction of OLPR	Successful	Factional leaders.	Fragmentation increased.
1984	Election of national congress delegates by regional lists instead of bottom-up PR	Successful	Party leader De Mita wanted to reduce the number of small factions.	Factional coalitions formed

actors in intraparty politics. Second, the statutory modifications that factional leaders promoted kept confirming the primacy of the centralized leadership selection process as the driving force of factional activities. Factional leaders tried to change the translation of support at the national congress into party council and, ultimately, party leadership seats in favor of their respective factions. Both points correspond to path-dependent rather than path-reversing change (Greif 2006, 195–205).

In 1962, the leaders of large factions pushed a statutory change that made all former party leaders and prime ministers from the DC ex officio members of the party leadership.[43] This might seem to go against my argument as the reform formally implied a slight decentralization of the leadership selection by increasing the number of ex officio members. However, this episode corresponds to my theoretical prediction that factional leaders would pursue statutory reforms that aimed to secure their influence vis-à-vis intraparty rivals without, however, eroding the factional playing field. The 1962 statutory change ensured the influence of factional leaders, such as Fanfani and Andreotti, for decades as the leaders of large factions usually held the positions of party leader and prime minister. Moreover, the supremacy of central party bodies in the party leadership election remained untouched.

The role of the party congress and party council as the two main arenas of intraparty competition was also confirmed by the introduction of PR. For almost twenty years, large factions had been rejecting PR for fostering division.[44] Their argument, however, had become absurd because factionalism had emerged despite the use of a majority system for internal elections. Instead, small factions' previous framing of PR as a tool to better reflect intraparty pluralism made it increasingly appear as a potential solution to the ongoing conflict over the DC's coalition strategy for the national government.[45] If PR allowed for a better translation of factions' strength within the party into factions' seat share in the party leadership, the latter's decisions regarding the coalition format might be less subject to intraparty conflict and defection in parliament (Issar and Dilling 2022, 210). Large factions finally agreed to introduce PR in 1964.[46] Each faction presented a party manifesto motion at the provincial and national party congresses. They were then entitled to proportional representation at the national congress and party council, respectively, according to their motion's vote share (Leonardi and Wertman 1989, 113).[47] Factional competition thereby organizationally expanded to the provincial level and put an end to the influence of local notables because it was no longer possible to run for party leadership seats without a factional affiliation (Belloni 1978, 86). Moreover, PR improved the seat share of small factions, which incentivized new factions to emerge and reinforced the need for factional coalitions (Boucek 2012, 152–53).

The following episodes of institutional change were characterized by the leaders of large factions trying to prevent their factions from splitting and to reduce the appeal of small factions without, however, questioning factions' importance. To facilitate coalitions, the number of deputy party leaders was increased from one to four in 1965 (Belloni 1978, 95; Boucek 2012, 153–55). Moreover, the practice to link a manifesto proposal to the factional slate presented at the party congress was abandoned in 1967 to encourage coalitions despite ideological differences (Leonardi and Wertman 1989, 116).[48] Yet the leaders of large factions did not want the new coalitions to challenge their influence. They introduced that preference votes could be cast within the bounds of a slate of candidates, which fostered tensions between small factions that were running on a joint candidate slate (Leonardi and Wertman 1989, 117).[49] To protect the influence of large factions, the new party leader, Arnaldo Forlani, successfully proposed a 3 percent threshold that factions had to overcome to be represented at the national congress.[50] A 15 percent threshold for representation at the party council was added in 1972. Moreover, any faction that gained 54 percent of the vote would be awarded 64 percent of the seats and the remaining 36 percent would be distributed proportionally among the minority lists.[51] Concessions, however, had to be made when minority factions threatened to defect in parliament. The party council threshold was reduced from 15 percent to 3 percent. At the same time, accommodating factional competition "penetrated down to the basic building block of the party organization" as factional lists were introduced at the local level to elect the provincial congress delegates (Leonardi and Wertman 1989, 119).

Factions' strength in internal elections was also formally translated into the allocation of public offices. After his faction had secured 12 percent of the votes at the 1967 congress, Massimiliano Cencelli suggested, "If we have 12 percent, similar to the executive board of a company where positions are divided according to the shares held by the different stockholders, positions in the party and the government should be allocated proportionally according to the support by the party membership."[52] Following the *Manuale Cencelli* (Cencelli's Manual), the number and type of positions each faction received depended on its strength at the national congress. Public offices were ranked in relation to their importance and access to public funds. Ministerial portfolios were worth more (three points) than the prime ministership (two points) and undersecretaries of state (one point) (Boucek 2012, 129). The distribution of offices became a mathematical problem: If one out of two factions of equal strength received a portfolio of the first category, it would receive only two undersecretary positions, whereas the second faction, if receiving a portfolio of the second category, was compensated with a larger number of undersecretary positions.[53]

Factions thereby persisted as the dominant actors of intraparty politics despite individual promises to reduce their influence. Even so-called modernizers, like Benigno Zaccagnini and Ciriaco De Mita, owed their influence to factional support (Hine 1993, 139–49). Summits at which alternative ways of organizing the party should have been discussed, like the national assembly in November 1981, thus passed without major results (Leonardi and Wertman 1989, 120, 133–35). Introducing the direct election of the party leader by the national congress aimed at providing the party with a more democratic appearance.[54] Yet Zaccagnini's reelection as party leader in 1976 still depended on a coalition of five factions (Pridham 1979, 76–78; Boucek 2012, 158–60). As the number of factions had even increased since the introduction of the majority bonus in 1973, an open-list PR system was restored in 1978.[55] Factionalism ultimately peaked at the 1982 party congress, with twelve factions grouped in three coalitions (Boucek 2012, 166). When the new party leader De Mita tried to reduce the influence of small factions by changing the selection of the national congress delegates from bottom-up PR to regional lists,[56] small factions simply countered by forming coalitions.

In short, driven by the ambition to gain power within the DC, the leaders of large and small factions pushed for statutory reforms that underlined the importance of the national party congress and, subsequently, the party council as the main arenas of leadership competition. By doing so, they reinforced the importance of mobilizing support among delegates from different organizational branches of the party as the key resource to assume party leadership positions. Their statutory modifications entrenched factions as the primary organizational units of intraparty competition.

High Factionalism Undermining Adaptability before 1990

A PARTY DROWNING IN FACTIONS

The DC's high level of factionalism was not necessary to integrate the various interests within the party and establish its dominant position in government during the Cold War. It was linked neither to the number of ideological groups within the party nor to the number of social groups within the electorate (Pridham 1979; Zuckerman 1979; cf. Zariski 1965). Instead, the Christian Democrats' position in power was based on anticommunism, the Catholic

Church, and women's suffrage (Hine 1993, 85; Bardi and Morlino 1994, 245–50). With the beginning of the Cold War, the Italian Communist Party (PCI), Italy's second largest party during the Cold War, became the DC's "natural antagonist" (Capperucci 2010, 168). To avoid a communist takeover, the United States entrusted the DC with important financial resources for Italian reconstruction. The Vatican used its strong local presence to urge all Catholics to vote for the DC (Hine 1993, 84, 90–94; Capperucci 2010, 168–71).[57] Pope Pius XII even excommunicated the millions of PCI voters and members in 1949 (Ignazi and Wellhofer 2012, 38). For both the Catholic Church and the US government, the DC was the only available partner (Warner 2000, 105–10). The Italian Socialist Party was initially quite Marxist itself, and the remaining political center was fragmented into the secular center-left Republicans (PRI) and the center-right Liberals (PLI). The latter were also discredited for their role in the advent of fascism. As a result, no minimum-winning coalition that excluded both the PCI and the DC was possible during the Cold War (D'Alimonte 2005, 253–54). The DC would have benefited from both anticommunism and the Catholic Church's initially strong influence even if it had been much less factionalized. Factionalism was also not linked to the DC becoming the main beneficiary of the enfranchisement of women in 1945 (Rossi-Doria 1996).

Instead, the DC's high level of factionalism undermined the party's ability to integrate and mediate between the party's diverse internal interests. As predicted in chapter 2, factionalism spilled over from the intraparty to the parliamentary level (Zuckerman 1979, 158). Factions that were dissatisfied with their share of posts or benefits sabotaged legislative votes to pressure the party leadership into responding to their demands. Benefiting from the secret ballot in the Italian parliament, these so-called *franchi tiratori* (snipers) contributed to the dramatic number of fifty-two governments between 1946 and 1994 and paralyzed the DC's actions in government (Zariski 1965, 14; Bardi and Morlino 1994, 265). Trying to separate internal power struggles from the business of running the government, factional leaders adopted a code of practice in 1969 known as the Pact of San Ginesio. They agreed that "internal shifts in the balance of power within the DC would result from time to time in changes in the choice of coalition partner but would not be allowed to affect the external unity of the DC" (Furlong 1996, 61). However, by detaching internal competition from governmental responsibility, the pact encouraged further factional splits without preventing five different governments between 1969 and the legislative period's end in 1972 (Boucek 2012, 156).

The 1971 presidential election underlined that frictions within the DC rather than the DC's coalition partners or Italy's investiture vote were largely responsible for this instability. Ten Christian Democrats tried to obtain support from other parties for their own candidacy. For an entire year, "this rivalry crippled the normal process of decision-making" and required twenty-three ballots to elect Giovanni Leone as the compromise candidate of the DC's various factions (Smith 1997, 458). The magazine *Tribuna Italiana* adequately depicted the DC as drowning in a sea of factions and factional elites.[58]

GRIDLOCK IN THE FACE OF A CHANGING SOCIETY

Factionalism thus not only was self-reinforcing but also undermined party adaptation long before the dramatic changes of the early 1990s (Hine 1993, 135; Boucek 2012, 165). The centrifugal pressure from competing factions kept party leaders from finding a response to the gradual erosion of their traditional support base. Weekly church attendance decreased from around 50 percent in 1968 to less than 35 percent in the early 1980s (Vezzoni and Biolcati-Rinaldi 2015, 103–9).[59] In addition, agricultural-sector employment declined dramatically while civil marriages, education, service-sector employment, and urbanization increased (Ignazi and Wellhofer 2012, 35–37). These changes eroded the DC's rural-Catholic base, as the two referenda in 1974 and 1981 indicated. Millions of Catholics ignored the Christian Democrats' plea and instead endorsed the legalization of divorce and abortion. Their increasing political independence contributed to the Communists rising from 22.6 percent in 1953 to 34.4 percent in 1976 and winning control over most big cities (Smith 1997, 460). All this raised what Giovagnoli (1996, 164) called "the Christian democratic question": In such a profoundly changed country, was there still room for the DC?

However, factional competition prevented any major changes in the DC's programmatic emphasis (fig. 3.2). The at times vivid reactions the party leadership received in favor of or against the divorce referendum emphasized the pressure the party faced.[60] They had to reconcile demands for socioculturally more progressive positions and those emphasizing the party's Catholic identity. Reconciling such conflicting demands would have been difficult for any party, but factional divisions sabotaged any substantive reforms.

The party leadership often struggled to make any decision at all. No single faction succeeded in winning a majority of party council seats after 1959 (fig. 3.3). Instead, coalitions between several factions were necessary to form a majority, which, however, were highly unstable. Because the high level of factionalism encouraged party elites to form their own factions and to look for alternative coalitions in case of disagreement, initial agreements were frequently contested and renegotiated (Hine 1993, 135). The importance of

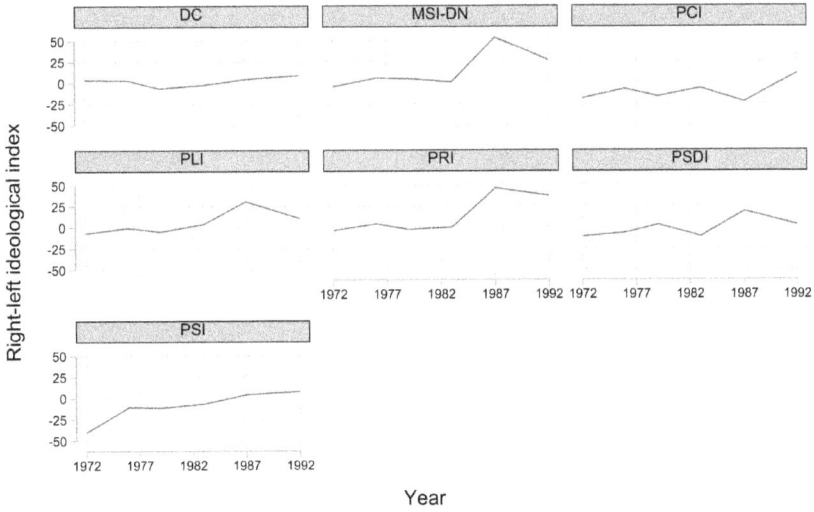

FIGURE 3.2. Italian parties' left-right positions over time

Source: Lehmann et al. (2023), using the Comparative Manifesto Project's summary Right-Left scale (RILE). Negative values indicate an emphasis on left-leaning positions, whereas positive values indicate an emphasis on right-leaning positions. Following the breakaway of its orthodox-Marxist faction, the PCI transformed into the PDS for the 1992 election.

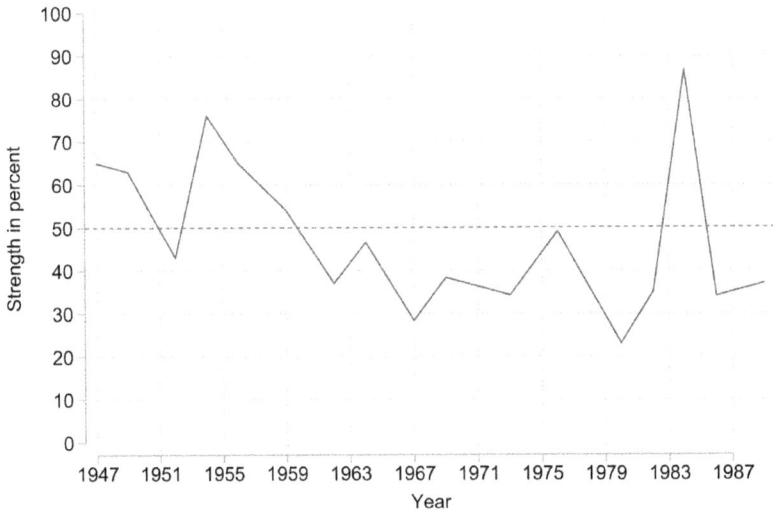

FIGURE 3.3. Plurality list at DC party congresses

Source: Boucek (2012, chap. 7). In 1984, a coalition between seven factions was required to carry 84 percent of the votes in the party council election.

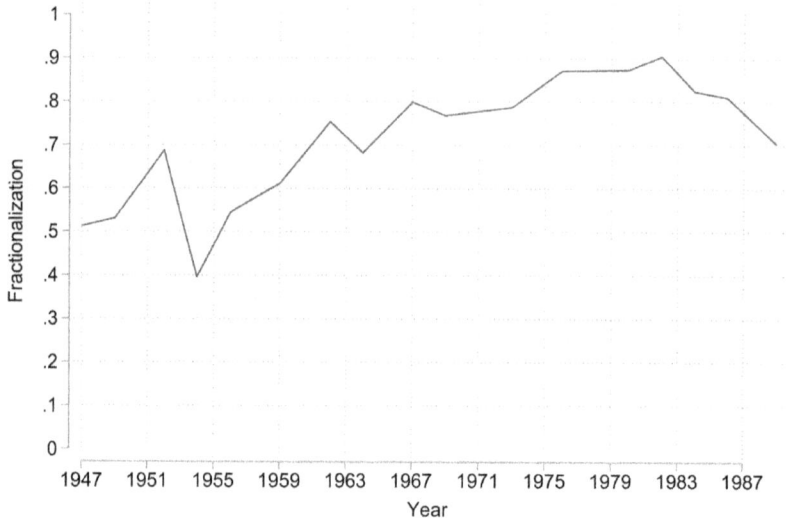

FIGURE 3.4. Fractionalization of the DC party council

Source: Figure from Dilling (2023), based on data from Boucek (2012, 148–71) and using Rae's (1967) fractionalization index to capture the extent to which the party council is split across different factions. It ranges from 0 to 1. Higher values express a higher level of fractionalization.

clientelism and patronage in the reinforcement of factionalism meant that ideological differences played an increasingly minor role in these conflicts. Factional leaders were less constrained by policy positions or ideology and could simply play off competing factions against each other and defect whenever a more lucrative offer came up. Under the headline "The DC in Search of a New Equilibrium," the newspaper *La Stampa* illustrated this nearly continuous rearrangement of factional coalitions that made intraparty majorities inherently unstable. In the run-up to the party council in October 1975, it published a figure showing the different factions and factional elites and indicated by using solid or dotted arrows whether the latter had already or were expected to defect to another faction.[61]

At the 1984 party congress, De Mita succeeded in integrating seven of the eleven factions into a single coalition, which won a sweeping majority at the party council election, but when the party congress later confirmed De Mita as party leader, his result was 30 percent lower than his coalition had votes (Levi 1984, 269–70, 284–86). Forming a stable and coherent party leadership was further complicated by increasing fractionalization. Using Rae's (1967) fractionalization index, we can see that an increasing number of factions had an increasingly similar seat share at the party council (fig. 3.4). As a result, negotiations between factions often ended in gridlock, and "cycling majorities from excessive factionalism" paralyzed the party (Boucek 2012 165).

Factionalism also continued to divide the DC in parliament despite increasing electoral pressure. The 1976 general election had left the party with only a 4.3 percent margin ahead of the Communists. Even though Italy had been shattered by a series of terrorist attacks, Aldo Moro gained his factional rivals' support for a government of national solidarity, which was also backed by the PCI, by giving all DC factions governmental positions. The result was a sixty-nine-member Christian Democratic minority cabinet. And still, 100 of 263 DC parliamentarians dissented at the investiture of this so-called historic compromise (*compromesso storico*) (Pridham 1979, 83; Smith 1997, 455–62; Boucek 2012, 161–62). In consequence, voters started distancing themselves from the DC, as a decline by more than 10 percent in the share of voters identifying with the DC in the 1980s illustrated (fig. 3.5).

Party reform had thus been repeatedly on the DC's internal agenda, without, however, resulting in substantive changes. Since the mid-1970s, the Christian Democrats had widely acknowledged that factionalism prevented the necessary modernization of the DC.[62] While the party's organization allowed for factions to serve as "promoters of special interests," it provided too much room for such groups which severely limited the "capacity of the DC . . . to aggregate interests, and to make clear choices" (Hine 1993, 135). Fighting

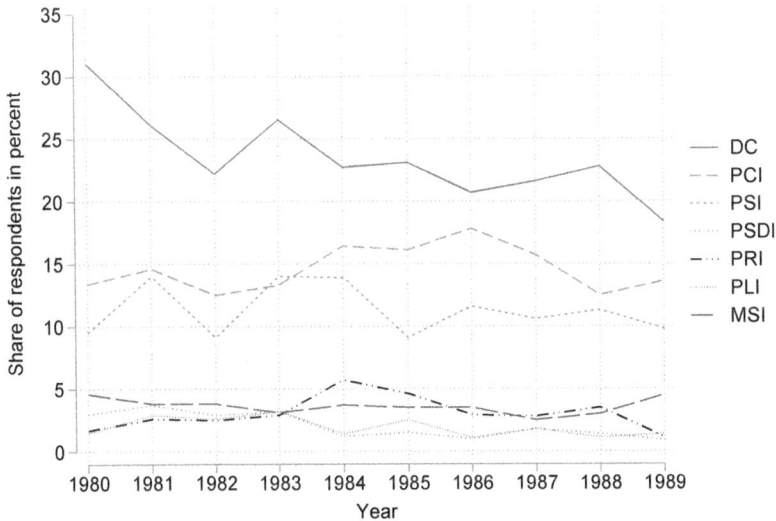

FIGURE 3.5. Party identification in Italy in the 1980s
Source: Bardi and Morlino (1992, 477).

factionalism by, for example, enhancing rank-and-file participation and empowering the party's regional branches were frequently expressed proposals (Leonardi and Wertman 1989, 131, 144). However, while the rhetoric of party reform was widespread, party elites' commitment to reform was much lower "because it would undercut their own power within the party" (Leonardi and Wertman 1989, 131). Even reformers like Zaccagnini depended on multifaction coalitions to assume leadership positions to begin with, which de facto heavily constrained their room for maneuver once in office (Leonardi and Wertman 1989, 131–32). Zaccagnini achieved a higher-than-usual turnover among the DC's parliamentary candidates (26 percent in 1976 compared to 10 percent or less in most elections) (Wertman 1988, 152). Under his leadership, the DC saw some changes to membership registration, which aimed to counter factions' tendency to inflate local membership figures to enhance their seat share at party meetings and to prevent people affiliated with a rival faction from joining the party. The party also briefly experimented with formats to stimulate engagement in the party that sought to bypass the formal party and factional structure, such as the local and national friendship festivals (Feste dell'Amicizia) and party sections organized in the workplace. However, these reforms feel markedly short of the initially discussed proposals and failed to bring any substantive change (Leonardi and Wertman 1989, 132–33).

The second and last more serious reform attempts before 1990 followed the Propaganda 2 scandal and the DC's loss of the premiership in 1981 against the backdrop of deteriorating relationships with the church.[63] A National Assembly was called in November 1981, bringing together an equal number of party members, parliamentarians, and nonpartisan representatives of Catholic civil society (so-called *esterni*), to discuss the DC's "revitalization" (Leonardi and Wertman 1989, 133). It led to the temporary incorporation of *esterni* at the party congress (around 10 percent of the delegates) and De Mita's direct election as party leader (Leonardi and Wertman 1989, 133–4). Similar to Zaccagnini, De Mita achieved a higher than usual level of turnover among parliamentary candidates (17 percent in 1983) and placed some well-known *esterni* on the party's list (Wertman 1988, 152). But again, these changes were rather moderate and also quickly abandoned. The *esterni* played only a marginal role at the party congress and, together with the direct election of the party leader, were again quickly abolished, and De Mita primarily focused on strengthening his own factional power base rather than seeking to abandon or weaken factionalism (Leonardi and Wertman 1989, 134–35).

Unable to reform the party's appeal, the Christian Democrats relied on bribes and clientelism to mobilize support in a system of corruption that became increasingly difficult to sustain (Warner 1996, 134–35; Smith 1997, 475; Boucek 2012, 171). The DC increasingly depended on support from Bettino Craxi's similarly factionalized Socialist Party. Together with the PSI, the DC became associated with a system emptied of political meaning (Scoppola 1991, 399). Elections were about exchanging material favors to confirm parties in office that were too divided to handle the country's problems. The Cold War environment largely kept the DC in office (Leonardi and Wertman 1989, 179; Smith 1997, 457). Italy was deeply rooted in the Western bloc, and the PCI failed to convince other parties and large parts of the electorate that it had wholeheartedly endorsed parliamentary democracy. The death of PCI leader Enrico Berlinguer, who had credibly tried to open his party toward Western democracy, and the (re)establishment of good relations with the Soviet Union and China fostered this impression by the mid-1980s (Bufacchi and Burgess 1998, 19; Smith 1997, 456–76; see also Agosti 1999 and Fanti and Ferri 2001).

Internal Paralysis and the DC's Demise

THE CONFLICTING SIGNALS OF FACTIONALISM

If growing electoral pressure, the rise of new rivals, and leadership change unequivocally triggered party adaptation, the DC should have implemented substantive reforms following the collapse of European Communism. However, when the party council met around a week after the fall of the Berlin Wall, the DC's plan for the future equaled the well-known agenda of the past: European integration, a social-Catholic version of market economy, and the continuation of the DC's coalition with the Socialists, Social Democrats, Liberals, and Republicans, known as the *Pentapartito*, to keep the Communists out of office.[64] According to Forlani, who had retaken the party leadership from De Mita in 1989, there was little reason for change, and Giulio Andreotti concluded: "If they [the PCI] change their name, we will need to call anticommunism differently. I don't know, anti–something else."[65] They had clear incentives to avoid any debate about party reform because it would have risked jeopardizing the precarious internal balance of power.[66] At the 1989 party congress, Forlani's and Andreotti's factions had defeated De Mita's left-wing bloc. While Forlani was rewarded with the party leadership and Andreotti became prime minister, the left had been appeased by making De Mita president of the party council.

However, Forlani's hope that by doing business as usual the Christian Democrats would prevent factional conflicts proved to be flawed. Already in January 1990, a conflict erupted between De Mita's left-wing coalition and

Forlani's and Andreotti's factions. Officially, the disagreement was over a series of policies on local autonomy, immigration, and privatization, but policy
differences hardly played a role in this quarrel, which was, once again, predominantly a struggle for power. His faction had challenged De Mita to demonstrate strength, and the dispute ultimately led to his resignation as president of the party council.[67] Well-documented by the media, the fragile truce
between the three main factional leaders had fallen apart—hardly a year after
it had been forged and even without trying to respond to the changes in Italian politics.[68]

In the post–Cold War environment, politicizing the old DC-PCI antagonism was unlikely to generate similar levels of support for the Christian Democrats as it had before 1990. This became particularly apparent when the PCI
transformed into the more moderate Democratic Party of the Left (PDS) following the breakaway of its orthodox-Marxist faction, and voters had started
to move away from the DC toward regionalist parties (Bufacchi and Burgess 1998, 19–20). The Northern Leagues had been campaigning on greater
autonomy (sometimes including separatist claims) for the economically advanced North.[69] While their results had been hardly impressive in the 1980s,
they experienced a substantive rise in the regional elections in May 1990 (e.g.,
growing by 5.3 percent in Liguria and 18.5 percent in Lombardy), drawing
considerable support from the DC (Diamanti 1996, 117).[70] Addressing some
of the country's urgent problems could have helped the DC to ensure ongoing
electoral support, but its high level of factionalism prevented any substantive
steps. Since the late 1970s and early 1980s, Italy had witnessed an escalation
of organized crime (Smith 1997, 468). By the late 1980s, the southern third of
Italy, according to a judge in charge of the anti-Mafia campaign, was under
"'absolute control' of the criminal underworld" (Smith 1997, 472). However,
many major factional leaders with a power base in the south, like Andreotti
(Sicily) and Antonio Gava (Naples), heavily depended on votes provided by
the mafia (Smith 1997, 468, 472–74). They repeatedly used their influence in
public office to pressure prosecutors and courts, and even threatened the local authorities that they would lose financial grants from Rome if they did not
go easy on some investigations. Uncooperative investigators, like Giovanni
Falcone, were simply transferred to other posts (Smith 1997, 472–74).

Electoral system reform was another issue that illustrated how factional
interests prevented the DC from modernizing. The old open-list PR system
was (rightly) perceived as one of the key institutional features that had eroded
party unity, undermined governmental stability, and nurtured clientelism
and corruption (D'Alimonte 2005, 254). Yet as outlined earlier, the electoral
system had helped reinforce factions' influence. Consequently, Forlani and

Andreotti rejected any electoral reform. In contrast, De Mita, under pressure from some reform-willing second-rank elites from the DC's left-wing factions (e.g., Mario Segni, Mino Martinazzoli), at least formally demanded institutional change.[71] The conflict led to the resignation of those affiliated with De Mita's faction from the Andreotti government.[72] Yet two months later, De Mita suddenly returned as president of the party council. Officially, he had managed to obtain Andreotti and Forlani's agreement to put electoral reform on the party's agenda—without, however, entailing any concrete plans.[73] De Mita's comeback was criticized by Carlo Donat-Cattin's Forze Nuove (New Forces) faction and reform-oriented members within De Mita's own faction as yet another deal at the expense of modernization.[74]

Reform pressure continued to grow in early 1992, when the news that Italy was nearly certain to miss the European Union's fiscal conditions for a common European currency "forced into every home an awareness of the mismanagement" in the country (Ginsborg 1996, 36). Leading businesspeople and industrialists, like Gianni Agnelli who was the president of the Italian automobile manufacturer Fiat, came out strongly against the DC's handling of the ineffective and inflated public sector.[75] Many of the economic actors who criticized the DC had heavily benefited from the system in place. However, the pool of spoils was exhausted, and the complex patronage and clientelism network increasingly caused delays in payment. This frustrated businesspeople and industrialists, who were eager to teach the DC a lesson (Bufacchi and Burgess 1998, 100–101). Moreover, with economic growth in decline, it had become obvious that the system that had allowed so many political and economic elites to enrich themselves had become unsustainable. Having to choose between their own profit and loyalty to the DC, many businesspeople chose the former. The social coalition which had tied the Christian Democrats to Italy's large industrial and business associations had begun disintegrating (Van Kersbergen 1999, 362–63).

However, instead of promising reforms, Andreotti blamed his critics for the poor state of Italy's economy.[76] A public-sector reform was undesirable (and probably also unfeasible) for Andreotti and other factional leaders. It would have required reducing the state bureaucracy and cutting down offices and positions, which factional leaders needed to pay their supporters and appease rival factions (Smith 1997, 471). The *vecchi capicorrente* (established factional leaders) consequently blocked reform-willing party elites, who, in response, started breaking away from the DC. Leoluca Orlando, the mayor of Palermo who was frustrated by the high levels of clientelism and organized crime in Sicily, had been promoting a reform of the DC's factional system, an end of the coalition with the similarly corrupt PSI, and an opening toward the reformist wing of the Communists.[77] When the DC's factional elites ultimately forced him out of office (Smith 1997, 476),[78] he left the DC together with his Sicilian supporters and formed the party La Rete (the Network) (Bufacchi and Burgess 1998, 29–30; Leonardi and Alberti 2004, 111–13).[79] Similarly, because Andreotti, Forlani, and De Mita were eager to preserve the existing electoral system, some reform-oriented Christian Democrats chose to pursue their agenda independently. Mario Segni, a previously rather unknown parliamentarian, became the leading voice of the electoral reform movement. His campaign ultimately succeeded in pushing through a referendum that reduced the number of preference votes from three to one in June 1991 (Bufacchi and Burgess 1998, 26, 66, 152). This was a serious blow to the factional system and increased the pressure on the DC leadership to reform the party (Ginsborg 1996, 25–26).[80] Moreover, Francesco Cossiga, then president of the Republic, left the DC, blaming Andreotti, De Mita, and Forlani for the governmental instability and sabotaging essential reforms (Bufacchi and Burgess 1998, 34, 63).

Still, factional leaders made only minor changes to the party's internal organization at the party council in January 1992. Although the factions' national leaders had a joint interest in reducing their dependence on local brokers, who provided factional leaders with members and votes at internal elections in exchange for money, offices, and public contracts, factions remained the key organizational unit of intraparty politics. Their decision that delegates who were elected by the DC's lower-level organizational strata would represent only 50 percent of party congress delegates was far from being a revolution of intraparty decision-making.[81] The remaining 50 percent (i.e., delegates from the DC's parliamentary groups and representatives from Catholic civil society organizations) still reflected factional loyalties. A second reform focused on the electoral system. To facilitate internal decision-making, the party council decided that the factional slate that won between 45 percent and 60 percent of the votes at party council elections would get a majority bonus of 10 percent.[82] This, however, was unlikely to change anything. As figure 3.3 shows, a single list, usually encompassing several factions, at had been able to win more than 45 percent of the votes only three times in the previous thirty years.

With the Christian Democrats failing to send a clear sign of renewal, the DC experienced a painful decline in the 1992 election. Although the DC still managed to win a plurality, the fact that its vote share fell under 30 percent for the first time was a serious wake-up call. The Christian Democrats had substantially lost ground in its former strongholds, losing voters especially to the Lega Nord and Orlando's La Rete.[83] In its own election analysis, the DC understood its losses as at least partially due to voters perceiving the Christian

Democrats as an "inadequate party to govern the changes" that had been unfolding in Italy and Europe.[84]

The relative autonomy DC leaders enjoyed should have been conducive to
adaptive reforms. Centralizing power and weak formal accountability mechanisms can help leaders bypass internal opposition and introduce reforms
(e.g., Levitsky 2003; Kitschelt 1994; Ziblatt 2017), and for most of its history,
the DC had actually been a formally quite centralized party. The party executive approved the party's budget, established dues and fixed the percentage of
contributions devoted to the provincial and regional party branches, enjoyed
various powers allowing interference in provincial and regional branches'
decision-making, selected the head of the party's lists (*capolista*) for Lower
Chamber elections, and directly chose about one-sixth of the party's Senate candidates in Italy's symmetrical bicameral system (Bardi and Morlino
1992, 538–40, 589; Wertman 1988, 150, 159).[85] Although the DC's statutes formally weakened some of these powers in favor of the provincial and regional
party levels in 1984 (Bardi and Morlino 1992, 543–44), Wertman's (1988) interview and newspaper analysis indicated that the party's practice had hardly
changed. The party leadership also enjoyed the freedom to cancel or postpone
party council and national congress meetings in the early 1990s. The national
congress had last met in 1989; a meeting was long overdue in mid-1992. The
party council was postponed several times and, as a result, did not meet for
six months (Furlong 1996, 66). Postponing these meetings was not the result
of the Christian Democrats simply being overwhelmed by the magnitude of
the challenge. Instead, it was a strategy that party leaders had already used in
the past to deal with factional conflicts.[86]

The party leaders' inability to translate this autonomy into adaptive reforms was due to the DC's high level of factionalism. By the summer of 1992,
it was undeniable that Italy was paying the price for decades of people entering politics because it was financially rewarding (Smith 1997, 471).[87] There
was increasing confirmation that the Christian Democrats, and the Socialist Party, had not only been involved in corruption and patronage but also
had completely lost control of the system they had created. Andreotti, who
had been forced to cede the prime ministership to the Socialist Giuliano
Amato after the election, confessed: "For many things we did in the past,
we deserve hell. May the Lord forgive us."[88] The extent to which factional
leaders in the DC (and PSI) required forgiveness was revealed by the *mani*

pulite or Tangentopoli scandal (Wertman 1995, 136; Smith 1997, 483–85).[89] Andreotti and PSI leader Bettino Craxi had been working together for years to resist prosecution, but the prosecutors possessed enough public support to act (Smith 1997, 474). The investigations had initially been concentrated on Socialist wrongdoings in northern Italy after Mario Chiesa, a Socialist from Milan, had been arrested while concluding a bribery deal. When Craxi, under pressure from the investigators, tried to put all the blame on Chiesa, the latter started to share his insights with the magistrates. In June 1992, the scandal reached the top level of the Christian Democrats' hierarchy when Giovanni Prandini, the DC's former minister of public works, and Severino Citaristi, the party's administrative secretary, were notified that they were under investigation for corruption (Furlong 1996, 65).

While it became clear that the old factional system was irreconcilable with ongoing party success, suggestions, like giving more power to the DC's organizational branches in Italy's regions and making them the key players in intraparty politics, were not followed.[90] Factional leaders were unwilling to sacrifice their own influence, and the DC's high level of factionalism impeded renewing the party leadership. The repeated changes in who was holding different party and public offices and the short life span of DC-led governments should not distract from the fact that the same people kept rotating through key positions. Andreotti had been part of the DC leadership since the first party council meeting in September 1944. Forlani had been part of the factional elite since at least 1952, and the rise of De Mita had begun with the formation of the Base faction in 1953 (Mattesini 2012, 2). When Forlani offered his resignation as party leader at the first party council after the 1992 election, he was immediately asked to remain in post because the other factional leaders were unable to agree on a successor.[91] The question of who should lead the DC split almost all factions. De Mita was challenged in his faction by Mino Martinazzoli's Group of 40 (I Quaranta). The conflict between Franco Marini and Sandro Fontana divided the Forze Nuove faction. Scotti abandoned Gava's Grande Centro. Andreotti was challenged by the Andreottiani Ribelli behind Sbardella, and Segni had organized his followers as Trasversali (transverse) (Leonardi and Alberti 2004, 113).[92]

When the Lega Nord replaced the DC as the largest party in Mantua in September 1992, factional leaders finally compromised on Martinazzoli as new leader, but without agreeing to substantive reforms.[93] Martinazzoli had not been discredited by the corruption scandal, and his power base in northern Italy promised to win back voters from the Lega (Bufacchi and Burgess 1998, 109; Leonardi and Alberti 2004, 116). Yet the old factional leaders were unwilling to step aside and accept reforms that jeopardized their influence.

Andreotti simply noted that the election of a new party leader did not mean "We all need to retire now."[94] The old guard had sufficient power to block, for instance, the regionalization of the party organization that, Martinazzoli hoped, would diminish factional power (Furlong 1996, 66–67; Leonardi and Alberti 2004, 111, 116). When Martinazzoli tried to downsize the party executive from forty-eight to around fifteen members in March 1993, the established factional cadres ensured that their representation at the DC's highest levels remained secure (Donovan 1994, 79; Wertman 1995, 144).[95] While the Christian Democrats under legal investigation were ultimately excluded from deliberations, the long-awaited Constituent Assembly in July 1993 nearly ended in a complete disaster as Martinazzoli barely managed to prevent a party split between modernizers and traditional factional elites (Wertman 1995, 135, 141). Factional divisions also crystallized among the reformists, with Martinazzoli preferring a left-leaning course and Clemente Mastella promoting a center-right coalition. Factional struggles prevented an agreement on electoral alliances for the local elections in November and December 1993, which was one of the key factors for the DC vote dropping to 11 percent (Wertman 1995, 136–38, 144; Bufacchi and Burgess 1998, 155).

With factionalism preventing any serious change, there was little holding the DC together. Segni had ultimately formed his own party in March 1993, and Ermanno Gorrieri left some months later to help found the Social Christians Party (Wertman 1995, 138, 142, 147; Furlong 1996, 68–69; Ginsborg 1996, 32; Leonardi and Alberti 2004, 114–17). In January 1994, when a general election was announced for March, the DC was a mere shadow of its former self. Andreotti and other traditional leaders had left politics for good due to the investigations against them. The remaining DC ultimately split over the strategy for the upcoming election, which was held under the new electoral system passed in August 1993 and encouraged parties to run as cartels. Mastella and his supporters left the party to form the Christian Democratic Center (Centro Cristiano Democratico, CCD), while Martinazzoli transformed the remaining DC into the Italian People's Party (Partito Popolare Italiano, PPI) (Bufacchi and Burgess 1998, 167–68; Leonardi and Alberti 2004, 118; D'Alimonte 2005, 257). However, this happened not because the dynamics of the electoral competition made it impossible to hold the party together but because there was nothing left worth holding together.

Conclusion

The case of the DC has generated some important insights for the study of party adaptation. First, while election defeats, changes in rival parties, and changes in a party's dominant internal coalition certainly matter for adaptive reforms, they are more accurately theorized as necessary rather than sufficient conditions. Especially the fundamentally transformed issue space, rival parties, and electoral system after 1990 put immense electoral pressure on the DC. However, changes in its dominant factional coalition did not translate into substantive reforms because of the conflicting incentive structure the DC's high level of factionalism had created for its leaders. On the one hand, a dramatically changed issue space, new political rivals, and a new electoral system required reforms in how the DC mobilized votes, and its high factionalism was an obstacle to such reforms. On the other hand, factional leaders continued to have an interest in keeping the factional system in place because they had built their political lives on it. The result: half-hearted changes that came nowhere near addressing the party's problems.

Second, analyzing the DC also allows refining the leadership autonomy account. Levitsky (2003) is right that the routinization of formal accountability mechanisms constrains party leaders, which can delay or even block adaptive reforms, but we cannot conclude that informal party organizations necessarily provide leaders with substantively more flexibility. Although factional competition led to repeated changes in the DC's formal organization, factions existed independently of the DC's organization. It was leaders' accountability toward their factions that prevented reforms even though the DC leaders could safely postpone or cancel formal party meetings.

Instead, the evidence has supported the book's argument. Political actors were free to decide on the DC's organization in 1946, and they made what, a posteriori, might be considered the wrong choice for party adaptation. The centralized selection process meant that party elites depended on support across different organizational branches of the DC to get elected to the party leadership, which encouraged the formation of factions. The resulting level of factionalism was reinforced over time as factional leaders changed the internal playing field in their favor and used public resources to strengthen their factions' appeal. The high level of factional competition paralyzed the party's internal decision-making, prevented the rise of anybody not associated with a faction, and made clientelism the dominant way of linking people to the party. Factional competition therefore prepared the corruption scandal that discredited the DC in the 1990s. When the transformations of the early 1990s challenged the DC to adapt, factional leaders were unwilling to compromise on their factions' influence and the extent and direction of reform. Eventually, splitting five times in three years, the DC ultimately ceased existing in 1994. Andreotti's prediction proved right: "If it must break apart, the DC will not do so in two but in a thousand pieces, like a crystal" (qtd. in Damato 1979, 5).

4

Austria's ÖVP: Decentralized Leadership Selection, Low Factionalism, and Organizational Rigidity

It is about cutting back the influence of the three previously dominant Leagues . . . and the Land organizations. . . . Interests of less noted groups . . . must be emphasized more within a new ÖVP.

HARRY HIMMER (1990)[1]

While the previous chapter showed how a centralized leadership selection can undermine party adaptation by allowing for too much factional competition, this chapter evidences that giving no room to factions also weakens a party's ability to adapt. Unlike Italy's DC, the Austrian People's Party (Österreichische Volkspartei, ÖVP) did not collapse; it even returned to office after sixteen years in opposition and again became the major governing party after thirty years. However, despite this recovery, the ÖVP is a clear case of weak party adaptation. For almost fifty years, its leaders discussed very similar reforms in response to their shrinking core constituencies but passed only very small and notably watered-down changes. Since the mid-1960s, party elites have identified the need to change their inflexible corporatist organization and rural platform. However, despite an extended stay in opposition, a rising radical-right competitor, repeated replacements of the party leader, and a dramatic decline in electoral support, more far-reaching reforms were introduced only in 2017.

At first glance, the ÖVP's weak adaptability seems to support the leadership autonomy argument. The ÖVP has been widely described as a highly decentralized party with a routinized set of internal rules and procedures (e.g., Müller 1994; Müller and Steininger 1994b; Ableitinger 1995; Müller, Plasser, and Ulram 2004; Wagner 2014, chap. 7.2). My factionalism argument helps improve our understanding of the ÖVP's trajectory in three ways. First, it shows that the ÖVP's high level of institutionalization was, at least partially, driven by the type of resources that were valuable given its decentralized leadership selection and low level of factionalism. Second, it shows the value of moving beyond the leadership autonomy account's focus on the individual party leader. Although the nominal party leader matters (e.g., Rahat and

Kenig 2018), many parties, including the ÖVP, are de facto led by a small clique of elites, with the party leader being a primus inter pares. In such parties, even if that group enjoyed a high level of formal autonomy from lower party levels (as in the DC; see chapter 3), adaptive reforms are still unlikely if they represent conflicting interests, as was the case in both the DC and ÖVP. My argument thus helps explain why parties with very different levels of formal institutionalization still ended up experiencing similar difficulties around party adaptation. Third, my argument helps sharpen our understanding of causal mechanisms by shifting the attention from parties' internal playing field to the actors active on that playing field. While the DC's struggle to mediate between rival party elites was the result of the extreme flexibility entailed by the proliferation of potential factional coalitions, gridlock in the ÖVP resulted from a lack of flexibility. It resulted from the absence of factions and its decentralized leadership selection, which entrenched the influence of internal groups that had quite different preferences and were increasingly ill suited to reflect Austrian society.

This chapter outlines these points by following the same steps as in the previous case study. It begins by showing why the ÖVP's decentralized leadership selection was neither a legacy of prewar politics nor the result of Austria's postwar political system. The choice of a decentralized leadership selection rather than choices regarding candidate recruitment and internal party financing best explains the ÖVP's low level of factionalism. Majority elites used resources from Austria's corporatist system and changes to the ÖVP's organization to reinforce the low level of factionalism. It prevented the rise of any new leaders and ideas who did not have a power base in the ÖVP's territorial and auxiliary branches, which constrained innovation of the ÖVP's manifestos and organization. While majority elites acknowledged the low level of factionalism as an important obstacle to party adaptation, it also protected their own position of power within the party. This dilemma resulted in a very slowly unfolding reform process, leaving the basis of the ÖVP's low level of factionalism largely untouched.

The Origins and Consequences of a Decentralized Leadership Selection

TOWARD THE PARTY OF LEAGUE AND LAND ORGANIZATIONS

The ÖVP is a good case for illustrating the analytical value the critical juncture framework can offer in the analysis of party organizations. It initially adopted a decentralized leadership selection process, which guaranteed the representation of majority elites from the party's auxiliary branches for particular occupational groups (i.e., the so-called Leagues, or *Bünde*) and the party's territorial branches in Austria's states (*Länder*) on the party's leadership board. Tracing key actors' decision-making process leading to the decentralized leadership selection underlines that actors' prewar experiences and postwar structural conditions did not determine the party's organizational format. Felix Hurdes's idea to form a catch-all party that mediated between different social and political interests was surely inspired by his prewar and wartime experience. He had been politically socialized in the Catholic youth movement during the 1920s in Vienna, where he had experienced the tensions between the Marxist Socialists, the increasingly authoritarian Christian Social Party, and the paramilitary Home Guard. The tensions had eventually culminated in violence, the replacement of democracy with an authoritarian-corporatist system (the Ständestaat), and Austria's annexation by Nazi Germany in 1938 (Reichhold 1975, 54, 62–63; Bruckmüller 1995, 286–94). Hurdes wanted to save postwar Austria from a similar fate by forming a political party that went beyond the Christian Social Party's confessional appeal and integrate blue- and white-collar workers, farmers, and the middle class (Kriechbaumer 1995a, 13–15).[2]

Hurdes had initially planned to set up only working committees for agricultural, labor, and economic policy, which would aggregate the interests of their respective constituency without interfering too much in the party's decision-making (Reichhold 1975, 77). Although they should be "represented" within the national leadership (Reichhold 1975, 77), it is unclear whether Hurdes was thinking about ex officio members with full voting or only advisory rights (Ableitinger 1995, 142–44). However, he sought a party "that was to be represented by central [party] bodies" (Reichhold 1975, 77) and not "constituted along corporatist [*bündisch*] lines" (Kriechbaumer 1985, 146). This might indicate that Hurdes was planning on making central party assemblies, like the national congress, key arenas in the selection of the party leadership. The historical data, unfortunately, do not permit less speculation.

Hurdes's plan started to be amended in 1939–1940, when he met with a group of trade unionists around his old friend Lois Weinberger and prewar Catholic labor leader Leopold Kunschak (Weinberger 1948, 92–93; Reichhold 1975, 32).[3] Weinberger quickly endorsed Hurdes's catch-all party idea but expected Kunschak to "gently show him the door" when he suggested reaching out to the farmers and the middle class, because Kunschak had suffered under the dominance of agrarian and middle-class interests in the Christian Social Party before the war (Weinberger 1948, 110). To Weinberger's surprise, Kunschak agreed to seek support for the new party among groups situated on the political right rather than the left. Yet he insisted that the influence of the different occupational groups should be formally built into the party's organization. This differed from the loose organization of the Christian Social Party, which had maintained ties to the associations of farmers, Christian trade unionists, and tradespersons without guaranteeing their equal say in the party leadership (Boyer 1981, 351; 2010, 323–24; Gottweis 1983, 55; Ableitinger 1995, 149; Müller 1994, 56; Bruckmüller 1995, 228–29). This had marginalized labor interests, which Kunschak wanted to avoid in the new party (Kriechbaumer 1985, 52).

Plans for organizing occupational groups at all levels of the ÖVP were thus not an institutional legacy of the Christian Social Party but originated from Weinberger and Kunschak's political calculations before they had even contacted representatives of the farmers and the middle class (Weinberger 1948, 112; Kriechbaumer 1985, 52). Gaining the farmers' support for their project proved difficult. Their most obvious spokesman, Josef Reither, president of the Chamber of Agriculture before Austria's annexation, was under observation by the Nazi secret police (Weinberger 1948, 95–96; Kriechbaumer 1985, 54–55). Prospects improved when Leopold Figl, who had been director of the farmers' association in Lower Austria and enjoyed some freedom to travel thanks to his job as a road engineer, was released from Dachau in May 1943 (Kriechbaumer 1985, 55–57). At Easter 1944, Weinberger, Hurdes, and Figl agreed to reestablish the farmers' association and integrate it into the new people's party (Reichhold 1975, 59). It would also include Vinzenz Schumy, former leader of the prewar Rural Federation Party (Landbund), whom Figl convinced to join to prevent the fragmentation of the agricultural vote (Kriechbaumer 1985, 143; 1995a, 20; 1995b, 87). To appeal to the middle class, the group reached out to Julius Raab, who had been a member of the Federal Economic Council (Kriechbaumer 1985, 55). While Hurdes and Weinberger had initial reservations about Raab, given his career in the authoritarian Ständestaat, his network and reputation were important for the new party (Kriechbaumer 1985, 56, 60–62). Aware of the preparations to formally entrench labor and agricultural interests into the party's organization, Raab began preparing an organization that represented employers' interests. This differed from Raab's prewar efforts, when he had aimed to integrate both employees and employers from the same occupational branch into a single association (Kriechbaumer 1985, 62).

The ÖVP's corporatist structure therefore predated the reestablishment of Austria's neo-corporatist system, which emphasizes that the ÖVP did not adapt it to align its organization with the wider political system (cf. Bruckmüller 1995, 286–94). When the ÖVP constituted on 17 April 1945, its first leadership committee included representatives from all the groups that the new party aimed to integrate: Kunschak, Hans Pernter and Weinberger for the Workers and Employees' League (ÖAAB), Figl for the Farmers' League (ÖBB), and Raab to represent the Business League (ÖWB).[4] The party's corporatist structure and guaranteed representation of occupational interests in the party leadership thus predated the reestablishment of the Austrian Chamber of Labor, Chamber of Agriculture, and Federal Economic Chamber in August 1945 and 1946, which actually followed intense pressure from the ÖVP's Farmers' League (i.e., Leopold Figl) and Business League (i.e., Julius Raab) (Tálos 1985, 60–66; Kriechbaumer 1995a, 29). Rather than causing the ÖVP's League structure, the occupational chambers in 1945–1946 were thus, at least partially, endogenous to the Leagues' interests. Reestablishing the occupational chambers, in turn, was the foundation for the development of Austria's neo-corporatist system in the 1950s and 1960s (Tálos 1985, 60–66).

The founders' willingness to accept a party that was organized along occupational lines was likely inspired by their personal background (Reichhold 1975, 61; Ableitinger 1995, 142). Raoul Bumballa, representing the liberal part of the Austrian resistance, and Hurdes were the only members of the leadership board without a power base in the occupational groups.[5] Hurdes was thus relatively alone with his hope to minimize their influence within the party leadership (Gottweis 1983, 56; Ableitinger 1995, 143). In contrast, Figl's and Raab's former involvement in the Farmers' Association and the Federal Economic Council, respectively, has already been mentioned. Kunschak had been leader of the Workers' Association (Blenk 1966). Weinberger had worked as secretary of the employees' association and, from 1934 to 1938, as chairman of the trade union for employees in the banking and insurance sector (Weinberger 1948, 88). In their view, a corporatist organizational structure was not discredited by the Ständestaat but instead in line with Catholic teaching, like in *Quadragesimo anno* (1931), which had influenced their political socialization (Weinberger 1948, 52–69, 88, 92–93; Reichhold 1975, 32, 52–54, 62–63; Bruckmüller 1995, 290).

However, this does not explain why the occupational structure remained a constituent part of the ÖVP's organization when the latter expanded to the entire Austrian territory. The Allied powers (i.e., Soviet Union, United States, United Kingdom, and France) had divided Austria into four occupation zones (Rauchensteiner 1979, 24–41), and all decisions regarding the ÖVP's organization were initially restricted to Soviet-controlled Vienna and northeastern Austria (Reichhold 1975, 93). The Christian Democrats in the Soviet zone could not be certain that their idea to form the ÖVP, not to speak of their organizational choices, would be accepted nationwide. Contact with the western Länder had stopped with the imprisonment of Hurdes, Figl, and Weinberger in July 1944, and once the war had ended, the Allies strictly prevented any travel or communication between occupation zones (Reichhold 1975, 100; Kriechbaumer 1985, 62, 109–11, 144). The formation of competing parties in the western zones was a serious risk for the Viennese ÖVP, and rumors were spreading that the Allies were considering establishing a provisory government and maybe even a separate state in the western Länder (Rauchensteiner 1979, 66–67, 73–74; Kriechbaumer 1985, 142–44; 1995a, 23–25; 1995b, 87–88).[6]

While upholding its 1933 decision to not participate in party politics (Reichhold 1975, 74), the Catholic Church played an important role in facilitating contact with the western zones. After Raab had tried in vain to pass from the Soviet to the American zone, the ÖVP elites agreed on more dramatic measures and chose Herbert Braunsteiner, the most physically fit member of their group, to cross the zone border by swimming the river Enns.[7] Braunsteiner had been equipped with a letter from Cardinal Innitzer asking the clergy in the western Länder to help Braunsteiner, and Bishop Fliesser in Upper Austria and Bishop Rusch in Tirol importantly mediated between Braunsteiner and the local political elites (Kriechbaumer 1985, 145–46).[8]

Braunsteiner's report showed how uncertain it was whether the western groups would follow the Viennese ÖVP. In Tirol, former resistance partisans and members of the Christian Social Party had already formed the Democratic Austrian State Party (Reichhold 1975, 99).[9] Moreover, the Tirol People's Party, which had been the Christian Social Party's name in Tirol, discussed maintaining their political and organizational independence.[10] The Christian workers' association also expressed reservations against joining the ÖVP.[11] In Salzburg, political elites had formally reconstituted the Christian Social Party, and the Democratic Party had been formed in Carinthia (Reichhold 1975, 96–97; Kriechbaumer 1985, 145). In contrast to the ÖVP's Leagues, many western organizations, like in Salzburg and Upper Austria, included only occupational working committees, which did not participate in the decision-making at the leadership level (Reichhold 1975, 94, 96).[12] This reveals that the experience of corporatism and Catholic teaching did not have an unequivocal effect on the preferences of all actors involved in party formation.

While the occupation zones and Austria's tradition of federalism had surely encouraged such scattered power centers prior to the creation of a national party (Panebianco 1988, 50–65), they did not automatically translate into the Land and League organizations gaining the right to autonomously select seats on the party's leadership board.[13] The first attempt to unite the different groups failed on 23 June 1945 (Kriechbaumer 1995a, 25). Many western

representatives feared that by joining the ÖVP, they would surrender themselves to Soviet control, because the ÖVP was participating in the predominantly Marxist provisory government in the Soviet zone. While this first of
four federal conferences resulted in the establishment of a separate head office for the western Länder, it remained uncertain whether this would be the
first step toward merging the western organizations into the ÖVP or toward a
separate political party (Kriechbaumer 1985, 89; Reichhold 1975, 115).[14]

Important progress had been made toward party unification when the
Land representatives from western and southern Austria met on 29 July 1945.
Karl Gruber's Democratic Austrian State Party had agreed to merge with the
ÖVP on the condition that Gruber become foreign minister after the first
national election (Reichhold 1975, 115–16).[15] Moreover, the Tirol workers' association had decided to join the new party after their leader Hans Gamper
negotiated the guaranteed representation of his group in the ÖVP's Land
leadership.[16] However, it was still contested whether the representation of
occupational groups should be guaranteed at all party levels (including the
party leadership). Salzburg's party secretary August Trummer wanted to integrate such interests as mere expert committees rather than constituent pillars
of the party organization alongside the territorial branches (Reichhold 1975,
97; Ableitinger 1995, 146). It is likely that the delegations from Upper Austria,
Lower Austria, Vienna, Burgenland, and Tirol, which also included League
representatives, foiled Salzburg's initiative.[17] Yet in the run-up to the third
conference on 19 August 1945, Salzburg's position had won support among
the western delegates (Ableitinger 1995, 146).[18]

To turn things around, leaders of the Viennese ÖVP (e.g., Figl, Raab,
Weinberger) visited the western Länder between 20 and 22 September 1945 to
promote the corporatist structure and organizational unity (Ableitinger 1995,
147; Kriechbaumer 1995a, 25). Their efforts benefited from the Allies' decision
on 11 September to allow the nationwide operation of political parties. They
also invited representatives from the SPÖ, ÖVP, and KPÖ from all Länder to
meet on 24 September to discuss the western Länder's integration into the
provisory government and the date for the first national elections (Reichhold
1975, 107). The Land representatives chose to show unity at the fourth Länder
conference on 23 September 1945 (Kriechbaumer 1995a, 25). All Land organizations acknowledged the ÖVP leadership in Vienna around Figl and the representation of the Leagues in the national executive. In return, all Land leaders
also became ex officio members of the party leadership (Reichhold 1975, 116).[19]

As the national party leadership ratified the ÖVP's first party statute
in early 1946, it is not surprising that the decentralized selection process
changed only marginally (table 4.1).[20] The party congress elected the party

TABLE 4.1. Composition of the ÖVP's leadership board (Bundesparteileitung) in 1945–1946

Party branch	National executive seats
National congress	7
Leagues	3x1
Women's movement	1
Land organizations	9x2
Total	29
Rae's fractionalization index	0.89

Source: Müller (1992, 76). To recap, I adapt Rae's (1967, 53–8, 62) fractionalization index to measure the degree of centralization of the leadership selection process: $F = 1 - \Sigma(S_i)^2$, where S_i refers to the proportion of full members (i.e., those with voting rights) of the national executive that party branch i is entitled to select. It ranges from 0 to 1, with higher values expressing a higher degree of decentralization.

leader, party secretary, treasurer, an administrator for organizational development, and two policy spokesmen as members of the national executive.[21] The three Leagues, the women's movement, and the nine Land organizations autonomously elected their respective leaders, who were ex officio members of the national executive.[22] The leadership selection was thus highly decentralized (Rae's fractionalization index: 0.89). The ÖVP's national executive's decentralized selection was also mirrored in the selection of the smaller and less influential executive committee (Bundesparteivorstand, later called Bundesparteipräsidium), which included, in addition to the party chairman and party secretary, the leaders of the Leagues and the women's movement (Müller 1992, 80).

FROM DECENTRALIZED LEADERSHIP SELECTION TO LOW FACTIONALISM

The ÖVP's Leagues were not factions. As shown in chapter 3 on the DC, factions can form, merge, and split according to whatever alliance party elites were willing and able to form. The ÖVP's Leagues, in contrast, have not had this flexibility. Instead, they are more accurately described as basic building blocks of the ÖVP's organization. Any merger, split, or formation of a League would have involved an organizational reform of the entire party. Instead, factionalism has been low in the ÖVP even though power has been decentralized, which, following Carey (2007), should have been conducive to higher levels of factionalism. Candidate selection for parliamentary elections was initially controlled by the Land organizations (Müller 1992, 102–3).

The national party initially depended on financial transfers from the League branches at the Land level. The latter also controlled the recruitment of party members, who almost exclusively joined the ÖVP indirectly via one of its Leagues (Müller 1992, 46–48; Müller and Steininger 1994b, 11–13). The national party, finally, was understaffed and underresourced compared to the League and Land organizations (Kriechbaumer 1995a, 29).

Carty (2010) might suggest that party elites did not form factions because there was nothing worth competing for at the national level, but there is evidence that the decentralization of power in the ÖVP was endogenous to the incentive structure created by a decentralized leadership selection. By 23 September 1945, it had been decided that the party's national executive would mainly be composed of the Land and League leaders. This decision predated the discussion between the political parties and the Allies about the first postwar election, the candidate selection for that election, and the ratification of the ÖVP's first party statute in early 1946. The party statute was ratified by the national executive, where the ÖVP's Land and League leaders had a solid majority. Although no minutes of the national executive meetings in 1945 and 1946 are available, a comment by Hurdes in April 1946 indicated that the decision to provide the Land and League organizations with substantive powers was the result of their majority elites' attempt to consolidate their influence.[23]

The rules that regulated the ÖVP's leadership selection entailed important dynamics for the two sets of party elites introduced in chapter 2. The decentralized leadership selection process established two essential arenas of intraparty politics: the party's Land and League organizations. Majority elites (i.e., actors who managed to assume leadership positions in their Land or League branch) enjoyed guaranteed access to the party leadership. As they could take part in all important party decisions, they had few incentives to form factions. Minority elites (i.e., actors who were not elected to leadership positions within their party branch) did not have direct access to the party leadership. Their minority status would not have changed if they had cooperated with actors from other Land branches.[24] Yet the ÖVP corresponds closely but not perfectly to the ideal type of a party with a decentralized leadership selection process described in chapter 2. Although the vast majority of leadership positions were elected autonomously by the different Land and League branches, around 24 percent of the positions (seven of twenty-nine seats) were elected by the national party congress.[25] We might thus expect minority elites to form factions in their attempt to win these seven seats.

As expected, minority elites tried to form factions but ultimately failed to gain much traction with these efforts. While Bumballa had been included in the national executive in April 1945 to attract former members of the resistance movement (Kriechbaumer 1995b, 87), his future place among the party's leaders was not guaranteed as he lacked a power base within one of the Land or League branches. He tried to organize support by forming the "Democratic Union," which can be considered the first step toward forming a faction.[26] The ÖVP's leadership selection process, however, made Bumballa's efforts likely to fail. To see why, recall from chapter 2 that the party congress included majority and minority elites from different party branches. To win the seats elected by the party congress, Bumballa's group would have needed to unite a share of minority elites across party branches and also win the support of some majority elites and their followers.

As expected by my framework, majority elites were not incentivized to support factional activities because they enjoyed ex officio membership in the party leadership. Even if supporting a faction had helped them to win the seven seats elected by the national congress, it would not have got them even close to a majority in the national executive. Moreover, engaging in factional activities would not have directly helped them strengthen their base within their own party branch. Such a base, however, was their key resource in intraparty politics. Majority elites were encouraged to focus on strengthening those networks rather than forming factions across party branches.

Consequently, the choice in favor of a decentralized leadership selection was momentous for the low level of factionalism that followed. Party elites who wanted to gain influence within the ÖVP built a power base within a Land or League organization. Viktor Müllner, for instance, who was, like Bumballa, a former member of the resistance movement, succeeded in gaining influence within the ÖVP by building a strong network within the ÖAAB and Lower Austria (Kriechbaumer 1995b, 334). The Land and League majority elites quickly established an organizational structure that allowed communicating their positions to lower-ranked elites and the party's rank and file, thereby consolidating their influence relative to potential competitors.[27] By October 1945, Land majority elites had constituted leadership committees for the ÖVP's Land branches.[28] By the same time, the ÖBB had established a head office with different departments for organization, policy, media and culture, and administration.[29] The ÖAAB and ÖWB followed suit.[30]

Thus, the ÖVP's eventually high level of institutionalization, which, for example, Müller and Steininger (1994b) and Wagner (2014, chap. 7.2) discuss, seems to have been at least partially driven by the party's initial internal playing field. It might be argued that Austria's Christian Democrats did not have much of a choice than to build quickly a highly organized party if they wanted to prevent the Socialists from winning the national election in November 1945. The so-called red threat, however, was not less pressing in Italy.

Still, Italy's Christian Democrats built their organization at the subnational level much more slowly than the ÖVP (Panebianco 1988, 123–30). My theory helps explain the different tempi of party formation. Unlike in the DC, majority elites in the ÖVP were incentivized to invest in and consolidate their network within their party branch to ensure their representation in the national party leadership.

The ÖVP's low level of factionalism started consolidating when conflicts manifested themselves along Land and League lines. For instance, when discussing the law on the formation and influence of works councils, Eugen Margarétha, a leading figure of the early ÖWB, noted in his diary: "We had maybe ten rounds of negotiations and in-between again and again discussions between the Labor (ÖAAB) and Business (ÖWB) League. The latter were even fiercer than those with the . . . Socialists and Communists" (qtd. in Bruckmüller 1995, 297). Already by 1947, controversies between the Leagues were not limited to the policy areas concerning their respective occupational groups.[31] The need to reconcile between the different League and Land branches became a persistent feature of the ÖVP. The dominance of the League and Land branches in internal decision-making was, for instance, debated at the national party congresses in 1951, 1963, 1972, 1979, 1980, and 1995.[32] It also was at the core of the reform initiatives in the 1990s and 2000s (Stirnemann 1993; Müller, Plasser, and Ulram 2004).[33]

How does the ÖVP's level of factionalism compare to Austria's other main parties after the war? The Socialist Party (later Social Democratic Party, SPÖ) and radical-right Freedom Party (FPÖ) initially adopted a more centralized leadership selection process (Müller 1992, 71–73, 86–87; 1996, 251–52), and we would consequently expect higher factionalism in both parties compared to the ÖVP. At first glance, the evidence is ambiguous. Austria has not seen the factional machines that characterized Italy's main parties (chapter 3), and as we might expect in federal countries, the provincial party branches have played an influential role in both the SPÖ and FPÖ (Luther 1991, 253; Müller 1994, 59; 1996, 252–55). However, we find cross-party variation in line with the book's argument. Similar to Italy's Socialist Party in the postwar years, a strong norm existed in the SPÖ emphasizing that "outsiders should not be given any insight into ongoing internal disputes," which de facto suppressed factionalism (Müller 1996, 296). Instances when this norm was not honored led to open rebuking and even expulsion (Grießler 2007, 273; Secher 1959, 294n87). Underneath this formal unity, however, scholars have identified divisions between networks that were not sponsored by the central party and expanded across party levels (Grießler 2007, 275–76; Secher 1959, 290–93). In turn, Luther (1991, 253–54) seminally described the FPÖ as "consisting of a wide range of formal and informal groups" beyond the party's territorial and auxiliary organizations such as the Atter Lake Circle (Atterseekreis) or Lorenzer Circle (Lorenzer Kreis). Factionalism temporarily subsided after Jörg Haider's election 1986 before again erupting forcefully and resulting in the party's split in the early 2000s (Luther 2003, 203, 205–7).

Reinforcement of Low Levels of Factionalism

LÄNDER, LEAGUES, AND THE AUSTRIAN STATE

Like the factional leaders in Italy's DC, the leaders of the ÖVP's Land and League branches used the opportunities and resources the wider political system provided to strengthen their support base within the party, thereby reinforcing a low level of factionalism. The Leagues strengthened their status within the ÖVP by becoming important links between the party and civil society. The aforementioned Austrian Chamber of Labor, Chamber of Agriculture, and Federal Economic Chamber represented occupational groups in the policy-making process. To determine the latter's interests, the chambers held elections. The campaigns and slates for the Christian Democrats were organized by the Leagues. Because membership within their chamber has been compulsory for all working adults, the chambers provided the Leagues with an exclusive access to a large pool of potential members.[34] This strengthened their influence within the ÖVP because the Leagues' membership size affected their number of delegates at party meetings, like the national congress (Ableitinger 1995, 157). Moreover, the more members a League had, the more legitimacy it had in demanding more seats in the party leadership. An increase in their membership also provided the Leagues with financial resources, as the Leagues kept 90 percent of the membership fees (Müller and Steininger 1994b, 13). All this confirmed the value of building a strong network in one of the League branches and helped introduce new members into the ÖVP's low level of factionalism.

The Austrian chambers system also allowed the Leagues to gain political influence. In particular, the Farmers' and Business League benefited from the ÖVP's strength in rural Austria and among employers and businesspeople to gain a dominant position in the Chamber of Agriculture and the Federal Economic Chamber (Gottweis 1983, 56–57; Stirnemann 1981, 419, 426). The chambers allowed them to influence policy making even when they did not find much support for their positions within the ÖVP and even when the ÖVP was in opposition thanks to the consultations over economic and social policies between the three chambers, the Trade Union Federation (Österreichischer

Gewerkschaftsbund), and the government.[35] Becoming influential political figures in Austria's political system, in turn, helped strengthen their role as important players within the ÖVP.

Furthermore, League and Land majority elites strengthened their position by rewarding new members and supporters with titles and jobs.[36] The practice of allocating jobs profited from many public companies, banks, and insurance trusts being close to either the SPÖ or ÖVP in general and a specific party branch in particular (Müller 2000, 148).[37] Majority elites also used their access to public resources to siphon off money for their own party branches. This has been revealed by Land- and League-related scandals over misappropriation of public funds, like the scandal around Viktor Müllner and the ÖAAB and ÖVP's Land branch in Lower Austria in 1966.[38] The access to such sources of patronage and clientelism was enhanced by the system of power sharing and rent sharing, known as *Proporz*, which the Christian and Social Democrats had introduced in December 1945. Governmental, administrative, and other public-sector positions were allocated in proportion to the ÖVP's and SPÖ's vote share (Rauchensteiner 1987, 539). Even after the ÖVP was ousted from the national government in 1970, the system prevailed at the Land level until the late 1990s. Seven of the nine Länder constitutions even included an article requiring that each political party, if it so desired (and it usually did), was included in the government proportional to its electoral strength (Fallend 1997, 23, 25). This system helped the Christian Democrats to remain almost permanently in government in eight of nine Länder, and thereby provided them with contacts and resources (Fallend 1997, 28).

So while close links between a dominant political party and the public and private sector helped reinforce high levels of factionalism in the DC, similar structural conditions contributed to the reinforcement of low levels of factionalism within the ÖVP. The different coalition formats do not help account for these differences in factionalism. Whereas the DC had always been the major party in Italian coalition governments between 1946 and 1992, the ÖVP spent seventeen years in opposition before returning to the national government from 1987 to 2000 as junior partner of the Social Democrats. It could be argued that the DC was more factionalized than the ÖVP because, as the major governing party, it controlled more ministerial portfolios. This increased the set of spoils to be distributed across intraparty groups, which could have stimulated factional competition. However, the ÖVP had been the dominant party in Austrian politics for twenty-five years before losing the 1970 election. By that time, the DC had already developed its high level of factionalism, whereas no such development occurred in the ÖVP. Moreover, the ÖVP's level of factionalism remained low regardless of its coalitional status.

TABLE 4.2. Preference voting in Austrian Lower Chamber elections, 1947–1986

Year	Share of valid votes in %	Party share of total PV in %			Share of party votes in %			Mandates allocated through preferential voting
		ÖVP	SPÖ	FPÖ	ÖVP	SPÖ	FPÖ	
1949	3.0	91.0	3.0	6.0	6.3	0.2	1.5	1
1953	4.2	93.1	2.3	4.6	9.5	0.2	1.8	1
1956	3.8	54.0	14.0	27.0	4.4	1.7	15.6	2
1959	0.2	72.6	21.0	6.4	0.3	0.1	0.1	0
1962	0.2	76.3	17.5	5.9	0.4	0.1	0.2	0
1966	0.5	79.0	18.0	2.9	0.9	0.2	0.3	0
1970	1.7	55.8	44.2	.	2.1	1.5	.	0
1971	1.1	48.3	46.7	5.0	1.3	1.1	1.0	0
1975	0.1	49.7	40.5	9.8	0.2	0.1	0.2	0
1979	0.1	44.9	45.1	7.6	0.1	0.1	0.1	0
1983	2.5	19.8	64.9	11.9	1.1	3.4	6.0	1
1986	2.7	37.5	32.6	19.6	2.5	2.1	5.5	0

Source: Müller (1989a, 675). 1959, 1971 and 1975: only including ÖVP, SPÖ and FPÖ; 1970: only ÖVP and SPÖ, excluding repeated elections in the Viennese constituencies.

Similarly, although preferential voting played an important role in reinforc-ing the DC's high level of factionalism, no factions emerged in the ÖVP despite a similar electoral system. In fact, while the ÖVP usually gained the highest share of preference votes relative to Austria's other parties, preference votes have generally played a negligible role (table 4.2). Pointing to the differences between Italy's open-list and Austria's flexible-list system does not fully explain the dif-ference in factionalism. In Italy, candidates required a relatively small number of preference votes to get elected because the order of candidates in which they filled the seats the party won was determined solely by their respective number of preference votes rather than their rank on the party list. In contrast, Austria's flexible-list system took the party-provided rank into account. It consequently required more preference votes for a lower-ranked candidate to move up into an electable position, and that number also varied depending on district mag-nitude (Katz 1986, 94; Shugart 2005, 42–43). This made preference votes more valuable for candidates in Italy than in Austria and thus incentivized Italian Christian Democrats more than their Austrian counterparts to campaign for preference votes against the other candidates from their own party (Kreuzer 2000). However, Austria introduced this system only in 1970. While the 1970 electoral reform allowed voters only to express their preference toward a single candidate, the pre-1970 electoral system allowed voters to alter the entire party list by ranking or crossing out some or all candidates on the list (Müller 1984, 84–86).[39] In fact, containing conflicts among candidates from the same party was an important driver of electoral reform (Müller 1984, 87).

To understand why a stronger preferential vote component before 1970 did not lead to greater use of preference votes and levels of factionalism, we need to look at the incentive structure created by the ÖVP's organization. To recap, in the DC, factions' competition for preference votes started as a reaction to their lack of representation in the party leadership. In contrast, majority elites in the ÖVP enjoyed a guaranteed similar seat share in the party's national executive and consequently did not need to campaign for preference votes as much to make their voice heard within the party. As expected, they only occasionally campaigned for preference votes to correct (in their view) ill-designed party lists (Müller 1989a, 678; Müller and Steininger 1994b, 14). Minority party elites, in contrast, did not have ex officio membership in the national executive and could have been incentivized to use the preference vote component to make their voice heard through the party's parliamentary group. Some of the cases in which local notables ran a preference vote campaign may fit this pattern (Müller 1989a, 684). However, as already shown, League and Land majority elites had benefited from their guaranteed representation in the party leadership to introduce a decentralized selection process for parliamentary candidates. This reinforced the value of strong networks within party elites' own party branch, as they were a prerequisite not only to assume leadership positions but also to be nominated as parliamentary candidates. Thus, preferential voting is not unequivocally linked to high levels of factionalism but instead depends on a party's preexisting level of factional activities (cf. Pasquino 1972; Morgenstern 2001).

ORGANIZATIONAL REINFORCEMENT BEFORE 1990

Majority elites also reinforced the low level of factionalism by modifying the ÖVP's organization. At the 1947 national congress, the party leadership diverted criticism against the Leagues' power by delegating organizational reforms to a separate committee.[40] It brought together majority elites from the Leagues and Land branches and the national executive, which ratified the new party statute.[41] In other words, those who had benefited from the organizational structure in place controlled its modifications. The few changes made to the national executive's composition even increased the level of decentralization. The party's parliamentary groups in the Lower and Upper House gained guaranteed representation in the national executive. In addition, the influence of the Leagues relative to the Land organizations was strengthened by grant-ing the ÖAAB and ÖWB an additional seat each. The ÖBB even received four additional seats, which reflected its initial importance for recruiting members, mobilizing voters, and running the party (Reichhold 1975, 172–74; Kriechbau-mer 1995a, 18, 21). The Land organizations, in return, lost one seat each (Müller 1992, 76). Yet the importance of networks within the Land organizations was confirmed by adding their leaders as ex officio members to the executive com-mittee (Müller 1992, 80).[42] Moreover, the Land branches maintained control over selecting parliamentary candidates. While the national executive gained the right to veto the Land organizations' candidate slates, a two-thirds major-ity of the Land branch executive could override the veto (Müller 1992, 107).[43] The Land organizations' influence in the party's decision-making was also ac-counted for by the introduction of the Land council—a coordinating commit-tee that included the party leader, Land party chairmen, and the highest ÖVP member in each Land government (Müller 1992, 84).

The 1951 national congress confirmed the importance of a power base within one's own organizational branch. While a motion suggested cutting the Leagues' power and another even demanded their disbandment, majority elites succeeded in getting the motions rejected.[44] The main controversy that emerged concerned the influence of the ÖAAB, which underlined the impor-tance of the Leagues within the ÖVP and the value of intrabranch networks. Weinberger and others criticized the ÖAAB's marginal role. They successfully demanded that the ÖVP representative in the Austrian Trade Union Federa-tion, who was obviously an ÖAAB member, could be co-opted to the national executive.[45] Moreover, by presenting it as a simplification and professionaliza-tion of the party's organization, Weinmayer gained support for reducing the number of executive positions elected by the national congress.[46] This meant a further decentralization of the leadership selection process. Also, the fre-quency of national congress meetings was reduced from annually to every two years and, in 1958, to once every three years (Müller 1992, 96–97).

Additional statutory changes in the late 1950s and early 1960s even further disincentivized party elites from forming factions (table 4.3). While a group of fifty congress delegates had previously been allowed to propose a motion at the national congress, that right became reserved to the national execu-tive and the Land, League, youth, and women's organizations (Müller 1992, 96–97). Also, a party council was introduced, which included majority elites from the different party branches (Müller 1992, 85). Although the council's influence was negligible, it confirmed that members of the national party bodies were predominantly chosen within rather than across party branches. It was proposed that the Leagues' influence on the ÖVP's policy positions be

reduced by introducing a party committee for each of the government departments when the ÖVP received for the second time fewer votes (though not
fewer seats) than the SPÖ, but the League leaders ensured that this proposal
went nowhere (Müller and Steininger 1994b, 14–15). Although the decision to
put the Leagues in charge of collecting the ÖVP membership fees was meant
to improve the national party's financial situation, the latter continued to depend on transfers from its constituent organizations (Müller and Steininger
1994b, 14). The Land council was abolished in 1960 (Müller 1992, 84), but the
Land leaders had not needed it to influence the party's decisions, as they had
been ex officio members of the national executive. Moreover, even though it
was reintroduced that a group of around forty delegates (i.e., 10 percent of
the delegates) could propose a motion at the national congress (Müller 1992,
97), this did not significantly incentivize party elites to form networks across
party branches.[47] The national congress elected only three positions of the
national executive, and majority elites hardly had interest in forming factions
because the members of the leading party bodies were still primarily selected
within the ÖVP's Land and League branches.

   Land and League majority elites continued to defend their conquered
sphere of influence. In 1966, they fought off an attempt by some national party
leaders to grant the national leadership the right to nominate some parliamentary candidates in electable positions (Müller and Steininger 1994b, 16).
While Peter Diem and Heinrich Neisser (1969, 22–53), two party hopefuls,
proposed far-reaching organizational reforms after the SPÖ had become the
strongest party in the ÖVP's stronghold of Upper Austria and was polling
ahead of the ÖVP for the 1970 general election, majority elites in the Land
and League organizations prevented any substantive changes. An age limit on
the holding of party and public office was adopted (Diem and Neisser 1969,
39–40), but a special majority was introduced to override it (Müller 1992, 70).
Diem and Neisser's (1969, 51–52) suggestion that the Leagues' seat share in the
party's committees and parliamentary groups depend on the relative size of
their respective occupational group in society was not realized. Nor was their
idea to explore other types of intraparty groups than the ÖVP's territorial
and occupational branches followed (Diem and Neisser 1969, 52–3). The only
noteworthy modification was an increase in the power of the executive committee, as the national executive had grown to fifty-seven members, which
made decision-making difficult. The executive committee, however, was
enlarged from nineteen to twenty-four members to include all Land leaders
(Müller 1992, 78, 81). A strong network within the respective Land branches
thus allowed majority elites to gain representation not only in the national
executive but also the executive committee.

TABLE 4.3. Main proposals and modifications of ÖVP party statutes, 1947–1965

Year	Modifications	Attempt	Proposal backed by	Effects
1947, 1951, 1958, 1960, 1963	Composition of the national executive and executive committee	Succeeded	Majority elites	Decentralized selection process and thus the value of intrabranch networks confirmed
1947	Land party executives could override the national executive's newly obtained veto over candidate selection	Succeeded	Statutory committee	Land organizations kept controlling candidate selection
	Introduction of Land council			Platform for Land majority elites to coordinate
	Representation at party congress depended on Leagues paying membership fees to central party			Attempt to improve financial situation of the federal party office failed
1951	National congress meets every two years instead of annually	Succeeded	Majority elites	Disincentivizing networks across party branches
	Abolishment of Leagues Decreasing Leagues' autonomy	Failed	Minority elites	Value of intrabranch networks confirmed
1958	National congress meets every three years and motions could only be proposed by national executive, Land, League, and auxiliary branches	Succeeded	Majority elites	Discouraging networks across party branches
	Introduction of party council			No substantive effect
1960	Abolishment of Land council	Succeeded	Majority elites	No substantive effect
	Leagues in charge of collecting fees		Central party officials	
1963	Representation at national congress depended on Land branches paying fees	Succeeded	Central party officials	Financial situation of the federal party office improved slightly
1965	10% of delegates could submit a motion at the national congress	Succeeded	Majority elites	Appeasing minority elites

While party reform returned to the agenda when the SPÖ won an absolute majority in 1971, majority elites maintained a tight grip on the organizational development (Müller and Steininger 1994b, 17). The statutory committee, which assessed the different motions, integrated them into a set of
suggestions for the national congress and had the right to speak last before
the vote, included the ÖVP's majority elites.[48] Consequently, profound reform
proposals, like making members join the ÖVP directly and not via one of
the Leagues, had no chance of being realized (Müller and Steininger 1994b,
17).[49] The groups that the party had identified as playing an increasing role
in deciding elections (i.e., youth, women, and the elderly) were integrated
into the existing League system (Müller and Steininger 1994b, 17). The party's
youth and women's movement and the organization for the elderly received the
same formal status as the Leagues in 1972 and 1977, respectively.[50] Their leaders thereby automatically became deputy party leaders and were, together
with their general secretaries, included in the national executive and executive committee (Müller 1992, 78; Ableitinger 1995, 160). The internal power
distribution, however, did not change significantly. The youth and women's
movement had already been co-opted in the national executive. The traditionally dominant Leagues (i.e., ÖBB, ÖWB, and ÖAAB) maintained their
control over nominating parliamentary candidates and even gained an additional seat in the national executive (Müller 1992, 78). More importantly, the
principle of gaining access to party leadership positions by building networks
within rather than across party branches was not called into question (Stirnemann 1980, 397; Müller and Steininger 1994b, 17–18).

The remaining modifications did not change the importance of forming
networks within party branches. Although primaries to select parliamentary
candidates, initially proposed by Diem and Neisser (1969, 22–31), were introduced on a voluntary basis, the Leagues and Land branches ensured that the
instrument never became relevant (Müller and Steininger 1994b, 18). Moreover, fifteen policy committees were introduced, reflecting in their composition the ÖVP's Land and League organizations. Finally, while the number of
ex officio members in the executive committee decreased, this did not change
the incentive structure motivating the existing low level of factionalism because it was accompanied by a power shift back from the executive committee to the national executive (table 4.4).[51]

After the SPÖ's third consecutive majority, ÖVP leader Josef Taus unsuc-
cessfully called for a reorganization of the party in 1979 (Müller and Steininger
1994b, 19). His proposal included the following: centralizing the leadership
selection process at all party levels, replacing the Leagues with policy-specific
working groups, expanding the powers of the national executive, replacing

TABLE 4.4. Main statutory modifications between 1966 and 1978

Year	Modifications	Attempt	Backed by	Effects
1966	National executive nominates some candidates in electable positions	Failed	Central party leaders	League and Land branches continued to control candidate selection
1969	Age limit for party and public office	Successful	Diem and Neisser	Negligible (could be overturned)
	Increasing power of executive committee			Negligible (countered by reform below)
	Increased representation of Land branches in the national executive and executive committee	Successful	Majority elites	High decentralization persisted
	Leagues' intraparty seat share should reflect the share of their occupational groups in society	Failed	Diem and Neisser	High decentralization persisted
1972	Replacing indirect with direct membership system	Failed	Minority and some majority elites	Leagues confirmed as key actors
	Youth and women's organization gaining League status; ÖBB, ÖAAB, and ÖWB gaining one seat in the national executive	Succeeded	Statutory committee	Leagues confirmed as key actors
	Land and League branches published membership lists; new membership cards indicated party in addition to League membership; fees collected by Land branches			Attempt to reduce importance of Leagues failed
	More centralized selection process of the executive committee			Unchanged incentives as power shifted back to national executive
	Formal increase in the national executive's power over party finances and candidate selection; possibility to conduct primaries to select parliamentary candidates			No substantive effect on intraparty politics
	Special majority for fourth/fifth reelection of party leader/MP			Attempt to encourage generational renewal with no substantive effect
	Introducing 15 policy committees reflecting in their composition the ÖVP's constituent organizations			Difficulty to reach compromise between Leagues; often vague policy proposals
1977	Organization for the elderly granted League status	Succeeded	Organization for the elderly	Value of intrabranch networks reinforced

TABLE 4.5. Statutory modifications in the 1980s

Year	Modifications
1980	Centralization of leadership election, while the internal structure of the party must remain respected
	Introduction of an extended executive committee, which included, in addition to the executive committee, the Land party leaders
	Abolishment of the party council
	Possibility of holding intraparty referendums
	All party members first join the party and then one of the constituent organizations
	Introduction of a central membership register
	National executive allowed to nominate 10% of parliamentary candidates in electable positions
	Introduction of an economic policy section in the party headquarters
1986	Increase in the number of deputy party leaders from four to six
1989	Shift of power from national executive and executive committee to extended executive committee, which was selected in a decentralized way

Source: Khol (1980, 453); Müller (1992, 76, 79, 82, 83, 85, 93); Müller and Steininger (1994b, 19–21).

the indirect with a direct membership system, centralizing finances, and giving the national executive the power to nominate 20 percent of the parliamentary candidates in electable positions (Khol 1980, 442; Müller and Steininger 1994b, 20),[52] While many minority elites and public opinion supported Taus's proposal, the Land and League majority elites rejected it (Khol 1980, 442).[53] Consequently, the proposal did not get enough support in the national executive and Taus resigned (Khol 1980, 443–45; Müller and Meth-Cohn 1991, 52).

Alois Mock, leader of the ÖAAB and the party's parliamentary group, became party leader but attached conditions to accepting the new role that resembled many of Taus's suggestions. Yet unlike Taus, Mock was "willing to operate within the given party structure, maintaining strong contact with the heads of the Leagues and the regional [i.e., Land] party organizations" (Müller and Meth-Cohn 1991, 52). He managed to convince the League and Land leaders to invite party members to express themselves on the most pressing reform questions (Khol 1980, 443–53).[54] The ÖVP's first internal referendum provided Mock with such a strong mandate for most of his ideas that the League and Land majority elites could not resist (Khol 1980, 453).[55] Although the Leagues were so deeply entrenched in the ÖVP's organization that the referendum yielded a clear majority in favor of keeping them (79.65 percent; Khol 1980, 453),[56] the adopted reforms in 1980 seemed far-reaching at first glance (table 4.5).

Although my theoretical framework would predict the emergence of factions had the decision to centralize the leadership selection process been taken at the moment of or shortly after party formation, it did not incentivize party elites to form factions in 1980. For thirty-five years, party elites had been in-centivized to build strong networks within their organizational branch. Those networks were not gone overnight. Majority elites could rely on their con-tacts and popularity to woo the national congress delegates to support their candidacy. Moreover, they could support their leadership bid by referring to the entrenched practice of ensuring the representation of all Land and League leaders in the national executive.[57] Minority elites, in contrast, were required to establish alternative networks—that is, factions—from scratch. This shows that timing and sequence matter in the path-dependent development of insti-tutions. An event that would have initiated a different incentive structure had it occurred at an early point on the path did not have such an effect at a later part of the sequence (compare Pierson 2000a, 263; Greif 2006, 190).

In fact, the organizational changes in the early 1980s did not alter the Leagues' and Land branches' predominance. While members could hence-forth join the ÖVP directly rather than via one of its Leagues, only 4 percent of party members had joined the party without being also a member of one of its Leagues by 1991 (Wagner 2014, 305). Recruiting and maintaining con-tact with party members remained in the hands of the Leagues (Müller and Steininger 1994b, 19). The Land and League majority elites also managed to introduce precautions to prevent the importance of networks within Leagues and Land branches from abating. The electoral committee that prepared and presided over the leadership elections was required to follow the proposals of the Land organizations for nine and of the League organizations for twelve of the forty-seven national executive seats elected by the party congress (Mül-ler 1992, 79). In practice, this guaranteed at least one executive seat for each of the nine Land organizations and two seats for each of the six Leagues.[58] Moreover, an extended executive committee was established that was placed in the party hierarchy between the national executive and the executive com-mittee. The twenty-four-member body included, in addition to the executive committee, all Land leaders and assumed the function of deciding "questions of particular importance" (Müller 1992, 83).

The continuing importance of strong networks within the Land and League organizations was also reflected in the statutory development until the end of the 1980s. It was intraparty practice that the deputy party leader positions were held by the leaders of the constituent organizations. The deci-sion to increase the number of deputy party leaders from four to six in 1986 thus further strengthened the representation of majority elites in the national executive and executive committee (Müller 1992, 76, 82). Finally, the extended executive committee, which was chosen in a decentralized way, practically became the most important leadership board in 1989. Substantive powers in terms of deciding on the party's strategies, finances, personal appointments, candidate selections, and preparations for the national congress were shifted from the national executive to the extended executive committee. The latter, moreover, henceforth included ex officio both the Land and League leaders (Müller 1992, 76, 83). In sum, changes in the ÖVP's organization between 1947 and 1989 reinforced the importance of networks within rather than across party branches to gain representation in the party leadership. The ÖVP's organization thereby left little room for factional activities.

Low Factionalism and Weak Party Adaptation before 1990

THE LIMITED INTEGRATIVE CAPACITY OF AN ASPIRING CATCH-ALL PARTY

The ÖVP's low level of factionalism entailed problems for party adaptation long before the changes of the 1990s and early 2000s. Like Italy's Christian Democrats, one of the ÖVP's first major challenges after the war was to consolidate the coalition of labor, agrarian-conservative, and liberal groups coming together within the new party. Yet in contrast to Italy's DC, where, for example, Andreotti's faction was so important for internal coalition-making that he became one of Italy's most powerful politicians even though his faction never won a plurality in internal elections, minority elites were more marginalized in the ÖVP. There was basically no alternative for them to access leadership positions than through building a strong network within their Land or League branch. This pushed those out of the party who did not have such a power base. Bumballa and many of his resistance supporters, for instance, left the ÖVP in late 1945 to form their own party (Kriechbaumer 1985, 161).[59] Decentralizing power over candidate selection and party finances, while useful to tailor parties' offers to different subnational constituencies (Wills-Otero 2016), did not help redress this because it did not change minority elites' lack of power in internal party politics.

Minority elites tried in vain to improve their situation by pushing for the formation of new Leagues. Right-wing activists promoted introducing a separate League for war veterans after around 500,000 people whose involvement in the Nazi regime was judged as minor had been granted the right to vote in 1947. Their attempt, however, failed because of majority elites' opposition.[60] Another attempt to introduce a right-wing League was made in 1949, when Ernst Strachwitz (leader of the party's youth movement in Styria) and others formed the Young Front (Höbelt 1999, 87–88). The ÖVP leadership initially supported Strachwitz's initiative and co-opted representatives of the Young

Front to the party leadership because the veterans and NS sympathizers were also wooed by the new Federation of Independents (VdU) party (Reichhold 1975, 190; Höbelt 1999, 87). Their stance changed, however, when they realized that the VdU was a similar threat to the SPÖ and the ÖVP and the Young Front attempted to downplay the ÖVP's Christian-social profile (Reichhold 1975, 190–91; Höbelt 1999, 89, 95). Dissatisfied with its lack of influence, the Young Front eventually left the ÖVP in 1951 (Höbelt 1999, 152; 2000, 125).

Majority elites foiled minority elites' attempts to institutionalize new Leagues, warning that the ÖVP must not "disintegrate into umpteen constituent organizations," and fostered the uneven playing field.[61] While the Youth and Women's organization received League status in 1972, the leaders of both organizations had been part of the national executive since 1946. The ÖVP's organization for the elderly became a League in 1977 because majority elites could not make a convincing case for why the youth and women would gain League status but not the elderly.[62] However, subsequent attempts by the Association of Austrian Academics (ÖAKB) and others to gain League status failed.[63] At the party congress, minority elites were not provided with a printout of the proposed changes to the party statutes but needed to purchase a copy if they wanted to read the motions before voting on them in 1963.[64] Important votes, like on the new party statute in 1972, were scheduled late in the evening, when many delegates did not attend the session.[65] Bernd Schlicher, an MP in the Styrian Land parliament, summarized minority elites' alienation when exclaiming that "a few other people . . . , very few, . . . still live in 'democratic niches' within the party. . . . [O]nly when equality is established, it will be possible to identify with the party."[66]

While gridlock within Italy's DC resulted from the extreme flexibility entailed by the proliferation of competing factions and potential factional coalitions, the ÖVP's low level of factionalism also generated gridlock—albeit because of conflicts between rigid blocks rather than unstable factional coalitions. The ÖVP's decentralized leadership selection provided groups with different preferences with a similar seat share on the party's leadership board. The negotiations between Land and League majority elites were tedious and often did not result in an agreement. Already in 1947, it was considered necessary to reiterate that "public statements, also by League representatives, can only occur under the condition that they follow the premise of party unity."[67] While skillful leaders, like Julius Raab during the 1950s, managed temporarily to appease the tensions between League and Land organizations, such tensions were institutionally built into the ÖVP. Conflicts between the ÖAAB and ÖWB and between the ÖVP's Land branches in Vienna and Lower Austria, on the one hand, and those from the western and southern Länder, on the other hand, became recurring conflict lines among the party leadership (Reichhold 1975, 151–52, 195, 208–9; Stirnemann 1981, 436–42). Frustrated, Hermann Withalm, party secretary from 1960 to 1970, urged: "I also need to say quite frankly that the party secretary cannot constrain his activities to simply adding up the wishes of the constituent organizations and Leagues and presenting the mere sum of th[eir] opinions. This would mean to confuse integration with summation."[68] When discussing the same problem in 1979, MP Wolfgang Blenk remarked that this was due not only to the behavior of the League leaders but also to a lack of solidarity of the party's Land branches.[69] Party elites acknowledged that the failed integration of competing positions within the party contributed to the series of election defeats in the 1970s, but the Land and League leaders were not willing to compromise on their influence.[70] The same problems that had been discussed at the beginning of the 1960s thus continued to exist.[71]

Without factions' flexible emergence and rearrangements, new party leaders nearly always came from the same set of internal interest groups. When a new leader was to be elected, majority elites usually negotiated a common solution during the meetings of the national executive (Reichhold 1975, 210). The meetings would be interrupted for talks among the delegates from the same League or Land to agree on their strategy. The minutes of the national executive meeting on 14 June 1951 illustrate this well. The Leagues were unable to agree on a successor for Leopold Figl. After Weinberger requested several breaks to consult with his ÖAAB colleagues, they finally settled on Julius Raab (ÖWB) as new party leader—on the condition that the ÖAAB would nominate the party secretary.[72] The ÖVP's decentralized leadership selection allowed majority elites to strike deals at the national executive. This disincentivized them from engaging in factional activities when national congress delegates elected the party leader, leaving minority elites in a marginalized position.

LACKING FLEXIBILITY IN THE FACE OF INCREASING SOCIAL DIVERSITY

Giving no room to factions also undermined the ÖVP's ability to incorporate the changing composition of Austrian society. In the first years after the war, the inclusion of representatives of agricultural, business, and labor interests in the leading party bodies might have enhanced the ÖVP's integrative power (Reichhold 1975, 172; Gottweis 1983, 57–59). Over time, however, the principle of granting a roughly similar seat share in all decision-making bodies to each of the three Leagues failed to correspond to the declining proportion of farmers and self-employed people and the growing share of employees among the working population (fig. 4.1). Overall, farmers and self-employed people were highly overrepresented among the ÖVP's party and public office holders, whereas blue- and white-collar workers were underrepresented (table 4.6; Stirnemann 1981, 418–25).

Majority elites acknowledged that the underrepresentation of workers and employees was the party's "death coming in small steps" and increased the ÖAAB influence in the national leadership, but this did not resolve the problem (Stirnemann 1981, 433).[73] The ÖAAB, ÖBB, and ÖWB were built on the assumption of group homogeneity, which did not adequately reflect increasing heterogeneity among employees, farmers, and employers. In other words, "the Austrian population cannot simply be split into thirds."[74] The ÖAAB encompassed civil servants, executive staff, and white- and blue-collar workers. The ÖWB included entrepreneurs and representatives of multinational corporations, as well as local innkeepers and grocers. Finally, traditional farmers, alpine farmers, part-time farmers, and smallholders gathered in the ÖBB.[75] The power structure within the Leagues did not reflect these groups' share in society. The interests of civil servants rather than white-collar workers dominated the ÖAAB (Müller 1991, 236). Part-time and alpine farmers were marginalized relative to large- and medium-scale farmers in the ÖBB,

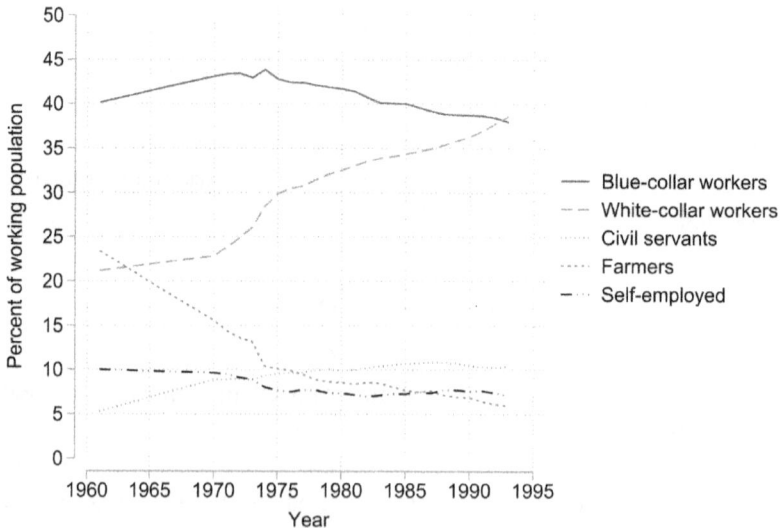

FIGURE 4.1. Occupational structure in Austria
Source: Bundesanstalt Statistik Österreich (2017, 36–37; 1995, 80). Percentage of working population. Self-employed and farmers including family workers.

TABLE 4.6. Occupational structure, Austrian population and ÖVP in 1969

	Self-employed	Farmers	Blue- and white-collar workers
Overall population[a]	5.5	10.0	44.2
ÖVP voters	8.0	22.0	32.0
ÖVP members	18.0	39.3	42.7
ÖVP party groups	23.4	35.7	35.7

[a] Diem and Neisser (1969) provide the values for the overall population (i.e., those working and those not working), whereas figure 4.1 refers to the working population only. This explains the different values in table 4.6 and figure 4.1.

Source: Diem and Neisser (1969, 44–49); Müller (1992, 46–48); Müller and Ulram (1995, 150–54). Population and ÖVP voters missing to 100%: unemployed or household; ÖVP members and party groups: not including family members (ÖBB) and associate members (ÖWB) because they could be affiliated with several organizations.

and the ÖWB predominantly represented the interests of self-employed people (Gottweis 1983, 61, 65).

The classification of voters and party members in one of the three traditional Leagues also became decreasingly clear. Alois Mock acknowledged in 1979: "Today, many farmers do not work anymore exclusively on their farm. For two, five, ten years, they have [also] worked in a factory. . . . To what extent are they still farmers? When should they be considered employees? Many employees . . . engage in entrepreneurial activities. How should they be classified?"[76] Territorial branches and auxiliary organizations for different occupational groups were also ill suited to incorporate the growing share of secular voters and so-called postmaterialists and progressive liberals (Gottweis 1983, 65–66).[77] Although Austrian parties had historically built on three mutually distinct and clearly separate milieus (i.e., Catholic, socialist, and German nationalist), the modernization of European societies in the 1960s and 1970s stimulated the gradual erosion of those pillars (Müller, Plasser, and Ulram 2004). A growing share of floating voters and party shifters indicated the importance for parties to adjust quickly to short-term swings in issue salience and voter preferences (Müller, Plasser, and Ulram 2004, 148). The ÖVP's reliance on inflexible territorial and auxiliary branches was ill suited for such an environment. While trying to broaden the range of groups and actors involved in formulating the party platform in the 1960s and the party's 1972 program, tensions between the Leagues and Land branches blocked substantive innovation (Wagner 2014, 239–41).

Analyzing the ÖVP's defeat in 1979, Ludwig Reichhold criticized the organizational rigidity of the ÖVP's League structure and noted that the ÖVP suffered from "a lack of political dynamics."[78] Peter Ulram recommended a "strengthened manifestation of intraparty positions which should crystallize around political elites but not stick to the Leagues' limits of thought and actions."[79] However, as Kurt Jungwirth, member of the Styrian Land government, acknowledged in his desperate plea for reform: The Leagues were "not abolishable."[80] The previous section outlined that attempts failed to abolish the Leagues, to make their influence depend on their share in society, or to create new groups that reflected more adequately the changes in the electorate. Forming additional subcategories, like for managerial employees in the ÖWB or academics in Tirol's ÖBB, was the main notable attempt to incorporate newly relevant social groups. Yet this only added to the fragmentation of minority elites and helped maintain the Leagues' dominance (Wagner 2014, 304–5). Devoting more resources to strategic planning, the party headquarters' equipment, and the printing of a smiley on campaign material remained the most substantive changes (Fallend 2005, 201; Müller, Plasser, and Ulram 2004, 156; Wagner 2014, 302–3).

Organizational Rigidity and Weak Adaptive Reforms

STRATEGIC INCENTIVES BUT WEAK RENEWAL

The 1990s and early 2000s should have been a busy period of adaptive reforms for the ÖVP given the growing strategic incentives for reform. The 1990 election initiated a period of prolonged decline. The party lost more than 9 percent and dropped for the first time under 40 percent, and almost even under 30 percent. It lost another 4 percent in 1994, and, in 1999, the party fell to third place for the first time—behind the Freedom Party (FPÖ, i.e., the renamed VdU). The FPÖ managed to attract votes from the new middle class and gained among the ÖVP's core groups of shopkeepers and other self-employed (Müller, Plasser, and Ulram 2004, 149; Plasser, Sommer, and Ulram 1991, 124; Sully 1991, 77, 79). Its right-wing populist strategy under Jörg Haider's leadership thrived on voters' dissatisfaction with the oligarchic structure of Austrian politics, to which the ÖVP's League and Land barons had importantly contributed (Sully 1995, 220–21; Müller, Plasser, and Ulram 2004, 153–54, 157; Luther 2009, 1052–55). Although the ÖVP celebrated a vigorous comeback in 2002, it again lost dramatically in 2006 and, by 2013, its vote share had fallen to 24 percent (fig. 4.2). A series of poor Land election results underscored the ÖVP's crisis (Müller, Plasser, and Ulram 2004, 147). However, only in 2017, when the ÖVP was polling around 19 percent and had elected its eighth party leader since 1990, were more substantive reforms introduced.

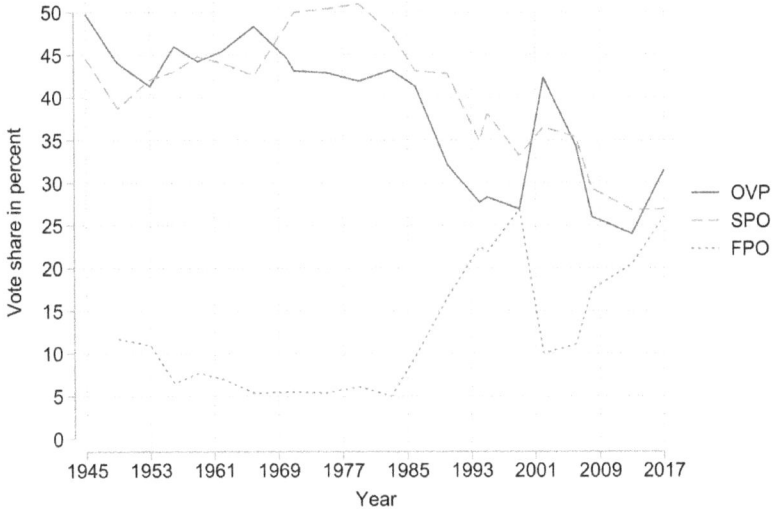

FIGURE 4.2. ÖVP, SPÖ, and FPÖ election results, 1945–2017
Source: Bundesinnenministerium. *Note:* FPÖ results in 1949 and 1953 referring to VdU/WdU.

Analyzing the ÖVP's reform process in terms of an antagonism between the party leadership, on the one hand, and the League and Land branches, on the other hand, as the leadership autonomy account would suggest, would be misleading. It would imply that they were mutually distinct actors. However, the same people who were leading the Land and League organizations were ex officio members of the national party executive (Kriechbaumer 1985, 147; 1995, 29). The national party leadership has therefore been more of an arena rather than an actor within the ÖVP. In the early 1990s, in fact, majority elites increased this arena's autonomy vis-à-vis the rank and file and minority elites by reducing the frequency of party congress meetings from once every three years to once every four years. This increased autonomy, however, did not facilitate adaptation (cf. Kitschelt 1994; Levitsky 2003).

Instead, the ÖVP's low level of factionalism importantly sabotaged party adaptation. In an analysis of the 1990 defeat, Erhard Busek (leader of the Viennese ÖVP) identified the Leagues as outdated, as failing to incorporate important societal groups, and as only contributing to the ÖVP's image as a divided party (Fallend 2005, 190–91; Wagner 2014, 305). The conflicts between them prevented coherent positions on salient issues. Between 1990 and 1996, voters judged both the SPÖ (on socioeconomic issues) and the FPÖ (on immigration, fighting corruption) as more competent than the ÖVP to address the country's most salient issues (Fallend 2005, 200). Clemens Auer, head of the party's political strategy committee, echoed that new constituencies

had no reason to vote ÖVP.[81] Harry Himmer, then leader of the ÖVP's youth
wing, analyzed that the most imminent reforms needed to be "about cutting
back the influence of the three previously dominant Leagues . . . and the Land
organizations. . . . Interests of less noted groups . . . must be emphasized more
within a new ÖVP."[82]

However, even though some party elites agreed on the need for reform,
the ÖVP's low level of factionalism meant that they remained fragmented
across party branches. The election defeats strengthened the reform-willing
actors around the Styrian and Viennese Land branches (Wagner 2014, 151–52),
and journalists described internal infighting as pitting a traditionalist "steel
helmet" wing against a moderate-liberal wing (Müller, Plasser, and Ulram
2004, 163). Yet while factional alternation facilitated leadership change in the
early DC (before the proliferation of factions made this increasingly difficult),
the loose connections in the ÖVP never consolidated into factions. Attempts
to establish factions occurred, and when they did, they supported leadership
changes, like when Michael Spindelegger's Maria Plainer Circle helped replace Erhard Busek as party leader in 1995.[83] The Platform for Open Politics
and the Initiative Christian Democracy brought together minority elites like
Feri Thierry and Stefan Wallner and drew attention to reform proposals, like
moving the party into a coalition with the Greens or reducing the Leagues'
power (Wagner 2014, 307–8). However, these groups failed to develop much
of a presence in the party. After leaving the ÖVP, a former Platform for Open
Politics member complained that they had been waiting in vain for a positive
signal from the party leaders (Wagner 2014, 308).

New ÖVP leaders were usually the result of compromises between the
League and Land leaders, which heavily restricted their room for reforms
(Wagner 2014, 154–62). Consequently, while the Christian Democrats replaced their leader seven times between 1989 and 2017, leadership change
usually did not propel party adaptation (Fallend 2005, 192; Müller and Meth-
Cohn 1991, 60; Müller, Plasser, and Ulram 2004, 167). Reformers, like Siegfried Ludwig and Robert Lichal, failed in their attempts to elect outsider or
non-League candidates, like IBM manager Bernhard Görg, as party leader.
Only occasionally did majority elites succeed in outplaying their rivals, as in
1995, when Erhard Busek managed to push through Wolfgang Schüssel's election. In that case, renewal was not as quickly aborted—also thanks to Schüssel's talent for mediating between competing preferences (Ennser-Jedenastik
and Müller 2014, 72; Wagner 2014, 169–71). Still, Schüssel (ÖWB) was part of
the same circle of majority elites. The same applies to his successors Wilhelm
Molterer (ÖBB), Josef Pröll (ÖBB), Michael Spindelegger (ÖAAB), Reinhold
Mitterlehner (ÖWB), and even Sebastian Kurz (Youth League). The ÖVP's

record of elite renewal was not much better at the cabinet or parliamentary level. With the Land and League majority elites controlling the party's primaries, the proportional allocation of candidates across the ÖVP's constituting organizations continued (Wagner 2014, 161). Outsider candidates were rare and usually outranked by the Leagues' candidates.[84] In general, candidates continued to serve the traditionally dominant interests (Bruckmüller 1995, 314; Müller, Plasser, and Ulram 2004, 159–60).

Facing the pressure to perform well in the next election, party leaders like Josef Riegler and Michael Spindelegger proposed giving more control to the national party leadership, but their attempts failed given the resistance of most other League and Land leaders (Wagner 2014, 145, 305–6). Instead, majority elites agreed to reduce the number of members in the executive committee and national executive to facilitate decision-making. However, the small executive committee had little formal power compared to the national executive, and the selection process of the latter was again decentralized, thus ensuring majority elites' influence (Bruckmüller 1995, 314; Stirnemann 1993).[85] While the newly introduced policy committees helped formulate offers to target white-collar workers, the attempts to generate support among this large constituency increasingly frustrated the ÖWB. For a while, it publicly contemplated splitting from the party. The new 4 percent threshold discouraged them from pursuing the split, but the ÖWB sabotaged reforms by defecting in parliament (Fallend 2005, 198; Müller, Plasser, and Ulram 2004, 160; Wagner 2014, 158–59). The leaders of the Land branches also increasingly emphasized their own agenda. They removed the ÖVP logo from campaign posters, withheld funds to impose their agenda, and, in the case of Tirol, removed the word *Austrian* from their name in favor of highlighting their regional identity (Fallend 2005, 197; Müller, Plasser, and Ulram 2004, 160–61; Wagner 2014, 144). For a while, they even discussed the option of splitting the ÖVP into several regional parties (Fallend 2005, 197).

WATERED-DOWN REFORMS AND LATE COMPROMISES

Conflicts between the party's traditionally privileged groups meant that programmatic reforms often remained vague and incoherent. While Josef Riegler's concept of eco-social market economy in the late 1980s indicated that the party tried to combine new issues, like environmental protection, with Christian Democracy's traditional social market economy, the concept remained the subject of internal debates for almost twenty years (Wagner 2014, 243–44). Under Schüssel's leadership, the ÖVP then markedly turned toward market-liberal positions and, entering a coalition with the radical-right

FPÖ in 1999, embraced many radical-right positions on national identity, immigration, and security (Fallend 2019, 9–10; Luther 2009, 1051; Wagner 2014, 243–44, 380). However, his course quickly attracted criticism from other Leagues and Land branches (Wagner 2014, 154, 244). In exchange for accepting Schüssel's and the ÖWB's austerity measures, the ÖAAB secured the continuing state support for families and an expansion of employees' rights and protections. The ÖBB, in turn, received exemptions for the agricultural sector and ensured ongoing support for socially conservative positions on same-sex relationships and gun ownership (Fallend 2005, 201; Wagner 2014, 172, 244–45). The peace between the Leagues and Land branches usually was short lived and repeatedly collapsed after—or, as in 2008, even during—election campaigns (Fallend 2005, 201; Luther 2009, 1052; Wagner 2014, 242). ÖVP leaders tried to outsource some of the conflicts by opening up programmatic discussions to members and supporters. Inclusive initiatives like the Alpbach Process between 2001 and 2004, Molterer's Perspektivengruppe 2010, and the Evolution People's Party between 2013 and 2015 aimed to create momentum for reform (Fallend 2005, 197; Rois 2016; Wagner 2014, 252). While these initiatives attracted much media attention, many proposals were watered down or not followed up on to avoid internal conflicts (Wagner 2014, 253–54).

Disillusioned by the ÖVP's failure to reform and the continuing dominance of the ÖBB in his Land, Fritz Dinkhauser, who had been a leading figure of the ÖABB in Tirol, left and formed his own party.[86] While his List Fritz failed to break through at the national level, it gained 18.35 percent in the Land election in the ÖVP's former stronghold of Tirol (Luther 2009, 1052). The NEOS (i.e., The New Austria) was another party that emerged out of a group of discontent ÖVP minority elites and quickly became the focal point for many former ÖVP members (table 4.7).[87] This also hurt the Christian Democrats, who, for example, lost 6 percent of their voters to the NEOS in the 2014 European election.[88] The ÖVP was increasingly limited to its traditional rural strongholds in Lower Austria, Vorarlberg, and Upper Austria. In the rest of the country, where its Leagues did not as easily map onto the population's social structure, it suffered heavy losses, shrinking, for instance, to around 14 and 17 percent in Vienna and Carinthia, respectively.

For decades, League and Land leaders tried to have it all—power within the party and the wider polity. It was only when the ÖVP was polling under 20 percent and well behind the SPÖ (28.5 percent) and FPÖ (30.5 percent) that Land and League leaders accepted reducing their branches' influence. They gave Sebastian Kurz, then leader of the party's Youth League, control over the party's manifesto, coalition negotiations, and the exclusive right to select the ÖVP's candidates for the national list and the cabinet, which he

TABLE 4.7. Survey on NEOS's membership composition

Former party membership	N	Percentage
None	288	69.90
Liberal Forum	40	9.71
ÖVP	34	8.25
SPÖ	15	3.64
Greens	4	0.97
FPÖ/BZÖ	4	0.97
Others, several parties, no answers	27	6.56
Total	412	100.00

Source: Ennser-Jedenastik and Bodlos (2019).

used to nominate political newcomers (Fallend 2019, 17–19, 21). Yet many of the reforms seemed mainly symbolic. In Austria's electoral system, most seats are allocated at the constituency or regional and not the national level (Müller 2005, 402–3). At these levels (and in the party's leadership board), the state and League branches maintained their influence. Moreover, Kurz's popularity and, in 2019, an FPÖ scandal were important for the ÖVP's success (Fallend 2019, 19). Party adaptation returned to the agenda after Kurz's resignation over corruption allegations in 2021 and the ÖVP's drop to 24 percent in the polls, with the party again facing many of the problems that it had been struggling to respond to for decades.

Conclusion

At first glance, dividing a party into different organizational branches and giving each branch a similar seat share in the national leadership might appear as a promising strategy to integrate all groups in the decision-making process and help the party adapt when political and social conditions change. The ÖVP shows that this is not the case. Austria's Christian Democrats had decided to select their national leaders by primarily co-opting the leading elites of their Land and League branches. As a result, internal competition has predominantly taken place within these branches and between the branches themselves. The resulting low level of factionalism was reinforced over time as majority elites, who had benefited from the rules in place, dominated the party's organizational development. In their efforts to strengthen their own networks, they also benefited from Austria's corporatist system, the ÖVP's long-standing participation in federal and Land cabinets, and the available means of patronage and clientelism. Because similar factors contributed to the reinforcement of high levels of factional competition in Italy's DC, they seem to be better theorized as reinforcing rather than causal factors in theories of factionalism.

The absence of factions undermined the substance and speed of party adaptation. Its organizational rigidity divided the party into winners (i.e., those who had a strong network in their party branch) and losers (i.e., those who did not). The absence of factions made the integration of groups that did not fall within one of the ÖVP's traditional branches ill fated. This prevented the extent of innovation often associated with changes in the person of the party leader. The same special interests that had dominated the party's organization and platform in the 1940s and 1950s continued to prevail in the 1990s and early 2000s. Despite recognizing the need to give room to new and more flexible groups, conflicts among ÖVP Land and League leaders complicated and slowed down adaptation, often embracing mostly vague and limited reforms to not jeopardize their influence.

Germany's CDU: Mixed Leadership Selection, Moderate Factionalism, and Adaptation

> Its European sister parties have often worked themselves into the ground over the con-
> sequences of secularization, scandals or the resignation of their great party leaders. Not
> so the CDU: So far, the CDU has succeeded in coping with social change as well as
> scandals or leadership changes.
>
> BÖSCH (2001,7)

Chapter 3 showed that a centralized leadership selection can undermine the speed and substance of party adaptation by giving too much room for fac-tional competition, whereas chapter 4 outlined that a decentralized leadership selection process can weaken party adaptation by discouraging the formation of factions at all. This suggests that a mix of both procedures could yield the necessary balance between flexibility and rigidity to help a party adapt to a changing environment. The case of Germany's Christian Democratic Union (CDU) supports this. Beyond the gradual secularization and modernization that challenged Christian Democrats across Western Europe, the CDU faced changes in the electorate that went beyond those in other cases. The end of the Cold War and sudden accession of the Communist German Democratic Republic required integrating more than sixteen million new citizens and the remnants of an ailing planned economy. Initially praised for its role in achieving German reunification, the CDU quickly entered difficult times and was ousted from government in 1998. Within five years, the party passed far-reaching reforms. Its 2003 program marked a dramatic market-liberal turn, "snuffing out" any social-Catholic programmatic remnants and marking the "most radical change of course" in years (qtd. in Clemens 2009, 130). When these changes proved less popular than anticipated, the Christian Democrats moderated their economic platform and adopted a more socially progressive course. This was not the first time the CDU reinvented itself, with program-matic and organizational adaptation already taking place in the 1950s and 1970s.

In contrast to what the leadership autonomy argument would expect, these reforms have been realized with rather than against party activists. Leaders like Konrad Adenauer, Helmut Kohl, and Angela Merkel managed to introduce far-reaching reforms not without but because of their engagement with and integration of varying intraparty coalitions. Similar to the DC and ÖVP, organized intraparty organizations in the CDU played an important role in connecting the party with society, aggregating special interests, and giving party elites a platform to make their voice heard. Unlike in the DC and ÖVP, factions alongside the party's Land and auxiliary branches were key actors in the CDU's reform processes. This provided the party with more flexibility to respond to changing societal conflict lines as a moderate level of factionalism supported the integration of interests not mapping onto the party's formal territorial and sociodemographic structure. It also supported innovation by facilitating the decline of old interests and the rise of new ones without entailing the fractionalization paralyzing the highly factionalized DC.

As in the previous case studies, this chapter traces the origins of the CDU's mixed leadership selection process and its impact on a moderate level of factionalism before outlining the latter's reinforcement over time. It will then show how its moderate level of factionalism already supported party adaptation long before the transformations of the 1990s and why Germany's Christian Democrats did not face the dilemma that undermined the DC's and ÖVP's adaptation.

The Origins and Consequences of a Mixed Leadership Selection

STRUCTURAL DIVISIONS AND
POLITICAL ENTREPRENEURSHIP

Similar to the ÖVP, the Allies' restrictions on postwar politics in combination with the country's historical conflict lines encouraged actors with different views and backgrounds to come together in the CDU. Germany's partition into four occupation zones supported the emergence of territorially scattered power centers (Kaack 1971, 159; Panebianco 1988, 116). Because the Allies had focused on their own interests rather than Germany's traditional divisions when deciding on the shape of the occupation zones and the reestablished Länder, quite different social groups ended up in the same territory (Bösch 2001, 21–22; Mosley 1950, 590–600; Sharp 1975, 1). In the first five years after the war, these groups depended on the Allies' approval, granted in the form of a license, to form political parties. The Allies' decision to license initially only one Christian-conservative party incentivized many Catholics and Protestants to overcome their prewar fragmentation (Ritter 1990, 34–46; Kleinmann 1997, 123–24).[1] Three main groups characterized the CDU's founding period.

First, Catholic and Protestant trade unionists, including Jakob Kaiser and Andreas Hermes, founded the CDU in Berlin and the Soviet zone in June 1945.
Their vision of a social-Christian party resonated with the founding circles in
Württemberg and Hesse (both US zone) and Catholic trade unionists behind
Karl Arnold from the Rhineland (UK zone; Bösch 2002, 13; Gurland 1980, 40–
46; Kaack 1971, 171–72; Rovan 1956, 268–69, 274). Second, the Rhineland was
also home to centrists, often with roots in the prewar Catholic Center Party,
like Konrad Adenauer and Léo Schwering (Bösch 2001, 22–34; Rovan 1956,
268). Third, in Northern Germany and Westphalia (both UK zone), middle-
class and conservative Protestants around Hans Schlange-Schöningen and
Friedrich Holzapfel, former members of the national-conservative German
National People's Party, designed the CDU as an anti-Marxist union of the
political right (Bösch 2001, 40–45; Rovan 1956, 272).[2]

However, structural antecedents do not explain why these groups adopted
a more centralized leadership selection process than the ÖVP. Both parties
largely decentralized control over candidate selection and internal funds. The
occupation zones also existed longer in Germany than in Austria, and the
German, unlike the Austrian, Christian Democrats differed in terms of not
only their class but also their denominational background. All this pointed
toward a more or at least similarly decentralized process for selecting the
CDU leadership compared to the ÖVP. The German Basic Law, adopted in
May 1949, did not predetermine the CDU's leadership selection process, as
it only required parties to be organized democratically without specifying
further organizational details. Instead, Kaiser's left-leaning group made the
first bid for the party leadership, setting up a national head office and inviting
representatives from the other zones to a national party meeting in December
1945 (Bösch 2001, 61; Schwarz 1995, 346). This meeting established an interzone committee to prepare for the creation of a national organization (Kaack
1971, 170).

Political maneuvering helped Adenauer to assume a leading position
in the CDU's organizational development. With the British occupation authorities lifting Adenauer's ban from political activities just in time for the
CDU's leadership elections, he formed a temporary alliance with Arnold and
his supporters worked behind the scenes to oust Schwering and secure the
leadership of the Rhenish CDU in early February 1946 (Schwarz 1995, 318–
26, 343, 347, 351).[3] At the zone level, Adenauer outmaneuvered Hermes by
insisting that he and his supporters who had left Berlin after conflicts with
the Soviets were not members of the CDU in the British zone (Schwarz 1995,
345, 348–49). At the start of the meeting to elect a new leader in January
1946, Adenauer stunned Holzapfel, who as leader of the hosting Westphalian

Land branch might have expected to preside, by declaring: "I was born in 1876 so I am probably the oldest person here. If no-one contradicts, I will regard myself as president by seniority" (Schwarz 1995, 438–39). As chair, Adenauer had room to outline why his roots in political Catholicism appealed to the social-Catholic left, why his anticommunism and procapitalism made him acceptable for many conservatives, and why his advanced age made him the ideal compromise candidate (Bösch 2001, 59). His strategy played out, and he was elected CDU leader in the British zone (Bösch 2001, 58; Schwarz 1995, 349). Adenauer strengthened his leadership by integrating the ideas of the different groups in the British zone into the so-called Ahlen manifesto (Bösch 2001, 61–62; Schwarz 1995, 368–75). When the working committee of the CDU-CSU, which had replaced the interzone committee in August 1946, met some days after the Ahlen manifesto's proclamation, it elected Adenauer as its provisory leader.[4]

Adenauer strategically delayed the creation of a national organization on terms that would have favored his opponents. A national organization seemed imminent in 1948, when, following intense negotiations, the working committee adopted a formal set of rules.[5] Its statute included a congress (*Hauptausschuss*) that would bring together delegates from the Land branches, meet at least annually, and elect the national executive.[6] If the working committee's statute had guided the CDU's national organization, the party's leadership selection process would have been highly centralized.[7] A centrally elected national leadership entailed the risk of his opponents gaining control as long as Adenauer had not consolidated his leadership beyond the British zone. While Holzapfel had become Adenauer's loyal deputy for the time being (Schwarz 1995, 437), the left around Kaiser, Arnold, and the trade unionist Johannes Albers remained a powerful rival, enjoying support among the occupation authorities, Josef Müller's CSU, and the CDU's Land branch in Hesse (Schwarz 1995, 362, 367). To delay party formation, Adenauer forged an alliance with the southwestern CDU leaders, who, though suspicious of Adenauer's ambitions, shared his skepticism about a central organization (Bösch 2001, 67–71; Strauß 1989, 104).

While the Allies ultimately decided that the three western zones and the Soviet zone would go separate way, Adenauer shifted toward promoting a national organization only after asserting his views on the CDU's economic policies, coalition strategy, and chancellorship (for a detailed account, see Schwarz 1995, 353–448; see also Bösch 2001, 91, 253–54; Patch 2018, 106; Strauß 1989, 111). The first national election in 1949 supported Adenauer's efforts to reach an agreement over the CDU's national organization. Although the Christian Democrats had won, the result had been much closer than expected, which

many observers attributed to the lack of a national party organization (Kleinmann 1993, 122–25).[8] Many Land leaders ultimately accepted a national party
leadership, but they succeeded in partially decentralizing its selection process
(Kleinmann 1993, 125). Alois Zimmer, who chaired the working group on organizational questions, proposed a statute that differed markedly from the one
introduced for the working committee and split the party leadership's election
between two party bodies (Grau 2011, 51). The newly created party council
would elect seven members. It aimed to guarantee the Land majority elites'
influence, with each Land branch sending two to eight delegates to the party
council depending on their results in the most recent federal election. The
national congress would elect the party leader and deputy leaders. Adenauer
wanted to introduce three deputy party leaders, arguably to have an additional
ally, as the left and right were likely to receive a deputy position each (fractionalization index: 0.42).[9]

Two conferences with Land majority elites in November 1949 and February 1950 did not notably advance the decision over the party's statute. Instead, Ernst Bach (mayor of the city of Siegen) proposed in April 1950 that the
party congress elected the party leader, deputy leaders, and the party council,
with the latter then electing the rest of the leadership (Grau 2011, 52–53). Had
Bach's proposal been accepted, the CDU's leadership selection process would
have resembled the DC's more centralized process (see chapter 3). While the
CDU Land leaders rejected Bach's proposal and endorsed Zimmer's proposed
basic setup in May 1950, the centralization of the leadership selection process
remained contested. Kaiser and Albers tried to include a representative of
the left as ex officio member in the party leadership. Adenauer foiled this
by convincing the Land leaders, who voted on the statutory draft, that the
party's youth and women's movement would also not receive ex officio representation.[10] This backfired because the youth and women's movement then
also demanded ex officio membership, which Zimmer prevented by reassur-
ing that their representation would be guaranteed informally.[11] In turn, Land
majority elites advocated an increase in the number of leadership positions
elected by the party council (Grau 2011, 65).[12]

While Adenauer's allies managed to repel another attempt to add an ex
officio member to the party leadership, the procedure to select the national
party leadership was settled only on the eve of the CDU's first national congress in October 1950 (Grau 2011, 66–67, 70). By that time, Adenauer had
accepted that the party leadership would count sixteen rather than ten members and the party council would elect twelve instead of seven seats to ac-
commodate Land majority elites. Moreover, there would be only two deputy
leader positions, to which Kaiser and Holzapfel were confirmed. Still, with his

two main rivals becoming deputy leaders, Adenauer had cleared his path to becoming the CDU's national leader (Bösch 2001, 246).[13] The eventual leadership selection process combined elements of a centralized and decentralized selection process (Rae's fractionalization index: 0.40). The party congress elected the party leader and two deputy leaders. The party council elected twelve executive positions and was composed of the party's leadership board and two to eight delegates per Land branch, including the respective Land party and parliamentary leaders. Finally, the leader of the party's national parliamentary group (PPG), in a last-minute compromise by the Land leaders (Grau 2011, 70), became an ex officio member of the CDU leadership.[14]

FROM MIXED LEADERSHIP SELECTION TO
MODERATE FACTIONALISM

Several explanations would expect the CDU to develop a similar or lower level of factionalism than Austria's ÖVP. The dominant party approach, Ceron's (2019) argument on the size of the selectorate, and the federalism argument would expect similar levels of factionalism in the CDU and ÖVP. Both were their respective countries' main governing party for the first twenty years after the war, the large party congress rather than a smaller committee elected the parties' respective presidents, and both parties competed in federal systems. In fact, if federalism unequivocally dampened factionalism, the Austrian Christian Democrats should have been more incentivized to form factions than CDU elites because the level of subnational autonomy is relatively weak in Austria (Erk 2004; Gamper and Koch 2014; Obinger 2005). We would also expect the CDU and ÖVP to be similarly factionalized if party (de)centralization had an unequivocal effect on their level of factionalism (Carey 2007). Both parties' national leadership had little influence over candidate selection and party funds (Pridham 1977, 246; see chapter 4). In turn, the electoral system argument would expect higher factionalism in the ÖVP than in the CDU because Austria's flexible-list system encouraged more competition among candidates from the same party than the closed-list vote and large district magnitude in Germany's mixed system (Shugart 2005, 47).

Unlike in the ÖVP, however, several factions emerged in the CDU and the focus on parties' leadership selection process helps explain why. Despite the early CDU's reputation for being a mostly informally organized party (Bösch 2001), the minutes document that the party's national leadership board brought together most of the key party elites at that time and met relatively frequently to decide important issues.[15] Chapter 2 made two predictions about party elites' incentives under a mixed leadership selection process. Majority

TABLE 5.1. Party council delegates by Land branch, 1951

Land branch	Number of seats	Land branch	Number of seats
Rhineland	8	North-Württemberg	4
Westphalia	8	Württemberg-Hohenzollern	3
Rhineland-Palatinate	8	North Baden	3
Exile-CDU	8	South Baden	3
Berlin	6	Brunswick	2
Schleswig-Holstein	5	Oldenburg	2
Hesse	5	Bremen	2
Hanover	5	Hamburg	2
Oder-Neiße	5		

Source: Mitglieder des Parteiausschusses, 01.10.1951, ACDP-07-001-703.

elites from branches whose representation in the national party leadership is secured will be incentivized to invest in strengthening networks in their party branch. In contrast, majority elites whose party branch does not autonomously fill seats on the national leadership board and minority elites are likely to form factions. This incentive structure is likely to result in a number of factions that is higher than in a party with a decentralized selection process (e.g., ÖVP) but lower than in a party with a centralized selection process (e.g., DC). The CDU's process to select its national leadership yielded a very similar incentive structure.

Majority party elites who could be certain to sit on the CDU's leadership board were not incentivized to form factions. The leader of the CDU's parliamentary group was an ex officio member of the national executive. Building a strong network in the party's parliamentary group thus ensured representation in the party leadership. Moreover, the party council ensured the influence of majority elites from the CDU's Land branches in the selection of the national party leadership. Ties within party elites' own Land branch were therefore a valuable resource. Yet no formal guarantee existed in 1950 that ensured that Land majority elites were represented in the national executive. The maximum number of delegates per Land branch was limited to eight, which meant that no Land branch had a majority in the party council. The extent to which this incentivized majority elites to form factions was influenced by how far they could go by building on the support within their own Land branch. This depended on their position in the party council. The Land branches' number of seats reflected their varying strength in the most recent federal election (table 5.1; fig. 5.1).[16] Their impact on the CDU's performance in national elections not only provided the (south)western Land branches with an edge in terms of party council seats but also made them

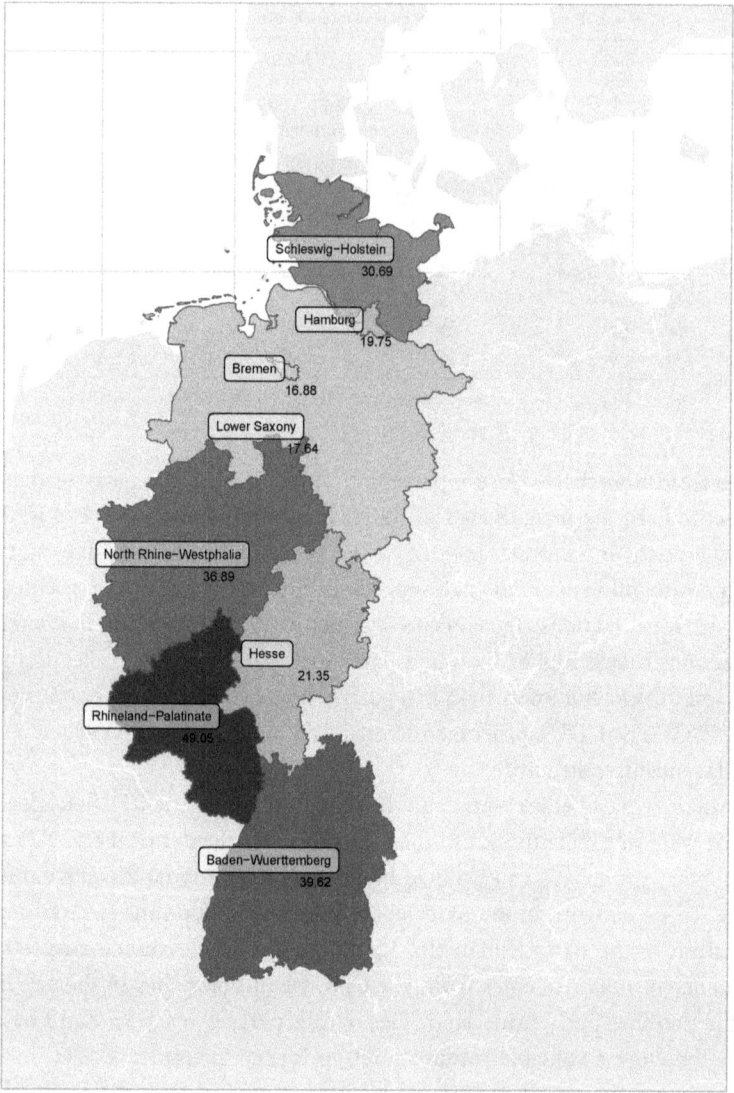

FIGURE 5.1. CDU vote share in 1949 federal election by Land
Source: Bundeswahlleiter (2016) and Hijmans (2015). The figure shows the current borders. Baden-Württemberg was only formed in 1952.

such heavyweights that their majority elites were practically ensured representation in the party leadership. Their strength also helped legitimize the claim of delegates from Baden-Württemberg to be represented on the party leadership.[17] Consequently, (south)western majority elites were incentivized to concentrate on strengthening their base within their Land branch. They were thus unlikely to form factions. This did not mean that majority elites did not cooperate, but these contacts were not formally organized as factions (Bösch 2001, 257, 262–67, 282; Hornig 2013, 90).

The situation was different for the majority elites from the northern Land branches, like Bremen, Hamburg, Hanover, Oldenburg, and Brunswick. While the support within their Land branch guaranteed access to the party council, they had fewer delegates in the council and could not build on a strong electoral record to justify their bids for national leadership positions. Consequently, in addition to maintaining a strong network in their Land branch, which guaranteed their representation in the party council, they were incentivized to build networks with other party branches to make their voice heard. As expected, they institutionalized this cooperation by forming the Soltauer Kreis (Soltau Circle). The Soltau Circle held formal meetings, had a spokesperson, and became more institutionalized and long lived than the networks occasionally formed by majority elites from the (south)west.[18] It was, however, restricted to the six northern Land branches and consequently organizationally less pervasive across different party levels than the groups formed by minority elites.[19]

Minority elites could not be certain to be among the delegates to the party council, and their prospects of getting elected to the national leadership depended on them either becoming majority elites in their respective party branches or building networks across party branches to pick up seats at the national congress. Attempts to establish factions were less ill omened than in the ÖVP because, unlike in the ÖVP, majority elites from smaller Land branches were incentivized to form, join, or support factions.

The emergence of factions in the early CDU corresponded to this incentive structure. In November 1951, Protestant party elites began to build a faction. The CDU was the first major political party in Germany that sought to integrate Catholic and Protestant Christians after centuries of conflict. While informal meetings among Protestants started as early as 1945, faction building started only once Protestants' minority position within the CDU risked being consolidated after the party's first national leadership election in 1950.[20] Although Protestants received six out of sixteen seats, they were clearly outnumbered by Catholics, whose dominance in the early CDU was

TABLE 5.2. CDU leadership board in 1950

Position	Name	Power base
Leader	Konrad Adenauer	Rhineland
Deputy leaders	Friedrich Holzapfel*	Westphalia
	Jakob Kaiser	CDA and Exile-CDU
Treasurer	Ernst Bach*	City of Siegen (Rhineland)
Other members	Anton Dichtel	South Baden
	Margarete Gröwel	Women's movement, Hamburg
	Werner Hilpert	Hesse
	Linus Kather	Expellees
	Kurt Georg Kiesinger	Württemberg-Hohenzollern
	Ernst Majonica	Youth movement
	Wilhelm Simpfendörfer*	Württemberg-Baden
	Walther Schreiber*	Berlin
	Carl Schröter*	Schleswig-Holstein
	Georg Strickrodt*	Brunswick
	Alois Zimmer	Rhineland-Palatinate
PPG leader	Heinrich von Brentano	Parliamentary party

* Indicate Protestant denomination.

Source: Bundesvorstandsmitglieder 1950–1966, https://www.kas.de/de/web
/geschichte-der-cdu/bundesvorstandsmitglieder-1950-1966.

widely acknowledged (Bösch 2001, 320–21; Dilling 2022, 15–18; table 5.2). Despite Adenauer's emphasis on the need to reach out to Protestants, the CDU leadership did not set up this group.[21] Letters from that time show that a small circle of primarily minority elites and majority elites from the CDU's smaller Land branches, concerned about their influence within the party, formed the Evangelischer Arbeitskreis faction (Protestant Working Group, EAK).[22] While increasing the share of Protestants in public office was certainly part of the EAK's motivation,[23] it does not in itself explain the faction's formation. If the EAK's formation had been driven by the CDU's candidate selection for federal elections, it is unclear why Protestants needed a national organization to represent their interests because candidate selection took place at the local and Land level. We would also have expected the EAK to emerge from the bottom up by Protestant candidates gradually joining forces. Instead, the top-down formation of the EAK is in line with Holzapfel's ambition to connect Protestants across Land branches and overcome their fragmentation within the CDU.[24] Demands to include Protestant politicians in the CDU's leadership board coincided with support for the idea of a Protestant faction.[25]

Another faction formed on the CDU's market-liberal right in the early 1950s. Ludwig Erhard's social market economy, supported by the Marshall Plan, revived Germany's economy and stimulated the growth of small and

medium-sized businesses (*Mittelstand*). Yet the *Mittelstand* was not represented among the CDU's leaders, and minority elites feared that their interests would be neglected as a result. Under the guise of the policy committees
within the Rhenish CDU, Horst Rheinfels and Fritz Etzel started building
a network that connected like-minded CDU members across Land and local branches, policy committees, and federal and Land public offices.[26] They
worked toward influencing candidate selection and expanding their local
presence, intensified their collaboration with the CDU's business-friendly
MPs around Kurt Schmücker, and started being active at party congresses.[27]
A joint committee formalized the collaboration between MPs and party elites
from Land and local branches in late 1954.[28] They started publishing circulars
(Kleinmann 1993, 145), and at the 1956 party congress, the group ultimately
formed the Bundesarbeitskreis Mittelstand faction under Schmücker's leadership (Federal Working Group Mittelstand, abbreviated *MIT* for its current
name Mittelstands- und Wirtschaftsunion). At the same congress, Schmücker
became a member of the leadership board.

The EAK and MIT followed two other factions that had emerged before
the CDU's 1950 statute but still reflected the dynamics of the book's argument. Already between October 1945 and February 1946, Johannes Albers
had formed the left-wing faction Sozialausschüsse (Social Committees, later
renamed Christlich-Demokratische Arbeitnehmerschaft). Albers was part of
the left-wing minority in the Rhenish CDU. The catalyst for Albers to form
the Social Committees was trade unionists' decision not to revive the separate
Christian trade unions.[29] This gave Albers and his allies no other choice than
to mobilize Christian workers through another organization (Kleinmann
1996, 197–98).

When the CDU's national organization started taking shape between 1948
and 1950, the Social Committees assumed the role that chapter 2 expects factions to play in a party with a mixed leadership selection by helping minority
elites like Albers, Arnold, and Kaiser to gain influence at the national party
level. While Arnold had been elected governor of North Rhine–Westphalia
in 1947, the CDU in North Rhine–Westphalia was divided into two Land
branches. Facing Adenauer in the Rhineland and Holzapfel in Westphalia,
Arnold's social-Catholic views did not have a clear majority in either Land
branch. Kaiser, in turn, lost his power base when the Soviet authorities dis-
missed him as CDU zone leader in December 1947 (Patch 2018, 87–88). With
national headquarters in Cologne and a group within the CDU's parliamentary group, the Social Committees helped Kaiser, Arnold, and Albers to mobilize support across CDU branches. Acknowledging the Social Committees'
influence, the party elected Kaiser as one of the two deputy leaders.[30] In the

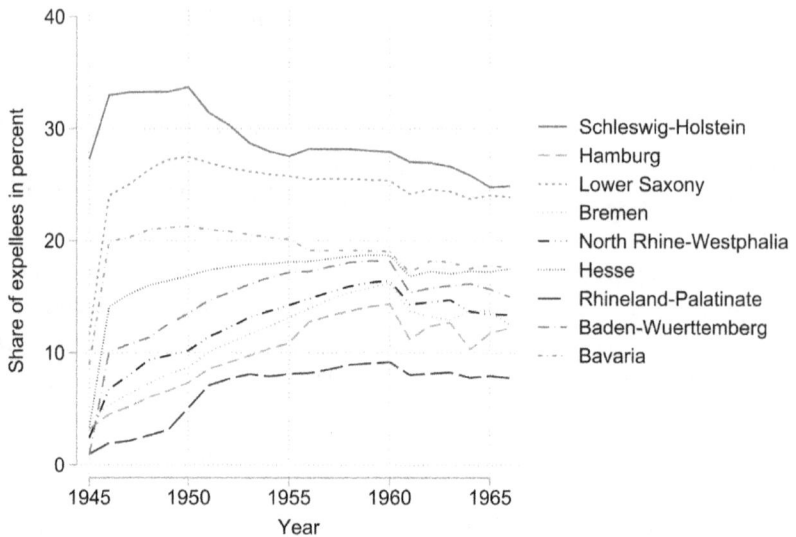

FIGURE 5.2. Share of expellees among resident population by Land
Source: Besser (2008).

run-up to the CDU's 1950 congress, the Land leaders around Adenauer also
agreed to recognize Kaiser and the old CDU leadership from the Soviet zone
as the Exile-CDU (Patch 2018, 113). The Exile-CDU received the status of a
Land branch with eight seats in the party council. Yet its membership was
scattered across West Germany, part of the CDU branch in the Land they
physically lived in, and shrunk notably as the number of people fleeing from
the Soviet zone declined over the years (Kleinmann 1993, 235–37).[31] Kaiser's
influence thus heavily relied on the Social Committees.

    Another faction around Linus Kather aimed to champion the interests of
those who fled or had been expelled from the territories Germany had lost as
a result of the war. Expellees represented a relatively small share of the population in Hamburg, where Kather helped cofound the CDU. Within that minority, Kather belonged to the small minority of Catholic East Prussians. Yet
expellees and displaced people were more numerous in other CDU branches in
the northwest (fig. 5.2), and Kather started organizing support among them in
1946. Starting from the special committee the CDU created for expellees in the
British zone, Kather built a tightly developed organization that spanned from
the group's Hamburg headquarters to the local level and increasingly appeared
like "a party within the party" (Kleinmann 1993, 110; Stickler 2004, 212). Kather
became deputy CDU leader in the British zone in 1947 and rose in expellee organizations outside the CDU. At the 1950 party congress, the CDU recognized

his faction's influence by electing him to the party leadership. Kather's faction received five seats in the party council and the status of a Land branch for the territories east of the rivers Oder and Neisse.[32] This established it as a "parallel organization" to the policy committees through which the CDU had initially intended to integrate expellees (Stickler 2004, 212).[33]

Thus, the dual incentive structure created by the CDU's initially mixed leadership selection process resulted in a moderate level of factionalism. Minority elites and majority elites from smaller party branches made their voice heard through factions. They differed from the CDU's Land branches and auxiliary organizations in that they were not set up or initially sanctioned by the party leadership and began recruiting followers across party levels and Land boundaries relatively quickly after their formation.[34] They expanded into parliament to coordinate the activities of "their" parliamentarians and, over time, gained notable influence over particular policy fields, like social and labor policy for the Social Committees, and some authority over the allocation of offices (Dümig, Trefs, and Zohlnhöfer 2006, 107; Schmid 1990, 263–64; Bösch 2001, 288).[35] At the same time, Land majority elites ensured that factional activities would not undermine their influence. Kather faced opposition in Schleswig-Holstein and Lower Saxony where many expellees had settled and CDU leaders saw their influence at risk. Their opposition, in addition to Kather's pugnacious nature, helped contain his factions' influence (Stickler 2004, 213–14).[36] While Kather ultimately left the CDU in 1954, second-rank elites assumed the factional leadership and accepted their place within the CDU (Stickler 2004, 213–35).[37]

How does the CDU's moderate level of factionalism compare to Germany's other main parties during that time? We should find higher levels of factionalism in German parties with a more centralized leadership selection process and lower levels of factionalism in parties with a more decentralized leadership selection process than the CDU. Overall, the level of factionalism has generally been lower in German than in Italian parties (e.g., Ceron 2019, 35), plausibly reflecting the presence of more favorable factors reinforcing high levels of factionalism in Italy (see chapter 3). Country-specific factors thus clearly play a role in the development of parties' level of factionalism. However, variation in German parties' level of factionalism echoes this book's strategic-institutional argument. While Germany's Social Democrats (SPD) readopted a centralized leadership selection process when reestablishing their party after the war, the party's Marxist "principle of unity" initially subdued factionalism, expelling those too openly engaging in factional activities (Braunthal 1994, 46–49; Heimann 1984, 2029, 2061, 2114, 2140–41). Nevertheless, internal politics developed along identifiable tendencies across party branches, which started working together in a more coordinated way in the 1950s by publishing programmatic position papers and, similar to the DC's early factions, rallying around their own newspapers (Heimann 1984, 2043–44, 2054, 2059, 2112–15). When the "principle of unity" weakened—though without disappearing—in the late 1960s (Heimann 1984, 2147–48, 2152), the SPD saw the emergence of several factions and has been described as more factionalized than the Christian Democrats (Braunthal 1994, 48, 108–111; Ceron 2019, 36–38; Heimann 1984, 2120–22, 2192–94; Klotzbach 1982, 84–86; Merkl 1978, 250).[38]

In contrast, the Liberal Party's (FDP) level of factionalism, with its more decentralized leadership selection process (Rae's fractionalization index: 0.696), was lower than in the more centralized CDU. Despite intense divisions between left- and right-wing liberals, the divisions did not result in factions, and the leaders of the party's parliamentary and Land branches have traditionally been the key actors in internal politics (Dittberner 1984, 1311–20; 1987, 31–34, 94–95). Networks between party elites across Land branches, like the Naumann Circle in the 1950s, the National-Liberal Action in the 1970s, and the Schaumburg Circle, were short lived or limited to the party's parliamentary group or some few Land branches, making them camps rather than factions (Dittberner 1987, 105–7; 117–18; 2010, 230–31). The only notable exceptions were the short period when two youth groups competed for being the party's officially "recognized" youth association in the late 1970s and early 1980s and the Freiburg or Sylt Circle—a loose network of left liberals in the 1960s, which, however, declined after the end of the SPD-FDP coalition (Dittberner 1987, 121–23; 2010, 228–29). In turn, the Bavarian Christian Social Union (CSU) adopted an even more decentralized leadership selection process (Rae's fractionalization index: 0.822) and experienced its first organized faction only in 2014.[39] Finally, the "youngest" party of the so-called Bonn Republic—the Greens—formed in the early 1980s, did not repress internal competition, adopted a centralized leadership selection process, and has usually been characterized as highly factionalized (Kitschelt 1989b, 95, 204, 217; Kolinsky 1989, 6–7).

Reinforcing a Moderate Level of Factionalism

ORGANIZATIONAL INCORPORATION AND ADENAUER'S INFORMAL QUOTA

Dümig, Trefs, and Zohlnhöfer (2006) argued that the CDU kept factionalism at a moderate level by incorporating these early factions into its organization—a process inseparably linked with Konrad Adenauer. Accusing the Social Committees of forming a party within the party, Adenauer negotiated to curb their expansion.[40] While Adenauer would not fight the faction, the trade unionists agreed to their faction being incorporated into the CDU's organization as a so-called association (*Vereinigung*). Although the faction emphasized that it was not simply a CDU branch or committee, the party statutes henceforth named it alongside the CDU's youth and women's movements.[41] As an association, the Social Committees received the party's financial support and formally required its approval for all leadership elections and press releases (Dümig, Trefs, and Zohlnhöfer 2006, 101–5). However, they often ignored this constraint and also found independent sources of income (Patch 2018, 86). The MIT was another faction that was incorporated in that way (Spary and Lehnen 2000, 13–14), and a similar approach was taken toward Kather's expellee faction.[42] Among the CDU's early factions, only the EAK kept a higher level of autonomy and refused "association" status. Organizational incorporation did not change that these groups were factions but instead reflected Adenauer's strategic response to existing factions within the CDU. The left-wing, middle-class, and expellee faction were all a reality within the CDU before being organizationally incorporated, had not been set up by the central party, and did not depend on the party's approval to be active. However, by recognizing these factions as groups representing special interests within the party, Adenauer created incentives for the groups to not splinter (as happened with factions in the DC) and for party elites to join already recognized groups rather than to form their own factions.

Adenauer's maneuvering was important, but its scope of action should be theorized within the institutional constraints under which leaders act. The creation of such a leadership space has been the main outcome of the process outlined so far. It explains why there were no incentives for party elites to create further factions at that time, which made Adenauer's incorporation strategy possible. The CDU's moderate level of factionalism had provided each set of party elites with a way of gaining power. Majority elites from (south)western Germany could rely on their powerful position in the party council to access the national executive. Majority elites from the northern Land branches benefited from their majority status to be delegated to the party council. If they were dissatisfied with their share of national executive seats via the party council, they could rely on factional activities. This also provided minority elites with some potential coalition partners at the national party congress in their attempts to gain leadership positions. This institutional playing field set the stage for Adenauer. He saw that it would be almost impossible to ignore these different groups in the party leadership, and trying to strike deals before party meetings between the groups that had already become reality became his trademark strategy (Bösch 2001, 239). He promoted a well-balanced concordance system in which positions were informally apportioned based on class, region, and denomination (Bösch 2001, 116, 245, 328–32). This was, for instance, reflected when the party leadership created the positions of managing board members (*geschäftsführende Vorstandsmitglieder*) in late 1951: Kurt Georg Kiesinger represented the southern Land branches, Robert Tillmanns the Protestants and northern Land branches, and Franz-Josef Wuermeling the Catholic Land branches in the west and southwest, respectively (Kleinmann 1993, 198).

Analyzing the incentive structure created by the rules to select the party leadership clarifies why Adenauer's incorporation strategy prevailed while De Gasperi's similar approach failed to keep the DC from becoming highly factionalized. In contrast to the CDU, support from delegates from different party branches was the key resource for both majority and minority elites in the DC to get elected to the party leadership. The party congress delegates could be divided, arranged, and rearranged into numerous potential coalitions. This incentivized party elites to form their own factions and factional coalitions and create incentives (e.g., pork) for delegates to support their coalition. The result was a proliferation of virtually continuously rearranging factions, which made their more structured incorporation into the DC's organization impossible. De Gasperi's strategy of trying to informally guarantee key groups' representation and thereby discouraging factionalism thus had no chance of permanently succeeding. In contrast, the institutional incentive structure in the CDU resulted, as chapter 2 made us expect, in a relatively similar number of factions, which supported Adenauer's incorporation strategy. Scholars of German, Austrian, and Italian Christian politics have therefore rightly highlighted the impressive leadership skills of Adenauer, Raab, and De Gasperi (e.g., Bösch 2001; Kriechbaumer 1995a; Capperucci 2010). Yet the ÖVP and DC's limitations in integrating their diverse internal groups already became manifest under Raab and De Gasperi. This was not because they were less talented leaders than Adenauer but because their parties had adopted an institutional design that created a specific incentive structure for party elites.

FORMAL AND INFORMAL INSTITUTIONAL CHANGE

As in the previous cases, organizational changes contributed to reinforcing the CDU's moderate level of factionalism. While the leadership selection process was increasingly decentralized between 1950 and 1966, this was rebalanced by incentives of factionalism. Although the Social Committees had failed to gain ex officio membership in the party leadership in 1950, it realized this in 1956. The faction benefited from many majority elites from smaller Land branches also seeking to formalize their influence. Together, they succeeded in making all factional and Land leaders ex officio members of the national executive.[43] The smaller Land branches had previously fought hard to keep a vote-based component in the allocation of party council and national party congress seats. They could, however, not prevent the (south) western Land branches from adding a membership-based component.[44] The new system provided the Rhenish and Westphalian Land branch with more than twice as many party council seats as most other branches.[45]

In return, the Rhenish and Westphalian majority elites cooperated with the smaller Protestant Land branches, the EAK, and the Social Committees to increase the number of deputy party leaders from two to four. They wanted to provide Karl Arnold, whose Land government had been overthrown in early 1956, with a national-level position. They gained Protestant support for this by emphasizing that half of the deputy leaders needed to be Protestants (Kleinmann 1993, 198; Bösch 2001, 294).[46] This alliance led to Kaiser (Social Committees), Arnold (Westphalia, Rhineland, Social Committees), von Hassel (Protestant Land branch of Schleswig-Holstein), and Gerstenmaier (EAK, CDU's parliamentary group) becoming Adenauer's deputies (Kleinmann 1993, 198). Adenauer (the federal chancellor since 1949) and parliamentary party leader Heinrich von Brentano countered these changes for the party in public office. They used the increased size of the national executive resulting from the ex officio membership of the Land and factional leaders to justify the introduction of an executive committee.[47] Its twelve members mostly consisted of delegates from the party in public office.[48] Their attempt also to make the governors of the CDU-led Land governments and all federal ministers ex officio members of the party leadership was, however, repelled by the Land leaders.[49]

The Land majority elites struck back at the 1958 party congress. They gained authorization to elaborate on reforms to the CDU's national leadership.[50] As a result of deliberations, the executive committee no longer primarily included members of the party in public office but was elected by the national executive. This helped the Land branches and factions ensure their representation (table 5.3).[51] The national executive even elected nineteen executive committee members, in addition to Adenauer as party leader, because the sixteen seats designated by the party statutes proved insufficient to grant comprehensive representation.[52] Adenauer managed to counter this reform only partially by making the CDU chancellor and the ministers in the federal government ex officio members of the national executive.[53]

TABLE 5.3. CDU executive committee in 1960

Name	National PPG	Land branch	EAK	MIT	Social Committees	Expellees	Women's group	Youth group
Konrad Adenauer	X							
Heinrich von Brentano	X							
Ludwig Erhard	X		X	X				
Franz Etzel	X		X	X				
Gerhard Schröder	X		X					
Peter Altmeier		X						
Kurt Georg Kiesinger		X						
Franz Meyers		X						
Franz-Josef Röder		X						
Erik Blumenfeld		X	X					
Josef Hermann Dufhues		X						
Wilhelm Fay		X						
Otto Fricke		X	X					
Wilhelm Johnen		X						
Johann Baptiste Gradl		X				X		
Klaus Scheufelen		X	X					
Hans Katzer					X			
Aenne Brauksiepe							X	
Luise Rehling		X					X	
Gerhard Stoltenberg		X	X					X

Source: *Bundesparteitag*, 1962, pp. 311–14, ACDP, https://www.kas.de/c/document_library/get_file ?uuid=71e5e6c1-101a-ea75-776a-772011cedb37&groupId=252038.

These changes occurred against the backdrop of public and internal con-cerns about Adenauer's age (Kleinmann 1993, 181–86). Many party elites real-ized that the CDU was not prepared for the case of Adenauer's resignation or death.[54] On the basis of a proposal by the Land leaders to increase organiza-tional independence, the executive committee was replaced with a smaller presidium in 1962, which included the party leader, the executive party leader, his deputies, and four other members (table 5.4).[55] While the absence of rep-resentatives from Rhineland-Palatinate and Baden-Württemberg was strik-ing, the presidium reflected the main internal conflict line at that time. It was almost equally divided between those demanding the CDU's greater in-dependence from Adenauer and those loyal to the eighty-six-year-old chan-cellor. Theodor Blank's membership is likely to have been the result of the only controversy that emerged over the new presidium. The leader of the Social Committees, Hans Katzer, complained that the presidium's proposed composition would not represent all intraparty groups (i.e., arguably refer-ring to his faction).[56] He proposed keeping the old executive committee in addition to the new presidium. However, his motion was opposed by several Land leaders and ultimately rejected.[57] It seems plausible that Blank, a Social Committees member and on good terms with Adenauer, was included in the presidium to prevent Katzer from bringing up the topic at the 1962 national congress.[58]

Table 5.5 summarizes these first episodes of organizational development. They illustrate that the different strategies party elites had been incentivized to adopt helped them to gain influence at the leadership level. They therefore had little reason to change them. The fact that factional leaders had been given ex officio membership in the national executive also incentivized factional elites, in addition to maintaining their network across party branches, to maintain a strong network within their own faction. This helped keep factionalism at a moderate level.

A ruling by the Constitutional Court triggered "the most far-reaching" organizational reform in the CDU's history (Poguntke 1994, 190). The ruling is rightly considered an exogenous shock. While the parties controlled the process of selecting constitutional judges, candidates were required to be elected by a two-thirds majority, which forced the parties to agree on politically moderate candidates, and consequently, partisan political jurisdiction did not play a major role (Poguntke 1994, 188). The ruling compelled lawmakers to devise a party law that dramatically reduced the share of ex officio members in the national party leadership. The party law of 1967 demanded that parties' respective leadership boards were elected by the national party congress and restricted the percentage of ex officio executive members to 20 percent. These restrictions led to the CDU's statute of 1967, which cut the number of executive members nearly in half and excluded the party council from electing the party leadership. Since then, the party congress has elected most seats in the national executive and presidium.[59]

TABLE 5.4. CDU presidium in 1962

Name	Position	Power base
Konrad Adenauer	Party leader	Party in government, Rhineland
Josef-Hermann Dufhues	Acting party leader	Westphalia
Kai Uwe von Hassel*	Deputy party leader	Schleswig-Holstein
Heinrich Krone	Ordinary member	Party in government, Exile-CDU
Ludwig Erhard*	Ordinary member	Party in government, MIT
Eugen Gerstenmaier*	Ordinary member	Party in parliament, EAK
Theodor Blank	Ordinary member	Party in government, Social Committees

* Indicate Protestant denomination.

TABLE 5.5. Main organizational changes within the CDU until 1966

Year	Proposal	Backed by	Effect
1956	Leaders of Land branches, Social Committees, MIT, and youth and women's movement ex officio members of the national executive	Land majority elites and Social Committees	Guarantee of Land and factional representation in the national executive. Increase of national executive from 16 to around 50 members
	Adding a membership-based component to the allocation of party council and national congress seats	Large Land branches	Increased seat share of large Land branches
	Introduction of an executive committee (12 members)	Party in public office and Adenauer	Ensuring Adenauer's influence and the ongoing importance of the party in public office
	CDU members in government participate at party leadership meetings		
1960	Executive committee as subunit of national executive and expanded to 20 members	Land majority elites	Land majority elites regained influence at the national level
	Chancellor and federal ministers (if CDU members) became ex officio members of the national executive	Adenauer	Ensuring representation of party in public office

Note: An acting party leader and a presidium were introduced in 1962. This reform was mainly driven by concerns over Adenauer's age.

However, while the Constitutional Court's ruling and the ensuing party law imposed a centralization of the leadership selection process, this was absorbed by the self-reinforced moderate level of factionalism. A committee including majority elites from the Land branches and the party in public office as well as factional leaders ensured that the internal balance of power would not be affected (Schönbohm 1985, 260–62; Schmid 1990). Moreover, the national executive usually kept inviting the Land and factional leaders to their meetings, and the number of deputy leader positions in the presidium was increased to reflect intraparty diversity.[60] Consequently, majority and minority elites' incentives did not change markedly (Haungs 1983, 69–70; Kleinmann 1993, 264). Majority elites from the (south)west and the party in public office focused on their power base within their party branch and only occasionally cooperated when they saw their influence at stake (Schmid 1990, 175–76). The majority elites from the smaller Land branches in northern Germany continued to rely on the Soltau Circle to make their voice heard.[61] Finally, factional activities remained the strategy of minority elites. The Social Committees and the MIT usually maintained representation in the party leadership, parliamentary committees, and ministerial departments (Haungs 1995, 190; Bösch 2001, 294; Dümig, Trefs, and Zohlnhöfer 2006, 108–11, 122). While their relative strength has varied over time, affected by the CDU's governmental status, actors' political skills, and issue salience (Poguntke 1994, 208–9), they have remained important for intraparty decision-making (Haungs 1995, 191). As in the ÖVP, behaviors associated with an initial institutional setting that was reinforced over time had proved quite robust to external shocks (Pierson 2000a, 263; Greif 2006, 190).

Reform-Friendly Factionalism and Party Adaptation before 1990

FACTIONAL INTEGRATION AND THE CDU'S DOMINANCE

Factional integration played an important role in overcoming denominational hostilities and establishing the CDU's dominant position on Germany's political (center-)right.[62] Many Protestants feared that the Catholic majority in the new Adenauer government would exploit the dramatic decrease in the Protestant population due to Germany's postwar partition and territorial losses and abandon efforts to reunify with the predominantly Protestant East (Bösch 2001, 118–19; Hehl 1999, 167, 177–78; Mitchell 2012, 188; Pearson 2010, 271; Sauer 1999, 1–2, 47). The conflict over West German rearmament became a focal point for these fears (Hehl 1999, 178; Pearson 2010, 272–73).[63] The Korean War in mid-1950 intensified discussions over rearming West Germany as part of a Western defense alliance, which would entrench both German states on opposite sides in the Cold War. While Catholics rallied behind rearmament, several Protestant state churches rejected it for jeopardizing reunification (Bösch 2001, 119–20). The opposition was particularly strong in areas with a reformed Protestant tradition and brought together a broad Protestant coalition that cut across prewar divides (Bösch 2001, 120; Dietzfelbinger 1984, 97–150; Jobke 1974, 116; Klein 2005, 342–45; Koch 1972, 279–80; Pearson 2010, 271). The issue divided the German public. Forty-two percent of people rejected rearmament before national reunification in September 1951, and support for German neutrality ranged from 30 percent to more than 50 percent between 1950 and early 1953.[64] More than half of the respondents repeatedly named "the German question," referring to rearmament, the East-West conflict, German reunification, and national sovereignty, as the country's most important problem between the fall of 1951 and 1953, vastly exceeding the share of respondents concerned about the country's economy (Noelle and Neumann 1975, 392).

Tensions between Protestants and Catholics were high in the CDU. Between November 1950 and March 1952, Adenauer rejected three initiatives

by the Soviet and East German government to negotiate Germany's reunification. While many people were skeptical of the initiatives' sincerity, Adenauer's decision to not even consider negotiations provoked intense opposition by CDU Protestants and the Christian Democrats exiled from the
Soviet zone (Koch 1972, 347; Volkmann 1988, 185–201). The risk of losing the
"CDU's Protestant circles," Adenauer said, was his "greatest concern."[65] In addition to disagreements over rearmament, Protestants and Catholics clashed
frequently over the distribution of national- and state-level posts.[66] In this
environment, the CDU's vote share collapsed in the state elections in many
Protestant areas.[67] The party lost on average 12.93 percent, excluding the two
Länder where electoral alliances most likely concealed even higher losses.[68]
As most observers expected neither the CDU's imminent recovery nor the
rival parties' disappearance (Bösch 2001, 139), the development pointed toward the resurrection of the Weimar Republic's highly fragmented political
right. Journalists and party elites considered the party's disintegration along
denominational lines a serious possibility.[69]

Attributing the CDU's success in integrating Catholics and Protestants
to the path-setting effect of the Allies' licensing policy does not fit the high
level of uncertainty in the early 1950s (cf. Loewenberg 1971, 268–76; Pridham
1977, 21–39; Rogers 1995, chap. 6). When the Allies abolished the restriction
in March 1950, the CDU suddenly faced competition from other centrist and
right-wing parties that provided voters with an alternative to the CDU's inter-
denominational and cross-class coalition.[70] It allowed the German Party
(DP), with its roots in prewar Protestant conservatism, and the social-
Catholic Center Party (Center) to expand beyond the British zone, where
they had achieved notable results.[71] The end of party licensing also allowed
for the emergence of the League of Expellees and Deprived of Rights (BHE),
which became a serious electoral force winning up to 23.4 percent in Land
elections and 5.9 percent in the 1953 federal election.[72] Finally, Gustav Heinemann (CDU minister of the interior and lay leader of the Protestant Church)
resigned in protest of Adenauer's rearmament course and formed the All-
German People's Party (GVP) (Dilling 2022).

The new electoral law in 1953 certainly helped the Christian Democrats in
consolidating the union between Protestants and Catholics and absorb most
of their new rivals until the end of the 1950s, but it cannot tell the full story.
As the Christian Democrats had intended, the new law disadvantaged small
parties.[73] Parties henceforth needed to win at least 5 percent of the valid party
list votes in the entire federal territory rather than a single Land, although
they could bypass the threshold by winning one constituency seat.[74] Deliberations on the new law had started in the spring of 1953, and after tedious

negotiations, it passed on 26 June 1953 (Pollock 1955, 107). But before all that, in January 1953, most of the DP's parliamentarians in Schleswig-Holstein had already joined the CDU (Bösch 2001, 144). Merging with the CDU was not the only option. The Center Party had common socioeconomic ground with the SPD and, in fact, formed a coalition with the SPD and FDP in North Rhine–Westphalia in 1956 (Cary 1996, 261–62). Alternatively, it could have merged with the Bavarian Party (BP), which had gained 20.9 percent of Bavarian votes in 1949 and continued to have notable support in Bavaria in the 1950s, and indeed, both parties formed a joint parliamentary group in 1951 and an electoral alliance in 1957 (Cary 1996, 267; Kaack 1971, 199). Moreover, the SPD wooed the BHE (Strickler 2004, 222–25), and cooperation between the DP and FDP, which was much more national-liberal than in later years, could have revived the interwar German National People's Party (Bösch 2001, 159).

Church support did not predetermine the CDU's integrative success. While the Catholic Church supported the CDU in fighting off the Center Party (Warner 2000, chap. 9), the Protestant Church refused to favor the CDU in identifying candidates for the 1949 election, did not endorse a political party, and remained divided for large parts of the 1950s (Conway 1992, 834–35; Klein 2005, 446–48). While Lutheran elites supported the CDU (Bösch 2001, 36; Sauer 1999, 80–104), opposition especially to the CDU's rearmament course was pronounced at the grassroots level (Hoeth 2007, 49–50; Pearson 2010, 283–85).

Adenauer's maneuvering is important for explaining why most of the smaller parties did not turn to the CDU's rivals, and his autonomy in offering posts to rival politicians without them having to climb the party hierarchy lends some support to the leadership autonomy argument (Bösch 2001, 244, 247, 268). His absorption strategy usually began by forming an electoral alliance with the smaller parties. While they benefited from the sharing of financial resources, constituency seats, and offices, they increasingly struggled to differentiate themselves from the CDU (Bösch 2001, 146, 160, 183–84; 2002, 205). When the smaller parties risked failing to reenter parliament, their elites were offered influential positions in exchange for changing sides (Bösch 2001, 172–76; Kaack 1971, 223–24; Stickler 2004, 211). Their reputation was then used to reach out to and finally incorporate their supporters (Stickler 2004, 232, 283–84), while the CDU stopped its help for the smaller parties (Kaack 1971, 259).[75]

However, the focus on leadership autonomy starkly underrates Adenauer's dependence on the CDU's moderate level of factionalism. Adenauer had to work with the CDU's internal groups to maintain the party's complex internal coalition (Bösch 2001, 105–6, 236–37, 268–69; Haungs 1986, 48; Schmid 1990,

56; cf. Heidenheimer 1961). Responding to the anti-rearmament campaign by Heinemann's GVP, the EAK operated among Protestants as a vocal defender of Western integration (Müller 1990, 270).[76] It closely monitored Heinemann's and the GVP's activities and implemented countercampaigns.[77] In Hamburg, for example, it distributed 150,000 flyers among attendees at GVP events.[78] The EAK also directly approached Protestant church officials, voters, and CDU members at the local level.[79] The faction was widely credited for the substantive increase in the CDU's share of Protestant voters in 1953 (Hehl 1999, 169; Oppelland 1998, 112–13). The EAK's campaigns for Protestant expellees and the refugee faction's rallies for Catholic expellees also helped counter the BHE.[80] Factions also helped promote their constituency's ideas within the CDU. While the CDU moved toward market economy positions in line with Adenauer's strategy to consolidate the party's dominance on Germany's political right (Bösch 2001, 86–88), the Social Committees called for a return to Christian-social ideas after the CDU's losses in the 1951 Lower Saxony election. The faction campaigned for this as an internal block among the public and CDU leaders and achieved several important welfare legislations, like the 1957 pension reform (Patch 2018, chap. 4).[81]

Factions also helped recruit members and elites from the CDU's rivals and target groups. Albers already called on the Social Committees' members during the 1949 campaign to convince members of the Center Party to join the CDU.[82] Kaiser and Albers confirmed this strategy in June 1951, inviting the representatives of the Center Party's left wing to a meeting in the faction's headquarters.[83] Incorporating these new and their own members among the CDU's office holders became one of the factions' key activities. The EAK leadership named influencing the distribution of posts at the federal, Land, and local level as one of its "most urgent tasks."[84] It kept a surgical denominational breakdown of CDU members in public office at the federal and Land level and built a personnel database to name "appropriate" Protestant candidates.[85] *Appropriate* did not refer only to candidates being Protestant and professionally qualified. Ehlers emphasized that they also needed to represent the faction's political views, over time giving the EAK the reputation of Ehler's "personal power base" (Oppelland 1998, 132).[86] The faction achieved close to denominational parity in the second Adenauer cabinet and ultimately a balanced leadership board (Dilling 2017, 99; Hehl 1999, 169). Similarly, the Social Committees kept a close eye on the share of labor representatives among CDU candidates and office holders.[87]

Factional integration helped decrease opposition to party reform. As Kraske elaborated in his report to Adenauer, the fact that the different voices within the CDU had been heard in internal decision-making reduced reservations against a more tightly organized central leadership. Even contested elections would pose less of a threat to the party's cohesion than it might have done in the CDU's early years.[88] At the same time, because many majority elites were not incentivized to join or form factions, the CDU avoided the fragmentation that paralyzed Italy's more factionalized DC. The leaders of most CDU's Land branches contended themselves with informal meetings to discuss their ideas and coordinate some initiatives. The so-called conference of the Land branch leaders (Konferenz der Landesvorsitzenden), without being a formal part of the CDU's organization, helped resolve internal tensions.[89] Majority elites then used their networks within their Land branch to implement the adopted strategies (Bösch 2001, 142–47).

FACTIONAL INNOVATION AND LEADERSHIP RENEWAL

The discussion so far has shown how organized groups within the CDU played a crucial role in the party adapting to its first crucial challenge—the end of party licensing and the (re)emergence of centrist and right-wing rivals. They did so by integrating key actors and their interests in the party and achieving outcomes in terms of both the distribution of posts and policy changes that echoed that different voices were heard within the CDU. Thus, rather than against party activists, as the leadership autonomy argument would expect, party adaptation was achieved together with party activists. It echoes Sarah Wiliarty's (2010, 2, 16, 42–46) finding that parties incorporating vertically organized subgroups that represent different political orientations on its decision-making bodies can importantly facilitate party adaptation. The ÖVP pursued a similar approach to interest incorporation (Wiliarty 2010, chap. 8), but it struggled to adapt once the societal conflict lines on which its auxiliary organizations for labor, agricultural, and business interests were built started changing. Distinguishing between the different types of intraparty groups and the dynamics they entail is powerful to explain why the CDU struggled less with internal innovation when similar processes of societal change unfolded in Germany.

In the 1960s and 1970s, the CDU's weak institutionalization started posing problems. Similar to the ÖVP, the co-optation of a large number of ex officio members had made the CDU's leadership board and party council too large to act. As a result, decision-making gradually shifted to Adenauer, who led the party through informal exchanges (Bösch 2001, 244–67). This practice increasingly struggled to resolve disagreements because decisions were often seen as lacking legitimacy, and the CDU's "behind-closed-doors" politics repelled party members at a time when the CDU's weak membership became a problem (Schwarz 2014, 140).[90] The SPD's transformation from a Socialist workers' party into a center-left catch-all party in 1959, the rise of the extreme-right NPD, and the far-left extraparliamentary opposition put further pressure on the CDU. The secularization of German society weakened the mobilizing power of the Catholic Church and increased the need for party members to mobilize support (Bösch 2002, 207).[91] Losing the 1969 and 1972 election to a Social Democratic–Liberal coalition, the Christian Democrats were under pressure to catch up.

Factions' flexibility supported innovation by facilitating the decline of "outdated" interests and the rise of elites and interests reflecting the changed societal conflict lines. With the decreasing salience of the rearmament issue following Germany's membership in the North Atlantic Treaty Organization in 1955, the EAK lost its focal point in the denominational conflict (Oppelland 1998, 123). While the CDU's internal foreign policy disagreements in the early 1960s again broadly mapped onto denominational differences, the EAK benefited only briefly, with the formation of the Catholic Political Working Group "Church and World," indicating a short-lived resurgence of denominational divisions (Oppelland 1998, 138–39). Similarly, with the decreasing relevance of the expellee issue, the expellee faction lost in relevance. The abolition of the Land branch for the territories east of Oder and Neisse deprived the faction of its guaranteed party congress and party council seats in 1968 (Dümig, Trefs, and Zohlnhöfer 2006, 109; Hehl 1999, 186–87). Instead, against the backdrop of Germany's growing middle class, the MIT grew to become the largest group in the parliamentary party (Kleinmann 1993, 273–74, 283–84).[92] With the generational conflict gaining in relevance, as illustrated by the 1968 student rebellion, the CDU's youth movement (Junge Union, JU) also became a vocal driver of reform, encouraging some scholars to label it as a faction (Merkl 1978; Dümig, Trefs, and Zohlnhöfer 2006). Opposing views on foreign policy concentrated in the discussions between "Gaullists" and "Atlanticists," of which the Gaullists, as the minority camp, developed more faction-like organizational pervasiveness (Geiger 2008, 531).

Although leadership changes in the ÖVP and DC often left the underlying dominant coalition untouched, changes in the factions' strength facilitated the alternation of different leadership coalitions in the CDU. In contrast to the rigid Land and League branches in the ÖVP, factions' flexibility facilitated responding to shifting political conditions. In contrast to the DC, majority elites from strong Land branches did not join or form their own faction, thereby limiting factional fractionalization. Following their success with the pension law in 1957, the Social Committees found itself on the backseat in the first half of the 1960s. While the 1961 election returned the faction with around 16 percent among the Christian Democrats' members of parliament (subsequently growing to 23 percent), it failed to prevent Erhard's rise to the chancellorship (Patch 2018, 224–34). The Social Committees had supported a center-left coalition with the SPD, whereas most Land leaders and the MIT backed Erhard's center-right coalition with the FDP (Kleinmann 1993, 186, 252). The foundation of the Wirtschaftsrat der CDU (Business Council of the CDU) in December 1963 further strengthened the center-right leadership. While formally setting up a separate organization for tax purposes, the Business Council quickly became "a fund-raising machine" and pushed back the Social Committees (Patch 2018, 235).

Power shifted again toward the left in 1966. Vatican II and shifting attention toward socioeconomic issues increased the CDU's vulnerability to lose Catholic workers to the SPD (Patch 2018, 242–51). When Erhard's government succumbed to conflicts over how to handle Germany's first (relatively small) postwar recession, the Social Committees actively nurtured the conflicts. It joined forces with Kurt Georg Kiesinger (governor of Baden-Württemberg) to form Germany's first national coalition between the Christian and Social Democrats and to achieve, among others, its long-standing demand for employers to continue paying wages to sick blue-collar workers (Kleinmann 1993, 302; Patch 2018, 252–54, 266–67). Yet the faction's collaborative stance toward the SPD also provoked a backlash when party congress delegates denied the faction's leaders Hans Katzer and Konrad Grundmann election to the CDU's leadership board in 1966 (Patch 2018, 259, 267). When a SPD-FDP coalition ousted the Christian Democrats from power in 1969, the Social Committees regained influence. Katzer joined Helmut Kohl (CDU leader in Rhineland-Palatinate) and Gerhard Stoltenberg (Schleswig-Holstein) as the "reform trio" elected as deputy party leaders (Patch 2018, 270). However, Kohl and other CDU leaders abandoned the Social Committees on the issue of workers' codetermination on factories' corporate boards in January 1971 (Patch 2018, 274–76). Rainer Barzel, leader of the Christian Democrats' parliamentary group, subsequently forged positive relations with the faction when securing the incorporation of its demands into the CDU's response to the government's codetermination bill (Patch 2018, 277–78). Backed by the Social Committees, the party's parliamentary group, and the Rhenish and Westphalian Land branches (with their social-Catholic strongholds), Barzel defeated Kohl to become CDU leader in October 1971 (Kleinmann 1993, 324).

Following Barzel's failure to retake the chancellorship, the CDU shifted back to more ordoliberal positions in 1973 and began a notable modernization process. Secularization and the growing share of white-collar workers among the population undermined the appeal of the Social Committees' emphasis on Catholic social teaching and trade unionism and resulted in a notable membership decline (Dilling 2017, 109–14; Kleinmann 1993, 273–74, 468). The rising MIT alongside the Land branches in the country's southwest and the party's youth movement backed Helmut Kohl's leadership bid and his selection of Kurt Biedenkopf, a relative political newcomer, as party secretary (Kleinmann 1993, 353–55). Organizationally, Kohl emphasized decision-making in the party's leadership board over the informal elite circles used by his predecessors (Schwarz 2014, 135–43, 173). He modernized the party's headquarters, streamlined internal processes, brought in a new generation of party elites loyal to his reform course, and secured greater influence for the central party by gaining a say over the nomination of the Land branch managers. His goal to stimulate party activism proved successful, as the CDU increased its membership from 422,968 in 1972 to 652,010 in 1976 (Hornig 2013, 90–91; Schwarz 2014, 174–75). Programmatically, Kohl and Biedenkopf worked to make the CDU more appealing to white-collar workers, self-employed people, and young voters (Schwarz 2014, 172). With the SPD drifting left, Kohl and Biedenkopf's emphasis on ordoliberalism helped unite the (center-)right (Schwarz 2014, 172–73), culminating in the CDU's first basic program in 1978 and ultimately succeeding in gaining the FDP's support to return the CDU to power in 1982.

Factional integration and innovation thus supported party adaptation long before the profound transformations of German society in the early 1990s. Factions helped integrate important voices, and their flexibility allowed old interests to decline and new interests to rise in response to changing conflict lines. They helped form alternative coalitions with the CDU's Land leaders without becoming as numerous and fragmented as in the DC, thereby supporting alternation in power within the party.

German Reunification and the New CDU

COALITIONAL ALTERNATION AND
PROGRAMMATIC REFORMS

The collapse of European Communism entailed far-reaching consequences for Germany. The role the CDU and, in particular, its leader and by then federal chancellor Helmut Kohl played in reunifying the two German states provided the Christian Democrats with a wave of public support in the early 1990s (Bösch 2002, 270; Clemens 2000, 39–40). Yet reunification meant that, practically overnight, more than 11.3 million voters from a very different and heterogeneous social and economic context joined the German electorate

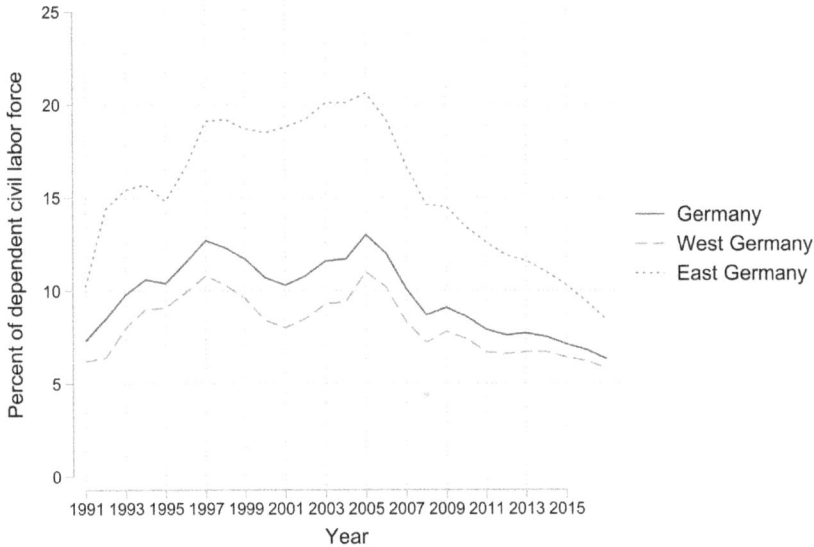

FIGURE 5.3. Unemployment rate in Germany after reunification
Source: Bundesagentur für Arbeit (2023).

(Mannewitz 2017, 221–32). Their integration increased the share of voters who did not have a strong attachment to one of the West German political parties and also intensified the existing trend of secularization (Lois 2011, 186; Pollack and Pickel 2003).[93] The integration of two completely different economic systems also led to a sharp rise in unemployment (fig. 5.3). Beyond a widespread mood for change, more than 80 percent of voters named unemployment as their most important concern going into the 1998 election (Clemens 2000, 54). The Christian Democrats fell behind the SPD in perceived party competence for employment, pensions, health care, and social security and, consequently, finished a distant second, losing 1.6 million votes and 109 direct mandates to the SPD alone (Clemens 2000, 53).

As in the DC and ÖVP, the losses sparked reform discussions. Reform pressure initially eased as the new government's internal turmoil and controversial citizenship reform contributed to the CDU's victories in Land elections and improving national polls (Clemens 2005, 59). This changed in November 1999 when former CDU treasurer Walther Leisler Kiep faced charges of tax evasion. The investigations revealed that the CDU had received undisclosed donations, made inappropriate use of funds, and had maintained secret accounts. The scandal implicated Kohl and Wolfgang Schäuble (Kohl's successor as party leader), and the CDU suddenly faced hearings and the risk of penalties (Clemens 2000, 55–56). Within three months, the Christian

Democrats plummeted in the polls from close to 50 percent to almost 30 percent. Reminded of the DC's collapse some years earlier, several observers predicted the CDU's complete implosion (Clemens 2005, 58; Rensmann 2015, 144). When Kohl refused to name the donors, the CDU had to break ties with its long-standing leader. This came on top of pressure to redefine the party's platform after sixteen consecutive years in office (Clemens 2005, 56, 59). Unlike in the DC and ÖVP, the discussion centered on programmatic rather than organizational change.[94] In both the DC and ÖVP, substantive programmatic reforms without prior organizational reforms were practically impossible because of the extent to which the DC's factions and the ÖVP's Leagues and Land branches prevented adaptation. In contrast, the CDU's organization was much less connected to the party's electoral losses, which Hunter (2010) has shown to facilitate adaptation. Yet this was, in line with the book's framework, endogenous to the CDU's initially mixed leadership selection process and moderate level of factionalism.

The leadership autonomy argument does not explain why the CDU's record of adaptive reforms was much better than that of the DC and ÖVP. CDU elites disagreed on whether the CDU should follow an economically centrist and socially progressive, a market-liberal, or a Christian-conservative course (Clemens 2009). While the party's long tenure in office did not cause high factionalism (cf. Boucek 2012), it had intensified disunity (Wagner 2014, 186–87). Neither the eventual popularity of the CDU's new leader Angela Merkel nor a particularly noteworthy mastery of the party provided her with a free hand (Clemens 2011, 475–77). Clemens's (2011, 477–82) view that Merkel enjoyed substantial autonomy because of the absence of factional consensus neglects that the DC was also characterized by a lack of factional consensus without generating substantive reforms. Moreover, Clemens shows how different internal groups repeatedly managed to realize their preferences, which undermines the leadership autonomy thesis. Finally, the CDU's internal practices starkly differed from the leadership autonomy that characterizes weakly institutionalized parties (cf. Levitsky 2003; Freidenberg and Levitsky 2006). The Land and even local party levels have remained highly influential in internal decision-making and have held far-reaching powers over party financing, staffing, membership administration, national campaigns, and candidate selection (Turner 2013, 120–22).

Instead, the CDU's adaptation was rooted in its moderate level of factionalism, with alternating coalitions between the leaders of large party branches and factions facilitating reforms, without resulting in the highly unstable coalitions characterizing highly factionalized parties. While Kohl had kept Norbert Blüm from the Social Committees as labor minister, the faction was relegated from the party's leadership coalition after the 1998 election defeat (Clemens 2009, 125). Instead, the market-liberal MIT faction became the single-largest faction in the CDU, accounting for around a third of all members and reflecting the growing importance of the new secular middle class (Clemens 2009, 125–26). Other market liberals, like Friedrich Merz, rose from within the party's parliamentary group (Clemens 2005, 60). Angela Merkel, who had been a vocal supporter of (social) market economy throughout the 1990s, can also be initially located in this camp (Clemens 2006, 163–64). They faced conservative majority elites, like Roland Koch from Hesse, Jörg Schönbohm from Brandenburg, and Edmund Stoiber from the Bavarian CSU.

The CDU's dominant coalition initially shifted toward a more conservative profile. While Merkel lacked the support to secure the nomination for the 2002 election and poor public opinion ratings blocked Merz and Koch, Stoiber enjoyed support among the CDU's large (south)western Land branches (Clemens 2005, 61, 66; 2006, 170–71).[95] At a private meeting in January 2002, Merkel and Stoiber agreed that he would lead the Christian Democrats into the election (Clemens 2005, 67). Untarnished by the donation scandal, Stoiber's economic competence appealed to many market liberals and those dissatisfied with the government's record on unemployment. His right-wing credentials resonated with conservatives and seemed suitable to stop the rise of the right-wing populist Schill Party (Clemens 2005, 62–69). The 2002 manifesto included demands for lowering the top tax rate and employers' social security contributions, reducing the restrictions on laying off long-serving employees, expanding part-time and casual contracts, and investing in infrastructure and education (Clemens 2005, 71–72; Wagner 2014, 265). Yet while Stoiber's Christian Democrats led the SPD in polls on the economy, law and order, and education, they trailed the Social Democrats on all other issues (including by a 13 percent margin on family issues) (Clemens 2005, 31–32). The SPD's response to the Elbe floods and opposition to US plans for invading Iraq further turned the momentum in the government's favor (Clemens 2005, 74–77).

After the Christian Democrats narrowly missed returning to office, Merkel found new support to lead the CDU into adopting what editorials described as the "most radical change of course in social policy" in years (qtd. in Clemens 2009, 130). She cashed in a deal struck with Stoiber in exchange for supporting his candidacy to oust Merz and combine the roles of CDU leader and leader of the opposition in parliament (Clemens 2005, 80; 2006, 159). While her market-liberal course clashed with the Social Committees, Merkel found support among the MIT and Business Council. Yet more than on these factions, she relied on the so-called pasta band, a network of party elites from North Rhine–Westphalia, like Peter Hintze and Ronald Pofalla, with whom Merkel had forged ties while serving as cabinet minister in the early 1990s. Over time, other liberally minded MPs joined this trusted circle, and Merkel gradually succeeded in placing them in influential positions (Clemens 2006, 172–74).[96] With this new backing, Merkel put forward the 2003 Leipzig manifesto. While protests from the Social Committees moderated some of its proposals, the manifesto demanded a flat-fee instead of an income-adjusted health insurance premium and proposed reversing a care coverage program introduced under the previous CDU government, replacing the linear-progressive income tax with a simple three-stage model, slowing pension hikes, raising the retirement age, and cutting employer contributions to unemployment assistance and scaling it to workers' years of service (Clemens 2009, 129–30). The neoliberal course initially revitalized the Christian Democrats. They rose to 50 percent in the polls, celebrated a series of Land election victories in 2004 and 2005, and amid the SPD's controversial labor market reform, regained voters' confidence to handle the labor market (41 percent CDU-CSU, 21 percent SPD) and the economy (40 percent to 25 percent; Schmitt and Wüst 2006, 41).

The CDU changed course when a poor campaign and reservations about the scale of the proposed reforms resulted in only narrow victory in 2005 (Clemens 2006, 154–55; 2010, 27). The disappointing result left the MIT with few allies supporting a market-liberal course, and Merkel turned toward the Social Committees under its new leader Karl-Josef Laumann, who blamed the Leipzig manifesto for putting off centrist voters. Many conservatives also turned their back on the old manifesto (Clemens 2006, 172; 2010, 27). While Merkel still faced skeptical Land leaders, she developed an opposing network, dubbed the "midnight round" because it often met very late in the CDU headquarters. The network helped Merkel generate support among Land party elites in Baden-Württemberg (Annette Schavan, Tanja Gönner), Bremen (Bernd Neumann), Hamburg (Ole von Beust), Lower Saxony (Ursula von der Leyen), Rhineland-Palatinate (Christoph Böhr), and Thuringia (Dieter Althaus, Dagmar Schipanski). By late 2005, Merkel had built a majority in the CDU presidium (Clemens 2006, 174–76).

Pointing to the CDU's poor record among young and urban voters, the new leadership coalition moved the party's platform toward the center and a more progressive agenda. On economic grounds, the 2007 manifesto returned to emphasizing solidarity and justice alongside freedom (Clemens 2009, 132). The CDU's left-wing faction certainly benefited from Merkel's leading of a coalition with the Social Democrats, but centrist reforms continued after forming a coalition with the Liberals in 2009. Just eight years after its 2003 debacle, the Social Committees celebrated a notable victory when the 2011 party congress endorsed a mandatory minimum wage (Wagner 2014, 267). On sociocultural issues, unmarried parents would henceforth be allowed to pool and split their incomes for tax purposes, a right previously reserved for married couples. The party also agreed to triple the number of publicly funded day-care places and recognized same-sex partnerships for fostering important values (Clemens 2009, 132–33). Its 2007 manifesto also recognized Germany as a "country of integration" and supported "controlled immigration," and the CDU-led ministry of the interior undertook several initiatives to reach out to Muslim voters (Rensmann 2015, 140–49). Finally, the CDU-led government abolished compulsory military service, adopted more environmentally friendly positions, and passed a phaseout of nuclear power following the Fukushima nuclear disaster (Rensmann 2015, 133–34; Decker 2015, 28).

While criticized in later years, the reforms proved effective in reaching out to centrist voters in 2009 (Clemens 2018, 142; Conradt 2010, 59–61). In 2013, the CDU picked up two million votes from its ailing Liberal coalition partner and another half million from the center-left, coming within five seats of an absolute majority. Since the 1950s, no party had achieved larger gains. Merkel's high approval ratings and the resonance of the CDU's highly personalized campaign in 2013 that Langenbacher (2015) and Decker (2015) describe needs to be seen against the backdrop of her reform course. While the proliferation of factions undermined the DC's adaptation by requiring its leaders to consider a myriad of potential multifaction coalitions, the ÖVP's low level of factionalism meant that similar interests continued to constitute the party's dominant coalition. In contrast, the CDU's factions introduced an element of flexibility by facilitating the rise and decline of internal groups in response to changing political and societal conditions without leading to excessive factionalism. Building a coalition involving factions, less institutionalized camps, and the party's Land branches, Merkel led her party to formulate a neoliberal vision for Germany's economy before moving the party back toward the center and adjusting its platform to sociocultural developments.

OPPOSITION TO DILUTING THE PARTY'S PROFILE AND CONSERVATIVES' INTEGRATION

The CDU's turn toward more progressive and centrist policies provoked criticism from conservatives and market liberals. Their discontent intensified over the Merkel government's bailout programs for EU member states during the financial and Euro crisis. Opposition to the bailouts translated into the rise of the right-wing Alternative for Germany (AfD) (Schmitt-Beck 2014, 95).

The AfD initially promoted a Eurosceptic image, including antiestablishment, migration-skeptic, and national-conservative elements. It moved starkly to the far right in 2015, running on an antirefugee platform in opposition to the Merkel government's accepting of over a million refugees in 2015 and 2016. The AfD won 7.1 percent in the 2014 European Parliament election, had entered all Land parliaments by 2018, and became the first radical-right party to enter the Bundestag since 1957 (Dilling 2018). Still, the AfD was not a CDU split. AfD founders Bernd Lucke, Alexander Gauland, and Konrad Adam had all a CDU background, but they neither had an organized group of supporters with whom they had left the CDU (like Mario Segni with his Trasversali faction in the DC) nor were they CDU minority elites. Lucke and Adam were simply party members who, to my knowledge, had never held any noteworthy CDU office. While Gauland had been undersecretary under CDU governor Walter Wallmann in Hesse in the late 1980s, a patronage scandal had put an end to his CDU career more than twenty years earlier. Only Gerd Robanus, among the AfD's founding members, used to be part of the MIT leadership.[97]

Instead, the moderate level of factionalism helped conservatives and market liberals in the CDU to achieve programmatic reforms. While Martin Lohmann's Working Group of Dedicated Catholics disintegrated quickly, a more lasting conservative faction emerged when more widely known minority elites formed the faction Berliner Kreis (Berlin Circle).[98] Its leadership included Wolfgang Bosbach (a federal parliamentarian without strong backing in his Land branch of North Rhine–Westphalia), Christean Wagner (sidelined in his Hessian Land branch since Volker Bouffier had become leader in 2010), and Erika Steinbach, whose expellee faction had dramatically lost in influence.[99] The faction ultimately merged with other conservatives into the WerteUnion faction (Union of Values) in 2017.[100] The new faction, alongside the party's youth movement, supported the rise of a new generation of conservatives and market liberals. While the WerteUnion faction does not formally include more than 1 percent of the CDU membership, it allowed the previously widely unknown Alexander Mitsch to gain nationwide attention.[101] Together with the resurging MIT under Carsten Linnemann and the CDU's youth movement behind Paul Ziemiak and subsequently Tilman Kuban, they staged several rebellions against the party leadership.[102] At the 2014 congress, they succeeded in defeating Merkel's ally Hermann Gröhe and instead electing Jens Spahn, at that time a conservative hopeful, to the presidium.[103] Together with conservative majority elites, like Thomas Strobl and Guido Wolf (both Baden-Württemberg), Julia Klöckner (Rhineland-Palatinate), and Reiner Haseloff (Saxony Anhalt), they put pressure on the CDU leadership.[104] At the 2016 party congress, this coalition of conservatives and market liberals defeated the compromise on dual citizenship that CDU leaders had negotiated with the Social Democrats.[105]

Overall, the CDU's reform process was one of programmatic adaptation cushioned by integrating both majority and minority elites. By 2021, the CDU again completed its sixteenth consecutive year in office, and many challenges that had characterized the end of Kohl's tenure resembled those at the end of the Merkel era. Worn out after a long spell in government, the CDU lost badly and faced demands for far-reaching programmatic reforms. The conservative and market-liberal factions' success in replacing incumbent CDU candidates alongside Friedrich Merz's election as party leader after his unexpected return to politics illustrate the continuing influence of factions in facilitating elite integration and renewal.[106]

Conclusion

The CDU avoided many of the problems plaguing the Italian and Austrian Christian Democrats by giving way to a level of factionalism that was higher than in the ÖVP but lower than in the DC. This moderate factionalism was to an important extent the result of organizational choices. Five years of bargaining had resulted in a mixed leadership selection process in 1950. It incentivized majority elites from the strong (south)western branches and the parliamentary group, majority elites from the weaker Land branches in the north, and minority elites to rely on different types of internal groups to assume positions on the party's leadership board. The resulting moderate level of factionalism was reinforced over time and absorbed the exogenously imposed centralization of the leadership selection process in 1967. This illustrates, like in the case of the ÖVP, that timing plays a crucial role in understanding processes of institutional development.

The CDU's moderate factionalism helped the party adapt. In contrast to the expectations of the leadership autonomy argument, party adaptation happened with rather than against party activists. Factions importantly complemented the party's Land and auxiliary branches in integrating both minority and majority elites without leading to the proliferation of factions characterizing the DC. Factions also facilitated innovation. Once old conflict lines dissipated, old factions declined and different ones rose, supporting the rise of new elites and ideas. The resulting alternation of leadership coalitions of Land majority elites and factions made reforms more substantive and dynamic than in the ÖVP, with its inflexible leadership coalition, and the DC, with its highly unstable multifaction coalitions. Chapter 6 explores the portability of these insights to parties beyond Italy, Austria, and Germany.

PART III

Comparative Perspectives

Christian Democratic Adaptation beyond Italy, Austria, and Germany

Ultimately, political science needs to develop a comparative framework for explaining the historical development of Christian democracy and the cross-national variation in the movement's capacity to mobilize power.

VAN KERSBERGEN (2008, 260)

The previous chapters have shown that the book's argument accounts for the differences in factionalism and adaptation of Christian democratic parties in Italy, Austria, and Germany. The analysis has covered the entire time span these parties have existed while building on original primary data. It has explained the trajectory of three cases that have been highly influential in the political development of their own countries and Western European politics at large. Although these are already important contributions in themselves, the fruitfulness of my theory of organizational choices and organizational adaptation is reinforced by its value to accounting for the development of further cases. If the initially adopted leadership selection process affects the level of factionalism, which, in turn, guides party adaptation, my argument should be supported by other cases that are part of my sample.

This chapter explores the value of my argument to explain the varying organization, factionalism, and adaptation of the Christian Democrats in Portugal, the Netherlands, and Luxembourg as three additional cases that have been close to the fitted line in figure 1.2. When choosing among the cases close to a characteristic point of the line, I have, in accordance with the methodological approach presented in chapter 1, selected the cases that provided actors with a similar strategic setting. All three parties are from unitary polities. Power in the parties has been centralized in the hands of the national leadership, which helps address Carey's (2007) argument about the link between power centralization and factionalism and arguments connecting power centralization to leadership autonomy and party adaptation (Wills-Otero 2016; Ziblatt 2017).[1] Furthermore, the Portuguese and Luxembourgian cases have in common that the Christian Democrats formed their organization after party competition had been suspended (i.e., the Salazar-Caetano dictatorship in Portugal; German occupation of Luxembourg during World War II). A final reason for choosing these three cases is the importance of accessible secondary literature, in the light of both language barriers and the general problem that studies on Christian democratic parties are relatively scarce compared to other party families.

Centralized Selection Procedure and Lack of Unity: The Portuguese CDS-PP

INTRODUCTION OF A CENTRALIZED LEADERSHIP SELECTION PROCESS

A group of political elites around Diogo Freitas do Amaral formed the Portuguese Democratic and Social Center (CDS) around three months after the popularly backed military coup on 25 April 1974 had put an end to the authoritarian Estado Novo (Bruneau 1997, 3–4; Bruneau and MacLeod 1986, 3–4; Pappas 2001, 259; Van Biezen 2003, 61). Having previously been close to the late autocrat Marcelo Caetano, they regarded the formation of a Christian democratic party as a way of preventing the Socialists and Communists from assuming power (Bruneau and MacLeod 1986, 78, 81; Bruneau 1997, 4; Frain 1997, 79, 83–84; Van Biezen 2003, 58, 61).

Freitas do Amaral and his supporters designed the CDS's centralized procedure to select its national leaders. It was accepted as part of their statutory proposal at the party's constituent congress in January 1975. The national leadership was, like in Italy's DC, primarily chosen by a central party assembly. The national congress elected twenty out of twenty-three members of the national executive (Comissão Politica). Only the presidents of the party's youth movement, trade unionists' organization, and the party's newspaper were ex officio members (Rae's fractionalization index: 0.238).[2]

Structural or antecedent factors did not seem to have played a role in this process. The CDS did not have a predecessor party that could have served as organizational role model.[3] Moreover, it had adopted its initial statute before the party established formal relations with other Christian democratic parties in Europe (Bruneau 1997, 8; Frain 1997, 80–81; Magone 1999, 244). The Catholic Church had also not interfered in the process of party formation and, finally, the CDS had been founded before basic legislation was issued to regulate party activities (Bruneau 1997, 4, 7).

HIGH FACTIONALISM

The CDS became highly factionalized even though the larger party congress rather than the smaller party council elected the CDS's president, which goes against Ceron's (2019) argument on the size of the selectorate.[4] Similarly, we would have expected Portugal's closed-list proportional representation system to discourage factionalism in the CDS by encouraging party-centered rather than candidate-centered competition (Bruneau 1997, 12; Shugart 2005, 49). The closed-list PR system also underlines why the tradition of clientelism (*caciquismo*) did not explain the formation of factions in the CDS.[5] Clientelism has usually been theorized as encouraging the formation of factions when combined with an electoral system that allows for competition between candidates from the same party (see chapter 2). Such a system, however, was absent in Portugal. Moreover, the dominant party approach cannot account for the CDS's high level of factionalism. Unlike the DC, the Portuguese Christian Democrats have spent, for various reasons, most of their existence in opposition (Bruneau and MacLeod 1986, 78, 80, 89; Van Biezen 2003, 57; Pappas 2001, 259–60). If the history of factionalism under the First Republic (1910–1926) had destined Portuguese parties to be highly factionalized (see Magone 1999, 234), we would not expect the observed cross-party variation in factionalism in Portugal (Frain 1997, 87, 90; Van Biezen 2003, 56). Finally, the CDS became highly factionalized even though it had been formed by a fairly homogeneous group around Freitas do Amaral (Matuschek 2008, 88–89).

Instead, factions emerged as a tool for party elites to mobilize support at national leadership elections. Freitas do Amaral's authority and the attacks by the far left might have delayed the outbreak of factionalism in the CDS's early years. Yet disagreements over the party's coalition strategy; the extent to which the CDS should pursue a Christian-centrist, market-liberal, and national-conservative course; and personal quarrels between party elites translated into the formation of factions in the early 1980s (Frain 1997, 90–91, 102; Bruneau and MacLeod 1986, 89; Matuschek 2008, 88–89). Since then, and similar to the DC, factions rather than the party's parliamentary, auxiliary, and subnational branches have been the predominant unit of competition within the CDS, although the CDS has usually not included more than three to four major factions at a time (Bruneau and MacLeod 1986, 89; Frain 1997, 90–92; Van Biezen 2003, 58; Matuschek 2008, 84–98, 139–71, 204–16). The almost-complete split of the national party into two factional blocs in 1990 illustrated the high level of factionalism (Frain 1997, 92).

A series of statutory modifications helped reinforce the high level of factionalism over time. This included the acceptance of PR for internal elections as a concession to Freitas do Amaral's Freitistas faction when Lucas Pires tried to consolidate his party leadership at the 1985 national congress (Frain 1997, 86).[6] It also included attempts by the faction that had won a majority in the national executive to strengthen its control over the party further (Van Biezen 2003, 65–66, 74). This was particularly obvious under Manuel Monteiro, who wanted to oust rival factions from party organs by abolishing the internal PR system (Frain 1997, 86). Monteiro also continued the development toward an increased central control over the party's candidate selection and internal finances (Van Biezen 2003, 74–76). Moreover, the incentives to join a faction spread from the national to the subnational party level when the centralized selection process spread from electing the national leadership to selecting national and subnational party congress delegates (Bruneau and MacLeod 1986, 81; Van Biezen 2003, 66–70). Consequently, factionalism persisted despite the enhanced political significance of the Portuguese regions in the 1990s (Magone 1999, 245).

WEAK ADAPTATION

The shrinking of its core base in the conservative and Catholic northern and northeastern regions made it important to broaden the party's electoral appeal (Magone 1999, 246–47), and the CDS was also required to find a place in Portugal's party system after the tumultuous revolutionary years (Bruneau and MacLeod 1986, 78). Its low level of institutionalization and growing centralization would make us expect the CDS to be highly adaptable (Kitschelt 1994; Levitsky 2003; Ziblatt, 2017). The party lacked an extensive mass membership or deep roots within society given the absence of historical parties and the fact that the CDS emerged shortly after the 1974 revolution (Freire 2006, 375–76). The party leaders tried to make up for this by building on the preexisting network of patron-client relations on the ground (Frain 1997, 79). The CDS thereby developed only a weak organizational presence at the local level. Consequently, the national leadership was widely autonomous in its decision-making, and the CDS acquired the reputation of being "a party with a head and no body" (Bruneau and MacLeod 1986, 81; see also Frain 1997, 86; Van Biezen 2003, 61, 75; Matuschek 2008, 85).

However, continuous factional disputes prevented the party from defining an ideological space as a way of strengthening its electoral appeal (Bruneau and MacLeod 1986, 87). When Lucas Pires and his Pristas faction assumed the party leadership in 1983, they shifted the party from a centrist position to the neoliberal right, which was criticized by the Freitistas (Frain 1997, 84). Freitas do Amaral returned to the leadership in 1988, again moving the party to the center but without solving the factional conflicts (Frain 1997, 91). After the 1991 election, the old factions had lost ground, and Manuel Monteiro assumed the leadership. He managed to gain support for adding the term *People's Party* (PP) to the party name and positioning it on the (nationalist) right (Frain 1997, 84, 92; Pappas 2001, 262). The CDS's trajectory highlights that factions' alternation in power facilitates changes in the party's platform, but when factionalism is too high, leaders' decisions are likely to be constantly challenged and renegotiated, which hinders the implementation of reforms. Even "the charismatic and popular leadership of Monteiro could not quell internal divisions among [CDS-PP] elites" even though the party more than doubled its vote share in 1995 (9.1 percent) and tripled its seat share (from five to fifteen) (Frain 1997, 92). Internal opposition to Monteiro's course led to a "breakdown in party discipline in Assembly votes" (Frain 1997, 92). In 1998, Portas succeeded in replacing Monteiro, which meant the comeback of the party's centrist faction (Magone 1999, 244; Van Biezen 2003, 58). Thus, the CDS's attempts to find its place in the political spectrum were accompanied by a high level of internal problems between the different factions, which led former party leader Basílio Horta to call the CDS "a group of friends who cordially hate each other" (Van Biezen 2003, 57).

While the CDS replaced its party leaders quite frequently, the elected leaders depended on the support of their own and often also other factions, and these coalitions, similar to the DC, were inherently unstable. Conflicts between factions often reemerged shortly after the leadership election. They undermined the leaders' authority, limited their ability to implement reforms, and prepared the way for yet another leader replacement (Matuschek 2008, 86, 88–89, 140, 142–48, 204, 206–10). Conflicts between factions also resulted in several splits. For instance, the battles with the party's right-wing faction convinced moderate and pragmatic party elites, like Luis Barbosa, Victor Sá Machado, and Roberto Carneiro, to leave in the 1980s and set up the New Democracy Group (Frain 1997, 91). In the mid-1980s, Freitas do Amaral and some of his Freitistas temporarily withdrew from the party to protest the rising neoconservative factions. In 1992, Freitas do Amaral left for good after Monteiro's right-wing faction had gained power. With one of its key founders leaving the party, the CDS lost a key identification figure for the party's centrist cadres and voters (Matuschek 2008, 86–89, 146–48).

The CDS's inability to agree on a political strategy and prevent its voters from abandoning the party contributed to its mediocre electoral trend (fig. 6.1). The party declined from 16.0 percent in the 1976 election to 4.4 percent

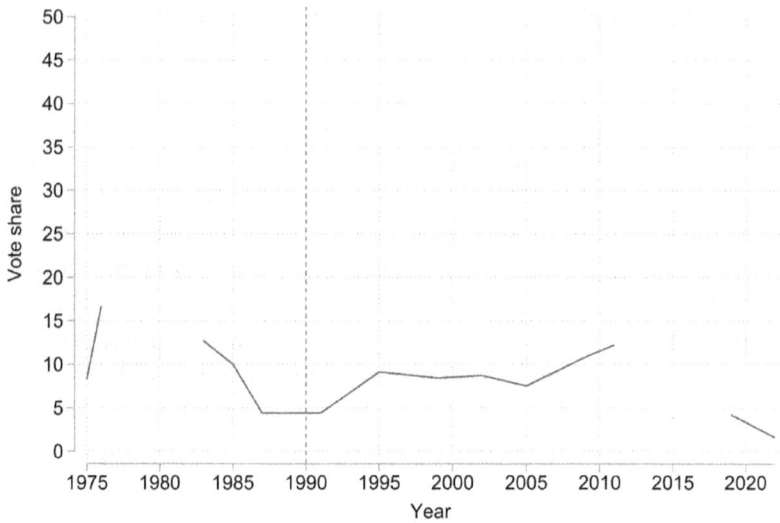

FIGURE 6.1. CDS vote share in Portuguese elections
Source: Armingeon et al. (2022) and Nordsieck (2021).

in the late 1980s and early 1990s after having tried to improve their prospects by forming an electoral alliance with the PSD (Frain 1997, 102–3). After the party celebrated a strong comeback in 1995 (9.1 percent), its vote share again declined to 7.3 percent in 2005. The Christian Democrats again succeeded in winning more than 10 percent (in 2009) and 11 percent (in 2011). However, the CDS lost six seats as part of an electoral alliance with the PSD in 2015 and declined to 4.3 percent and 1.6 percent in the 2019 and 2022 election, respectively. Overall, the development of the CDS shows notable parallels to the dynamics unfolded in Italy's DC (chapter 3). A centralized leadership selection process initiated a high level of factionalism that, in turn, undermined party adaptation.

Decentralized Selection Procedures and the
Lack of Flexibility: The Dutch CDA

INTRODUCTION OF A DECENTRALIZED
LEADERSHIP SELECTION PROCESS

The CDA resulted from a merger of the Catholic People's Party (KVP), the left-leaning Protestant Anti-Revolutionary Party (ARP), and the conservative Protestant Christian Historical Union (CHU) (Lepszy and Koecke 2000, 124, 137). The decreasing importance of religion in elections and the three parties' resulting decline had encouraged them to merge (Lepszy and Koecke 2000, 142–43).[7] Yet it took them eight years to agree on entering a federation and another five to merge into the CDA in 1980 (Bakvis 1981, 2; Lucardie and ten Napel 1994, 53; Evans 1999, 242; Lepszy and Koecke 2000, 143–48; Bosmans 2004, 57; Duncan 2007, 72). With no legal requirements regarding the party's internal structure (Lepszy and Koecke 2000, 154), party elites disagreed on, among other things, the extent to which the federative structure should give way to a single organization. Especially the ARP leadership had reservations against abandoning the three parties as distinct entities. It was the pressure from its own members who collected eighty thousand signatures in favor of the merger that convinced the ARP leaders to give in (Lepszy and Koecke 2000, 149).

The CDA ultimately adopted the model of a mass party with an influential national executive, which was selected in a highly decentralized way (Koole 1994, 280, 286, 299; Lepszy and Koecke 2000, 160–61). It included the party leader and two deputy leaders who were elected by the CDA local branches in combination with the party council (and confirmed by the party congress), ten members elected by the party council, between one and three delegates (depending on membership size) from each of the nineteen district branches, two delegates from the women's movement, and two delegates from the youth movement (Rae's fractionalization index: 0.922) (Lepszy and Koecke 2000, 160).

LOW FACTIONALISM

The decentralized leadership selection discouraged party elites from forming factions. Compared to the Christian democratic parties in Austria, Italy, Germany, and Belgium, Van Kersbergen (1995, 28–29) has ranked the CDA as being the least factionalized party (see also Lepszy and Koecke 2000, 161–67). This lends strong support to my theory because factionalism might have appeared to be quite likely given the existence of three predecessor organizations and the stark theological and political differences between them (Lepszy and Koecke 2000, 141, 148; Duncan 2007, 85; Wagner 2014, 113–16). Yet while people's former party affiliation was considered when distributing offices, the importance of this quota system fluctuated over time and has not resulted in factions (Lepszy and Koecke 2000, 196–97, 208; Wagner 2014, chap. 5.1).

The CDA's low level of factionalism also echoes the finding in chapters 3 and 4 that a preference vote component, which was included in the Dutch electoral system, does not unequivocally translate into high levels of factionalism (see Koole 1994, 283). An alternative explanation for the absence of factions refers to the CDA's incompatibility clause, which prohibited party elites from holding office simultaneously in the party in public office (i.e., in the parliamentary party group or the cabinet) and the extraparliamentary party organization (Lepszy and Koecke 2000, 161, 169). The incompatibility rule has surely been one of the reasons the CDA's parliamentary party leader and the prime minister, when the CDA was holding this position, have played a crucial role in internal politics (Lucardie and ten Napel 1994, 57). It does not imply, however, that factions did not emerge because there was nothing to compete for within the CDA (cf. Lepszy and Koecke 2000, 157). The national executive and executive committee have held far-reaching powers over the party's internal decision-making and financial resources (Krouwel 1993, 71–74; Koole 1994, 286, 299; Duncan 2007, 74). Still, factions remained largely absent, despite deep divisions within the CDA (Lucardie and ten Napel 1994, 53; Wagner 2014, chap. 5.1). Rather than giving rise to factions, conflicts were fought within the organizational branches of the party and between the branches themselves (Van Kersbergen 1999, 368–69; Lepszy and Koecke 2000, 186–93; Duncan 2006, 485).

Although the CDA's organization was already criticized in the 1980s for being overly rigid (Lepszy and Koecke 2000, 196), majority elites from its organizational branches prevented substantive changes to the internal playing field. They successfully opposed party leader Wim van Velzen, who wanted to make the internal selection and decision-making process more inclusive and facilitate the internal rise of new groups (Lepszy and Koecke 2000, 201–4). The initial low level of factionalism thus persisted.

WEAK ADAPTATION

The CDA initially appeared like a success in terms of stopping the decline of the confessional vote share (Bosman 2004, 57). Under the popular and charismatic CDA prime minister Ruud Lubbers, the Dutch Christian Democrats became the largest party and a pivotal player in the coalition system (Lepszy and Koecke 2000, 197–201; Van Kersbergen 2008, 260–61). Lubbers's influence was also essential in "integrating the still youthful party" and attracting "a greater proportion of voters distant from the church" (Duncan 2007, 74).

Yet Lubbers's great popularity distracted from serious structural problems (Lepszy and Koecke 2000, 180–86, 201; Duncan 2006, 471–82; Van Kersbergen 2008, 263–65). By the early 1990s, the extensive welfare regime, which the CDA had largely built and that was the basis of the party's social support coalition, had shown itself to be unsustainable (Van Kersbergen 1999, 366; Lepszy and Koecke 2000, 216). When the Christian Democrats announced that no social security scheme could be spared from retrenchments, two parties for the elderly formed to woo parts of the CDA electorate (Van Kersbergen 1999, 368–69; Duncan 2007, 75–76). Moreover, the issue of reforming the welfare state intensified tensions within the party's parliamentary group. Parliamentary party leader Elco Brinkman, who had succeeded Lubbers as the CDA's top candidate for the 1994 election, had proposed austerity policies that were heavily contested (Van Kersbergen 1999, 368–69; Duncan 2007, 75–76; Wagner 2014, 107–9). The quarrels in the CDA also facilitated the rapprochement of the liberal VVD and the Labor Party, which deprived the Christian Democrats of their pivotal position in coalition formation (Van Kersbergen 1999, 349; 2008, 262–63).

The CDA's relatively low level of institutionalization would make us expect the CDA to be more adaptable to such changes than the book's main cases. Although the CDA had been created as a mass party, with the ARP's strong organization providing a promising foundation (Koole 1994, 280), its member-voter ratio had remained below that of the book's main cases by the late 1980s (CDA: 0.04, CDU: 0.05, DC: 0.14, and ÖVP: 0.35).[8] The same point holds for the party's number of professional staffers (especially for the extra-parliamentary party) and local units (Koole 1994, 290).[9] Seawright (2012, 9) has rightly noted that Kitschelt's (1994) concept of organizational entrenchment is more inclusive than Levitsky's (2003) focus on the de facto importance of internal rules and bureaucracies. Still, while the CDA's territorial branches formally enjoyed some influence over candidate selection via the party council and party congress, with the latter meeting at least every two years and in election years (Koole and Van de Velde 1992, 673, 688–89), the party's parliamentary leadership de facto dominated (Koole 1994, 295). Leadership selection occurred by a small circle of majority elites (Koole 1994, 295). Compared to the ÖVP with its Leagues and the DC with factions' local brokers, CDA elites and candidates also depended much less on external support given the erosion of the Netherlands' religious pillars (Koole 1994, 285, 294). Unlike in Austria and Italy, a spoils system hardly existed (Koole 1994, 288).

However, the party's reform record has been rather poor. While the CDA repeatedly changed its leaders, new leaders, like in the ÖVP, were constrained in their reform attempts by competition with party elites from their own and other party branches (Duncan 2007, 76–77; Wagner 2014, 112–18). The internal divisions paralyzed the CDA (Duncan 2007, 84). The 1996 program New Ways, Firm Values contained relatively little in terms of policy change and particularly maintained the party's strong commitment to its religious identity (Duncan 2007, 78–81). The continuing emphasis on its religious identity was more a sign of the party's inability to pass substantive reforms than of internal agreement. The CDA had always had a stronger programmatic emphasis on the Bible than other Christian democratic parties (Hanley 1994, 5; Lane and Errson 1994, 151; Duncan 2007, 73). Yet there was clear evidence that this position would not be beneficial electorally, as the share of religiously active voters was in long-term decline and the CDA's support among the non-religious was low (Van Kersbergen 1994, 35; Duncan 2007, 83). While party elites were initially at least ambivalent about the option of chasing new voters (Duncan 2007, 73), the CDA tried to reach out to new voters and members, but its lack of factions made it too stiff to be able to succeed in doing so (Wagner 2014, chap. 6.1).

This is not to suggest the complete absence of reform. When the approaching 2002 election forced the CDA to decide on its lead candidate, the gridlock between parliamentary group leader Jaap de Hoop Scheffer and party leader Marnix van Rij allowed Jan Balkenende, a relative political newcomer, to secure the nomination (Wagner 2014, 118–20). As Levitsky (2003) and Kitschelt (1994) would make us expect, more substantive reforms followed the rise of an outsider to the leadership. Balkenende's communitarianism temporarily succeeded in reconciling the party's Christian-social tradition with more right-wing and market-liberal positions (Wagner 2014, 126–28, 224–25). Conflicts, however, soon remerged. Committees including majority elites from the party's parliamentary group and territorial and auxiliary branches were unable to reconcile their differences. Vague platforms were usually the result (Wagner 2014, 22–23, 233–36).

Efforts to resolve gridlocks through organizational reforms were tedious and had only limited success. Proposals centered on bridging the gap between the party leadership and the rank and file to stimulate membership participation and allow new groups and ideas to rise in the party (Duncan 2007, 81; Wagner 2014, chap. 7.1). Proposals to increase the independence of the CDA's auxiliary organizations, most notably the women's and youth organizations, and give them a more network-like structure points to party elites realizing the need for more flexible internal groups such as factions (Wagner 2014, 222, 287–94). Yet only very limited reforms were introduced, and they took a long time to pass. Similar to the ÖVP, the CDA solicited members' and nonmembers' input when formulating its platforms. Yet this had a notable effect only on the party's manifesto in the first Balkenende election in 2002 (Wagner 2014, 293–97). Like the ÖVP, the CDA also introduced primaries to select its parliamentary candidates, and it managed to increase the share of female and young MPs (Duncan 2007, 81–82). Yet as in the ÖVP, territorial party leaders maintained a tight grip on the actual selection (Wagner

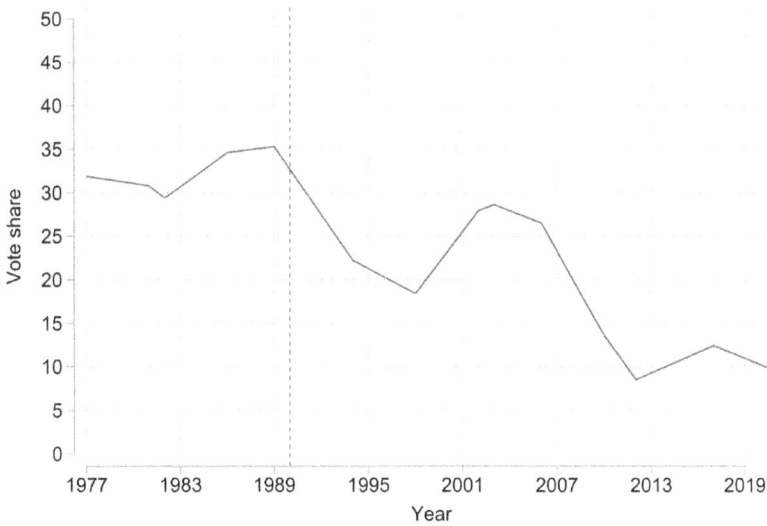

FIGURE 6.2. CDA vote share in Dutch elections
Source: Armingeon et al. (2022) and Nordsieck (2021).

2014, 136). A more profound reform with the introduction of a membership vote to select the party's lead candidate was introduced only in 2010—more than twenty years after van Velzen's first attempts to make candidate selection more inclusive (Lepszy and Koecke 2000, 201–4; Wagner 2014, 137).

Thus, although power has been similarly centralized in the CDA and the highly factionalized CDS, the process leading to the CDA's weak adaptation shows some important similarities to the development of the decentralized ÖVP. This follows the dynamics predicted by the book's argument: a decentralized leadership selection process discouraged the formation of factions, which made the party struggle to integrate new ideas and groups and thus to innovate in the light of a changing environment. Struggling to adapt, the CDA's vote share declined from 35.3 percent in 1989 to 22.2 percent in 1994 and 18.4 percent in 1998 (fig. 6.2). This trend had started before right-wing populist parties marked their noteworthy entry into Dutch politics. The rise of the right-wing populist Pim Fortuyn, the assassination of Fortuyn shortly before the election, and the CDA's antigovernment campaign helped the Christian Democrats to celebrate a comeback in 2002 (27.9 percent). The comeback, however, was short lived. The CDA's vote share again collapsed in 2010 (down 12.8 percent) and has remained relatively weak (i.e., 12.4 percent in 2017, 9.5 percent in 2021).

Mixed Selection Procedure and Successful Adaptation:
Luxembourg's CSV

Despite the small size of Luxembourg's territory, administration, and legislature, the Christian Social People's Party (CSV) is a suitable comparative case.
Like the book's main cases, it has been the dominant governing party for
most of Luxembourg's postwar history. It was built on strong anticommunism during the Cold War, and it emerged after party competition had been
suppressed as a result of Nazi German occupation (Schroen 2000, 344–45,
368–69; Grosbusch 2008, 332; Schoentgen 2008, 214–15, 259).

INTRODUCTION OF A MIXED LEADERSHIP
SELECTION PROCESS

The CSV resulted from the transformation of the prewar Party of the Right
(PdR) (Janssen 2006, 323–24). The structural conditions under which party
formation took place pointed to a decentralized leadership selection process.
Similar to Austria, Italy, and Germany, ongoing military activities in 1944 and
early 1945 restricted free movement and thus the ability to centrally direct
party formation. This contributed to strong cross-regional differences in
terms of party building (Schroen 2000, 346; Schoentgen 2008, 252).[10] The PdR
had also been a classic cadre party in which groups of notables representing Catholic Church, trade-unionist, or agricultural interests had substantive influence (Schoentgen 2008, 247, 254). We might thus expect the leadership selection process mainly to take place within the party's organizational
branches.

   However, the CSV's founding fathers Pierre Dupong, Émile Reuter, and
Émile Schaus designed the CSV as a mass party whose rules to select its
national leaders starkly differed from those of the PdR (Schroen 2000, 346;
Schoentgen 2008, 247). The PdR's national leadership had included an unspecified number of delegates who were autonomously chosen from the party's parliamentary group and the press and civil associations that endorsed
the PdR's principles (Schoentgen 2008, 254, 260). Ex officio membership in
the CSV's national executive, in contrast, was restricted to the leader of the
party's parliamentary group and the presidents of the four district branches
of the party. The national congress, in turn, elected seven national executive
positions. Although these seven positions had to include two representatives
each for the southern, northern, and central district and one representative for the eastern district, the national congress was sovereign in its choice
whom to elect.[11] Competitive elections for the positions were quite frequent

(e.g., Feltes 2008, 411–12). The elected national executive could then co-opt five eminent party elites and elected, among its own ranks, the party's president (Schoentgen 2008, 261).[12] The CSV thus introduced a mixed leadership selection process, which guaranteed regional representation while giving significant influence to a central party assembly (fractionalization index: 0.542).

MODERATE FACTIONALISM

If the size of the selectorate for the party leader position drove the CSV's level of factionalism, we would have expected the CSV to become highly factionalized, given the election of the party leader from the midst of the relatively small national executive (cf. Ceron 2019). Similarly, Luxembourg's PR system with a pronounced preferential voting component should have been conducive to high factionalism (Pasquino 1972; Katz 1986, 89, 98). Voters could cast as many votes as seats were available in their constituency (i.e., between seven and twenty-three). These preference votes could be distributed among candidates from the same or different parties, and a maximum of two votes could be given to the same candidate (Fry and Raymond 1980, 83; Schroen 2000, 354–55; Fehlen 2008, 479). Finally, the CSV's nearly permanent position in government should have encouraged high levels of factionalism (e.g., Boucek 2012). While it could be argued that Luxembourg's consensus-oriented political practice, including the outsourcing of contentious topics to referenda, discouraged factionalism (Schroen 2000, 338, 373), this does not pay sufficient attention to the rivalries among the Christian Democrats. Already in the 1940s and 1950s, the CSV was characterized by conflicts between party elites over the selection of parliamentary candidates, the allocation of offices, and the direction of policies. These conflicts often came into the open at the party's national congress (Schoentgen 2008, 315–19). This has not changed much over the past decades, as detailed accounts of the party's trajectory have outlined (Feltes 2008; Grosbusch 2008; Schoentgen 2008).

My argument helps explain why internal tensions have entailed a level of factionalism higher than in Austria's ÖVP and the Dutch CDA but lower than in Italy's DC and Portugal's CDS. Majority elites in the CSV's district branches and parliamentary group did not need to form factions because their guaranteed access to the national executive allowed them to promote their interests. Accordingly, the CSV's organizational branches in the districts and parliament became important actors in intraparty politics (Feltes 2008, 453; Schoentgen 2008, 265, 287–91, 327). Yet the CSV's mixed leadership selection process also provided opportunities to gain intraparty influence by forming networks across party branches. A left, an agricultural-conservative, and a middle-class camp became notable at the national congress, which elected around half of the executive positions, shortly after the CSV's formation (Schoentgen 2008, 299–300).[13] Actors from different party branches acted together by presenting joint motions and supporting specific leadership candidates (Feltes 2008, 411–12; Grosbusch 2008, 362, 365; Schoentgen 2008, 314, 317–19). Such networks were reproduced at different levels of the party organization (Feltes 2008, 449–50, 456; Grosbusch 2008, 391).

While the available sources do not allow naming the specific factions that solidified out of these conflicts, we know that factions have existed throughout the CSV's history. Janda (1980, 494) mentions factions that appeared after the CSV had gone into opposition in 1974. Moreover, the ongoing conflict between the middle-class, conservative, and left-leaning camp culminated in the formation of the socially and economically right-wing Cercle Joseph Bech in the late 1990 (Feltes 2008, 448–49). Finally, in Borz and de Miguel's (2019) expert survey, the CSV has received a score of 2.5, 2, and 2 on a scale from 1 to 5 for leadership, ideological, and issue factionalism, respectively. Internal politics are characterized by the party's district branches and the party in public office, which have enjoyed guaranteed representation in the national executive, and flexible networks that operated across party branches (Schoentgen 2008, 321, 326). Statutory changes confirmed the coexistence of ex officio members and centrally elected members of the national executive (Schoentgen 2008, 261, 264, 266; Grosbusch 2008, 338–39, 363).

HIGH ADAPTATION

Although the Luxembourgian electorate is socially quite homogeneous, and the country's economic development has been positive (Fry and Raymond 1980, 69; Janssen 2006, 321; Fehlen 2008, 492–94), the CSV still has faced important challenges that required adaptation (Feltes 2008, 437–43). The Christian Democrats' core constituencies have been shrinking dramatically (Schroen 2000, 339, 354; Fehlen 2008, 486; Feltes 2008, 436). Both the share of churchgoing Catholics and the CSV's vote share decreased by 15 percent between 1954 and 1974 (Grosbusch 2008, 370). The proportion of people attending church at least once a week subsequently dropped from 42.8 percent in the 1970s to 24.6 percent in the second half of the 1990s (Fehlen 2008, 485). Similarly, the number of farms in Luxembourg declined from 13,500 in 1950 to 5,200 in 1980 (Schroen 2000, 358–59; Grosbusch 2008, 370). Moreover, the instability in Eastern Europe after the collapse of Communism intensified concerns over growing immigration (Feltes 2008, 434). The right-wing Alternative Democratic Reform Party (ADR) surged between 1989 and the late 1990s and questioned the CSV's dominant position on the political right (Schroen 2000, 343, 359).

The CSV has adapted relatively well to these challenges. Unlike in the ÖVP, agricultural interests did not enjoy a guaranteed representation in the CSV leadership, so their influence in the party declined when their importance in society declined (Majerus 2008, 664). Although this surely triggered dissatisfaction and encouraged some party elites and voters from rural constituencies to turn their back on the CSV (Schroen 2000, 359; Majerus 2008, 637–73), it also allowed the party to modernize its image and policies. Young party elites, socialized in a transformed Luxembourgian society and representing the interests and values of a new generation, benefited from the elections taking place at the national congress to increase their influence in the party leadership (Schroen 2000, 347–48; Grosbusch 2008, 390). At the same time, the district branches' guaranteed representation added an aspect of continuity. This helped the CSV to diversify its electoral basis by reaching out to young voters and women, while maintaining its traditional strongholds (Schroen 2000, 351–52; Feltes 2008, 445, 459, 491).

As in all cases discussed in this book, leadership changes usually followed disappointing election results, but changes in the person of the party leader, similar to the CDU, usually reflected a shift in intraparty power (Schroen 2000, 353; Feltes 2008, 403; Schoentgen 2008, 322). The leadership elections since 1979, for instance, have reflected the strength of the party's left wing (Feltes 2008, 402, 455–56). The rise of new and young party elites might have contributed to the continuous increase in party membership, which is particularly noteworthy at a time when political parties have usually experienced a decline in membership (Schroen 2000, 353; Feltes 2008, 419).

Despite the strength of social-Catholic positions in the CSV's recent history, the party's moderate level of factionalism provided liberal-conservative party elites with influence, which helped the CSV to prevent major splits. Admittedly, the CSV lost a number of party elites to the right-wing ADR due to policy disagreements and personal quarrels (Feltes 2008, 431, 438–39; Majerus 2008, 665–66). While the ADR thus benefited to some extent from conflicts in the CSV (Schroen 2000, 358–59), it would be wrong to consider the ADR a split from the CSV (Majerus 2008, 670). In fact, the CSV's internal playing field might have prevented a breakaway of its right wing as it allowed for the Cercle Joseph Bech faction (Feltes 2008, 448–49). This also helps refine the leadership autonomy argument, which provides insights into understanding the substantive level of autonomy the party leadership enjoyed but does not explain why minority elites stayed in the party when the party leadership ignored (positions taken at) the deliberative party bodies (Feltes 2008, 409–11,

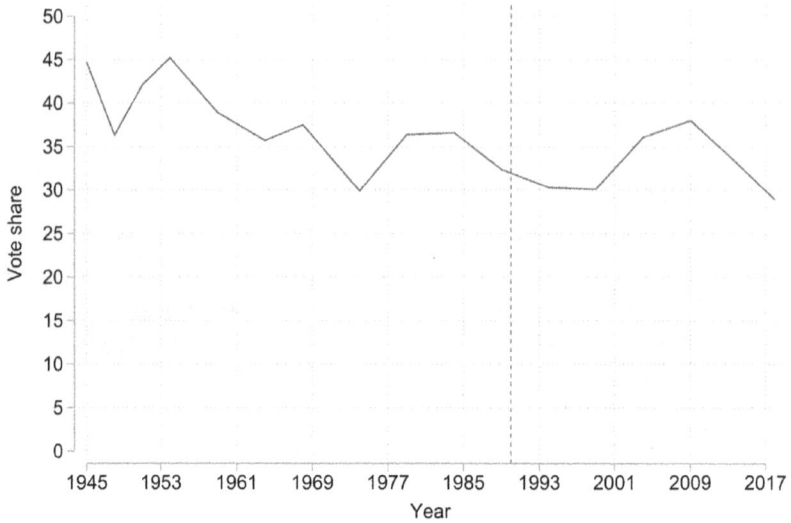

FIGURE 6.3. CSV vote share in Luxembourgian elections in percentage
Source: Armingeon et al. (2022) and Nordsieck (2021).

420–21, 424, 441, 452; Grosbusch 2008, 333, 338–39, 349, 388; Kraemer 2008, 748, 750; Schoentgen 2008, 268, 316). The party's moderate level of faction-alism allowed, unlike in the ÖVP, all intraparty groups to make their voice heard without giving way to the same level of paralyzing factionalism that we observed in Italy's DC.

Hence, similar to Germany's CDU, the CSV's moderate factionalism has supported party adaptation. It allowed, on the one hand, for changes in the party's internal power structure and the rise of new leaders as well as for mi-nority groups to influence the internal decision-making. All this facilitated programmatic reforms. On the other hand, the CSV did not develop exces-sive factionalism as its district branches and parliamentary group have re-mained important intraparty actors (Janssen 2006, 327). The result of this balancing of interests has been a party that "moves . . . between tradition and innovation" and thereby adopted quite successfully to social and political changes (Feltes 2008, 457). All these factors contributed to an electoral trend that has been much more positive than for most Western European Christian democratic parties (fig. 6.3). Although the CSV is no exception to the obser-vation that Christian Democracy has declined across the continent, its losses have been relatively moderate. While it needed to give up power to a So-cial Democratic-Liberal-Green coalition in 2013, the CSV remained Luxem-bourg's strongest party, more than 10 percent ahead of the Social Democrats.

Conclusion

The discussion of the Christian Democrats in Portugal, the Netherlands, and Luxembourg adds to the evidence presented in the three preceding chapters. As in the case of the DC, ÖVP, and CDU, actors had a choice when formulating the initial procedure to select their national party leaders, and their choice proved consequential for their parties' level of factionalism and adaptation in the medium and long run.

The development of the Portuguese CDS supports my findings on the trajectory of Italy's DC. The decision to adopt a centralized leadership selection process at the moment of party formation created an internal playing field that incentivized party elites to form factions. The resulting high level of factionalism provides strong support for my argument because competing approaches highlighting the role of the electoral system, the size of the selectorate to elect the party president, and the extent to which power has been centralized in the hands of the party leadership would have predicted a low level of factionalism. Instead, and in line with this book's framework, factions emerged as part of party elites' strategy to seize control over the party leadership. The importance of factions became entrenched and reinforced over time. It undermined the party's ability to settle on a position in Portugal's party system. While factions' alternation in power allowed leaders to change the party's platform, the high level of factionalism undermined uniting the party behind the new course. The Portuguese Christian Democrats experienced a breakdown of parliamentary unity, the breaking away of factions, and a mediocre electoral development. This underlines the limited explanatory power of the leadership autonomy argument as the high level of leadership autonomy would have predicted the CDS to be a highly rather than weakly adaptable party.

The case of the Dutch CDA has revealed important similarities to the ÖVP's trajectory. Its highly decentralized process to select its national leaders granted ex officio membership in the national executive to a wide range of majority elites. As expected, this created an internal playing field that made the formation of factions an unbeneficial strategy for gaining leadership representation. The resulting low level of factionalism was unexpected from the perspective of alternative explanations as the existence of three predecessor parties, intraparty conflicts, and preferential voting would have predicted high factionalism. The low level of factionalism was reinforced over time. Attempts to "democratize" the party's internal decision-making by giving more influence to party members remained limited. Similar to the ÖVP, the low level of factionalism made it difficult for new groups to rise. This complicated the CDA's efforts to attract new voters and party cadres. Conflicts between majority elites from the CDA's different district, parliamentary, and auxiliary branches often constrained new party leaders in the extent to which they could yield renewal. The Dutch Christian Democrats thus struggled to introduce reforms to respond to pressing ideological and organizational questions, which contributed to a long and steep decline.

Finally, Luxembourg's CSV echoes what chapter 5 outlined for Germany's CDU. Adopting a mixed selection process, the CSV gave space to both ex officio representation of party branches in the national executive and the election of party leaders by a central party assembly. The resulting incentive structure made networks both in and across party branches a valuable resource within the CSV. The party's moderate level of factionalism corresponds to the predictions by my framework but is unexpected from the point of view of competing theories. In particular, Luxembourg's preferential-list PR system would have led to expectations of a much higher level of factionalism than we actually observe, as would have the CSV's long tenure in government and small size of the party president's selectorate. Its moderate degree of factionalism gave minority groups space to make their voice heard without entailing excessive factionalism. Moderate factionalism also facilitated the rise of new leaders, changes in the party's internal power structure, and party reforms. The next chapter explores the book's argument beyond post-1990 Western European Christian Democracy.

7

Party Adaptation beyond Post-1990
Christian Democracy

Neither the attacks . . . of the political enemy, nor the most difficult situations destroy a
political force but the . . . suppression of its necessary and vital internal contradictions.
Men need two feet to walk. And you only have one.
ABBÉ PIERRE (14 MAY 1950)[1]

Most important, because factions can no longer perform as many roles for their members, loyalty to the factions seems to have considerably weakened.
KRAUSS AND PEKKANEN (2011, 138)

The book's argument that parties' initial rules to select their national leaders drive their level of factionalism and adaptation in the medium and long
runs has been evidenced by an in-depth analysis of Italy's DC, Austria's ÖVP,
and Germany's CDU and has further been supported by the development of
the Portuguese, Dutch, and Luxembourgian Christian Democrats. All these
cases have in common that they were challenged by social and political transformations in the early 1990s. This has allowed holding unobserved shock-
related characteristics relatively constant.

If I am right and the initial leadership selection process is momentous
for a party's level of factionalism and adaptation, my argument should also
be supported for cases that have been challenged by different transformations as long as they meet my argument's scope conditions.[2] France's Popular
Republican Movement (MRP) allows for the study of party adaptation before
1990 while keeping constant many party family- and region-related factors.
Founded after World War II, the MRP quickly became France's largest governing party, like the Christian Democrats in Italy, Austria, and Germany.
Unlike those parties, though, the MRP quickly declined. Unable to agree on
its political course amid major political upheaval, the MRP ultimately disintegrated in 1967. Based on the analysis of archival material from the French
National Archives and studies in history and political science, the MRP's
link between a decentralized leadership selection, low level of factionalism,
and weak adaptation displays striking similarities with the trajectory of Austria's ÖVP. This is remarkable given their differences. The ÖVP was a large
party with a large membership and strong societal roots in a federal system,

whereas the MRP was a medium-sized party with a relatively small membership and weak societal roots in a unitary system.

Japan's Liberal Democrats (LDP) extends the assessment of the book's argument to a different part of the world and cultural context while also revealing how parties might escape the long shadow of their level of factionalism. The LDP's struggle to adapt to gradual societal changes and a series of corruption scandals before 1994 echoes many of the findings on Italy's DC regarding the connection between a centralized leadership selection, high factionalism, and low adaptation. In turn, the LDP's post-1994 reform period supports many of the points chapter 5 revealed about Germany's CDU. Following an externally imposed electoral reform, this period suggests how, under the right circumstances, moving toward a mixed leadership selection can moderate factionalism and enhance adaptation. The chapter discusses each of these cases in turn.

Decentralized Leadership Selection, Low Factionalism, Failed Adaptation before 1990: France's MRP

TOWARD A DECENTRALIZED LEADERSHIP SELECTION

Despite emerging in unitary France and following a centralized, top-down formation, the MRP adopted a highly decentralized leadership selection process. The 1901 association law did not predetermine these rules because it did not specify the rules for parties to select their national leadership. Moreover, whereas the French Socialists (SFIO) served as role model in other organizational fields (Bichet 1980, 47), they had a centralized leadership selection process, unlike the MRP.[3] Similarly, while the labels for internal committees and assemblies suggest some continuity with the prewar Popular Democratic Party (PDP), the MRP adopted a more decentralized process to select its national leaders (Bichet 1980, 55; Bazin 1981, 215; Delbreil 1990, 49–60).[4]

The rules to select the MRP leaders were the outcome of politics. Unlike in Italy, Austria, and Germany, the Catholic Church did not notably influence party formation (Warner 2000, 179–83). Leaders of the prewar PDP around Auguste Champetier de Ribes wanted a cartel of Catholic organizations to maintain their advantage as the best-organized and most cohesive group (Bazin 1981, 169; Delbreil 1990, 195–204, 428–29). In contrast, Georges Bidault, one of the figureheads of the Catholic Resistance,[5] wanted to establish a party that would not be organized along the lines of preexisting organizations (Bazin 1981, 169, 174, 181, 200–203; Callot 1978, 95; Dalloz 1993, 17–21, 428; Letamendia 1995, 49, 63). Bidault gained momentum after being elected president of the National Resistance Council in September 1943 as André Colin's group from the Catholic Association of the French Youth (ACJF) started supporting him (Bazin 1981, 171–81, 200–203; Sa'adah 1987, 46–47). Following negotiations over the party's profile, Bidault also gained support for forming the MRP among other Catholic Resistance leaders (e.g., Maurice Schumann) and Catholic trade unionists (e.g., Paul Bacon) (Callot 1978, 95–97; Letamendia 1995, 63; Plaza 2008, 62, 65).

After discussions over the party's organization (Bazin 1981, 225–28), the showdown came at the constitutive party congress on 25 November 1944. Earlier that day, the PDP leadership decided to not join the MRP (Bazin 1981, 228–32; Delbreil 1990, 435). In response, some delegates wanted to postpone constituting the party (Bazin 1981, 233). Bidault and his allies managed to convince the delegates to go ahead by reserving a small number of seats on the MRP's leadership board in case the PDP and other groups joined eventually (Bazin 1981, 234, 256). Another controversy arose over the extent to which a central assembly should elect the party leadership. According to Robert Bichet (1980, 50–54), who was close to Bidault, Bidault and Colin's coalition feared the formation of a united opposition if they adopted a centralized process. Splitting the leadership selection across party branches was seen as "an admirable means of banishing democracy while pretending to apply it" (Bichet 1980, 50). At that stage, the structure of the French state might have played a role. Yet instead of imposing a centralized leadership selection, France's unitary structure might have encouraged subnational delegates to welcome the right to send representatives to the party's national leadership board. While the Bidault-Colin coalition wanted guaranteed leadership seats for MRP members holding cabinet positions, delegates from the French *départements* opposed that and instead wanted to expand their branches' representation.[6] Ultimately, numerous party branches sent their representatives directly to the national executive (table 7.1).[7]

LOW FACTIONALISM

If a party's internal heterogeneity unequivocally explained its level of factionalism (Matuschek 2008, 87–88; Capperucci 2010), we would expect the MRP to become highly factionalized. Its first leadership board included trade unionists, supporters of the social-Catholic Sillon movement, centrists, and actors on the center-right. They often clashed over the party's direction (Irving 1973, 77; Letamendia 1995, 59–63; Plaza 2008, 9–13, 82). While internal elections were held under a two-round majority system rather than a PR system (Letamendia 1995, 236), such a system has not been theorized to preclude

TABLE 7.1. Initial MRP leadership board

Party branch	Seats
Party in government	3 (the three ministers in de Gaulle's provisory government)
Party in parliament	3 (13 after the 1945 election)
Départements branches	39 seats allocated across 21 regional councils
	(1–4 seats depending on regional membership size)
Party council	13 seats
Auxiliary organizations	7x1 seats
TOTAL	65 members
Rae's fractionalization index	0.919

Note: Rae's (1967, 58) fractionalization index allows measuring how centralized the leadership selection process is (ranging from 0 to 1, with higher values indicating higher decentralization).

Source: Status, 1944, Arts. 40, 42–48, and *Tableau des Conseils Régionaux,* AN-681AP /10–1; *Bâtir la France avec le peuple: Les organismes directeurs,* AN-681AP/10–2; "Comité Directeur du MRP," *L'Aube,* 28, 1944, AN-457AP/166.

the formation of factions.[8] When assessing the effects of a two-round major-ity system on the party system, Elgie (2005) suggested that it was conducive to the consolidation of a right- and left-wing bloc. Applying this reasoning to the MRP's intraparty level, we would expect the consolidation of a left- and right-leaning factional coalition.

However, besides a loosely connected left-wing camp around Joseph Dumas and André Denis, we have seen only two short-lived and ultimately unsuccessful attempts to establish factions in the MRP. Jack Lanfranco and Félix Lacambre set up the Study and Action Group for a Larger MRP (Équipe d'études et d'action pour un plus grand MRP) as a response to France's eco-nomic difficulties and failing military endeavor to keep its southeast Asian colonies in the early 1950s.[9] While the Équipe attracted some attention (Plaza 2008, 470–71), it remained isolated to a few departmental branches.[10] Eventu-ally, it started supporting the slightly more influential Democratic Renova-tion (Rénovation Démocratique) faction.[11] Democratic Renovation operated between 1956 and 1961 in reaction to the escalating decolonization crisis, led by young activists of the Seine departmental branch (Plaza 2008, 129, 471). It held meetings, had an address, and published pamphlets.[12] Yet it also failed to generate widespread support (Plaza 2008, 472).[13] Eventually, the MRP leader-ship banned the faction.[14] Threatened by expulsion, Democratic Renovation was in the end nothing more than another name for the student group of the MRP's Seine departmental branch.[15]

The centralization of power argument would expect the highly factionalized DC and not the MRP to be more successful in enforcing the ban on factional activities (cf. Carey 2007). Both parties' statutes included such a ban.[16] In both parties, the national leadership had similar privileges and limitations regarding the selection of parliamentary candidates.[17] In comparison, the DC leadership had even more control over the party's finances. It received membership fees directly from the individual members, whereas the MRP leadership depended on the departmental branches' remittances (Letamendia 1995, 200–202).[18]

The book's argument helps explain the MRP's low level of factionalism. Similar to the ÖVP, the MRP corresponded very closely but not perfectly to the ideal type of a party with a decentralized leadership selection. The national executive delegates representing the party's departmental branches were sent by twenty-one regional councils, each of which brought together delegates from two to eight *départements*. It is possible that some cooperation took place between delegates from different *départements* coming together at the same regional council. The institutional setup to select the national leadership, however, did not incentivize them to expand and develop such contacts into factions, which, as conceptualized in chapter 2, are characterized by organizational pervasiveness. Moreover, while the MRP's organizational branches elected autonomously a vast majority of national executive positions (i.e., 80 percent in 1944–1945), twelve positions were elected by the central party council (Conseil National). This might point to the formation of factions, as it could have helped minority elites to gain representation and majority elites to increase their seat share in the leadership.

Similar to the ÖVP in chapter 4, the few attempts to establish factions outlined here show that, as predicted, minority elites tried to form factions, but their efforts were ill omened given the MRP's decentralized leadership selection. The party council included both majority and minority elites from different party branches, but the seat share of minority elites was likely fairly small, as the party council gathered only around two hundred delegates (compared to about a thousand delegates for the national congress) (Irving 1973, 100).[19] This also goes against Ceron's (2019) selectorate argument, which would have expected the emergence of factions when a smaller assembly elected the party leader. Finally, to pick up any of the twelve executive seats elected by the party council, minority elites would have needed to gain the support of some majority elites. The latter, however, were not incentivized to support factional activities because they enjoyed ex officio membership in the party leadership. Even if supporting a faction had helped them to win all twelve seats, it would not have brought them even close to a majority in the national executive.[20] While majority elites surely talked to one another and tried to make deals to forge a majority in the national executive, there was no need to develop such deals into factions. The latter would also not have directly helped them to strengthen their support within their own party branch, which was their key resource in intraparty politics.

Consequently, competition mainly occurred between party branches and within branches themselves rather than between factions. The MRP's party in public office emerged as the strongest branch. It benefited from the sliding scale in the allocation of national executive seats, which disadvantaged larger departmental branches (Irving 1973, 102). If such a scale had not been used, the party in public office would have faced stronger opposition from the larger departmental branches. Leadership positions, however, would have continued to be primarily chosen within rather than across party branches, and the level of factionalism would have thus remained low. This also refines the suggestion that a group that controlled party formation would be likely to prevent factionalism (see Panebianco 1988, 50–51). Bidault and Colin's group succeeded in translating their dominant role during party formation into a dominant position within the established party (Letamendia 1995, 233–38; Bazin 1981).[21] They managed to do this because the MRP had adopted a leadership selection process that rewarded holding public office and encouraged a fragmented opposition across departmental branches. The adaptation of such rules was the result of politics rather than the sequence of party formation.

REINFORCING LOW FACTIONALISM

Bidault, Teitgen, Schumann, and other majority elites built on their popularity as former Resistance partisans, personal networks, and ideological appeals to strengthen their control over the MRP's parliamentary group (Irving 1973, 104–5; Callot 1978, 238; 1986, 360; Letamendia 1995, 235–38).[22] Given the absence of state funding for political parties, those of them holding a ministerial portfolio also benefited from access to their ministries' funds to support candidates' campaigns and pay party officials (Callot 1978, 248; Letamendia 1995, 220–22). This entailed a remarkable level of parliamentary unity compared to the other parties during the Fourth Republic (Macrae 1963, 196, 199; Irving 1973, 104–5). The dominance of the party in public office was confirmed at the MRP's national congress and council meetings, which were usually chaired by the party's ministers and MPs (Irving 1973, 102). Over the years, delegates to the meetings could see that developing a strong presence in the MRP's parliamentary group was the way to intraparty power.

The leaders of the MRP's *département* branches also invested in their networks. They developed their organization, organized grassroots activities, lobbied national leaders to implement their branch's preferences, and built an ideological identity (Callot 1978, 286–87; Plaza 2008, 84). The Seine branch, in particular, gained the reputation of being the MRP's "left-wing conscience" (see, e.g., Callot 1978, 286–87). This underlined their status, besides the party in public office, as the MRP's main organizational unit of internal politics. Party branches' relative seat shares in the national executive, as outlined in chapter 2, mattered. Many regional councils, like that of Languedoc, sent only one delegate. In contrast to parties with a mixed leadership selection process, factional activities, as already explained, were unlikely to increase their seat share. Some majority elites from smaller departmental branches thus focused on striking deals with majority elites from other branches. For example, the leaders of the party in public office were often popular in rural *départements* and, consequently, supported by their majority elites (Callot 1978, 116). Others simply did not attend the national meetings (Callot 1978, 117–18). Their branches often merely existed on paper (Irving 1973, 91–98). Consequently, there was substantial variation in terms of size, activity, and organization across departmental branches.[23]

Finally, the leaders of auxiliary organizations played a vital role in the MRP's campaigns and provided the party leadership with policy briefs (Irving 1973, 99). Their leaders, like Paul Bacon from the workers' organization, often became influential figures in the MRP's leadership.

By enlarging the set of party elites who could be delegated to the national executive, more actors became rewarded for building a strong network in their own party branch, which reinforced a low level of factionalism. At the second national congress, the party's founding elites continued to emphasize how important the MRP's eighty-seven departmental branches were for becoming a real mass party.[24] This rhetoric risked losing credibility given the party in public office's overrepresentation in the national executive. Since centralizing the leadership selection would have jeopardized their dominant position, they agreed that the regional councils should elect two-thirds of the national executive members.[25] The allocation of executive seats across regional councils provided the large Parisian (i.e., Seine, Seine-et-Oise, and Seine-et-Marne) and northern *départements'* branches (i.e., Nord, Pas-de-Calais) with almost as many executive seats as the party in public office.[26] Yet the latter managed to introduce a clause that allowed it to send additional MPs to the national executive, depending on the MRP's share of legislative seats, thereby increasing its chances of remaining the largest group in the national executive.[27] In contrast, the number of executive seats elected by the party council dropped from 20 percent to around 12 percent. Although the national congress gained the function of approving the final list of national executive members, this was a matter of formality, as no procedure existed in case the national congress did not approve the suggested list.[28] Finally, the MRP's auxiliary branches, which the national executive had set up at the national level, would henceforth also be organized at the departmental level.[29] This was meant to integrate different groups into the party while discouraging the emergence of factions already at the departmental level.

Statutory modifications in 1947 gave the impression of making the MRP's leadership selection more centralized. The national congress henceforth elected the positions of national party leader and party secretary. The leaders of the party in public office had an interest in this proposal because a Gaullist minority within the MRP's group in the French Assembly questioned its decision to continue the coalition with the Socialists and Communists (Woloch 2007, 101–2). Knowing that many minority elites on the ground were left leaning, the central election of the party leader and party secretary allowed them to gain legitimacy. The congress's delegates reelected Schumann and Colin with a landslide, thereby confirming the left-wing coalition.[30] Moreover, the party council (renamed Comité National) elected the national executive (renamed Commission Exécutive), which subsequently elected most of the executive committee (now called Bureau).[31]

However, the changes were countered by modifications that ensured that the incentives to build a strong network within one's party branch rather than across branches prevailed. Quotas were introduced that formalized the distinction between delegates representing the party in public office and those representing the departmental branches at the national congress, party council, national executive, and executive committee.[32] Departmental delegates at the party council were not allowed to be members of parliament, whereas one-third of the party council seats were granted to delegates from the MRP's parliamentary group. The national executive had to include eighteen departmental representatives, who were not members of parliament, and fourteen members of parliament.[33] At the same time, the abolition of the regional councils deprived departmental party elites of a platform to at least partially coordinate their activities, thus strengthening the party in public office over a fragmented extraparliamentary party. The leaders of the party in public office also benefited from the clause that departmental delegates who were unable to attend party council meetings could be replaced only by members of their *département*, who, however, were allowed to be members of parliament.[34] As the party council met in Paris, many delegates from small and rural branches transferred their mandate to the only representative of their branch living in

Paris, their respective MPs.[35] Hence, as long as the party in public office remained united, it was well protected against pressure from the departmental branches.

The leaders of the MRP's departmental branches tried to counter. In 1950, they succeeded in reducing the quota for departmental branches to gain an additional council seat.[36] In 1952, the Seine branch tried to reduce the influence of the party in public office by proposing to make the position of the party secretary incompatible with a governmental position.[37] While this proposal failed to gain the necessary two-thirds majority at the national congress, it illustrates that even the MRP's internal opposition had accepted that competition in the MRP was structured along the lines of the party's organizational branches.

The reinforcing process of institutional development made the MRP's low level of factionalism persist even against the backdrop of the establishment of the Fifth Republic in October 1958. It replaced the old parliamentary system with a semipresidential regime and the use of PR for parliamentary elections with a two-round majority system without, however, affecting the MRP's level of factionalism (cf. Cox, Rosenbluth, and Thies 1999; Sartori 1976). While the party congress met in January 1959 to respond to the new political reality, its organizational measures continued on the well-known paths.[38] The Democratic Renovation faction's attempt to take hold within the party by giving more power to the national congress in the selection of the party leadership failed in early 1958 (Plaza 2008, 472).[39] The use of quotas specifying the composition of the national executive and executive committee also remained in place.[40] To improve the party's linkages with selected social groups, the auxiliary organizations gained the right in 1962 to name twelve and six members to be co-opted to the party council and national executive, respectively.[41] The move reinforced that access to the party leadership worked via generating support in the MRP's organizational branches, emphasizing that forming factions was an unbeneficial strategy.

LOW FACTIONALISM UNDERMINING PARTY ADAPTATION

The MRP's low level of factionalism rather than the leadership autonomy argument explains the party's serious problems when trying to adapt to the political upheavals in postwar France. With the Communists' exit from the government in 1947 and the rise of the Gaullist party, parliamentary democracy faced antisystem opposition from both the left and the right. It condemned the MRP to govern for most of the Fourth Republic, challenging it to adjust its platform in response to changing coalition formats, popular unrest, and an escalating (de)colonization crisis. The latter culminated in an attempted coup by French anti-independence deputies and officers in Algeria in May 1958, bringing France to the verge of a civil war and leading to the political comeback of Charles de Gaulle. De Gaulle accepted power under the condition of profound institutional changes, and the MRP had to adjust its policies and strategies to find its place in the new environment.

Although such an environment would have been challenging for any party, the MRP's weak internal accountability mechanisms would lead to expectations that it was relatively well equipped to adapt. Even though the statute provided its federation with notable influence over selecting candidates and collecting membership dues (Irving 1973, 97–99; Callot 1978, 110), power was de facto centralized in the party leadership in Paris. The MRP tried but never succeeded to build an active mass membership and lasting strong ties with civil society groups (Irving 1973, 96–98; Callot 1978, 104–5; Letamendia 1995, 193–213). While the statutes limited the party leader's tenure to three reelections, a small group of elites usually decided informally who would succeed as leader.[42] The term limit could be ignored if in the leaders' interest.[43] To say that party adaptation was doomed from the start given Christian Democracy's historical weakness in France is misguided (cf. Vinen 1995, 164). The deep entrenchment of the religious cleavage and Catholic civil society organizations during the Third Republic revealed that there was a social basis for Christian democracy (Irving 1973, 1–17; Kalyvas 1996, 9, 14, 114). Its absence as a strong political party before 1945 resulted, as Kalyvas (1996, 115–18) has outlined, from the strategic alliance between the Catholic Church and conservative elites (see also Rémond 1969, 264–66, 316). This alliance, however, had been discredited by 1944–1945 for its role in the breakdown of democracy (Rémond 1969, 318–21; Rioux 1987, 45–48). The blame for the latter was also attributed to the centrist Radical Party, which further improved the political prospects of leaders from anti-Vichy Catholic organizations like Colin and Bidault (Callot 1978, 103; Sa'adah 1987, 41). The MRP successfully filled this political space in the first postwar elections (table 7.2).

Instead, the MRP's low level of factionalism thwarted adaptive reforms and, in fact, contributed to many of the developments that challenged the party to adapt in the first place, as illustrated by the MRP's difficult relationship with Gaullism. The Christian Democrats initially benefited from their connection with de Gaulle. The leader of the exile government during the Vichy years and head of the provisory government was highly popular in postwar France. His announcement in March 1945 not to form his own party made his endorsement a valuable political good (Bazin 1981, 502). The MRP

TABLE 7.2. MRP election results during the Fourth Republic

Election	Result in percentage	Party ranking (percentage change)
Constituent Assembly, 1945	24.91	2nd
Constituent Assembly, 1946	28.22	1st (+3.31)
Parliament, 1946	25.96	2nd (−2.26)
Parliament, 1951	12.49	5th (−13.47)
Parliament, 1956	11.14	6th (−1.35)

Source: Laurent de Boissieu, France Politique, https://www.france-politique.fr/.

initially gained this asset. In the provisory government, they loyally endorsed positions close to those of de Gaulle and, in addition, gained the reputation of being the bulwark against the rising Communist Party (Bazin 1981, 534–38; Rioux 1987, 48–51, 56–59, 100–101). The link to de Gaulle persisted even though the MRP remained part of the provisory government after de Gaulle's resignation in January 1946 (Letamendia 1995, 81).[44] However, the MRP publicly broke with de Gaulle by accepting the only slightly modified second constitutional draft (Rioux 1987, 100–9).[45] De Gaulle came out strongly against the draft and the MRP (Bazin 1981, 534–35; Rioux 1987, 104–6; Letamendia 1995, 82–83; Woloch 2007, 103). Many political observers expected the MRP to lose significantly in the November 1946 election because Gaullist voters had the option to support René Capitant's Union Gaulliste and the numerous slates of Conservative and Radical candidates that had added the adjective *Gaullist* (Bazin 1981, 512, 532–33; Rioux 1987, 106–10; Letamendia 1995, 83–84). Yet the MRP roughly maintained its previous performance.

While the MRP initially included well-known Gaullists, its low level of factionalism prevented the integration of those right-wing elites. While de Gaulle's brother-in-law, Jacques Vendroux, had left the MRP before the election (Letamendia 1995, 83), the Christian Democrats, most notably, still counted among its ranks Edmond Michelet, minister of defense, and Louis Terrenoire, editor of the Catholic newspaper *L'Aube* (Michelet 1971, 150, 157–60). They and other right-wing party elites, however, opposed the executive committee's narrow decision to continue the tripartite coalition with the Socialists and Communists in January 1947 (Michelet 1971, 180; Woloch 2007, 101–2). While both Michelet and Terrenoire were part of the MRP's leadership at that time, they could not expect to reverse this decision in the near future. Michelet was no longer in charge of the ministry of defense and would thus not remain ex officio member of the national executive beyond the 1947 party congress. Terrenoire had been elected for one of the thirteen seats filled by the party council.[46] Yet even if they had managed to secure all thirteen seats elected by the party council for themselves and others sharing their views, they would have still been far from a majority in the national executive. Moreover, Michelet and Terrenoire were supported by only a minority of the MRP's branch in public office, which sent the largest group to the national executive (i.e., sixteen delegates in January 1947). While the party in public office delegated some few Gaullist sympathizers to the leadership board (i.e., Paul Coste-Floret, Marie Madeleine Dienesch), their influence was unlikely to improve in the near future.[47] Majority elites of the party in public office (i.e., Bidault, Teitgen, Lecourt) categorically refused to endorse a center-right strategy (Michelet 1971, 182–83), and did not renominate Dienesch as member of the national executive.[48]

Right-wing party elites' isolated situation drove them out of the MRP, and the party lost large parts of its internal right before its poor showing in the local elections in October 1947. Shortly after the MRP's congress in March 1947, de Gaulle had announced the formation of his own party (Rally of the French People, RPF) (Callot 1978, 263; Rioux 1987, 112–24). Michelet, Terrenoire, and other Gaullist MPs responded by creating, together with defectors from other parties, a Gaullist parliamentary group and finally left the MRP for the RPF (Letamendia 1995, 99; Michelet 1971, 182–91). While I do not claim that the defection of its Gaullist minority was the only reason the MRP won just 10 percent of the votes compared to the RPF's 38 percent, attracting Michelet and other right-wing elites certainly helped the RPF become the dominant force on the political right. The same can be said for its electoral downfall in the 1948 Senate elections and the 1951 parliamentary election (Vaussard 1956, 125; Vinen 1995, 159). The rise of parties on the political right of the MRP was thus at least partially endogenous to the MRP's failure to integrate its Gaullist minority.

The MRP similarly failed to integrate left-wing minority elites. They demanded that the MRP would withdraw from the government after the Communists had left the coalition in May 1947 (Callot 1978, 273; Sa'adah 1987, 42–43). Yet their weak position in the party council made their proposal fail (Callot 1978, 273). Many left-wing minority elites criticized their de facto exclusion from decision-making.[49] While some of them resigned, other left-leaning MPs tried to organize an opposition within the MRP for the 1950 party congress (Sa'adah 1987, 54; Letamendia 1995, 22, 242). Yet in contrast to the DC, where the national congress elected a large number of high-level party positions, which allowed even smaller factions to receive at least some seats, the MRP national congress elected only the party leader and the party secretary. Only large networks had a chance at these elections. Yet because almost all leadership positions were selected within rather than across party branches, factions were not a beneficial strategy for a sufficiently large share of party elites. The left's candidate consequently lost against Colin when running for party secretary in 1950.[50] The episode illustrates that attempts to build factions emerged around the election of the very few leadership positions centrally selected at the party congress. The MRP's low level of factionalism is therefore not uniquely explained by the Fourth Republic's closed-list PR system, which has been suggested to discourage factionalism (Ceron 2019, 69).[51]

When a trade unionist was shot by a policeman during a demonstration in April 1950, Abbé Pierre Groués, part of the left-wing minority in the parliamentary group rejecting the MRP's anti-strikes stance, left the party and condemned the leadership's inability to integrate the different opinions within the party: "Neither the attacks . . . of the political enemy, nor the most difficult situations destroy a political force but the . . . suppression of its necessary and vital internal contradictions. Men need two feet to walk. And you only have one."[52] Other left-wing MPs followed, leaving the MRP over the leadership's support for NATO and its refusal to join Pierre Mendès France's center-left coalition in 1954 (Vaussard 1956, 126; Callot 1978, 292–93; Sa'adah 1987, 54–56; Letamendia 1995, 103–4; Plaza 2008, 99).

Other minority elites saw no alternative to change the MRP's strategy than to leave the party, join a new one, and then seek to merge with the MRP.[53] The MRP's auxiliary organizations did not provide a promising avenue for minority elites. Similar to the ÖVP, the organizations formally represented the interests of the youth, women, and different occupational groups. The party leadership had set up the groups, maintained a tight control over them, and often had close personal ties to their leaders (Plaza 2008, 76, 87–88).[54] Except for the workers and agricultural team, they remained weak and static (Letamendia 1995, 202–7).[55] The auxiliary organizations lacked factions' flexibility and therefore were ill suited to integrate social and political groups in response to changing conflict lines within the party or society.

With minority elites marginalized or driven out of the party, party leaders emerged out of the same closed circle of majority elites from the party in public office (Callot 1978, 238; Letamendia 1995, 238, 241, 247–50). Stuck with the same circle of leaders, the MRP struggled to respond when the outbreak of the Algerian War of Independence in November 1954 intensified divisions within that circle. On the political right, Bidault refused to abandon Algeria and cooperate with the Socialists, whereas Menthon promoted left-wing and anticolonial positions.[56] Pierre Pflimlin took a moderate stance.[57] Pflimlin ultimately defeated Menthon in the MRP's only seriously contested party leader election in 1956 (Callot 1986, 286, 304–5; Letamendia 1995, 91).[58] His

TABLE 7.3. Difference between first-round vote and seat share, 1958 and 1962

		Communists	Socialists	Radicals[a]	MRP	CNIP and Moderates	Gaullists
1958	Vote share	18.9	15.5	9.2	11.1	22.1[b]	20.6
	Seat share	1.8	8.0	7.1	10.2	21.6	39.5
	Seats − votes	−17.1	−7.5	−2.1	−0.9	−0.5	18.9
1962	Vote share	21.9	12.4	7.4	7.9	11.5	31.6[c]
	Seat share	8.0	12.9	7.6	7.0[d]	6.8	45.4
	Seats − votes	−13.9	0.5	0.2	−0.9	−4.7	13.8

[a] Radicals including Socialist and Centrist Radicals

[b] Caramani reports 20.5%, which would turn the seats − votes share mildly positive

[c] Caramani reports 33.7%

[d] Based on Callot's reported number of seats. Höhne's results would give a seat share of 10.7%, but his reported number of seats almost certainly includes the independent republicans who joined the MRP's parliamentary group. Callot's reported first-round result of 8.9% for the MRP is most likely a typo.
Source: Höhne (2006, 184–85); Caramani (2000, 346, 347); Callot (1978, 407).

moderate attitude toward Algerian independence and his decision to join de Gaulle's government in 1958 attracted intense internal opposition and re-sulted in Georges Bidault, who hated de Gaulle, leaving the MRP to set up his own party (Callot 1978, 307–12; 1986, 287, 289; Letamendia 1995, 117, 122–28, 131, 136).

While the translation of first-round votes into seats indicated that the 1958 electoral reform was not biased against the MRP (table 7.3), gridlock among majority elites kept the party from agreeing on a strategy under the new envi-ronment. The 1963 party congress decided to seek an alliance with other par-ties (Callot 1978, 408), but Gaston Defferre's (Socialist) surprising proposal to form a socialist-centrist party revealed that the MRP leaders had very dif-ferent ideas about the partners for such an alliance. Majority elites from the MRP's branches in Seine and the Parisian region demanded a merger with the Socialists.[59] By contrast, the party in public office was divided into those advocating a cooperation with de Gaulle (e.g., Maurice Schumann), a conser-vative but non-Gaullist party (e.g., Pflimlin), and a centrist party around Jean Lecanuet (senator and MRP leader since 1963; Irving 1973, 244–50).[60]

Faced with internal gridlock, Lecanuet, who had secured the MRP's nom-ination for the 1965 presidential elections, ultimately resigned as party leader to run as a cross-party centrist candidate (Callot 1978, 409; Letamendia 1995, 146). He finished third and forced de Gaulle in a second ballot against Fran-çois Mitterand. The surprisingly strong performance seemed to give momen-tum to a new center party, and Lecanuet left the MRP and formed the Demo-cratic Center in January 1966 (Letamendia 1995, 146). Many MRP members followed him, while the Gaullists around Schumann joined de Gaulle's new party, and other party elites, like Paul Bacon, joined left-wing parties (Mayeur 1980, 172). The MRP itself ceased to exist in 1967 (Callot 1986, 368; Letamendia 1995, 146).

In conclusion, Christian Democracy had an actual chance in postwar France, but the MRP's decentralized leadership selection and resulting low level of factionalism proved highly problematic. It undermined the integration of the diverse interests coming together in the MRP, contributed to the rise of rival parties, and thwarted any renewal of an increasingly divided leadership. The result was internal gridlock in the face of profound social and political changes. France's MRP thus reveals notable similarities to the trajectory of Austria's ÖVP despite competing under very different political and institutional conditions. A similar statement can be made about Italy's DC and Japan's Liberal Democrats before 1994, which is the case to which I now turn.

Centralized Leadership Selection, High Factionalism, Weak Adaptation: Japan's Pre-1994 LDP

THE ORIGINS AND CONSEQUENCES OF A CENTRALIZED LEADERSHIP SELECTION

Japan's Liberal Democratic Party (LDP) moves the book's discussion beyond European Christian Democracy. Encouraged by a newly united Socialist Party, pressure from big business, and strategic considerations, the LDP emerged in November 1955 after almost two years of complex negotiations as the merger of Japan's conservative Liberal Party and Democratic Party (Krauss and Pekkanen 2011, 107; Thayer 1969, 11–12). Factions (*habatsu*) emerged shortly after the merger. They, rather than the party's branches in Japan's prefectures or auxiliary organizations for the youth, women, and occupational groups, quickly became the LDP's key internal players. Their meetings often predetermined the personnel and political decisions taken at formal party and parliamentary sessions (Thayer 1969, 14), and the LDP gained a reputation in the comparative politics literature as one of the seminal highly factionalized parties (e.g., Bettcher 2005; Boucek 2012).

Japan's cultural and institutional characteristics compared to the book's European cases do not provide a satisfactory answer to why the LDP developed such a high level of factionalism. A historically popular argument goes that Japan's history of hierarchically organized small groups would be conducive to factionalism (e.g., Baerwald 1986). However, scholars have rejected such a deterministic perspective for failing to account for the differences in factionalism across Japanese political parties and the organizational changes in the LDP factions' development outlined below (Kohno 1992, 377; Krauss and Pekkanen 2011, 103–4; Köllner 2004). Seeing the LDP's high level of factionalism as a mere legacy of previous parties does not provide a convincing explanation either. Divisions between supporters and opponents of party leaders characterized the very early LDP as well as previous conservative parties. Politicians' support groups often had some organizational pervasiveness because leaders held regular meetings with their supporters independent of party gatherings, intervened in the distribution of party and public posts, and rewarded their followers financially (Thayer 1969, 18–20). However, being mostly fluid, loose, and mostly informal, the groups were a far cry from the LDP's highly organized factional machines (Sveinsdóttir 2004, chaps. 2 and 3, 144–47; Krauss and Pekkanen 2011, 106, 110). Moreover, while the initial conflicts within the LDP unfolded along previous partisan lines, politicians soon started recruiting allies and followers across the old parties (Sveinsdóttir 2004, 144; Krauss and Pekkanen 2011, 110–11). Japan's single nontransferable vote system (SNTV), though important in reinforcing the LDP's high level of factionalism, does not account for these differences. Japan had already used the electoral system, which allowed candidates from the same party to compete with one another, between 1918 and 1925 and again since 1947. It thus cannot explain why the factions that started emerging in the LDP after 1956 differed so markedly from previous parties' internal groups (Krauss and Pekkanen 2011, 104–6).

Thayer (1969, 21) and Krauss and Pekkanen (2011, 108) have rightly highlighted that an institutional innovation in terms of how the LDP selected its top leadership resolves this puzzle. Earlier conservative parties had usually selected their party leader through informal consultations among senior party elites. Yet one of the conditions of the Liberal-Democratic merger was that an election would henceforth decide the LDP presidency (Thayer 1969, 21). The rules stipulated that the party congress would elect the party president. In this election, all LDP members in the Lower and Upper House, as well as a comparatively small number of prefectural delegates, formed the selectorate. Among the about five hundred selectors, Lower House members represented an overwhelming majority. If no candidate achieved a majority of the valid votes, a runoff election between the two leading candidates was required (Thayer 1969, 152, 159–60, 165). While the LDP compromised on a leadership collective composed of two Liberals and two Democrats at its constituting congress, the rules incentivized politicians who wanted to become LDP president to build support among this selectorate, which resulted in the formation of factions. Many analysts consider the 1956 party presidency election as the starting point for the LDP's high level of factionalism. The candidates recruited followers across the old party lines, and a deal between two former rivals helped defeat the initial front-runner Nobusuke Kishi in the runoff (e.g., Thayer 1969, 167; Krauss and Pekkanen 2011, 107–8). Thayer (1969, 168–74) has provided rich interview quotes from LDP politicians in support of this view, and Krauss and Pekkanen (2011, 108) have cited a 1963 survey that asked the leaders of the seven most important factions why factions were created. Four of them named the party presidency election.[61]

How does the role of the party president election reconcile with the book's argument about the selection of a party's leadership board? Thayer (1969, 21) and Krauss and Pekkanen (2011, 108) have reasoned that the party president election was so important for the emergence of high factionalism because it required candidates to win support among LDP members of parliament. This support was valuable to assume not only the party presidency but also the prime ministership given the LDP's dominant position in parliament. Yet in the first decades of all the book's main cases, a central party assembly elected the party leader, and this election basically decided who would lead the government given the initial dominance of Italy's, Austria's, and Germany's Christian Democrats. However, only Italy's DC experienced a high level of factionalism. Focusing on Ceron's (2019) suggestion that party leadership races with a small number of voters would facilitate faction building compared to larger selectorates does not resolve the puzzle. For the first twenty years of its history, the CDU had a similar and generally smaller selectorate (between three hundred and five hundred delegates) that elected its leader than the LDP without even remotely developing a similarly high level of factionalism (Thayer 1969, 159).[62] A similar statement applies to France's MRP and Italy's DC. In both parties, the smaller party council rather than the large party congress initially elected the party leader. And yet both parties dramatically differed in their level of factionalism.

Focusing on the particular sequence of leadership selection in the LDP helps clarify things and is in line with the logic of the argument outlined in chapter 2. The election of the LDP president was so momentous for the party's level of factionalism because the party president initially de facto filled a majority of the remaining top leadership positions.[63] The selection process started with the election of the party president who then appointed the party secretary and the chairperson of the LDP's leadership board (the Executive Council). The party secretary and chairperson then got together to select the eight Executive Council members that the LDP's statute entitled the party president to fill. They then chose, in consultation with the prefectural federations, fifteen additional members, even though the LDP statute reserved this right to the LDP's parliamentary group in the Lower House. The party president thus de facto controlled who would assume twenty-three of the thirty seats in the Executive Council, having little influence over only the seven seats filled by the LDP group in the Upper House (Thayer 1969, 254–57, 272).

Building factions was thus, as expected, a valuable strategy to assume party leadership positions in a party with a de facto centralized leadership selection. They became the "final arbiter" for leadership elections, with every vote being "committed" to a faction (Thayer 1969, 162). They established headquarters, held regular meetings, and even published membership lists (Thayer 1969, 15, 13–14). Their members came from across electoral districts and predominantly served as LDP members in the Lower and Upper House, although prefectural politicians also often joined a faction (Thayer 1969, 16, 47, 160). The effective number of factions increased from 5.2 in 1958 to 7.3 in 1974, and by 1986, only 5 percent and less than 2 percent of the LDP members in the Lower House and Upper House respectively were not members of a faction (Boucek 2012, 186, 189, 192).

REINFORCING HIGH FACTIONALISM

Similar to factions in Italy's DC, the LDP factions, once established, benefited from Japan's preferential voting system to reinforce their influence. As in Italy, copartisans directly competed for votes (Reed and Thies 2003, 155–56). Conservative candidates had historically organized their campaigns through their own formal membership organizations and overlapping sets of networks, called *koenkai* (Krauss and Pekkanen 2011, 30, 37, 46–47). These district-level camps were not formally part of the LDP. In fact, they predated the LDP and were a direct result of the incentive structure created by Japan's SNTV system (Krauss and Pekkanen 2011, 47). While the *koenkai* were essential to candidates' campaign efforts, maintaining them was expensive (Krauss and Pekkanen 2011, 41). Factions offered to provide funding for candidates' *koenkai* (with extra funding in election years), send well-known national politicians to help campaign, and support candidates in securing the LDP's nomination. They also connected candidates with businesses and, starting with Kakuei Tanaka's faction, provided policy expertise to support candidates in addressing district-specific problems (Krauss and Pekkanen 2011, 102, 115; Thayer 1969, 30, 37). In exchange, candidates pledged their loyalty to the faction. In this way, factions expanded from the national to the district level and counteracted the LDP leadership's attempts to establish local party branches since the factions had assumed the role these branches were intended to play.

Their establishment consequently failed (Krauss and Pekkanen 2011, 53–54, 57, also 115; Thayer 1969, 84–85).

Factions paid less and less attention to ideology because constraining their membership to those with a common ideological stance would have only limited the pool of potential members and thus risked disadvantaging a faction compared to its rivals (Krauss and Pekkanen 2011, 109; Sveinsdóttir 2004, 167; Thayer 1969, 47). Concentrating on strengthening the ties with their supporters through clientelism, factions benefited from the LDP's dominant position. They regularly met with members of the business community to learn about their interests and, in exchange, received financial backing. They established internal mechanisms to raise and process funds and increasingly involved companies in electoral politics (Bettcher 2005, 346–47; Krauss and Pekkanen 2011, 117–18; Reed 2011, 18; Thayer 1969, 66, 73–74).

While not being the cause of LDP factions, decentralizing power in the party certainly helped factional leaders strengthen the value of their networks (Köllner 2004, 93). The LDP president gradually lost the ability to shape policies, allocate posts, and nominate candidates as rival factions pushed for an unwritten code of practice and formal changes to the LDP's organization that expanded their influence (Krauss and Pekkanen 2011, 209–11). Initially, LDP presidents generously rewarded their supporters with cabinet and party posts, which triggered intense rebellions from the factions not allied with the party president and resulted in the failure of several important legislative proposals and a series of short-lived cabinets in the 1960s and early 1970s (Bouissou 2001, 590–91). When increasing factional fragmentation and the LDP's shrinking parliamentary majority intensified concerns that factional infightings might kick the LDP out of government, factional leaders eventually agreed on the proportional allocation of posts as a key norm (Krauss and Pekkanen 2011, 113). The top party positions (e.g., party president, party secretary, chairperson of the Executive Council) all went to different factions, and cabinet and other posts were allocated in proportion to factions' strength (Bettcher 2005, 347; Kohno 1992, 374). Though informal, the rule was highly consequential. When Tanaka violated it in 1972, rival factions forced him to reshuffle his cabinet to restore interfactional balance (Kohno 1992, 374).

To allocate positions within factions, a strict seniority principle developed over time. While so-called leap-frog promotions, whereby members of parliament became cabinet ministers after only a few terms, were relatively frequent in the LDP's early days, they had basically ceased to exist by the early 1980s (Kohno 1992, 378–79). Instead, factions allocated public offices and internal posts on the basis of their members' number of reelections (Kohno

1992, 373–74). Similar to the DC, LDP leaders tried to mediate factional conflicts by separating the competition for posts from policy discussions. The latter were delegated to the party's policy affairs research councils (PARC), further reducing the role of the party president in setting the LDP's course. The PARC brought together representatives from all factions and formulated the party's legislative agenda (Krauss and Pekkanen 2011, 3, 165–86). They helped ease the LDP's struggle to mediate between different factional interests in parliament and added PARC positions to the set of positions that factional leaders used to reward loyal supporters (Krauss and Pekkanen 2011, 182). The PARC mirrored Japan's parliamentary committee system, which helped reinforce their value for the LDP factions by helping connect their members with the bureaucracy (Krauss and Pekkanen 2011, 184). Serving on one of the main PARCs became connected to factions' promotion scheme and encouraged the development of internal policy experts (*zoku giin*), whose ties to interest groups and the bureaucracy helped strengthen factions' grasp on policy making and pork barreling (Krauss and Pekkanen 2011, 184–86; Kohno 1992, 373).

Factional leaders' efforts to reinforce their faction's position in the party also guided the development of the LDP's formal organization. In 1962, the influence of the prefectural federations, where factional ties were weaker albeit not absent, in the LDP president election decreased as the number of votes for each federation was reduced from two to one (Krauss and Pekkanen 2011, 159). Following the Lockheed scandal, factional leaders changed the rules for the 1978 party president election by introducing a primary across all party members to select the two front-runners between whom the LDP parliamentarians could then subsequently choose. While giving more power to the grass roots was aimed to improve the LDP's poor reputation for choosing the country's prime minister through backroom deals between factions, factional leaders prevented any real loss in influence by strengthening their relationship with candidates' *koenkai* and local businesses to improve their chances in the membership primary (Krauss and Pekkanen 2011, 58–59, 116).

Reformers in and outside the LDP made several proposals to transform the way the LDP chose its president to reduce factions' influence (Thayer 1969, 175–78), but the proposals had no chance of being realized. While several LDP presidents, once in office, attempted to eliminate (rival) factions and centralize power, their efforts failed (Krauss and Pekkanen 2011, 124). After another unsuccessful attempt to establish local party branches in the early 1960s, LDP leaders abandoned this plan and accepted the *koenkai* (and by extension, factions) in place of local party branches (Krauss and Pekkanen 2011, 58). A proposal by almost a hundred parliamentarians to reduce the number of Executive Council seats to facilitate decision-making failed because factional leaders refused to accept a shrinking of the pie they could use to reward supporters (Thayer 1969, 265–66). Instead, the party president lost even the prerogative to name the party secretary as the principle of allocating the party's top positions across the main factions institutionalized (Krauss and Pekkanen 2011, 212–13).

HIGH FACTIONALISM UNDERMINING
PARTY ADAPTATION

The LDP helps add conceptual nuance to the leadership autonomy argument. The LDP president certainly lost much of the role's power in the party. The most important functions and decisions with regard to allocating posts, selecting candidates, and campaigning had been delegated to actors other than the party president (Krauss and Pekkanen 2011, 15; Reed 2011, 17). Although the LDP presidents (and thus prime ministers) formally made the final decision over the composition of their cabinet, they had to follow factions' nominations. Decisions over policies did not originate in the cabinet but were the result of negotiations between factions in the PARC and the bureaucracy (Krauss and Pekkanen 2011, 15). However, with its decentralized candidate selection, district-targeted pork barreling, and candidates' *koenkai*, the LDP's local units enjoyed quite notable autonomy, which, following Levitsky (2003, 21), should have facilitated experimenting with new strategies and thus party adaptation (see also Wills-Otero 2016). Moreover, while many rules within the LDP—for instance, on seniority and factional proportionality—were primarily informal codes of conduct and norms, such informal institutions became highly impactful and constrained decision-making.[64] The development of these rules within the LDP was the result of the process suggested in chapter 2. It challenges the leadership autonomy argument to specify why informal organizations were conducive to leadership autonomy and party adaptation in some cases, as in Levitsky's (2003) seminal study of Argentina's Peronists, but not in others, like the LDP.

The book's argument provides a clearer picture as to why the LDP struggled to adapt. The party's increasing fractionalization into competing factions significantly undermined party adaptation already during its long tenure in government. Japan's SNTV with its small district magnitude (i.e., usually $M = 4$) created greater incentives for small factions to merge compared to Italy's open-list PR system, with its larger districts and around three preference votes for each voter (Kohno 1992, 383–84). Still, Boucek's (2012, 186–87), Kohno's (1992, 372–73), and Thayer's (1969, 16–17) studies point to a growing share of medium-sized factions that together controlled almost all the LDP's

Lower House seats. As a result, coalitions between factions were necessary to elect the party president. By virtue of their size, factions became increasingly similar in their bargaining power in internal negotiations, and smaller factions also often broke away from larger factions in the run-up to presidential elections and offered themselves as junior coalition partners (Boucek 2012, 187; Kohno 1992, 371n4). Consequently, while, like the DC, the LDP changed its leader often, the leader virtually always originated from the set of factional elites (Cox, Rosenbluth, and Thies 1999, 48–49; Kohno 1992, 371). The party president was "a mere first among equals in a collective leadership of factional bosses" (Krauss and Pekkanen 2011, 216). The factional elites actually allowed former party leaders to maintain influence even after their "turn" had been up, thus limiting their successors in terms of what they could achieve, but they readily dropped the leader if the latter became too popular (Reed 2011, 21). As a result, even popular and skillful politicians like Yasuhiro Nakasone in the 1980s were constrained in their scope of action, and many initiatives were quickly aborted or reverted after their tenure (Boucek 2012, 192; Krauss and Pekkanen 2011, 224).

While factions' lack of an ideological basis has often underpinned the LDP's reputation for being flexible in many policy areas (Köllner 2004, 247–48), factional competition actually heavily constrained the party's ability to innovate its policies (Krauss and Pekkanen 2011, 14–15; Reed 2011, 19). Factions' reliance on pork-barrel politics and clientelism translated into a policy agenda that focused on heavy public spending, overregulated industry, a large public sector, numerous construction projects, and tax cuts for supporters (George Mulgan 2002, 49; Park 2011, 273). This agenda contributed significantly to Japan's growing fiscal problems and gave rise to a large part of the challenges to which the LDP had to adapt. The budget deficits the LDP had been running for decades made Japan the most highly indebted OECD nation in terms of both gross and net liabilities (Park 2011, 273). Moreover, the need to finance their clientelist exchanges had increasingly pushed LDP factions to rely on corruption, resulting in several scandals and increased electoral pressure (Reed 2011, 18–19). The LDP had lost its majority of the votes in 1967 during the "Black mist" scandal, its majority of the seats (not counting independents) in 1976 during the Lockheed scandal, and its majority in the Upper House in 1989 during the Recruit scandal (Reed 2011, 19; Boucek 2012, 189–94). As in Italy, the end of the Cold War increased this electoral pressure by reducing the salience of anticommunism and opening up new cooperation between political parties (Boucek 2012, 194; Krauss and Pekkanen 2011, 230–33).

Although corruption scandals and the collapse of the bubble economy in the late 1980s and early 1990s put immense pressure on the LDP to change its policies and abandon pork barreling and corruption, the party stayed on the well-known path. Its stimulus package combined tax cuts with spending increases and thus contributed to ballooning deficit and debt (Park 2011, 273–74). The LDP's unaltered corrupt practices resulted in another major scandal. The 1992 Sagawa Express scandal implicated more than two hundred politicians, led to the resignation and arrest of the leader of the LDP's dominant Takeshita faction, and triggered a series of events that led to the LDP's split and an eight-party coalition's ousting it from government (Boucek 2012, 195–98).

As in the DC, LDP politicians acknowledged that the party's high level of factionalism prevented party adaptation. Already when writing in the late 1960s, Thayer (1969, 53) noted that often when new LDP presidents and prime ministers assumed office, they pledged to abolish the factions. The high level of factionalism undermined the leaders' ability to move in policy space by requiring them to appease a growing number of increasingly similarly seized factions. It damaged the country's economy by running large deficits to buy off supporters, pushed factions into corruption to maintain their clientelist linkages, and resulted in scandals and growing electoral pressure. Yet the factions were also the basis that allowed leaders to assume power to begin with and to maintain a say in politics after their tenure. As in the DC, reform initiatives thus did not seriously curtail factions' influence.

Mixed Selection Procedure, Moderating Factionalism, Party Adaptation: The LDP since 1994

THE 1994 ELECTORAL REFORM AND THE WEAKENING OF FACTIONS

The 1994 electoral reform importantly affected the dueling incentives LDP politicians faced regarding their party's high level of factionalism. On the one hand, the high level of factionalism had created incentives for party elites to abandon it by constraining LDP elites' decision-making at the executive and party leadership level and hurting the party's electoral prospects. On the other hand, factions had been instrumental for LDP politicians to assume party and executive positions and accumulate financial resources, thus incentivizing them to keep the LDP's system of factions. The balance of the two processes shifted in favor of change when the 1992 corruption scandal initiated a dynamic that culminated in the replacement of Japan's SNTV system with a mixed-member majoritarian system.

The LDP did not want electoral reform. It previously had only briefly (in 1956 and 1973) considered replacing SNTV with a single-member plurality (SMP) system to increase its seat share but abandoned those plans when election results improved (Boucek 2012, 194; Reed and Thies 2003, 157–63). However, the 1992 Sagawa scandal caused widespread demand to fight corruption, which many politicians linked with abandoning SNTV (Reed and Thies 2003, 156, 165–66). While opposition parties' initial proposal to replace SNTV with a mixed system failed, it increased pressure on the LDP, and prime minister and LDP leader Kiichi Miyazawa pledged on television to replace SNTV. Yet his plan to introduce an SMP system caused opposition from other parties and those Liberal Democrats with only weak factional backing, as they feared losing the nomination against candidates with well-developed *koenkai* and factional support (Krauss and Pekkanen 2011, 22; Reed and Thies 2003, 166). Ichiro Ozawa, who had failed to secure the leadership of the Takeshita faction, mobilized dissent within the LDP. Together with Tsutomu Hata, Ozawa appealed to the LDP's junior faction members threatened by an SMP system (Boucek 2012, 196–97). Together, they joined the opposition parties in bringing down Miyazawa's SMP bill and backed the Socialist Party's motion of no confidence the next day. Having triggered new elections, the rebels split from the LDP, set up two new parties, and joined an eight-party coalition that ousted the LDP and passed a bill replacing SNTV with a mixed-member system (Boucek 2012, 197). Although divisions in the new coalition gave the LDP some influence over the new system to get it through the Upper House, the fear of further defections and collapse for being the party that killed reform ensured that the LDP made only minor amendments (Reed and Thies 2003, 168).

The electoral reform's impact on factions' role within the LDP corresponds to Greif and Laitin's (2004) work on the shift from self-reinforcing toward self-undermining processes of institutional development. In their work, features (called quasi parameters) that exist independently of the institution of interest can endogenously influence the value of keeping or changing the institution over time (Greif and Laitin 2004, 639). Although the LDP's high level of factionalism had emerged independently of Japan's SNTV system, SNTV had contributed to reinforcing factional ties by expanding the value of factional support from national party leaders to LDP candidates at the district level. Factions had helped candidates in Japan's multimember districts to secure the nomination, develop pork-barrel-relevant policy expertise and connections, and accumulate resources to defeat rival LDP candidates in the same district. After the reform, however, there was only one LDP candidate per district race. This favored the renomination of incumbents and those candidates with already-strong *koenkai*. Because many of them also ran on the party list, which increased their chance of entering parliament even if they did not win their district, the incentives of many candidates and their supporters to join a faction declined (Krauss and Pekkanen 2011, 129–38).

Therefore, although national leaders continued to rely on factions (Park 2001, 448–51; Krauss and Pekkanen 2011, 132), "loyalty to the factions . . . considerably weakened" because factions no longer performed "as many roles for their members" (Krauss and Pekkanen 2011, 138). Studying the 1996 election (i.e., the first Lower House election after the reform), Cox, Rosenbluth, and Thies (1999, 44) found that the share of candidates with unknown factional affiliation had increased from an average of 7.8 percent for the 1960–1993 period to 38.31 percent. While "unknown" does not necessarily imply "unaffiliated" (Cox, Rosenbluth, and Thies 1999, 44), especially new candidates cared little about making their factional affiliation known, if they had any. The *Asahi Shimbun* newspaper, which traditionally documented LDP candidates' factional ties, confirmed that "factional involvement in the endorsement process was now negligible" (Cox, Rosenbluth, and Thies 1999, 43). District nominations were usually given to incumbents or candidates with a track record of winning, and only a few nonselected candidates challenged the LDP's nominee by running as independents (Cox, Rosenbluth, and Thies 1999, 45). The prefectural branches resolved quarrels over the PR lists by exclusively ranking candidates who agreed to be list candidates only. Candidates who ran both in a single-member district and on the list were subsequently ranked depending on their district race results (Cox, Rosenbluth, and Thies 1999, 46). The electoral reform rather than the LDP's loss of power drove this weakening of factions at the district and prefectural level, because conflicts within the new coalition allowed the LDP to return to government after only ten months.

CHANGES TO THE LEADERSHIP SELECTION, MODERATING FACTIONALISM, AND LEADERSHIP RENEWAL

Although the 1994 reform had reduced parliamentarians' dependence on factions for their reelection and consequently their loyalty toward their old factional bosses, on its own, it did not alter factions' importance in the election of the party president. Similar to the DC after Italy's electoral reforms in the early 1990s, the LDP saw junior faction members setting up new groups and coalitions in the party's 1995 leadership election (Cox, Rosenbluth, and Thies 1999, 49–51; Park 2001, 449–56), documented in a slight increase in the effective number of factions (Boucek 2012, 186).

Yet factions' weakening at the district level facilitated a change in the LDP's leadership selection. When the Liberal Democrats looked again for a new party president in 2001, it initially looked like they would again rely on either a party convention vote or, as in 1978, a membership primary with LDP parliamentarians subsequently choosing between the two front-runners (Krauss and Pekkanen 2011, 238). This time, however, the LDP's prefectural branches used their independence gained since the electoral reform to rebel. Fearing that the election of yet another factional puppet would result in a disastrous result in the upcoming Upper House election, they forced the LDP leaders to change the selection process. The prefectural branches received additional votes (albeit still fewer than given to the LDP parliamentarians) and, most importantly, scheduled their own separate primaries to decide which leadership candidate they would support before the parliamentarians would cast their vote (Krauss and Pekkanen 2011, 139–40, 238; Park 2001, 458).

The reform moved the LDP toward a mixed leadership selection process. On the one hand, networks across party branches were valuable for candidates for the party presidency to make a strong showing across prefectural primaries and have enough support at the party convention. This favored factional leaders. On the other hand, and similar to the logic of district races under single-member plurality, the separate prefectural primaries required candidates for the party presidency to build a strong network within prefectural branches. The geographical concentration of support thus mattered, too. This supported prefectural majority elites and improved their influence alongside factional leaders in party president elections.

The result was a decrease in the importance of factional support in party president elections. In 2001, many observers initially expected former prime minister Ryutaro Hashimoto to become party president because his own and allied factions were strong among party convention delegates. He faced Taro Aso from the Kono faction, Shizuka Kamei from the Eto-Kamei faction, and Junichiro Koizumi, who was supported by the YKK Group and Mori faction. Koizumi had been unsuccessful in the 1995 and 1998 leadership race but was popular among the public and rank and file for being reform oriented and clean of factional scandals (Park 2001, 457–58). The prefectural branches' move to hold separate internal primaries before the party convention changed Koizumi's odds dramatically (Krauss and Pekkanen 2011, 238; Boucek 2012, 200). Building his leadership bid on the support in the prefectural branches, Koizumi resigned as factional leader and instead sought the party presidency as an independent. He won in forty-two primaries, while Hashimoto and Aso won four contests and one, respectively. Koizumi's strong showing in the prefectures put pressure on several factions to support him, and he built a loose coalition that allowed him to defeat Hashimoto and Aso at the party convention, making him the first LDP president in decades who did not come from one of the major factions (Park 2001, 458).

In fact, for the first decade following the changed rules for the party's leadership selection, no leader of a major faction became party president (Krauss and Pekkanen 2011, 140). At the parliamentary level, the share of LDP parliamentarians unaffiliated with a faction increased from 9 percent in 2000 to 25 percent in 2003 (Boucek 2012, 1999). In 2005, only a small minority of parliamentary newcomers joined a faction before or right after the election, and the share of "unaffiliated" MPs ultimately grew to become the largest block among LDP parliamentarians (Krauss and Pekkanen 2011, 146–47; Endo and Pekkanen 2016, 46). At the same time, many hopefuls for the LDP leadership continued to woo members of parliament to join their faction, and around 57 percent of those initially unaffiliated in 2005 ended up joining a faction (Krauss and Pekkanen 2011, 147).

Subsequent organizational changes reinforced the dual logic of prefectural and factional influence. While only parliamentarians (where factions remained influential) were initially allowed to vote in the runoff between the two lead candidates, the 2013 party convention changed this rule, giving one vote to each of the prefectural branches. In 2014, the prefectural branches received the same total number of votes as the parliamentarians (Endo and Pekkanen 2016, 46–47). In short, as chapter 2 would make us expect under a mixed leadership selection process, factions continued to be valuable especially for those with little backing in the prefectural branches, "but they were no longer the whole game" (Krauss and Pekkanen 2011, 141).

Why did the shift toward a mixed-member majoritarian system facilitate organizational reform in Japan's LDP but not in Italy's DC? In both cases, factions had been entrenched for decades, intertwined with big business and the public sector, and delegitimized by major corruption scandals. Changing entrenched institutional behavior requires time—time that the LDP had and the DC did not. When Italy's new electoral law passed in August 1993, the DC had only two months to adjust before voters went to the polls for local and provincial elections. This was not enough time to change entrenched patterns of internal decision-making, and the party collapsed. In contrast, Japan's first elections following the reform in January 1994 only took place in 1995 (Upper House and local elections) and 1996 (general election). By that time, factions had already weakened in the LDP.

INNOVATION, INTEGRATION, AND PARTY ADAPTATION

While factions continued to support national politicians in assuming party and executive positions, their reduced influence in selecting the party president gave LDP presidents more autonomy (Krauss and Pekkanen 2011, 140–41). It underlines that the rise of Koizumi as a more autonomous leader was the result rather than the cause of the decrease in factionalism (Elgie 1995, 8; Burrett 2017, 401). Under Koizumi, the principle of factional proportionality in allocating cabinet posts significantly weakened (Köllner 2004, 253; Krauss and Pekkanen 2011, 143). Koizumi also included nonparliamentarians in his cabinet, which enhanced his autonomy because they often had no power base in the factions (Krauss and Pekkanen 2011, 144–45). While non–faction members remained less likely than faction members to receive major executive and party posts, the gap between them declined from 25 percent to less than 7 percent from before to after Koizumi (Krauss and Pekkanen 2011, 148). Moreover, Koizumi used his greater autonomy compared to pre-reform LDP presidents to shift policy making away from the PARC and policy tribes, which had been essential to broker agreements between factions, toward the cabinet and prime ministerial councils (Boucek 2012, 201). The weakening of long-held internal norms and practices emphasizes, as Levitsky's (2003) work suggests, the value of easing the institutional constraints on party leaders to pursue reforms. Flexibility and innovation are thus rightly conceptualized as important mechanisms of party adaptation. Yet the departure from long-held practices was the result of institutional reforms and moderating factionalism, thus highlighting flexibility and innovation as a mechanism rather than an independent variable in the LDP's reform process.

Koizumi went on to implement needed reforms. He had been elected on a policy agenda that pledged to turn away from heavy public spending, an overregulated industry and huge public sector, and pork-barrel construction projects (George Mulgan 2002, 49). Instead, he advocated relying on market forces to revitalize the economy and standing up for urban, young, and more highly educated voters, white-collar workers, and female employees, all of whom were long neglected by the LDP (George Mulgan 2002, 53; Park 2011, 275). Postal privatization was Koizumi's most talked about project. Factional elites had used the public postal system to reward loyalists by appointing them as postmasters in small towns and villages in their districts. In return, their appointees helped mobilize votes for their factional patron. The postal savings and insurance system also significantly contributed to the Fiscal Investment and Loan Program, which funded many infrastructural projects that factional elites used for pork barreling (Krauss and Pekkanen 2011, 247).

Unable to replace Koizumi as party president (as they did in the past when party presidents risked infringing on their interests), factional leaders organized defections in parliament that foiled Koizumi's bill. Yet backed by his reform coalition, Koizumi called new elections and ran a skillful campaign that focused on the issue of postal privatization. After winning the most decisive LDP victory in twenty-five years, his postal reform bill passed (Krauss and Pekkanen 2011, 248–49).

Similar to the factional alternation in the CDU, factions facilitated the alternation between different leadership coalitions while avoiding the long-term exclusion of particular interests. They continued to help integrate the party's old guard and support backbenchers in gaining seats on the PARC and parliamentary committees (Krauss and Pekkanen 2011, 257). While Koizumi's reforms had been popular among the rank and file in the prefectural branches, many factions expressed growing concerns over economic insecurity and wealth disparities. In 2006, Shinzo Abe secured the party presidency (and prime ministership) by building support on both sides of the divide, claiming to follow Koizumi's reformist agenda while promising to pay greater attention to economic security (Park 2011, 277). After losing in the 2007 Upper House election and Yasuo Fukuda's brief leadership spell, the LDP's internal pendulum swung back to the old guard, with factions backing Taro Aso's election to the presidency. Under Aso's leadership, the LDP abandoned its clear targets for budget cuts and instead resumed a stimulus-oriented course (Park 2011, 277–78). Voters punished the LDP's departure from its previous reforms in 2009, and the LDP entered a three-year spell in opposition (Krauss and Pekkanen 2011, 251–55; Boucek 2012, 202–4). A new factional coalition supported the return of Shinzo Abe to the party presidency, this time on a clear reformist agenda. Abe consolidated the party leader's greater autonomy compared to the pre-reform period (George Mulgan 2018, 66–71), and his economic platform, known as Abenomics, was important in revitalizing support. The LDP returned as the lead governing party in 2012 (Mark 2016).

Conclusion

This chapter explored the transferability of the book's argument beyond post-1990 Christian Democracy by studying the adaptation of parties that meet the book's theoretical scope conditions but competed in a very different cultural, institutional, and political environment. France's MRP allowed keeping many party family- and region-specific characteristics similar while studying party adaptation to very different environmental changes. Facing strong antisystem parties on the right and left, an escalating (de)colonization crisis, and a profound institutional overhaul of the political system, the MRP was unable to adjust its policy and coalition strategy and ultimately dissolved in 1967. The link between a decentralized leadership selection, a low level of factionalism, and weak adaptation displayed striking similarities with Austria's ÖVP. This is remarkable because both parties have varied substantively in other organizational characteristics, their societal rootedness, and the institutional context.

Studying Japan's Liberal Democrats has allowed exploring the insights of the book's argument beyond European Christian Democracy. The LDP has been a particularly insightful case because its history consists of two quite different parts. Until 1994, its development showed notable similarities with Italy's DC regarding the link between a centralized leadership selection, high factionalism, and weak adaptation. Regardless of many institutional similarities between Japan and Italy, the book's argument can teach us something about party organization, factionalism, and adaptation even in a very different cultural environment. Finally, the 1994 electoral reform, undesired by the LDP, was highly impactful in weakening its factions and facilitating a change in the leadership selection process that helped moderate its level of factionalism. The positive impact of its moderate level of factionalism on leadership renewal, policy innovation, and the alternation between competing blocks bears notable similarities to the development of Germany's CDU. This is remarkable given both cases' cultural and institutional differences.

Beyond providing rich empirical narratives of eight important political parties, the previous chapters have generated suggestions for the study of party organizations, factionalism, and adaptation. The next chapter discusses these lessons.

Conclusion: Lessons for the Study of Party Adaptation, Factionalism, and Party Organization

Under what conditions do Christian democratic parties adapt successfully to a new structural context increasingly affected by ongoing secularization and globalization? Under what conditions can Christian democratic parties adapt to new competitors such as populist parties?

KALYVAS AND VAN KERSBERGEN (2010, 203)

Especially at the level of the individual parties, it is a constant phenomenon, an ongoing process of continuous adaptation to changing social, political, and policy circumstances.

MAIR (1997, 16)

The puzzle that motivated this book is embedded in the varying substance and speed of party adaptation. When European politics entered a period of profound transformations in the early 1990s, Italy's Christian Democrats had known for years that their dependence on clientelism and pork barreling was a growing liability. For years, they had discussed empowering the party's regional branches to ease their dependence on factions' clientelist networks. Still, despite facing new and reformed challenger parties, a massive corruption scandal, and heavy electoral losses, the DC passed only minor reforms and eventually collapsed. Similarly, the ÖVP had known for decades that its corporatist organization and agrarian platform significantly undermined the party's ability to mobilize the growing and diversifying middle class, eventually culminating in a steep electoral decline in the 1990s and 2000s amid a rising right-wing rival. Still, the party introduced substantive changes only in 2017, after losing half of its pre-1990 vote share. In stark contrast, Germany's CDU passed more substantive reforms and did so more swiftly. Suffering a crushing defeat in 1998 for its handling of integrating more than sixteen million new citizens and two very different economic systems as a result of German reunification, the party initially abandoned long-held welfare positions and embraced a market-liberal course. When this strategy proved less successful than anticipated, the party moderated its economic positions and instead departed from its long-held social conservatism. Why these and other parties have differed so much in the substance and speed of their adaptation has been the topic of the previous chapters.

Their varying adaptation related to a broader puzzle in the literature on party politics. Mair (1997, 16) has rightly highlighted that political parties are in a state of tension. They compete in a permanently changing world, which requires them to almost continuously update their positions, strategies, and organization. The rise of populism seems to suggest that established parties are losing this battle, with many old parties appearing too static to counter radical challengers (e.g., Haggard and Kaufman 2021; Mudde 2007, 2019; Zielonka 2018). At the same time, election defeats, scandals, and party system changes have often been the catalyst for party reform (Gauja 2016; Bale 2012; Harmel and Janda 1994). However, why some parties are more adaptable than others has remained puzzling.

In response, this book has developed a theory that redeemed a concept with a historically bad reputation in the study of party politics—*party factions*. Its main argument can be summarized in three steps. First, factions, defined as organized internal groups with no formal ties to the central party, can enhance party adaptation. Parties have a tendency to oligarchize and entrench the dominance of special interests (e.g., Kitschelt 1994; Levitsky 2003; Michels [1911] 1959). Factions can help counter that tendency by providing the flexibility for old interests to decline and new interests to rise. Too much of this flexibility, however, risks leading to a proliferation of competing factions, unstable internal coalitions, and dependence on a class of factional brokers. Consequently, both extremely high and extremely low levels of factionalism undermine a party's ability to pass adaptive reforms, whereas a moderate level of factionalism facilitates adaptation. Second, parties' level of factionalism is importantly shaped by their initial rules to select their national leaders. They determine what selectorate party elites need to win over and thereby drives the type of intraparty groups party elites are incentivized to rely on. The more centralized the leadership selection process, the more incentivized party elites are to form and join factions and the higher the level of factionalism. Third, moving away from very high or low levels of factionalism becomes increasingly difficult. The level of factionalism tends to become deeply rooted in the party over time as actors in the position to introduce organizational change are likely to have benefited from it. However, the same level of factionalism puts their political career in jeopardy by sabotaging adaptive reforms. Very high and very low levels of factionalism thus leave key decision-makers in a dilemma, which makes changing the level of factionalism not impossible but difficult. Party elites in moderately factionalized parties are less likely to face such conflicting incentives.

The previous five chapters have tested this argument, developed in chapter 2, by providing in-depth analyses of eight parties and covering nearly

seventy-five years of history. Western European Christian Democracy served
as the book's main empirical focus. These parties were of crucial importance
in the emergence, consolidation, and resilience of postwar European democracies. Europe's social market economies, appeasing historical societal divisions, and European integration would have been unthinkable without their
doing. And yet, despite their importance, their varying fate against the backdrop of Europe's gradual secularization, internal disagreements, and the profound transformations of the early 1990s has received very scarce scholarly attention compared to parties on the mainstream and far left and radical right.
This book has addressed this lacuna by providing the first English-language
monograph on their internal lives and adaptation. Guided by a nested analysis, part 2 offered a structured focused comparison of Italy's DC (chapter 3),
Austria's ÖVP (chapter 4), and Germany's CDU (chapter 5). It traced their
trajectory from their beginnings in the 1940s until today (or until their collapse, as in the DC) by using a rich record of archival material. Against common expectations given these parties' internal diversity and catch-all approach, they have varied enormously in their level of factionalism and party
adaptation. To explain this variation, the book benefited from the similarities
across parties. While political challenges are never identical across cases, this
party family faced a similar strategic setting. The parties have faced intense
pressure to get their act together after the end of the Cold War, shared a similar ideology, and historically appealed to a similar membership and electorate. All this facilitated within-case analyses by ensuring that actors were
operating under similar contextual conditions, key concepts traveled across
cases, and the book's scope conditions were met. Part 3 then moved beyond
the main cases. Chapter 6 outlined that the book's argument provides important insights for understanding the varying adaptation of additional cases
from the same sample, and chapter 7 assessed its external validity by using the
French MRP and Japanese LDP as comparable cases challenged by different
contextual transformations.

The theoretical and empirical parts of this book have yielded important
implications for the study of party adaptation, factionalism, and party organizations. The remainder of this conclusion discusses these implications.

Implications for the Study of Party Adaptation

THE LIMITS OF ADAPTATION AGAINST ACTIVISTS

While providing insights into the understanding of individual cases, previous accounts have faced comparative limitations when trying to explain the

varying substance and speed of adaptation in the book's cases. A common starting point in the study of party adaptation has been considering how reform-willing party leaders can overcome the opposition of less reform-minded lower-rank elites and activists either through centralizing power or the weakness of internal accountability mechanisms (e.g., Levitsky 2003; Lupu 2016; Kirchheimer 1966; Kitschelt 1994; Ziblatt 2017). Yet as table 8.1 summarizes for the cases included in Katz and Mair's (1992) data handbook, there was actually relatively little variation in Christian democratic parties' organizational institutionalization and leadership accountability on the eve of these parties being required to adapt to the post–Cold War environment.[1] The qualitative analysis in the previous chapters further underpinned the comparative limitations of the leadership autonomy argument for the cases under investigation. Party centralization cannot explain the differences in adaptation of parties with a similarly decentralized control over candidate selection and party finances (e.g., the CDU and ÖVP). Moreover, it ignores the role of intensifying factionalism in bringing about an initially de facto and subsequently de jure decentralization of power in Japan's LDP and (to a lesser extent) Italy's DC. Power in the Dutch CDA has also been similarly formally centralized as in the highly factionalized CDS and early DC, while the party has experienced the dynamics and problems associated with low levels of factionalism that resembled those observed in the decentralized ÖVP. Such differences in the causal process undermine the credibility of the centralization argument for the book's cases.

While the highly institutionalized ÖVP has experienced serious problems when trying to adapt to a changing environment, France's MRP was only institutionalized on paper, and its leadership enjoyed a high level of autonomy from second-rank elites and the rank and file. Kitschelt's (1994) and Levitsky's (2003) findings would thus expect the MRP to be highly adaptable, which chapter 7 outlined to not be the case. Decisions by the national party congress, the formally prescribed frequency of national party meetings, and internal rules were repeatedly ignored in the (early) CDU and DC. Yet these parties starkly differed in their substance and speed of adaptation. Weak organizational entrenchment and leadership accountability have also not enhanced the CDS's and the CDA's adaptability. Exclusively focusing on party institutionalization thus leaves underexplored why parties vary in their ability to benefit from weak institutionalization.

The book's analysis has highlighted some areas for further research on the effect of party institutionalization and leadership autonomy on party adaptation. Compared to the ÖVP and the post-1970 CDU, formal rules and procedures played only a marginal role in Italy's DC and Japan's pre-1994 LDP,

TABLE 8.1. Institutionalization of Christian democratic parties, 1989

Variable	CDA	CDU	DC	ÖVP
(1) Member-to-voter ratio	0.0	0.5	0.5	1.0
(2) Importance of patronage	0.0	0.5	1.0	1.0
(3) Size of the party's middle apparatus	0.5	1.0	1.0	1.0
(4) Institutionalization of intra-party pluralism	0.0	0.5	1.0	1.0
(5) Local control over candidate recruitment	0.5	1.0	0.5	0.5
(6) Control of party conference	0.5	1.0	0.0	0.0
(7) Dominance of party executive over parliamentary leadership	0.0	1.0	1.0	1.0
(8) Dependence on external groups	0.5	0.0	0.5	1.0
Summary (1)–(4): Organizational entrenchment (0 to 4)	0.5	2.5	3.5	4.0
Summary (5)–(8): Leadership accountability (0 to 4)	1.5	3.0	2.0	2.5
Summary (1)–(8): Institutionalization (0 to 8)	2.0	5.5	5.5	6.5

Notes: Row (1): Member-to-voter ratio ≥20% =1.0; m/v ≥5% = 0.5; m/v <5% = 0.0. Rows (2)–(8) are my scoring following Kitschelt (1994, 221–25). The data underpinning this coding can be found in the supplementary material available on the author's website. I rescaled Kitschelt's leadership accountability variable so that higher values indicate higher organizational entrenchment and leadership accountability.
Source: Bardi and Morlino (1992); Koole and Van de Velde (1992); Müller (1992); Poguntke and Boll (1992); Koole (1994, 282–95).

which should have made the parties more adaptable. Although DC and LDP leaders were constrained by informal rules, this also applies to the seminal case for Levitsky's (2003) party institutionalization argument, Argentina's Justicialist Party (PJ). The PJ was a highly informally organized party, with formal rules mainly existing on paper (Freidenberg and Levitsky 2006). Demarcating party institutionalization conceptually from the (in)formality of party organizations and exploring why the triviality of formal rules helped the PJ to adapt but not the DC and pre-1994 LDP is a promising avenue for future research. The book's empirical analysis has also highlighted that studying party adaptation in terms of an antagonism between a reform-willing leadership and a reform-hostile rank and file risks being overly simplistic in parties with a collective leadership. The national leadership in all parties discussed in this book is better thought of as an arena rather than an actor in internal party politics. Increasing the autonomy of this arena vis-à-vis the rank and file and lower-rank elites does not automatically guarantee reform if members of the

TABLE 8.2. Strength of the book's and alternative theories of party adaptation

	Theory	DC (IT)	ÖVP (AT)	CDU (GE)	CDS (PT)	CDA (NL)	CSV (LU)	MRP (FR)	LDP (JP)	Cases
This study	Inverted U-shaped impact of factionalism	✓	✓	✓	✓	✓	✓	✓	✓	8
Alternative theories	Linear impact of factionalism	✓	—	—	✓	—	—	—	✓	3
	Party centralization	−1	✓	—	—	—	✓	✓	−1	3
	Party institutionalization	—	✓	—	—	—	✓	—	—	2

[1] Although power became increasingly decentralized across party factions.

leadership body are unwilling to reform the party or are divided over which course to take.

Finally, the trajectories of the ÖVP, CDA, and MRP highlight that parties do *not* become more adaptable as parties' level of factionalism continues to decrease. Table 8.2 summarizes the discussed findings.

PARTY ADAPTATION AND THE INVERTED-U-SHAPED EFFECT OF FACTIONALISM

In contrast, the analysis has shown consistent support for an inverted U-shaped relationship between factionalism and party adaptation. Italy's DC has emphasized that high factionalism weakens party adaptation. The proliferation of competing groups with an increasingly similar seat share in the party's internal assemblies gave way to almost constantly rearranging factions and multifaction coalitions. Consequently, while the DC repeatedly replaced its leaders, party leaders like Moro and Zaccagnini, who were elected on a reformist agenda, depended on broad factional backing, which substantially constrained the extent of reform they could bring. Factional splits, cycling majorities, and rearranging factional coalitions eroded parliamentary unity, importantly contributed to governmental instability, and complicated internal decision-making over programmatic and organizational reforms. Over time, the party got caught in the clientelist web that the factions had established. While acknowledging high factionalism as an obstacle to adaptation, factional leaders opposed reforms when the DC faced a massive corruption scandal and pressure to move beyond its anti-Communist and religious electorate. Despite suffering the breakaway of several factions and a sharp electoral decline in the 1992 national and 1993 local elections, the reform process unfolded only very slowly and resulted in few and minor changes before the DC's collapse in 1994. The development of Portugal's CDS and Japan's pre-1994 LDP have echoed many of these findings.

However, the DC would not have been better off by suppressing all factions. In Austria's ÖVP, the lack of factions effectively blocked the integration of social and political groups that did not easily map onto the party's territorial and occupational structure. Party elites who wanted to rise to the top of the party were required to build a strong power base within one of the party's territorial branches or auxiliary organizations. This prevented the innovation usually associated with leadership changes, as all new leaders came from the same closed circle of majority elites. Those without such a power base were de facto excluded and repeatedly driven out of the party. Given their secured influence, majority elites often did not have an incentive to compromise, and the ÖVP consequently struggled to agree on programmatic and organizational reforms. The same traditional interests continued to dominate in the party, increasingly putting the party out of touch with a changing and diversifying electorate. While party elites and political observers acknowledged the problem, it took the party more than forty-five years to reduce the dominance of its Land and League branches. Thus, adaptability does not linearly increase as factionalism decreases. The discussion of the Dutch CDA and the additional test of France's MRP support this conclusion.

Instead, the moderately factionalized CDU has been the most adaptable party included in part 2 of the book. On the one hand, the importance of the CDU's territorial branches helped keep factionalism at a lower level than in the DC by incentivizing some majority elites to not form or join a faction. On the other hand, the influence of some factions provided the CDU with more flexibility to integrate new or previously minor groups within the party and renew the party's dominant coalition in response to societal changes. While farmers maintained a formally guaranteed powerful standing within the ÖVP even after their share in society had decreased markedly, the CDU's expellee and Protestant factions declined when their relevance in reflecting Germany's social conflict lines decreased. Changes in factions' size and coalitions with the party's Land leaders facilitated more substantive leadership change than in the DC and ÖVP, often taking the form of an alternation between the CDU's market-liberal, social-Catholic, and conservative forces. Without any of those groups being relegated to the sidelines for long, this leadership alternation facilitated innovation, and new leaders were often able to pass substantive reforms relatively swiftly. The development of Japan's LDP after 1994 and of Luxembourg's CSV have further supported the link between moderate factionalism and party adaptation.

These results importantly refine what we know about the effects of factionalism and party adaptation with activists. Several recent books have highlighted the asset organized groups in political parties can be to identify and aggregate politically relevant interests and thus help the party keep up with public demands.[2] This book has built on these accounts and added that factions' organizational flexibility and pervasiveness make them particularly valuable for party adaptation. Unlike parties' territorial or auxiliary branches, factions are more flexible to form, split, and rearrange as socially and politically relevant conflict lines change. Unlike more locally concentrated groups like legislative caucuses and camps, they help connect like-minded people across parties' various different levels. Both features help incorporate interests not easily captured by parties' official organization and provide flexible coalition partners for leadership renewal. While previous studies have almost exclusively highlighted the negative consequences of (eventually) high levels of factionalism, Boucek (2009) and especially DiSalvo (2012) have suggested that factionalism, within limits, can facilitate integration and innovation.[3] This book set out to integrate the insights generated from both sides of this debate by including parties with no or only some few factions and providing, to my knowledge, the first systematic theorization and testing of the relationship between different levels of factionalism and party adaptation.

My results have also underlined the importance of the internal supply side in theories of party competition. Among others, changes in the social composition of the electorate and issue salience, the rise of new competitors, and changes in the electoral system have caused internal debates about parties' response to these changes. The extent to which the book's cases managed to get their act together in these debates depended on their level of factionalism. Analyzing intraparty politics, and thereby opening what has too often been treated as a black box, has shown to be crucial.

Implications for the Study of Factionalism

THE POLITICS OF LEADERSHIP SELECTION

The level of factionalism in the analyzed cases depended on the rules party elites adopted to select their national leaders when forming their organization. The Italian Christian Democrats chose a centralized leadership selection process, which led to a high level of factionalism. Delegates from the different provincial, parliamentary, and auxiliary branches of the DC came together at the national party congress to elect the majority of the party council, which then elected almost all positions of the party leadership. To get elected to the leadership, party elites depended on the support of delegates from different party branches. This incentivized party elites who lacked such a broad support base to form factions. While those who enjoyed sufficient support across party branches to be confident about assuming leadership positions were initially not incentivized to form factions, the emergence of the first factions increased pressure on them to also form or join a faction. The resulting high level of factionalism was reinforced over time, and factions became deeply entrenched as the dominant type of intraparty groups within the DC. When compared with the DC, the emergence and development of factionalism in Japan's pre-1994 LDP and Portugal's CDS have shown important parallels.

The decentralized selection process of the ÖVP's national leadership yielded a very different incentive structure. Austria's Christian Democrats had decided to select their national leaders by mainly co-opting majority elites from their Land and League branches. This meant that party elites primarily depended on support in their own organizational branch. Consequently, there was little to gain from forming networks with members from other party branches to get elected to the national party leadership, and the level of factionalism remained low. I observed a similar process in the Dutch CDA and the French MRP.

While majority and minority elites had eventually similar incentives under a very centralized and decentralized leadership selection process, incentives were more diverse in the case of the CDU. Most national leadership positions were elected by two committees.[4] Majority and minority elites came together at the national party congress to elect the party leader and the two deputy leaders. The remaining leadership positions were elected by the party council, which was primarily a meeting of majority elites from the CDU's Land branches. The party council provided majority elites from the strong Land branches from (south)western Germany with de facto secured seats on the party leadership. Leaders of these Land branches and the parliamentary party leader, who was an ex officio member of the party leadership, were thus, unlike in the DC and similar to the ÖVP, incentivized to focus on strengthening their network within their respective party branches rather than to form factions. Yet unlike in the ÖVP, majority elites from the weaker Land branches in the north(west) had a more diverse incentive structure. On the one hand, support within their party branch guaranteed access to the party council. On the other hand, they had fewer seats in that committee than majority elites from larger Land branches and could not build on an as strong electoral record to justify their bids for national leadership positions. In addition to maintaining a strong network within their Land branch, they were therefore incentivized to build networks across party branches. Minority elites, finally, could not be

TABLE 8.3. Findings on leadership selection process and factionalism

	DC	CDU	ÖVP
Centralization of leadership selection	Centralized (0.22)	Mixed system (0.4)	Decentralized (0.89)
Incentive structure			
Minority elites	Cross-branch networks	Cross-branch networks	Within-branch networks
Majority elites	Cross-branch networks	Within-branch networks (stronger Land branches) Within- and cross-branch networks (weaker Land branches)	Within-branch networks
Factionalism	High (6.82)	Medium (4.01)	Low (0.75)
Further support	CDS, LDP (pre-1994)	CSV, LDP (post-1994)	CDA, MRP

Note: Rae's (1967) fractionalization index as a measure of centralization and number of factions standardized by year as a measure of factionalism in parentheses. A list of the annual number of factions can be found in the supplementary material.

certain to be represented at the party council at all. Their chance to influence the composition of the national leadership was to forge alliances across party branches at the national congress. Overall, this resulted in a moderate level of factionalism. I observed a similar trajectory in Luxembourg's CSV and Japan's LDP after the new electoral system had allowed reformers to move the party's leadership selection toward a mixed process.

These findings, summarized in table 8.3, make important contributions to the study of intraparty politics and factionalism. The book tested its theoretical framework and competing arguments with regard to their power to explain different levels of factionalism. This is important, as the previous focus on highly factionalized parties has usually meant not investigating the full variation of the variable(s) of interest. The results highlight how essential it is to base comparative analyses on a clear conceptualization. Some of the groups discussed in this book could have been misinterpreted as factions (e.g., the Leagues within the ÖVP, the specialized groups in the MRP). By drawing on a new typology of intraparty groups in chapter 2, the case study chapters revealed important differences between these groups and factions. Defining a faction in terms of an intraparty group that acts collectively to realize some joint goals thus risks being too broad to uncover important differences in the dynamics of intraparty competition and allow for valid conclusions of what initiates different levels of factionalism.

By revealing the rules and procedures a party uses to select its national leaders as an important factor explaining different levels of factionalism, the book offers a better understanding of how a party's organizational setup can affect its internal competition. It has done so by providing important micro-foundations for a theory of factionalism and outlining how the rules struc-turing access to positions on the party's leadership board guided party elites' strategies to form factions. In doing so, this book helps resolve some of the conflicting findings and fragmentation that have characterized the study of factionalism. Previous case studies of highly factionalized parties have gener-ated a wide array of factors plausibly linked to the formation and development of factions (Coppedge 1994, 94–95; Boucek 2009, 456–57), and the few quan-titative studies in the field have assessed the extent to which various factors correlate with factionalism (Ceron 2019; Borz 2017). This book's comparative-historical analysis has identified at which stage of the causal process different factors played a role. This helped clarify some of the puzzling and conflicting results found in previous research, as the next section discusses.

DISTINGUISHING INITIATING FROM REINFORCING FACTORS

My findings on the important role of initial organizational choices in ac-counting for different levels of factionalism help clarify why, when, and how factors found to correlate with factionalism matter. Previous studies have rightly identified the electoral system, clientelism, governmental dominance, and federalism as important variables. The brief within-case comparisons with other parties competing in the same country have echoed this. German and Austrian parties with a similarly centralized leadership selection and unrestricted internal democratic competition have experienced higher levels of factionalism than parties with a more decentralized leadership selection but not the intensely high factionalism in similarly centralized Italian parties, where additional reinforcing factors were present. Yet it is important to iden-tify the correct stage of the causal sequence when these factors are influential.

Similar factors can help reinforce different levels of factionalism. The preferential vote component of Italy's electoral system proved to be an im-portant tool for minority factions in the DC to put pressure on the factions controlling the party leadership. By accumulating preference votes, minor-ity factions could increase their seat share in the DC's parliamentary group and threaten to sabotage parliamentary votes if their interests were not duly taken into account. An open-list PR system thus helped reinforce the value of factional networks and contributed to factionalism's spilling over from the competition for national party leadership positions to the competition over parliamentary seats at the district level. In contrast, the preference vote com-ponent of Austria's electoral system did not encourage ÖVP elites to engage in similar (factional) activities.[5] As shown in chapter 4, preference vote campaigns were rare, short lived, and predominantly autonomous endeavors by individual candidates. They looked nothing like the factional machines striving for preference votes in the DC.

To explain these differences despite a similar electoral system, we need to look at the incentive structure created by the party's leadership selection process. Unlike in the DC, majority elites in the ÖVP enjoyed guaranteed representation in the national party leadership. They were not incentivized to form factions. Instead, they only occasionally used preference vote campaigns to correct for ill-designed electoral lists. Minority elites, in contrast, were practically excluded from the ÖVP's leadership. They could have been incentivized to use the preference vote component to make their voice heard through the party's parliamentary group. Some of the cases where local notables campaigned for preference votes could fit this pattern. However, as shown in chapter 4, League and Land majority elites had benefited from their influence within the ÖVP to introduce a decentralized selection process for parliamentary candidates. This reinforced the value of strong networks within actors' own party branches, as they were not only a prerequisite to assume party leadership positions but also to be nominated as a parliamentary candidate. Factionalism was therefore not a valuable strategy for minority elites in the ÖVP. These findings resonate with what I have found in other cases. The CSV's mixed leadership selection process gave way to a moderate level of factionalism despite Luxembourg's preferential voting system, and the CDA, similar to the ÖVP, has been characterized by a low level of factionalism despite the Netherlands also using a preferential voting PR system. In contrast, the CDS's centralized procedure to select its national leaders triggered a high level of factionalism even though the party competed under Portugal's closed-list PR system.

My results thus help make sense of ambiguous results from previous studies on the impact of the electoral system on factionalism. While several studies have highlighted the link between preferential voting and factionalism (Pasquino 1972; Katz 1986; Cox and Rosenbluth 1993), large-N analyses have either found only a statistically weak relationship (Ceron 2019, 77) or no significant relationship (Borz 2017, 13). My analysis suggests that these results might appear ambiguous only at first glance. A party's organization, at least in the cases I looked at, had an important mediating impact on the link between the electoral system and factionalism. Future research would benefit from controlling for such interaction effects.

This discussion has also implications for the conclusions we can draw regarding the way party elites use available means of clientelism and patronage.

These have usually been theorized to encourage factionalism when combined with an electoral system that allows for competition between candidates from the same party (Ames 1995; Carey and Shugart 1995). Similar to the point made earlier about the reinforcing role of preferential voting, I have found that party elites can use clientelism and patronage to reinforce different levels of factionalism. Sources of clientelism and patronage were particularly present in the Italian and Austrian cases. Both Austria's and Italy's public sector and the links between politics and the economy provided the DC and ÖVP with access to substantive resources, like money, positions, and public contracts. While Italy's Christian Democrats used these resources to create incentives for party members and voters to support their factions, clientelism and patronage were focused on strengthening party elites' position within their Land or League branch in Austria. Thus, previous research has been right in saying that clientelism and patronage can matter a great deal for the development of factionalism (e.g., Zuckerman 1979; Ames 1995; Golden and Chang 2001). Yet party elites use such means to reinforce different levels of factionalism.

In turn, the book's analysis has not found support for the dominant party approach, which has suggested that factionalism in a governing party increases as the level of competitiveness of the party system decreases (e.g., Key 1949; Arian and Barnes 1974; Boucek 2012). The Portuguese CDS became highly factionalized despite spending most of its existence in opposition. Moreover, all remaining cases have been major governing parties for a long period of time while starkly differing in their level of factionalism. In fact, chapters 3–5 specified that the ÖVP's, CDU's, and DC's position in government was quite safe until the end of the 1960s, while no faction, four factions, and more than seven factions were established in those cases, respectively, during the same period. In addition, chapter 3 showed that factionalism in the DC increased when the party's dominant position was far from secure following its losses in the local elections in November 1946. Instead, parties' participation in government primarily mattered to the extent that it provided party elites with access to resources, which they used to strengthen the type of intraparty group that was valuable given their respective parties' internal playing field.

While the absence of factions in the ÖVP seems to support the argument that federalism would dampen factionalism, several factions have been established in the CDU from federal Germany. Moreover, if the level of factionalism decreased as the level of subnational autonomy increased, the ÖVP should have been more factionalized than the CDU given Austria's weakly federalized polity. Furthermore, some cases from unitary polities (i.e., CDA and MRP) have been as weakly or less factionalized than the ÖVP and CDU, respectively. Differences in the structure of a polity therefore do not have an unequivocal effect on a party's level of factionalism. Yet this is not to say that federalism did not affect the development of parties' internal competition. German federalism helped majority elites from Land branches to reinforce their influential position within the CDU (without, however, preventing majority elites from smaller Länder and minority elites from engaging in factional activities). In Austria, the Land level has substantial spending power, which has helped ÖVP Land leaders to strengthen their power base by facilitating Land-specific patronage.

Furthermore, in almost all cases, party formation was the result of very different groups coming together in the same party without predetermining a high level of factionalism. In fact, the CDS became highly factionalized even though it had been formed by a fairly homogeneous group. Moreover, the DC's founding groups started forming factions only once the party's centralized leadership selection process had left many of them with very little influence in the national executive and their attempt to gain ex officio membership in the national executive had failed.

My results resonate with previous findings that the use of a PR system for internal elections within the DC was part of the reinforcement process through which factions tried to increase their influence and thus the result rather than the cause of high factionalism (Leonardi and Wertman 1989, 109–10; cf. Sartori 1971). This book also adds to previous studies that have identified parties' procedure to select their president as influencing party elites' incentives to form factions. Thayer (1969) and Krauss and Pekkanen (2011) highlighted the direct election of the LDP president as an important reason for the party's high level of factionalism before 1994, and Ceron (2019) provided a refined argument by suggesting that factionalism would increase as the size of the selectorate for the party president decreased. I have found only limited support for the selectorate argument when applied to this book's cases. This might be because the metaphorical pie that party elites are competing for goes beyond the party presidency. Many parties, and all the parties discussed in this book, have a collective leadership, typically in the form of a leadership board that includes additional positions beyond the party president. The rules to select a party's leadership board rather than only the party president have been important drivers of actors' incentives to form factions within the studied cases.

This conclusion seems to hold regardless of the extent to which power has been centralized in the hands of the party leadership. Carey's (2007)

TABLE 8.4. Strength of this book's and alternative theories of factionalism

	Theory	DC	ÖVP	CDU	CDS	CDA	CSV	MRP	LDP	Cases
This study	Leadership board selection process	✓	✓	✓	✓	✓	✓	✓	✓	8
Alternative theories	Heterogeneity of founding coalition	—	—	—	—	—	—	—	—	0
	Federalism	n/a	✓	—	n/a	n/a	n/a	n/a	n/a	1
	Party dominance	—	—	—	—	—	—	—	—	0
	Preferential voting	—	—	n/a	—	—	—	✓	—	1
	Clientelism	—	—	—	—	✓	—	—	—	1
	Intraparty PR	—	n/a	n/a	[1]	n/a	n/a	n/a	n/a	0
	Selectorate for party president	✓	✓	—	—	✓	—	—	—	3
	Party centralization	—	—	—	—	✓	—	—	—	1

[1] As outlined in chapter 6, a factional compromise in the CDS also led to the introduction of PR for internal elections in the early 1980s. I could, however, not determine whether this was the first time that PR was used for internal elections.

suggestion that centralizing power might deter the formation of factions finds little support when applied to the book's cases. High levels (DC, CDS) and low levels (CDA) of factionalism emerged in initially centralized parties, and similarly decentralized parties have differed in their level of factionalism (e.g., ÖVP, CDU). In fact, the case of the DC and especially the LDP showed how the emergence of factions can lead to a party's gradual decentralization of power.

In short, the study of factionalism requires a historically sensitive approach to differentiate between variables affecting the origins and those influencing the development of factionalism. Party elites can benefit from similar structural conditions to reinforce different levels of factionalism. Consequently, while previous theories of factionalism are plausible for the trajectory of individual cases, they find less empirical support than my framework when applied to the book's cases (table 8.4). When building and testing theories, we are urged to differentiate variables that initiate a causal process toward a particular outcome from variables that are important in reinforcing that outcome over time.

Implications for the Study of Party Organizations

Despite an empirically rich scholarship on the organization of political parties, the most comprehensive efforts to integrate party organizations' origins, development, and effects within a single analytical framework still date from the seminal evolutionary approaches (Duverger 1951; Kirchheimer 1966; Panebianco 1988; Katz and Mair 1995).[6] These studies have been pathbreaking. However, the broad party types introduced by these studies do not (and have never been intended to) capture the persistent organizational variation between parties (Webb, Poguntke, and Scarrow 2017).[7] While Panebianco's (1988) work on the structure of a party's formative process has moved the literature toward a more fine-grained analysis, the focus on structural variables has left his framework blind for the role of actors and politics. Moreover, Panebianco was concerned about the driving forces behind the process of party institutionalization and, consequently, did not explore the origins, development, and effects of specific organizational characteristics.[8]

Recent historical and strategic approaches to studying party organizations have begun addressing this gap. On the one hand, historical approaches have used tools from path-dependence theory, like increasing returns and negative externalities, to explain the surprising stability of some party organizations amid the often tumultuous political context in Latin America and East Asia. In these cases, organizational characteristics introduced early in a party's history became entrenched over time by reinforcing the dominance of some actors over others, incentivizing the latter to adapt to the rules in place, and crowding out those unwilling or unable to comply (Bentancur, Rodríguez, and Rosenblatt 2020; Anria 2019; Krauss and Pekkanen 2011; Hellmann 2011). On the other hand, and often studying the historically more stable party systems in Europe, Australia, and North America, strategic approaches have studied the changes in many parties' internal procedures to select their policies, candidates, and leaders (Gauja 2016; Cross and Pilet 2014; Hazan and Rahat 2010).[9] Their work highlights that parties can change the power relationships between leaders, lower-ranked elites, and the rank and file. While often not using these tools explicitly, their focus on actors building coalitions, laying new rules on top of existing ones, and strategically reinterpreting existing regulations echoes theories of incremental institutional change (see Mahoney and Thelen 2010).

These studies have been important and set out questions for subsequent research. Why do parties adopt a particular organizational format in the first place? To identify the starting point of the causal process, we need to disentangle structural factors and actors' political maneuvering and carefully trace the political process that led to parties adopting specific organizational

characteristics. Moreover, considering historical and strategic approaches together highlights a theoretical paradox about the development of party organizations. If positive feedback effects or negative externalities explained the
stability of parties' organizational characteristics, we would expect attempts
to depart from these characteristics to dissipate over time as more and more
actors adapt to the practices in place. This view, however, does not account
for many parties' continual reform attempts and organizational innovations.
In turn, when party elites identify a part of their organization that requires reform, strategic approaches would expect these actors to pass such reforms—
particularly when their organization does not correspond to current political
demands. However, why actors often fail to pass such reforms, pass only a
small part of them, or require a long time to do so has remained puzzling.

The previous chapters have been a step toward answering these questions.
In doing so, they aimed to start bridging the strange fragmentation of the
party politics scholarship by drawing on historical approaches developed in
the study of Latin American politics and using them to investigate the organizational development of one of Europe's most prominent party families.
The book complemented historical approaches with strategic approaches' emphasis on politics and contingency by bringing in recent advances in theories
of critical juncture and self-undermining processes of institutional development. Though rare in research on political parties, these approaches have
been prominent in the study of political regimes, public policy, and political
economy.[10]

ORIGINS OF PARTIES' ORGANIZATIONAL CHARACTERISTICS

Critical juncture theory helps take issues of historical causality seriously.
When analyzing the origins of the rules to select the party's national leaders, several competing explanations came to mind. These rules could have
been endogenous to the structure of the political system, the organization of
predecessor parties, or the territorial divisions imposed by the Allied liberation and occupation strategies. These antecedent factors could have closed off
alternative options or determined actors' preferences in a way that one, and
only one, option seemed to be the natural way to go (Collier and Collier 1991,
27; Capoccia 2015, 168–69). If the evidence had confirmed this, the leadership
selection process would have been an intermediate rather than independent
variable and the true cause would have been the antecedent factors.

My analysis has systematically addressed such concerns by tracing the relevant decision-making process. I have followed what can be summarized in a

TABLE 8.5. Comparative summary, origins of leadership selection process

	DC	ÖVP	CDU
Variable	*Rules to select national party leaders*		
Key actors	Moderates in Southern and Central Italy (e.g., De Gasperi) Catholic trade unionists (e.g., Gronchi) Christian partisans and academics from Northern Italy (e.g., Dossetti) Roman youth group (e.g., Ravaioli) Catholic Church	Elites of prewar Catholic trade unions (e.g., Kunschak, Weinberger) Elites of prewar farmer organizations (e.g., Figl) Elites of prewar business groups (e.g., Raab) Political elites in Western *Länder* Catholic Church	Conservative Protestants in Northern Germany (e.g., Holzapfel) Left-leaning Catholics in Berlin, Hesse, and Rhineland (e.g., Kaiser, Arnold) Centrist Catholics in Rhineland (e.g., Adenauer) Catholic Church
Potentially relevant antecedent factors	Territorial divisions imposed by Allied liberation strategy Organization of PPI History of regional divisions and identities	Allied occupation policy Federalism Elite continuity and prewar experience Austrian corporatism Organization of Christian Social Party	Allied licensing and occupation policy Federalism Regional, social, and denominational conflicts Legal structure Organization of Center Party
Evidence for the importance of political choices	Four different statutory proposals between 1944 and 1946 Attempts to alter leadership selection process Political entrepreneurship by De Gasperi	League structure proposal as trade unionists' strategic choice Divergence from the structure of prewar organizations ÖVP's organization preceded resurrection of corporatism Coalition engineering during four party conferences	Competing proposals Political entrepreneurship by Adenauer Compromise solution after five years of bargaining

set of questions that can also be used to study the origins of the same or different organizational characteristics in other parties. First, what is the organizational variable that is hypothesized to do the causal work?[11] Second, who are the key actors whose preferences and choices are consequential for the institutional selection process? Third, which antecedent factors can constrain the set of options available to actors? Fourth, are actors able to choose among different options when specifying the value of the variable of interest? My results highlight that the Italian, Austrian, and German Christian Democrats' initial leadership selection process was not endogenous to antecedent factors (table 8.5). Analyzing the CDS, CDA, CSV, MRP, and LDP has yielded further support for the importance of political choices in explaining the origins of parties' rules to select their national leaders.

STABILITY AND CHANGE IN

PARTY ORGANIZATIONS

Institutional theories are based on the premise that institutions affect what strategies seem to be the most promising to actors to achieve a predefined goal. When moving from the origins to the consequences of party organizations, we are thus required to spell out the following questions: What goal do actors pursue? What resources do actors need to achieve their goal given the institutional playing field? How does the institutional playing field direct actors' strategies to obtain these resources?

In chapter 2, I assumed that party elites seek leadership positions within their organization. This was plausible because intraparty power has been theorized as being beneficial for achieving rent- and ideology-related goals (Schlesinger 1984, 381–89). My findings back this initial assumption. Some conflicts between party elites were primarily driven by ideological concerns, like between left-, right-wing, and centrist groups in the early CDU, whereas rent-seeking motivations fueled other conflicts, like in the mature DC. To achieve any of these goals, party elites tried to gain influence within their party. An important way of ensuring influence in the party was to be part of its national leadership. This made the selection process of the party leadership an important set of rules. It affected where party elites were required to look for support and whether they were incentivized to build factions.

Their initial level of factionalism became deeply rooted within parties' internal practices and organization. This process was driven by actors trying to expand and strengthen the networks they had been incentivized to form. This entailed, for instance, campaigning, ideological appeals, or clientelism, and the party organization determined at which internal selectorate efforts were targeted. At this stage, actors took advantage of surrounding institutional and structural conditions to acquire the resources valuable under the level of factionalism in place. Moreover, party elites tried to increase the value of their networks by modifying the party organization in their favor. Because party organizations are modified all the time (e.g., Janda 1980; Katz and Mair 1992), I built on Capoccia and Ziblatt's (2010) episode analysis to identify the relevant moments of actual and potential organizational changes. Guiding questions for the analysis were as follows: How does the party's initial internal playing field drive actors' attempts to modify the party organization? How do these organizational modifications influence party elites' incentive structure?

Organizational changes reinforced actors' incentive structure and the corresponding level of factionalism. In the DC, small factions successfully promoted the introduction of a PR system for internal elections not only at the national but also at the subnational level. Larger factions, in return, tried to dampen small factions by introducing an electoral threshold that factions needed to overcome to be represented at the national party congress and party council. Both statutory changes emphasized the importance of factional ties and reproduced it at different levels of the party organization. The case studies have underlined that a process of institutional (self-)reinforcement entailed behavioral rather than institutional stability (Greif 2006, 168). The parties' organizations continued to be modified but thereby confirmed rather than altered the level of factionalism.

Earlier organizational changes were more momentous for party development than changes implemented at a later point in time, which is in line with predictions from the path dependence literature (e.g., Pierson 2000a, 263). For example, as part of an attempt to reform the ÖVP, Austria's Christian Democrats centralized the leadership selection process in 1980. Had that decision been taken at the moment of party formation, my theoretical framework would have predicted the emergence of factions. In 1980, however, party elites had been incentivized to build strong networks in their respective organizational branches for thirty-five years. These networks were not gone overnight. Majority elites could rely on their influence and contacts to counter that organizational change and shifted power to another executive committee that was still selected in a decentralized way. Similarly, the entrenched internal practices allowed CDU elites to counter the German Constitutional Court's ruling to centralize the process to select national party leadership positions.

Yet parties' initial level of factionalism endogenously created incentives not only for party elites to maintain and reinforce the level of factionalism but also to change it. By undermining parties' ability to integrate different social and political interests and innovate its platform or organization, a very low and very high level of factionalism threatened party elites' political career, because a lack of party adaptation increased the risk of electoral decline. Lupu (2016) has rightly highlighted that electoral defeats were a particular threat to the party president, who was likely to be replaced as leader after a defeat, whereas lower-ranked elites had a longer time horizon. The book's analysis echoed this observation. Yet changing the level of factionalism risked entailing imminent costs and only uncertain and more midterm benefits even for the party president. Resolving gridlock and integrating new social and political groups would certainly have been conducive to implementing programmatic and organizational reforms. Yet it was uncertain whether and, if yes, when the party president would benefit from these reforms, while moving power away from factions in highly factionalized parties or making space for factions in weakly factionalized parties risked jeopardizing the president's own power base. While other party elites might have had less to lose and even benefited from an election defeat by one of them becoming the new party president, a lack of party adaptation was hardly an acceptable outcome for them either. Their careers, too, were on the line because ongoing electoral decline entailed the risk of losing, among others, ministerial portfolios and legislative seats for themselves and members of their network.

The interplay between both processes helps understand the change (attempts) and stability in political parties. Electoral decline strengthened the call for reform by minority elites in weakly factionalized parties and those without factional backing in highly factionalized parties. While often unable to completely ignore the reform pressure from lower-rank elites, majority elites and factional leaders respectively often responded with changes that left the level of factionalism untouched. Where changes appeared far-reaching at first, like with the introduction of primaries to select the ÖVP's candidates or the replacement of the party's decentralized leadership selection process,[12] countermeasures were often introduced to protect those in power. To break this antireform coalition, institutional reformers often sought institutional change outside the party. In Japan, LDP defectors joined a multiparty coalition that replaced the country's SNTV system, which had been an important part in the reinforcement of factionalism from the national to the local level. Under the new electoral system, local brokers and parliamentarians had little reason to continue supporting factions. This strengthened the LDP's prefectural branches in their push for party reform, which resulted in the change from a centralized to a mixed leadership selection process, a moderation of the level of factionalism, and more substantive party adaptation. Similar developments also started within Italy's DC, with Mario Segni and others leaving the DC to campaign successfully for abolishing the preferential voting system that had been an important reinforcing factor behind the party's high level of factionalism. Had the reformers in the DC had more time before the next election to capitalize on these external changes to expand their coalition within the party, the DC might have taken a trajectory similar to the LDP's.

Moving beyond the Book's Cases and Final Remarks

This book has shown the theoretical and empirical efforts necessary to comprehensively explain the varying adaptation of a well-defined set of parties. The importance of rules and internal competition in my account of party adaptation has implications for the scope of my argument beyond the cases discussed in this book.

Application of formal rules.   An organization needs to have a set of rules and procedures that actually structures the selection of its leadership to develop the dynamics I have described. This usually involves the existence of a formal party statute and the general agreement that the specified rules will be applied and respected when choosing the national leaders. Actors are certainly reluctant to follow regulations that do not serve their interests (Duverger 1951, 76; Sartori 1976, 84; Panebianco 1988, 35). Still, the formal procedures that organize how national party leaders are selected have been generally followed in the parties under investigation, arguably because party elites have been incentivized to detect rivals who are not playing by the rules (see Katz and Mair 1992, 6). There are, however, parties where formal rules have less of an impact. Argentina's Peronists have been one such case of an informally organized and weakly institutionalized party in which the lack of routinized procedures and rules entailed a high level of fluidity and unpredictability (Levitsky 2003). In many personalistic or charismatic parties, like Silvio Berlusconi's Forza Italia or Ecuador's Partido Roldosista, leaders can often bypass formal rules, if the latter exist at all (Freidenberg and Levitsky 2006, 192–95; McDonnell 2013, 220–24). In these cases, intraparty politics is usually not particularly rule-bound, and they consequently do not fall within my universe of cases.

Democratic intraparty competition.   The parties discussed in this book held internal elections to select their leaders and party elites who wanted to gain power were required to win over a particular selectorate. The variation in the selectorate they needed to win over explained party elites' varying incentives to form factions in my framework. However, some parties do not hold internal elections to select their leaders. Candidates for leadership positions or public offices are sometimes not elected but appointed by a single party leader or a closed elite circle (Chandra 2004, 246–61; Wills-Otero 2016, 762, 766). We are thus unlikely to see similar dynamics as described in the previous chapters. In the parties discussed in this book, party elites have also been free to form and join factions if the latter were deemed useful to advance their interests. Yet this freedom to promote one's own interests, even when the latter goes against the position of the incumbent leadership, is absent in some parties. Many communist and socialist parties, as highlighted in the brief within-country comparisons in part 2, applied the Leninist principle of democratic centralism. It prohibited any critic toward or defection from the party line once the latter had been established. While such rules may be in place only temporarily, like in Italy's PSI between 1949 and 1953 (Zariski 1962, 374; Barnes 1967, 45–48), they can entail an important legacy. The suppression of factionalism can also be based on informal institutions, like socially acceptable conducts of behavior. For instance, despite the absence of formal democratic centralism, norms of unity and conformity in Germany's SPD and Austria's SPÖ de facto blocked the open manifestation of dissent and led to the expulsion of the (small) left-wing opposition to the parties' transformation into more moderate center-left parties. As such institutions restrict intraparty pluralism and constrain actors in their efforts to compete for their preferences within the party, such cases would not fulfill my scope conditions.

However, although my theoretical framework is not applicable to all parties, we would not expect it only to apply to the parties discussed in this book as long as those two conditions are met. Anecdotally, we can see some support for my argument in parties in other parts of the world that operate based on a set of formal rules and allow for democratic intraparty competition. The Chilean Christian Democratic Party (PDC) meets the two scope conditions and displays the characteristics predicted by my argument. The PDC has used a centralized leadership selection process, has experienced intense factionalism, and has shown a rather low level of adaptation (Huneeus 2003). In fact, there is no reason to expect the dynamics predicted by my framework to unfold only in political parties. Rule-based and competitive leadership elections also take place in other organizations, like nongovernmental organizations and trade unions. While systematically assessing this point would go beyond the scope of this book, my argument makes a quite general prediction beyond the realm of party politics. First, the type of networks actors will build in their ambition to assume leadership positions in a specific organization will depend on whether positions on this leadership board are primarily elected either by an assembly that brings together delegates from different branches of the organization or by these branches autonomously. Second, the existence of a mix of networks both within and across organizational branches enhances the organization's ability to adapt to a changing environment.

In conclusion, historical institutionalism in general and theories of critical juncture and self-reinforcing and self-undermining institutional development in particular have proven to provide a valuable tool kit for the analysis of party adaptation, factionalism, and party organizations. They are helpful to move "beyond the crude classification of party organization" in terms of mass, catch-all, or cartel party and redress many of the challenges that Mair (1997, 42–43) identified more than twenty-five years ago: focusing our analysis on a concrete organizational variable we expect to affect the internal life of parties, specifying the causes and effects of organizational change, and developing and testing hypotheses that "might account both for the diversity of" and "change within party organizations." My findings suggest a perspective on party adaptation that combines a focus on the demand- and supply-side-specific challenges to which political parties need to adapt with the entrenched institutional legacy that constrains their decision-makers when making strategic choices. It is only by disaggregating party organizations into specific institutional variables and laying out how those variables drive actors' behavior that we can systematically understand what guides a party's ability to adapt to profound societal and political transformations.

Acknowledgments

This book is the result of several years of research and work across eight countries. I am deeply grateful to fellow researchers and colleagues at the University of Oxford, Yale University, the University of Vienna, and Swansea University for their intellectual and moral support. A special thanks goes to Oxford University's Department of Politics and International Relations, Magdalen College, Nuffield College, and Pembroke College as well as Swansea University's Department of Politics, Philosophy, and International Relations and School of Social Sciences for the generous material support and working environment during the development and completion of this project. I also want to gratefully acknowledge the support of the International Association for the Study of German Politics. I also owe a debt of gratitude to the staff at the Archivio Storico and Archivio Andreotti dell'Istituto Luigi Sturzo in Rome, Historical Archives of the European Union in Florence, the archive at the Karl von Vogelsang-Institut in Vienna, the Archiv für Christlich-Demokratische Politik in Sankt Augustin, Bundesarchiv in Koblenz, the archive of the Stiftung Bundeskanzler Adenauer-Haus in Röhndorf, as well as at the Archives Nationales in Pierrefitte-sur-Seine for their help, patience, and expertise. I am also thankful to the Austrian ÖVP, Luxembourgian CSV, Portuguese CDS, and Swedish KD, the Austrian Bundesanstalt Statistik, the Belgian Centre Permanent pour la Citoyenneté et la Participation, the Portuguese Instituto Amaro da Costa, the Swedish Riksarkivet, and the Swiss Bundesarchiv for kindly scanning some archival documents and transferring them digitally.

Many colleagues have provided invaluable feedback and encouragement over the years. I want to express my sincere and heartfelt gratitude to Giovanni Capoccia, Amel Ahmed, Ben Ansell, Nancy Bermeo, Michael Bernhard,

Nicole Bolleyer, Elias Dinas, Noam Gidron, Jane Gingrich, Ezequiel González Ocantos, David Hine, Stathis Kalyvas, Heidi Maurer, Wolfgang C. Müller, Peter Pulzer, Petra Schleiter, Jürgen Selke-Witzel, Stephen Whitefield, two anonymous reviewers, and numerous participants at conferences, talks, and workshops at APSA, CES, DVPW, ECPR, PSA, and beyond. I am deeply grateful for their advice and hope I have done it justice. Moreover, I am thankful to Urs Altermatt, Gabriela Borz, João Carlos Espada, Luís Gouveia Fernandes, Tim Frey, Magnus Hagevi, Hanspeter Kriesi, Jon Pierre, and Anders Widfeldt for their help in accessing data on several parties discussed in this book.

Behind every book, there is a publisher who believes in it, and I am immensely grateful to the University of Chicago Press and especially to my editors, Sara Doskow and Erika Barrios. They were excited about this book from the moment I proposed it and engaged with it at a level that I would have not dared imagine. I also thank Michaela Luckey, Stephen Twilley, Katherine Faydash, and David Robertson. I could not have wished for a better publishing experience.

Parts of this book draw on material I published earlier, and I thank *Political Research Quarterly*, *Social Sciences History*, the *Political Studies Review*, and the *MIP Zeitschrift für Parteienwissenschaft* for the opportunity to reuse (and significantly expand) on this material as part of this book.

Last but not least, I want to express my personal gratitude to my wife, Tabea, for her continuous encouragement, understanding, and selfless support during the challenging moments of this project; to my parents, Daniela and Rudibert; to my sister, Franziska; to my family-in-law for always believing in me; to my friends for enduring endless conversations about party adaptation; and to God. Without them, this book would not have been possible, and it is dedicated to them.

Appendixes

Appendix A: Primary Sources for Figure 1.2 and Alternative Cutoff

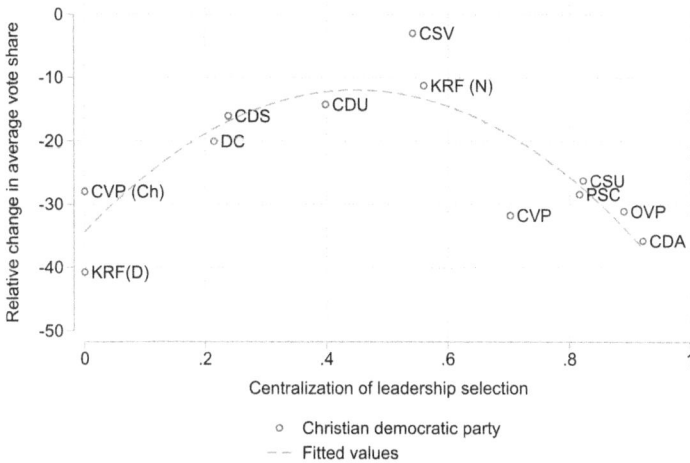

FIGURE A.1. Christian democratic leadership selection and relative electoral change, 1960–2013
Source: Election data from Armingeon et al. (2022) and Nordsieck (2021). Centralization: parties' first party statutes. See the data description in appendix A for further details.

Data on the first party statutes of the Austrian ÖVP, the Belgian CVP, the Danish KRF, and the Dutch CDA have been taken from the respective country chapters in Richard S. Katz and Peter Mair, *Party Organizations: A Data Handbook on Party Organizations in Western Democracies, 1960–90* (London: Sage, 1992).

Electronic or printed copies of the first party statutes of the remaining parties have been kindly provided for the Belgian PSC by the Belgian Centre Permanent pour la Citoyenneté et la Participation (CPCP); the German

CDU: Archiv für Christlich-Demokratische Politik; German CSU: Flech-theim, Ossip Kurt 1962. Dokumente zur parteipolitischen Entwicklung in Deutschland seit 1945. Berlin: Dokumenten-Verlag; the Italian DC: Archivio della Democrazia Cristiana of the Istituto Luigi Sturzo; the Luxembourgian CSV: Archives of the Christian Social People's Party; Portuguese CDS: Insti-tuto Amaro da Costa and the Portuguese People's Party (CDS-PP); the Swiss CVP: Schweizerisches Bundesarchiv; Swedish KDS: private data collection of Magnus Hagevi, Anders Widfeldt and the Swedish Riksarkivet.

Data on the Norwegian KRF have been available only since 1960 and have been taken from the chapter in Katz and Mair (1992). I am thankful to Urs Altermatt, Nancy Bermeo, João Carlos Espada, Tim Frey, Magnus Hagevi, Hanspeter Kriesi, Wolfgang C. Müller, Jon Pierre, Anders Widfeldt, and the Swedish Christian Democratic Party for their support in gathering the data.

Appendix B: Note on the Archival Material and Data Collection

To trace the origins and development of parties' organization, level of faction-alism, and adaptation, I conducted archival research in eight archives in four countries. The archival sources are referenced in the footnotes in the empiri-cal chapters in the following format: *Title/name of source*, date, page(s), archi-val code or collection or box/folder *or* author, year of the published collection.

The archives, the used archival acronyms, the years in which the research was conducted, and any additional primary document collection used are listed below. Translations from Italian, German, and French into English are my own.

Supplementary material online provides a breakdown of all archival col-lections and boxes that I consulted. It indicates whether material from a spe-cific box has been referenced in the book's chapters. The decision whether to reference specific material was made on the basis of the material's proba-tive value to assess the book's argument against competing explanations. In a separate tab in the supplementary material, I then list all referenced archival documents by box, archive, and case.

CHAPTER 3: ITALY'S DC

Archives

Archivio Storico of the Istituto Luigi Sturzo in Rome (ASILS 2013, 2015)
Archivio Giulio Andreotti of the Istituto Luigi Sturzo in Rome (AGA 2016)
Historical Archive of the EU in Florence (HAEU 2019).

Published Collections

Damilano, Andrea, ed. 1968, *Atti e documenti della Democrazia Cristiana, 1943–1967.* Vols. 1 and 2. Rome: Cinque Lune.

Salvi, Franco, ed. 1959. *Atti e documenti della Democrazia Cristiana, 1943–1959.* Rome: Cinque Lune.

Trotta, Giuseppe. 1995. *Giuseppe Dossetti. Scritti politici, 1943–1951.* Geneva: Marietti.

CHAPTER 4: AUSTRIA'S ÖVP

Archive

Archive of the Karl von Vogelsang-Institut in Vienna (KVV 2016–17)

Published Collections

Diem, Peter, and Heinrich Neisser. 1969. *Zeit zur Reform. Parteireform, Parlamentsreform, Demokratiereform.* Vienna: Wedl.

Gehler, Michael. 1994. *Karl Gruber. Reden und Dokumente 1945–1953. Eine Auswahl.* Vienna: Böhlau.

Kriechbaumer, Robert. 1995b. *Von der Lagerstraße zum Ballhausplatz. Quellen zur Gründungss- und Frühgeschichte der ÖVP 1938–1949.* Salzburg: IT-Verlag.

Weinberger, Lois. 1948. *Tatsachen, Begegnungen und Gespräche. Ein Buch um Österreich.* Vienna: Österreichischer Verlag.

Wohnout, Helmut. 1997. *Demokratie und Geschichte. Jahrbuch des Karl-von-Vogelsang-Instituts zur Erforschung der Geschichte der christlichen Demokratie in Österreich.* Vienna: Böhlau.

CHAPTER 5: GERMANY'S CDU

Archives

Archiv für Christlich-Demokratische Politik in Sankt Augustin (ACDP 2013, 2020)
Bundesarchiv in Koblenz (BA 2020)
Archive of the Stiftung Bundeskanzler Adenauer-Haus in Röhndorf (StBKAH 2020)

Published Collections

Buchstab, Günther. 1998. *Adenauer: "Stetigkeit in der Politik." Die Protokolle des CDU-Bundesvorstands 1961–1965.* Düsseldorf: Droste.

Buchstab, Günther. 1994. *Adenauer: ". . . um den Frieden zu gewinnen." Die Protokolle des CDU-Bundesvorstands 1957–1961.* Düsseldorf: Droste.

Buchstab, Günther. 1990. *Adenauer: "Wir haben wirklich etwas geschaffen." Die Proto-kolle des CDU-Bundesvorstands 1953–1957.* Düsseldorf: Droste.

Buchstab, Günther. 1986. *Adenauer: "Es musste alles neu gemacht werden." Die Proto-kolle des CDU-Bundesvorstandes 1950–1953.* Stuttgart: Klett-Cotta.

Noelle, Elisabeth, and Erich Peter Neumann. 1975. *Jahrbuch der Öffentlichen Meinung, 1947–1955.* Allensbach: Verlag für Demoskopie.

Reigrotzki, Erich. 2015. *Bundesstudie 1953.* GESIS Datenarchiv, Köln. ZA0145 Datenfile Version 2.0.0: https://doi.org/10.4232/1.11992.

CHAPTER 7: FRANCE'S MRP

Archive

Archives Nationales in Pierrefitte-sur-Seine (AN 2013, 2016)

Published Collection

Michelet, Claude. 1971. *Mon père Edmond Michelet. D'après ses notes intimes.* Paris: Presses de la Cité.

My analysis combines the archival material with comparative and country-specific literature in political science and history, online and media sources, and public opinion data. I began the research by drawing on secondary sources to establish a timeline of key events and identify key actors. Descriptive accounts of events and individuals provided a first set of causal process observations.

Questions remained, which guided the primary archival research. I entered the field with a set of questions based on my prior research. Theoretical considerations guided the selection of archives, collections within archives, boxes within collections, and documents within boxes. To test the observable implications presented in chapters 1 and 2 for the book's and alternative accounts, two types of archival collections were particularly relevant: (1) collections of political organizations, most notably of the relevant parties (e.g., CDU), party factions (e.g., EAK), and party meetings (e.g., minutes of the party congress, minutes of the party leadership board), and (2) collections of individual politicians who were key actors during theoretically relevant events of the parties' history. For example, I visited the Historical Archives of the European Union to consult the files of Alcide De Gasperi, the German Federal Archive to access the Jakob Kaiser collection, and the archive of the Stiftung Bundeskanzler Adenauer-Haus to study the files of Konrad Adenauer.

I consulted online and hard-copy inventories of the archival collections of relevant organizations (e.g., CDU federal party, EAK) and individuals (e.g., Adenauer, Kaiser). I double-checked my selection of archival collections through communications with the respective archivists. In this correspondence, I did not specify the arguments that I sought to test to avoid selection bias. Instead, I focused on case-specific empirical questions. To probe the existence of additional relevant material, I switched from specific empirical questions to broader topics, inquiring whether other collections might hold material on a particular topic (e.g., German rearmament).

I selected documents on the basis of their relevance to test the observable implications of the book's framework and the alternative theories specified in chapters 1 and 2. If case-specific alternative explanations emerged during the archival or case-specific research, they were included and tested. The insights generated through the archival research were included in the timeline of key events.

In a final step, I embedded the newly gained insights and refined timeline in the broader historical context through an additional survey of secondary sources on topics, events, and individuals I felt I needed more contextual information on. I used studies from political science and history in English, German, Italian, and French. I followed the recent suggestions in J. Møller, "Feet of Clay? How to Review Political Science Papers That Make Use of the Work of Historians," *PS: Political Science & Politics* 53, no. 2 (2020): 253–57. These suggestions include using classic as well as recently conducted studies, branching out into political and ecclesiastic history, and providing explicit page numbers when using accounts of specific events as evidence.

Overall, the collected evidence was deemed to be sufficiently detailed and comprehensive to test the observable implications of the book's main competing accounts.

Notes

Chapter One

1. See, among others, case studies by Bale (2012), Gauja (2016), and Levitsky (2003).

2. Madison did not refer to political parties or party factions in today's sense but to the inevitability of any society to fragment into groups with opposing interests. Scholars of political parties and political representation have often drawn on this when describing the competition between and within parties.

3. Proposals by the rank and file primarily gain in importance by influencing discussions among party elites.

4. For more recent empirical tests and rebuttals of May, see Van Holsteyn, Den Ridder, and Koole (2017) and Norris (1995).

5. See Dilling (2023) for an in-depth elaboration of this point.

6. These characteristics are echoed in DiSalvo's (2012) description of factions as "engines of change."

7. See, e.g., Boucek (2012).

8. See Levitsky (2003) and Hunter (2010) for the few exceptions.

9. Van Kemseke (2006), Kaiser (2007), and Accetti's (2019) history of political thought are the few exceptions. See also the edited volumes by Kselman and Buttigieg (2003), Gehler and Kaiser (2004), and Van Hecke and Gerard (2004).

10. To ensure that the results in figure 1.2 are not driven by Christian Democrats' victories in the immediate postwar era, appendix A provides the figure showing the relative change for 1960 and 2013. The curvilinear pattern persists.

11. The only complete outlier is the Swedish KDS. Its average vote share increased from 1.83 to 6.99 percent. As a complete outlier, it is not included in figure 1.2. Data on the Finnish case has been missing.

Chapter Two

1. See Wiliarty (2010, 2–4) for the development of the adaptation-against-activists point. Similar to Levitsky, Kitschelt (1994) proposed an argument that highlights organizational entrenchment and power centralization (coined leadership accountability). Seawright (2012, 9)

has rightly noted that Kitschelt's concept of organizational entrenchment is more inclusive than Levitsky's (2003) focus on the de facto importance of parties' internal rules and bureaucracies.

2. The following paragraph draws on Dilling (2023).

3. Freidenberg and Levitsky (2006) have highlighted that local units in informally organized parties often emerge without the central party's knowledge or approval. Their lack of formal ties with the central party make them more similar to local cliques or caucuses than to territorial party branches in formally organized parties.

4. The following paragraphs draw partially on Dilling (2014).

5. The leadership board varies across parties in its level of formal and de facto power (e.g., Ziblatt 2017; Wills-Otero 2016). I discuss later what this means for my study.

6. Here, it is important to remember the two scope conditions of my argument: political parties need to allow for internal competition and have formal rules that regulate the selection of the party leadership.

7. Alternative terms to describe a centralized and decentralized selection process would be indirect (i.e., centralized) and direct (i.e., decentralized). Yet this would risk causing confusion with the terminology used by Hazan and Rahat (2010) and Cross and Pilet (2014). They described methods to select the individual party leader and candidates for public office in terms of direct and inclusive selection procedures. The inclusiveness of the leadership selection process reflects a continuum ranging from a single person or small group of elites to all party members or the entire electorate. I discuss the potential impact of variation in inclusiveness on the level of factionalism later.

8. I do not consider the case in which a party branch does not have a leader. While leadership struggles in subnational party branches or the party's parliamentary group are interesting, my focus is on the interaction between party elites coming from different organizational branches at the national level. I thus assume that organizational branches that are involved in the leadership selection at the national level have a leader. This is a plausible assumption for the parties belonging to my set of cases.

9. This is because majority $= ([D_A + D_B + D_C + D_D + \ldots D_N]/2) + 1$, whereby $D_A, \ldots D_N$ denotes the total number of delegates that party branch A . . . N sends to the NC. It does not need to be an absolute majority system for my model to work. The election system used for NE elections simply affects the threshold $M+_i$ and $M-_i$ are required to overcome to gain representation in the NE. My model also yields unambiguous predictions regardless of whether the number of delegates is constant across party branches. This is not the case in many political parties where the number of delegates depends on, for instance, the membership size or the electoral performance of the delegating party branch N. If the share of delegates varies across party branches to such an extent that a single party branch N sends a majority of delegates to the NC, which is a very unlikely scenario, then my model would predict that $M+_N$ would focus on building a strong network among the delegates from their own party branch, whereas $M+_{non-N}$ and $M-_i$ would try to break $M+_N$'s network and gain support among N's delegates. If $M+_{non-N}$ and $M-_i$ manage to do this, $M+_N$ are expected to try to gain support from delegates from other party branches. The reasoning for these predictions is outlined in the following sections in the main text.

10. Krauss and Pekkanen (2011) have made a similar point on SNTV and the LDP's factionalism.

11. See Cross and Blais (2012), Gauja (2016), Scarrow (2014), and Wauters (2014).

12. Also termed *positive feedback* or *increasing returns processes* (Pierson 2000b, 74).

13. This point is consistent with the coalition shifting described by the endogenous institutional change literature (Thelen 2004, 33, 295; Streeck and Thelen 2005, 9, 19; Mahoney and Thelen 2010, 10). Of course, minority factions could simply leave the party. Indeed, threatening to leave might be part of minority factions' bargaining strategy to increase their influence in the party leadership. Yet defection implies costs. Actors face, for instance, the uncertainty over being potentially worse off by leaving the party. While Ceron (2015) has provided theoretical underpinning for the likelihood of factional splits, for my argument, it suffices to say that if minority factions leave the party, the party's institutional playing field is unlikely to change in a path-reversing manner. Indeed, there is likely to be even less opposition to majority factions seeking to reinforce their dominance.

14. While minority elites can threaten to defect in parliament to put pressure on the majority coalition, such rebellion is unlikely to develop into high factionalism given the low benefits of cross-branch networks to assume party leadership positions.

15. To reiterate, passing reforms does not guarantee electoral success (Gauja 2016, 56-57). Yet failing to respond to changing public concerns weakens parties' connection with voters and increases the risk of declining levels of party identification and electoral support (Morgan 2011, 75). This does not mean that parties that do not pass reforms cannot survive or revive. If contextual conditions make their traditional programmatic or organizational resources valuable again, electoral recovery can occur (Cyr 2017). Yet this suggests that the electoral prospects of weakly and highly factionalized parties depend more on contextual conditions than is the case for moderately factionalized parties.

16. Appendix B and supplementary material 1 provide an overview of the archives, data, and data collection.

Chapter Three

1. On the groups forming the DC, see Magri (1954, 221-24), Webster (1961, 129-70), Chassériaud (1965, 272-73), Pombeni (1976, 151-52; 1979, 380-81), Scoppola (1991, 109), and Capperucci (2010, 26-27, 45).

2. *Congresso Interregionale*, 29-30.07.1944, p. 49, in *Atti e documenti della Democrazia Cristiana, 1943-1959*, ed. Franco Salvi (Rome: Cinque Lune). Primary data is referenced as follows: title, date, page(s), archive or collection or box/folder, (if applicable) URL.

3. *Direzione Provvisoria del Partito to Comitati Regionali di Milano, Torino, Genova, Bologna, Venezia*, 29.04.1944, Archivio Storico della Democrazia Cristiana of the Istituto Luigi Sturzo (ASILS), Fondo Spataro Sc. 9/Fasc. 41; *Mozione della Direzione Centrale*, 28.04.1945, in Salvi (1959, 119-20).

4. *O.d.g. della Direzione Centrale*, 30.05.1945; *Direzione Centrale*, 09.06.1945, in Salvi (1959, 126-27); *Le decisioni del Convegno del Consiglio Nazionale dei Segretari provinciali e del Comitato provvisorio Alta Italia*, in *Democrazia. Cristiana. Bollettino della Direzione del Partito*, 19.08.1945, pp. 1-2, Historical Archives of the EU (hereafter HAEU), Fondo Alcide De Gasperi (hereafter ADG) 77; *De Gasperi from Salerno*, 15.04.1945, pp. 1, 6-7, HAEU-ADG-76.

5. *Idee Ricostruttive della Democrazia Cristiana*, 1943, p. 6, HAEU-ADG-76; *La Convocazione del Consiglio Nazionale and Norme per la designazione dei Consilatori Nazionali, in Democrazia Cristiana. Bollettino della Direzione del Partito*, 14.07.1945, pp. 1-2, HAEU-ADG-77; *Consiglio Nazionale*, 01.03.1945, pp. 14-15, HAEU-ADG-81; *Indirizzi politico-sociali della Democrazia*

Cristiana, April 1945, p. 53; *Convegno Nazionale Democrazia Cristiana, Seduta pomeridiana*, 31.07.1945, pp. 10–11; *Convegno Nazionale, Seduta antimeridiana*, 01.08.1945, p. 21; *Convegno Nazionale, Seduta pomeridiana*, 01.08.1945, pp. 4–5, all in HAEU-ADG-80; *Il progretto di statuto e le mozioni sulla riforma costituzionale, sulla riforma agraria, e sui problem sindacali presentate da "Tendenza" e "Politica d'oggi" al I Congresso Nazionale della Democrazia Cristiana*, 24–27.04.1946, HAEU-ADG-78.

6. *Partito Popolare Italiano, Statuto*, 18.01.1919, http://www.altavillahistorica.it/vita-civile /amministrazione/amministratori/propaganda-e-risultati-elettorali/241-partito-popolare-iatliano.

7. *Congresso Interregionale*, 29–30.07.1944, in Salvi (1959, 49); *Verbale*, 31.07.1944, ASILS-Consiglio Nazionale-Sc. 1/1; *Lo Statuto*, 1945, Art. 14, 16, ASILS-DC Statuti.

8. For instance, Dossetti became deputy party leader. See *Direzione Centrale*, 04.08.1945, in Salvi (1959, 117–18, 136).

9. *Lo Statuto*, 1945, Art. 16; *Progetto di Statuto*, 1946, Art. 98, ASILS-DC Statuti; *Direzione Centrale*, 17.04.1946, in Salvi (1959, 177–78).

10. *Il progretto di statuto e le mozioni sulla riforma costituzionale, sulla riforma agrarian, e sui problem sindacali presentate da 'Tendenza' e 'Politica d'oggi' al I Congresso Nazionale della Democrazia Cristiana*, 24–27.04.1946, p. 1, HAEU-ADG-78.

11. *Il progretto di statuto e le mozioni sulla riforma costituzionale*, pp. 3–4, 13–14, 17; Art. 22, 24, 44, 45, 47.

12. *Il Consiglio Nazionale eletto dal I Congresso Nazionale*, 24–27.04.1946; *Consiglio Nazionale*, 29.04.1946, in Salvi (1959, 215–18).

13. *Statuto*, 1947, p. 3, ASILS-DC Statuti.

14. *Consiglio Nazionale*, 18–22.09.1946, in Salvi (1959, 239).

15. The selection process taking place within the different organizational branches of the party only accounted for a small part of the seats. Each regional and ancillary branch was entitled to one seat (1.7 percent) and the party's parliamentary group chose five delegates (8.5 percent).

16. Only the leader of the party's parliamentary group and a representative of the Italian General Confederation of Labor (CGIL) were granted ex officio membership.

17. *Una commissione di studi politici dei Democratici Cristiani*, 30.07.1943, HAEU-ADG-76; *Consiglio Nazionale della Democrazia Cristiana*, 01–02.08.1945, HAEU-ADG-80.

18. *Consiglio Nazionale*, 31.07.1944, in Salvi (1959, 52).

19. *L'ampliamento del Consiglio Nazionale e la nuova Direzione del Partito*, in *Bollettino della Direzione del Partito*, 19.08.1945, p. 3, HAEU-ADG-77.

20. *Consiglio Nazionale*, 10–11.09.1944; *Consiglio Nazionale*, 28.02–02.03.1945, HAEU-ADG-81; *Indirizzi Politico-Sociali della Democrazia Cristiana*, April 1945, pp. 52–53, HAEU-ADG-77; *Convegno Nazionale*, 31.07–01.08.1945, HAEU-ADG-80; *Consiglio Nazionale*, 06–09.01.1946, in Salvi (1959, 158–59).

21. On the trade-unionist base, see *Vittorino Veronese to De Gasperi*, 23.04.1946, HAEU -ADG-77.

22. A. Grandi, "Saluto al Congresso," in *Politica Sociale*, 21.04.1946, p. 1, ASILS-Gronchi Primo Parte-Sc. 11/41.

23. *Segretario Politico Piccioni to Dirigenti del Partito*, 15.11.1946, in Salvi (1959, 251–54).

24. *Dossetti to De Gasperi*, 28.02.1946, 07.03.1946, and 04.09.1946, HAEU-ADG-533.

25. V. Zincone, "Preminenza del Governo sul partito riaffermata a Venezia dal Segretario della D.C.," *Il Tempo*, 04.06.1949, HAEU-ADG-78.

26. "La Convocazione del Congresso Nazionale," *Bollettino della Direzione del Partito*, 20.01.1946, p. 2, HAEU-ADG-77.

27. *Il progretto di statuto e le mozioni sulla riforma costituzionale, sulla riforma agrarian, e sui problem sindacali presentate da 'Tendenza' e "Politica d'oggi" al I Congresso Nazionale della Democrazia Cristiana,* 24–27.04.1946, p. 1, Art. 11, HAEU-ADG-78.

28. *Consiglio Nazionale,* 18–22.09.1946, in Salvi (1959, 239).

29. The beginning of the Cold War made the election in April 1948 a critical moment for Italy. The DC promoted the integration with the West and Italy's entry into the NATO, whereas the Socialists and Communists advocated an opening toward the Soviet bloc. As the latter formed an electoral alliance, De Gasperi and the Vatican urged all Catholics to stay united. Eventually, the DC won with 48.5 percent, compared to 31.0 for the PCI-PSI alliance (Capperucci 2010, 169–209).

30. *Statuto,* 1947, Art. 89, ASILS-DC Statuti; *Verbale,* 14.03.1947, ASILS-Direzione Nazionale-Sc. 1/4.

31. *Direzione Centrale,* 08.03.1946, in Salvi (1959, 171); *Statuto,* 1948, Art. 8, 12, ASILS-DC Statuti.

32. *Il Discorso di Gronchi, Pesaro,* 21.11.1948, ASILS-Gronchi Primo Parte-Sc. 14/64; Appunto I and Appunto II con riferimento ai Gruppi di Studio di "Politica Sociale" e del Convegno di Pesaro, 17.11.1948; *Dichiarazione della Direzione Nazionale,* 18.11.1948, ASILS-Direzione Nazionale-Sc. 3/23; *Verbale Seduta Serale,* 20.12.1948, ASILS-Consiglio Nazionale-Sc. 4/11.

33. *Renzo Ascani to Battistini and Gronchi,* 02.02.1948, ASILS-Gronchi Primo Parte-Sc. 14/64.

34. *Samartino Salvatore to Gronchi,* 27.07.1946, ASILS-Gronchi Primo Parte-Sc. 11/41. Moreover, it seems unconvincing that actors' experiences under the truncated form of prewar parliamentary democracy could have helped them to anticipate the dynamics of an open-list PR system with regard to intraparty competition. PR was only used for the last two free elections before the advent of fascism. Furthermore, the system used in 1919 and 1921 allowed allocation of preference votes across party lists—an aspect that encouraged candidate-centered rather intraparty competition and that was not restored in 1946.

35. This included artificially inflating membership figures by retaining members who had died, quit, moved, or had been recorded without their knowledge.

36. Between 1946 and 1992, the DC won a plurality in all general elections and participated in every cabinet.

37. Rae's fractionalization index: PSDI: 0.272, PLI: 0.258, PRI: 0.151, PSI: 0.000. Data from Bardi and Morlino (1992).

38. *Resconto sommario dell'Ufficio Stampa della D.C. Seduta Pomeridiana,* 23.11.1952; *Seduta Antimeridiana,* 24.11.1952; *Seduta Notturna,* 25.11.1952; "Viva Lotta per l'Elezione del Consiglio Nazionale D.C.," *La Stampa,* 27.11.1952, ASILS-Congresso Nazionale-Sc.3.

39. The folder ADG-78 at the HAEU includes De Gasperi's various drafts of his slate of candidates. They were structured along factional lines and cross-checked with the size and membership lists of the different factions. The folder also includes some letters De Gasperi received from factional leaders stating their conditions for joining his slate.

40. *Proposta di Modifica dello Statuto; Seduta Notturna,* 28.06.1954, pp. 3–5; *Seduta Antimeridiana,* 29.06.1954, p. 1, ASILS-Congresso Nazionale-Sc.5/6.

41. *Seduta Pomeridiana,* 15.10.1956; *Seduta Antimeridiana,* 16.10.1956, ASILS-Congresso Nazionale-Sc.6/7-1.

42. *Statuto*, 1957, Art. 72, ASILS-DC Statuti.

43. *Statuto*, 1962, Art. 68, ASILS-DC Statuti.

44. *Seduta Antimeridiana*, 27.04.1949, p. 7, ASILS-Consiglio Nazionale-Sc.5/14.

45. *Seduta Antimeridiana*, 27.04.1949, pp. 8–9; *Seduta Pomeridiana*, 28.04.1949, p. 7, ASILS-Consiglio Nazionale-Sc.5/14.

46. *Verbale*, 24.01.1964, pp. 10–12; *Verbale*, 25.01.1964, pp. 104–7; 27.01.1964, pp. 367–69, ASILS-Consiglio Nazionale-Sc.51/73.

47. *Nuovi Articoli dello Statuto*, Art. 5, 1966, ASILS-DC Statuti.

48. *Statuto*, 1968, Art. 14–16, 95, 99, ASILS-DC Statuti.

49. *Statuto*, 1970, Art. 83, ASILS-DC Statuti.

50. *Statuto*, 1970, Art. 83, ASILS-DC Statuti.

51. *Statuto*, 1972, Art. 89, ASILS-DC Statuti.

52. Quoted in "Che cosè il 'manuale Cencelli,'" *Il Post*, 18.02.2014, http://www.ilpost.it/2014/02/18/manuale-cencelli/.

53. "Fanfani contro i dosaggi DC," *La Stampa*, 106 (239), 23.10.1974, p. 7.

54. *Statuto*, 1976, Art. 86, ASILS-DC Statuti.

55. *Statuto*, 1978, Art. 61–65, 68, ASILS-DC Statuti.

56. *Statuto*, 1984, Art. 20, 74, ASILS-DC Statuti.

57. One parish for every 1,800 to 1,900 inhabitants (Ignazi and Wellhofer 2012, 38).

58. *Caricature*, in *Tribuna Italiana*, 09.10.1971, Archivio Giulio Andreotti (AGA).

59. This is a conservative estimate as survey data usually overreport church attendance (Rossi and Scappini 2012; Vezzoni and Biolcati-Rinaldi 2015).

60. See the collection of letters in DC ASILS-Segretaria Politica-Sc.188/12-1-Forlani.

61. L. Furno, "I dc sono alla ricerca d'un nuovo equilibrio," *La Stampa*, 26.10.1975, AGA.

62. For instance, *Resoluzione Ravaioli*, 20.12.1974, ASILS-Consiglio Nazionale-Sc.56/104; *Relazione del Segretario Politico*, 06–07.12.1980, ASILS-Consiglio Nazionale-Sc.62/132; *Verbale*, 31.07.1981, pp. 1–2, ASILS-Consiglio Nazionale-Sc.64/139-1.

63. Propaganda 2 was a criminal and secret society associated with illegal shares dealing, corruption, assassinations, and conspiracies against the Italian state. Its discovery implicated numerous politicians and led to the resignation of the Forlani government (Boucek 2012, 164; Smith 1997, 466–67).

64. *Intervento del Presidente del Consiglio Giulio Andreotti al Consiglio Nazionale della DC*, 18.11.1989, pp. 3–22, AGA-Democrazia Cristiana-Busta 1038.

65. *Sintesi della Relazione del Segretario Politico Arnaldo Forlani, Consiglio Nazionale*, 17–18.11.1989, pp. 3–4, 6, AGA-Democrazia Cristiana-Busta 1038; F. Proietti, "Andreotti: Il Pci non mi pare in liquidazione," *Corriere della Sera*, 19.11.1989, p. 2, AGA-Democrazia Cristiana-Busta 1038.

66. *Sintesi della Relazione del Segretario Politico Arnaldo Forlani, Consiglio Nazionale*, 17–18.11.1989, p. 8., AGA-Democrazia Cristiana-Busta 1038.

67. "Non sarà una vera spaccatura," *Il Tempo*, 21.02.1990, p. 2, AGA-Democrazia Cristiana-Busta 1038; F. Summonte, "Un interrogativo. Quale riflesso a Palazzo Chigi?," *Il Tempo*, 21.02.1990. p. 2, AGA-Democrazia Cristiana-Busta 1038.

68. A. Minzolini, "De Mita lascia: Non è piu la mia DC." *La Stampa*, 21.02.1990, p. 3; F. Damato, "Anche il governo rischia la cinese," *Il Giornale*, 21.02.1990, p. 1; "Andreotti deluso. Non vedo proprio motivi insuperabili di divisione," *Il Mattino*, 21.02.1990. p. 2; G. Compagna, "Dc, lascia De Mita governo più debole," *Il Sole 24 Ore*, 21.02.1990, p. 1, AGA-Democrazia Cristiana-Busta 1038.

69. In 1991, this group of regionalist parties formed a joint federation called *Lega Nord* (Northern League).

70. V. Spini, "Il terremoto del 6 maggio," *La Repubblica*, 22.05.1990, https://ricerca.repubblica .it/repubblica/archivio/repubblica/1990/05/22/il-terremoto-del-maggio.html.

71. E. Scalfari, "Il ritorno di De Mita," *La Repubblica*, 27.11.1990, p. 12, AGA-Democrazia Cristiana-Busta 1038.

72. "La Dc si ricuce sulla Riforma," *Il Giorno*, 07.09.1990. p. 2, AGA-Democrazia Cristiana-Busta. 990.

73. In addition to the factions' interest in keeping the preference vote component, Andreotti and Forlani were also unwilling to break with the PSI which opposed any changes to the electoral system. See E. Scalfari, "Il ritorno di De Mita," *La Repubblica*, 27.11.1990, p. 12, AGA-Democrazia Cristiana-Busta 1038.

74. M. Franco, "Il santo di Ciriaco," *Panorama*, 03.12.1990, p. 46, AGA-Democrazia Cristiana-Busta 1038.

75. F. Geremicca, "Andreotti consuma la sua vendetta," *La Repubblica*, 11.01.1992, p. 3, AGA-Democrazia Cristiana-Busta 1038.

76. F. Geremicca, "Andreotti consuma la sua vendetta," *La Repubblica*, 11.01.1992, p. 3, AGA-Democrazia Cristiana-Busta 1038.

77. S. Marroni, "Sinistra Dc, ascoltami o morrai," *La Repubblica*, 26.08.1990, https://ricerca .repubblica.it/repubblica/archivio/repubblica/1990/08/26/sinistra-dc-ascoltami-morrai.html.

78. V. Spini, "Il terremoto del 6 maggio," *La Repubblica*, 22.05.1990, https://ricerca.repub blica.it/repubblica/archivio/repubblica/1990/05/22/il-terremoto-del-maggio.html.

79. A. Ziniti, "Orlando ha deciso," *La Repubblica*, 06.11.1990, https://ricerca.repubblica.it /repubblica/archivio/repubblica/1990/11/06/orlando-ha-deciso-ora-lascio-la-dc.html.

80. Following another referendum in 1993 against the use of PR for Senate elections, a new electoral law was passed in August 1993. Seventy-five percent of the seats would be elected in single-member districts, while a PR system was used for the remaining seats (Bufacchi and Burgess 1998, 152; D'Alimonte 2005, 255–56). The DC, however, collapsed three months before the first election under the new system.

81. *Modifiche allo Statuto approvato dal Consiglio Nazionale, Consiglio Nazionale*, 09–10.01.1992, p. 61, Art. 17, AGA-Democrazia Cristiana-Busta 1038.

82. *Modifiche allo Statuto approvato dal Consiglio Nazionale, Consiglio Nazionale*, 09–10.01.1992, p. 61, Art. 20, AGA-Democrazia Cristiana-Busta 1038. The same rule also applied to the local, communal, provincial, and regional party level.

83. The Lega Nord won up to 29 percent and became the strongest party in several northern constituencies, whereas La Rete won 7.8 percent of the votes in Sicily (and no less than 25.8 percent in Palermo) (Bufacchi and Burgess 1998, 30). *Relazione del responsabile organizzativo sull'analisi del voto del 5–6 aprile, Luigi Baruffi, Consiglio Nazionale*, 14–15.04.1992, p. 24, AGA-Democrazia Cristiana-Busta 1038.

84. *Relazione del responsabile organizzativo sull'analisi del voto del 5–6 aprile, Luigi Baruffi, Consiglio Nazionale*, 14–15.04.1992, p. 24, AGA-Democrazia Cristiana-Busta 1038.

85. Wertman (1988, 159) estimates this to represent around one third of the DC's elected candidates.

86. For example, G. Dossetti, "Fisionomia del II Congresso della DC," *Cronache Sociali* 13, 30.11.1947, in Trotta (1995, 184, 187); "Dinanzi al Congresso," *Politica Sociale*, 23.11.1952, ASILS-Congresso Nazionale-Sc.2; *IX Congresso Nazionale della D.C.*, 12.09.1964, in Damilano (1968, 1794).

87. Even though most of the illicit profits went toward paying for elections, political favors and party administration (Smith 1997, 471).

88. G. D'Avanzo, "E Andreotti ammette: Meritiamo l'inferno," *La Repubblica*, 12.05.1992, AGA-Democrazia Cristiana-Busta 990.

89. *Mani pulite* is Italian for "clean hands." Tangentopoli is an Italian neologism that can be translated as "Bribe City."

90. *Relazione del responsabile organizzativo sull'analisi del voto del 5–6 Aprile, Luigi Baruffi, Consiglio Nazionale*, 14–15.04.1992, p. 26, AGA-Democrazia Cristiana-Busta 1038.

91. *Relazione del Segretario Politico Arnaldo Forlani, Consiglio Nazionale*, 14–15.04.1992, p. 16, AGA-Democrazia Cristiana-Busta 1038. On agreeing on a successor, see *Seduta del 14 Aprile 1992, Interventi*, p. 29; *Il documento approvato*, p. 67, *Consiglio Nazionale*, 14–15.04.1992, AGA-Democrazia Cristiana-Busta 1038.

92. "Gli uomini della Balena Bianca," *L'Unità*, 18.04.1992. p. 4, AGA-Democrazia Cristiana-Busta. 990.

93. A. Minzolini, "Salta il triumvirato Forlani–Gava–De Mita," *La Stampa*, 25.09.1992, ASILS-Segretaria Politica-Sc. 240.

94. F. Geremicca, "Sipario su notabili e rampanti," *La Repubblica*, 14.10.1992, ASILS-Segretaria Politica-Sc.240.

95. The new rules still guaranteed that the leaders of the party's parliamentary group (e.g., Gava) and all former party leaders (e.g., De Mita) would remain ex officio members of the party executive. I. Drioli, "Martinazzoli prova a liquidare la vecchia Dc," *La Nazione*, 23.03.1993. p.2, AGA-Democrazia Cristiana-Busta 990.

Chapter Four

1. H. Himmer, "Zeit und Mut zur Reform," *ÖMH* 7/1990, p. 18.

2. W. Hämmerle, "Der Letzte der Generation 1945," *Wiener Zeitung*, 24.12.2001, https://web .archive.org/web/20011224235210/http://www.wienerzeitung.at/linkmap/personen/hurdes.htm.

3. Kriechbaumer (1995a, 14) dates the first meeting in mid-1939, whereas Weinberger (1948, 87) recalled that it happened "at some point after 1940."

4. The ÖAAB, ÖBB and ÖWB were founded on 9 and 12 April and 8 May 1945, respectively (Kriechbaumer 1995a, 18).

5. The group around Bumballa had joined the ÖVP shortly before the party's constitution (Kriechbaumer 1995b, 87). On the Austrian resistance, see Rauchensteiner (1979, 58–70) and Kriechbaumer (1985, 118–42).

6. They distrusted the provisory government set up by the Soviets because it did not include any representatives from their occupation zones and was based on a two-thirds majority for the Communist (KPÖ) and Socialist Party (SPÖ) (Kriechbaumer 1995a, 23).

7. H. Braunsteiner, "So blieb mir nichts anderes übrig, als die Enns zu durchschwimmen," in Wohnout (1997, 80–86).

8. H. Braunsteiner, "So blieb mir nichts anderes übrig, als die Enns zu durchschwimmen," in Wohnout (1997, 80–86).

9. *Programm der Demokratischen Österreichischen Staatspartei in Tirol. 15.05.1945*, in Gehler (1994, 38–40); *Quelle 84*, in Kriechbaumer (1995b, 140).

10. *Major political developments*, in Kriechbaumer (1995b, 118–21).

11. Kriechbaumer (1995b): 119.

12. *Bericht der Salzburger Volkszeitung vom 29.Oktober 1945 über den 1. Landesparteitag der Salzburger ÖVP*, in Kriechbaumer (1995b, 132).

13. F. Bock, "Das Problem des Bundesstaates," in *Österreichische Monatshefte* (henceforth: ÖMH), December 1945, p. 97, KVV.

14. *Quelle 86*, in Kriechbaumer (1995b, 141).

15. *Quelle 84*, in Kriechbaumer (1995b, 140); *Protokoll über die Bundesländerkonferenz der Vertreter der ÖVP in Salzburg*, 29.07.1945, in Gehler (1994, 63).

16. *Die Volkspartei*, in Kriechbaumer (1995b, 125–6).

17. *Protokoll über die Bundesländerkonferenz der Vertreter der ÖVP in Salzburg*, 29.07.1945, in Gehler (1994, 60–61, 65–66).

18. *Protokoll über die zweite Bundesländerkonferenz der ÖVP in Salzburg*, 19.08.1945, in Gehler (1994, 69–71).

19. *ÖVP-Pressedienst 24.09.1945*, in Kriechbaumer (1995b, 157–58).

20. "Aus dem Leben der Partei," *ÖMH*, February 1946, p. 208; F. Hurdes, "Ein Jahr Österreichische Volkspartei," *ÖMH*, April 1946, p. 269, KVV.

21. The seven leadership board seats elected by the national party congress were presumably an attempt to appease Hurdes who still favored a stronger role for central party bodies.

22. The leader of the women's movement became an ex officio member of the national executive probably toward the end of 1945. "Aus dem Leben der Partei," *ÖMH*, December 1945, p. 129, KVV.

23. It is only mentioned that a draft of the statute was discussed in February 1946. See "Aus dem Leben der Partei," *ÖMH*, February 1946, p. 208, KVV. However, when discussing the ÖVP's eventual statute, Hurdes remarked that it "had found a prosperous unity of . . . an adequate independence of the Leagues and the clearly acknowledged primacy of the central party." The statement indicates that the balance of power between the Leagues, Länder, and the central party had been a point of contention when formulating the statute. Hurdes, Felix. "Ein Jahr Österreichische Volkspartei," *ÖMH*, April 1946, p. 269, KVV. See also Kriechbaumer (1985, 146–47).

24. It is noteworthy that party members were usually members of both a Land and a League organization. Being backed by, for instance, the Farmers' League in Lower Austria would have thus helped minority and majority elites in Lower Austria in their efforts to assume/maintain the Land leadership. Consequently, majority elites, like Raab (ÖWB and Lower Austria) and Weinberger (ÖAAB and Vienna), built a power base within both a League and Land organization. This, however, did not encourage factional activities because forming networks that were organizationally reproduced across Land branches would not have been beneficial to assume leadership positions within their own Land branch. "Aus dem Leben der Partei," *ÖMH*, October 1945, p. 43, KVV. See also Kriechbaumer (1995a, 29).

25. The de facto role of the party congress in selecting the party leadership was lower. While the party leader and the general secretary were important positions, the remaining five positions were mainly administrative in nature. However, I do not pursue this reasoning any further because the framework presented in chapter 2 does not distinguish between more and less "important" members of the national executive but only focusses on whether they are entitled to vote.

26. "Memorandum von Martin F. Herz vom 14. Dezember 1945 über die Österreichische Volkspartei"; "Bericht des amerikanischen Geheimdienstes OSS vom 21. November 1945"; "Bericht des amerikanischen Geheimdienstes OSS vom 03. Dezember 1945," in Kriechbaumer (1995b, 351–53).

27. "Die Bünde," *ÖMH*, October 1945, pp. 43–45, KVV.

28. "Aus dem Leben der Partei," *ÖMH*, October 1945, p. 43, KVV.

29. "Aus dem Leben der Partei," *ÖMH*, October 1945, p. 44, KVV.

30. "Die Bünde," *ÖMH*, November 1945, p. 28–29; "Die Bünde," *ÖMH*, February 1946, p. 208; "Die Bünde," *ÖMH*, August 1946, pp. 500–501, KVV.

31. *Bundesparteitag*, 1947, p. 19/11,55/Mo/2 and 19 1220 kn1–2, KVV.

32. *Bundesparteitag*, 1951, p. 84; 03.03.1951, pp. 109–39, KVV; *Bundesparteitag*, 1963, pp. 61–62, 135–36, 162–66; 20.09.1963, pp. 213–59, KVV; *Bundesparteitag*, 1972, pp. 27–41, 342–435, KVV; *Bundesparteitag*, 1979, pp. 11–25, 54–66, 93–95, 101–32, 139–40, 172–73, 195–212, KVV; *Bundesparteitag*, 1980, pp. 105–69, KVV; *Speech Wolfgang Schüssel*, 22.04.1995, p. 5, KVV.

33. H. Himmer, "Zeit und Mut zur Reform," *ÖMH* 7/1990, pp. 16–18; K. Wilfing, "ÖVP-Reform an Haupt und Gliedern," *ÖMH*, 7/1990, pp. 23–27, KVV.

34. Except for civil servants.

35. See Engelmann (1962, 657, 661), Müller (1985, 165), and Pelinka (2009, 628–30) on the so-called social partnership system.

36. See Müller (1989b, 337–41). Titles have been held in high esteem in Austria. It is not rare for a farmer to hold the title of a "councilor of the economy," for businessmen to be called "councilor of commerce" and "professor" is often used for intellectuals and artists. These titles have usually been awarded by the relevant cabinet minister after conferring with the occupational associations (Müller 2000, 148).

37. For instance, the Raiffeisen banking group has had close ties with the ÖVP's Farmers' League and the Newag (i.e., Lower Austrian Electricity Corporation) has been close to the ÖVP's Land branch in Lower Austria (Müller 2000, 148).

38. *Biographisches Handbuch des NÖ Landtages und der NÖ Landesregierung*, p. 94, https://noe-landtag.gv.at/fileadmin/sites/noe-landtag/dokumente/biographisches_handbuch/1921-dato .pdf?msclkid=73b410b5a20111eca30ef442212941df; "Aufstieg und Fall des Viktor Müllner," *Die Presse*, 05.02.2010, http://diepresse.com/home/innenpolitik/zeitgeschichte/537896/Spendenaf faereAufstieg-und-Fall-des-Viktor-Muellner?vlbacklink=/home/politik/zeitgeschichte /index.do.

39. Until the official ballot was introduced in 1959, voters could also (often without being aware of this) change the party list by using special ballots that ranked the candidates in a different order compared to the official party list. These special ballots were provided by the candidates and/or intraparty groups (Müller 1984, 86).

40. *Bundesparteitag*, 1947, pp. 19 1150kn1–19 1230 A2, 21 1220 A1, KVV.

41. *Bericht des Ausschusses für Organisation, Finanzen und Personalpolitik*. Bundesparteitag 1947, pp. Mo 1–3, KVV.

42. They were again excluded in 1951 before Land representatives were again included in 1958 (Müller 1992, 80).

43. It was reduced to a simple majority in 1964 (Müller 1992, 107).

44. *Bundesparteitag*, 1951, pp. 121–22, KVV.

45. *Bundesparteitag*, 1951, pp. 114–15, 135.

46. *Bundesparteitag*, 1951, pp. 111, KVV.

47. *Bundesparteitag*, 1963, p. 214, KVV.

48. *Bundesparteitag*, 1972, pp. 339–40, 418–33, KVV; *Referat Herbert Kohlmaier, Bundesparteitag*, 1972, pp. 31–33, KVV.

49. *Bundesparteitag*, 1972, 31, KVV. Also, *Bundesparteitag*, 1972, pp. 342–48, 353–60, KVV.

50. Renamed constituent organizations (*Teilorganisationen*).

51. *Bundesparteitag*, 1972, p. 361, KVV.

52. *Bundesparteitag*, 1979, pp. 8–25, KVV.

53. *Bundesparteitag*, 1979, pp. 12, 120, KVV.

54. *Bundesparteitag*, 1979, pp. 55–56, KVV.

55. *Bundesparteitag*, 1980, pp. 105–6, 115–69, KVV.

56. *Bundesparteitag*, 1979, pp. 61–62, 93–95, 101, 115–17, 172–13, KVV.

57. Compare *Bundesparteitag*, 1979, pp. 150–51, KVV.

58. *Bundesparteitag*, 1979, pp. 148–49.

59. *Memorandum von Martin F. Herz vom 14 Dezember über die Österreichische Volkspartei; Bericht des amerikanischen Geheimdienstes OSS vom 21 November 1945; Bericht des amerikanischen Geheimdienstes OSS vom 03 Dezember 1945; Aus einem Schreiben des amerikanischen Gesandten in Wien, John G. Erhardt, vom 06 Oktober 1948*, in Kriechbaumer (1995b, 351–53).

60. Speech by Staatssekretär Graf, 19.04.1947, Bundesparteitag, p. 19 1230 A1, KVV.

61. *Bundesparteitag*, 1972, p. 400, KVV.

62. *Bundesparteitag*, 1972, pp. 416–17, 420.

63. *Bundesparteitag*, 1979, pp. 132, 135–93, KVV.

64. *Bundesparteitag*, 1963, p. 153, KVV.

65. *Bundesparteitag*, 1972, pp. 364, 377–78, 381, KVV.

66. *Bundesparteitag*, 1979, pp. 110–11, KVV.

67. *Bundesparteitag*, 1947, p. A3, KVV.

68. *Organisatorischer Rechenschaftsbericht*, Bundesparteitag 1963, pp. 61–62, KVV.

69. *Bundesparteitag*, 1979, pp. 94–95, KVV.

70. S. Knafl, "Primat der Partei—kein Lippenbekenntnis," *ÖMH*, July/August 1979, p. 36, KVV.

71. *Bundesparteitag*, 1979, p. 93, KVV.

72. *Bundesparteileitung*, 14.06.1951, KVV.

73. H. Schutzenhofer, "Praktische Politik für den Nächsten," *ÖMH*, September 1979, p. 25, KVV.

74. *Bundesparteitag*, 1979, p. 132, KVV.

75. *Bundesparteitag*, 1979, p. 132, KVV.

76. *Bundesparteitag*, 1979, pp. 57–58, KVV.

77. The share of regular church goers declined from 30 percent in 1951 to 18 percent in 1989. G. Wilfinger, "Technokratischer Zentralismus," *ÖMH*, May–June 1979, p. 21; K. Jungwirth, "Die Chancen der ÖVP," *ÖMH*, May–June 1979, pp. 24–25, KVV.

78. L. Reichhold, "Krise und Chance der ÖVP," *ÖMH*, July–August 1979, p. 23, KVV.

79. P. Ulram, "Progressive Mitte oder programmatische Mittelmäßigkeit," *ÖMH*, May–June 1979, pp. 28–29, KVV.

80. K. Jungwirth, "Die Chancen der ÖVP," *ÖMH*, May–June 1979, pp. 24–25, KVV.

81. C. Auer, "ÖVP neu?," *ÖMH*, 8/1990, p. 13, KVV.

82. H. Himmer, "Zeit und Mut zur Reform," *ÖMH*, 7/1990, pp. 16–18, KVV.

83. C. Zöchling, "Welches Umfeld die Spitzenkandidaten der Parteien geprägt hat," *Profil*, 20.08.2013, https://www.profil.at/oesterreich/welches-umfeld-spitzenkandidaten-parteien-364350.

84. One of the very few notable exceptions was the 1996 European election when the Christian Democrats nominated a popular TV journalist as their top candidate (Müller et al. 2004, 168). Primaries were eventually abandoned after the 1994 election (Fallend 2005, 193).

85. *Bundesparteiorganisationsstatut*, 28.06.1991, Art. 27–30, ÖVP federal office.

86. See Liste Fritz Tirol, https://listefritz.at/parteigeschichte/.

87. E. Linsinger, "Warum die ÖVP sich zu Recht vor den Neos fürchtet," *Profil*, 11.02.2013, https://www.profil.at/oesterreich/parteigruendung-warum-oevp-recht-neos-352329; "Nach dem Spindelegger-Abgang will sich die ÖVP erneuern wieder einmal," *Profil*, 06.09.2014, https://www.profil.at/oesterreich/nach-spindelegger-abgang-oevp-377869; O. Pink, "Von der ÖVP zu den Neos," *Die Presse*, 19.08.2017, https://www.diepresse.com/5271430/von-der-oevp-zu-den-neos-die-wandlung-des-nikola-donig?msclkid=54bba1b0a20411ecadcfc5df55f8f896.

88. SORA: https://www.sora.at/themen/wahlverhalten/wahlanalysen/waehlerstromanalysen/eu-wahl14.html.

Chapter Five

1. Although the British authorities quickly allowed the (re)emergence of the Catholic Center Party and conservative German Party (DP) (Bösch 2001, 52–53), the Allies disadvantaged the few smaller parties they licensed (Rogers 1995, chap. 6). Some liberals also joined the CDU, but their anticlericalism encouraged most of them to affiliate with the FDP (Bösch 2001; Klein 2005).

2. A founding group also existed in Bavaria. It, however, ultimately formed its own party, the Christian Social Union (CSU). While forming an electoral alliance and joint parliamentary group with the CDU since 1949, the CSU is an independent party with a distinct organization and level of factionalism.

3. Although the British authorities were sympathetic toward the CDU's left, they adopted a positive attitude toward Adenauer, who, unlike Kaiser and Hermes, did not push for reunification with the Soviet-controlled East (Schwarz 1995, 319–20, 363–67). The British also valued Adenauer's anti-Nazi past and anti-Communism (Bösch 2001, 75, 193; Foschepoth 1986, 410–11; Schwarz 1995, 293, 326–28).

4. *Arbeitsgemeinschaft der CDU/CSU*, 05–06.02.1947, pp. 3–4, ACDP-01-021.

5. *Protokoll Organisations-Ausschusses*, 12.10.1948, p. 2; *Auszug Protokoll über die Sitzung des Vorstandes der Arbeitsgemeinschaft*, 24.09.1948; *Dr. Lenz*, 13.11.1948; *Dörpinghaus*, 13.11.1948, all ACDP-01-021.

6. *Statut der Arbeitsgemeinschaft*, October 1948, Art. 2–6, ACDP-07-001-14001.

7. Rae's fractionalization index: 0.00. To recap, I adapt Rae's (1967, 58) fractionalization index to measure how centralized the leadership selection process is. It ranges from 0 to 1. Higher values express a higher degree of decentralization.

8. *Konferenz der Landesverbandsvorsitzenden und Landesverbandsvertreter*, 11.05.1950, p. 2; *Deutschland-Union-Dienst: Gründung der Gesamtdeutschen CDU*, 11.05.1950, ACDP-07-001-3204.

9. *Statutenentwurf*, 09.10.1949, Art. 9, ACDP-07-001-14001.

10. *Konferenz der Landesverbandsvorsitzenden und Landesverbandsvertreter*, 11.05.1950, p. 3; *11.09.1950, pp. 3–4, ACDP-07-001-3204*.

11. *Konferenz der Landesverbandsvorsitzenden und Landesverbandsvertreter*, 31.07.1950, pp. 2–7, ACDP-07-001-3204.

12. See the letters in ACDP-07-001-3204. Also, *Protokoll vorbereitender Ausschusses*, 21.07.1950, ACDP-07-001-3204.

13. *Konferenz der Landesvorsitzenden der CDU gemeinsam mit dem vorbereitenden Ausschuss*, 13.10.1950, pp. 2–3 and 9–12, ACDP-07-001-3204.

14. *Statut der CDU*, 21.10.1950, Art. 4–9, ACDP.

15. The minutes are available in Buchstab (1986, 1990, 1994). Between December 1950 and July 1953, the leadership board convened twenty-one times (an average of every 1.67 months). There were times between 1953 and 1957 as well as 1957 and 1961 when the board did not meet for several months. Yet the number of meetings (twenty and twenty-one, respectively) and their frequency (an average of every 2.38 months and 2.5 months) underline its continuing relevance.

16. *Statut*, 21.10.1950, Art. 6, ACDP.

17. Party branch boundaries have not always corresponded to Germany's administrative boundaries due to regional conflicts. The Land branches of Rhineland and Westphalia-Lippe existed in North Rhine–Westphalia until 1982. The Land branches of North Baden, South Baden, North Württemberg, and Württemberg-Hohenzollern existed in Baden-Württemberg until 1972, and Hanover, Brunswick, and Oldenburg continue to maintain formally separate Land branches in Lower Saxony (Schmid 1990, 55; Bösch 2001, 269–74).

18. "Unbehagen über Soltauer Kreis," *Die Welt*, 21.01.1969; "Nach bayrischem Muster," *Donauer Kurier*, 27.08.1969; "Soltauer Kreis," *Die Welt*, 29.10.1970, ACDP press archives.

19. Hanover, Brunswick, Oldenburg, Hamburg, Bremen, Schleswig-Holstein (and later Berlin). "Verstärkte Zusammenarbeit," *Union in Deutschland*, Nr. 38, 26.09.1968; "In und um Soltau," *Rheinischer Merkur*, 7.2.1969; "Keine Landesgruppe Norddeutschland der CDU," *Hamburger Abendblatt*, 15.08.1969; "Der Traum von der norddeutschen CSU," *Handelsblatt*, 20.08.1969, ACDP press archives.

20. See, e.g., the collection of letters and minutes in ACDP-04-001-024/1.

21. E.g., *Bundesparteiauschuss*, 09.11.1951, pp. 2–3, StBKAH-I.05.13/082–3.

22. *Bach*, 04.12.1951; *Bach to Ehlers*, 07.12.1951; *Ehlers to Tillmanns*, 20.12.1951; *Holzapfel to Tillmanns*, 28.12.1951, ACDP-04-001-008/1; *Holzapfel to Adenauer*, 31.10.1951, StBKAH-11.04.

23. *Bach to Adenauer*, 17.04.1952, StBKAH-11-04-032.

24. *Holzapfel to Tillmanns*, 28.12.1951, ACDP-04-001-008/1; *Holzapfel to Ehlers*, 28.12.1951, ACDP-01-369-002/1.

25. *Bach to Adenauer*, 13.11.1951, ACDP-04-001-008/1.

26. *Rheinfels to Roelen*, 03.11.1952 and 08.11.1952, ACDP-01-083-005/2.

27. *Rheinfels to Hellwig*, 26.11.1952, 01-083-005/2; *Bundesausschuss für Wirtschaftspolitik*, 04.10.1953 and 26.01.1954, ACDP-01-083-176/2, *Schmitz and Schmücker to members of Landesmittelstandsausschuss Rheinland*, 21.12.1953, ACDP-01-083-005/2; *Pohle to Hellwig*, 25.02.1954; *Brand to Pohle*, 03.03.1954, both ACDP-01-083-164/1; *Etzel to leadership board Bundesausschuss für Wirtschaftspolitik*, 06.05.1954, ACDP-01-083-176/2.

28. *Bundesausschuss für Wirtschaftspolitik der CDU / Unterausschuss Mittelstandsfragen*, 10.11.1954, ACDP-01-083-176/2.

29. *Albers*, 14.12.1945, ACDP-04-013-170/1.

30. See *Bach to Adenauer*, 27.09.1950, StBKAH-11-03-049.

31. *Bundesvorstand*, 03.06.1955, pp. 535–56, 543–49, in Buchstab (1990).

32. *Statut*, 1950, Art. 6, ACDP.

33. *Bundesvorstandsmitglieder 1950–1966*, https://www.kas.de/de/web/geschichte-der-cdu/bundesvorstandsmitglieder-1950-1966; *Tagung des Geschäftsführenden Ausschusses des Evangelischen Arbeitskreises*, 29.09.1952, p. 6, ACDP-04-001-002/2.

34. See, for example, the early drafts of the CDA's contact lists in ACDP-01-329-002/1 and the documents in ACDP-01-57-024/1. For the EAK, see the letters and minutes in ACDP-04-001-002/2.

35. *Kaiser to Arndgen*, 31.12.1951, ACDP-01-343-001/2; EAK leadership, 11.12.1953, p. 2, ACDP-04-001-002/2.

36. The correspondence between Kather and Adenauer and Adenauer and Holzapfel in StBKAH-B1–09.01. Also *Hernmarck to Ehlers*, 04.11.1952; *Ehlers to Adenauer*, 31.10.1952, both ACDP-04-001-002/1; *Kather to Adenauer*, 25.07.1952, StBKAH-10.23a/167–170. *Lukaschek*, 14.12.1951, StBKAH-B3-021-539.

37. *Kather to Adenauer*, 14.06.1954, BA-NL-18/17a-Fiche1.

38. Examples include the Kurt Schumacher Circle, Godesberg Circle, Julius Leber Society, Mayors' Wing (*Bürgermeisterflügel*), Sewer Workers' Squad (*Kanalarbeiterriege*), Seeheim Circle, and Frankfurt Circle.

39. A.-M. Meister, "Warum die CSU noch konservativer werden soll," *Die Welt*, 13.07.2014, http://www.welt.de/regionales/muenchen/article130053232/Warum-die-CSU-nochkonservativer-werden-soll.html.

40. *Adenauer to Albers*, 19.06.1946, in Kleinmann (1996, 200); *Adenauer to Albers*, 14.07.1946, in Kleinmann (1996, 203).

41. *Speech Albers*, ACDP-04-013-088/6; *Speech Katzer*, ACDP-01-057-24/1; *Statut der CDU*, 1950 and 1956, Art. 12, ACDP.

42. *Statut der CDU*, 1950 and 1956, Art. 4, ACDP.

43. *Statut*, 1956, Art. 9, KAS/ACDP.

44. *Bundesvorstand*, 03.06.1955, pp. 535–36, 546–50.

45. *Mitglieder des Bundesparteiausschusses*, ACDP-07-001-703.

46. *Bundesvorstand*, 26.04.1956, pp. 908–14; *Bundesparteitag*, 1956, pp. 112–35; *Statut*, 1956, Art. 9, ACDP.

47. *Statut*, 1956, Art. 9, ACDP.

48. *Bundesvorstand*, 03.06.1955, pp. 553–54; *Bundesvorstand*, 10.11.1955, pp. 691–92.

49. Similarly, Adenauer also failed to increase central control over the candidate selection process (Bösch 2001, 268–69). *Bundesvorstand*, 03.06.1955, pp. 538–39; 26.04.1956, pp. 915–18.

50. *Bundesvorstand*, 10.05.1962, pp. 206–7, in Buchstab (1998).

51. *Statut*, 1956, Art. 9, ACDP.

52. *Bundesvorstand*, 23.05.1960, p. 670–72, in Buchstab (1994).

53. *Statut*, 1960, Art. 25, ACDP.

54. Confidential note, Adenauer, Globke, Krone, von Hassel, 09.07.1959; *Bericht Kraske an Adenauer über Zustand der Gesamtpartei*, 24.07.1959; Meeting notes, Kraske und von Hassel, 05–06.08.1959, ACDP-01-157.

55. *Bundesvorstand*, 10.05.1962, pp. 207–8, in Buchstab (1998); *Bundesparteitag*, 1962, pp. 310–14, 329–30, ACDP; *Statut*, 1962, Art. 21, 25, 26, ACDP.

56. *Bundesvorstand*, 10.05.1962, pp. 211, 213.

57. *Bundesvorstand*, 10.05.1962, pp. 212–14.

58. *Bundesparteitag*, 1962, pp. 306–7, ACDP.

59. *Statut*, 1967, Art. 29, 33, ACDP. At the same time, the position of a party secretary was finally established. This was part of the organizational professionalization process that will be discussed in the main text.

60. To guarantee the representation of the new Land branches from East Germany in 1990, this informal agreement was formalized. Land leaders who were not elected to the national executive became ex officio members. *Statut*, 1990, Art. 33, ACDP; *Statut*, 1967, Art. 29, 33, ACDP.

61. "Norddeutsche CDU-Politiker unzufrieden," *Frankfurter Allgemeine Zeitung*, 15.01.1968; "Der Soltauer Kreis tagt wieder," *Hannoversche Allgemeine*, 01.07.1968; "Der Traum von der norddeutschen CSU," *Handelsblatt*, 20.08.1969; "CDU Spitzentreffen der CDU Norddeutschlands," *Dpa*, 21.08.1981, ACDP press archives.

62. On denominational conflicts, see especially the letters in ACDP-01-369-010/1 and also Bösch (2001, 109–10). This section draws on Dilling (2022).

63. Disagreements also existed in other fields, like over the role of confessional schools (Bösch 2001, 109–33; Cary 1996, 254–55).

64. Opposition to rearmament remained between 14 percent and 30 percent, depending on the question, even after the Soviet Union quelled an East German uprising in June 1953 (Noelle and Neumann 1975, 175, 359; Reigrotzki 2015). See the survey results in Noelle and Neumann (1975, 175, 318, 332, 353, 355, 358, 360–61, 372–73, 377).

65. *Bundesvorstand*, 29.10.1951, p. 87, in Buchstab (1986).

66. *Bundesvorstand*, 03.07.1951, 06.09.1951, 27.09.1951, 09.11.1951, 17.10.1952, 22.05.1953.

67. Hesse: from 31 percent to 18.8 percent, Württemberg-Baden: 40.9 to 26.3 percent, Bremen: 22 percent to 9 percent.

68. For instance, in Lower Saxony, the CDU-DP alliance only won 23.7 percent compared to the CDU's previous 19.9 percent and the DP's 17.9 percent.

69. *Kaiser to Toussaint*, 21.11.1950, BA-NL 18/460–1; *Lehr to Dibelius*, 24.11.1950, StBKAH-B3-021-298; P. Sethe, "Arnold gegen Adenauer. Und Heinemann?," *Frankfurter Allgemeine Zeitung*, 05.12.1950, BA-NL 18/460–2.

70. I do not discuss the FDP. Although Adenauer initially hoped it might merge with the CDU, the anti-clerical FDP competed for a different electorate (Kaack 1971, 239, 261–62; Bösch 2001, 190–92).

71. The DP achieved 14.7 and 16.6 percent in the 1951 and 1955 Bremen election. In Lower Saxony, its results included 17.9 percent in 1947 and 12.4 percent in 1955, and in Schleswig-Holstein, it achieved 9.6 percent in 1950. The Center achieved 9.8 percent and 7.5 percent in the 1947 and 1950 election in North Rhine–Westphalia respectively.

72. The figure was 23.4 percent in Schleswig-Holstein in 1950.

73. *Bundesvorstand*, 26.01.1953, p. 357, and 22.05.1953, pp. 531–66.

74. This number increased from one to three in 1956.

75. *Bundesvorstand*, 30.09.1955, in Buchstab (1990, 648–49).

76. H. Ehlers, "Keine evangelische Partei," *Frankfurter Allgemeine Zeitung*, 17.03.1952; *Entschließung der Siegener Tagung*, 18.03.1952, ACDP-01-483-053/3.

77. *EAK Vorstand*, 03.02.1953, p. 7, ACDP-04-001-002/2. See also the letters and reports in ACDP-04-001-040/2.

78. *Blumenfeld to Ehlers*, 09.05.1953; *Zunker to Ehlers*, 19.09.1953, both ACDP-01-369-007/1.

79. *Brand*, 12.06.1953, ACDP-01-369-002/2; *EAK Vorstand*, 29.09.1952 and 03.02.1953, p. 7, ACDP-04-001-002/2; *EAK Vorstand*, 27.05.1952, ACDP-04-001-002/1.

80. *Beyer to Ehlers*, 16.09.1952; *Hernmarck to Ehlers*, 04.11.1952, p. 3, ACDP-04-001-002/1; *EAK Vorstand*, 29.09.1952, ACDP-04-001-002/2.

81. See, e.g., Report, *CDU leadership meeting*, 01.06.1951, p. 1, ACDP-01-57-24/1; *EAK leadership meeting*, 03.02.1953, p. 3, ACDP-04-001-002/2; *Kaiser to Albers*, 08.03.1956, BA-NL18/160–1/407.

82. *Albers*, 12.04.1949, ACDP-01-329-002/1.

83. *CDA leadership meeting*, 01.06.1951, ACDP-01-057-24/1.

84. *EAK Vorstand*, 27.05.1952, p. 8, ACDP-04-001-002/1.

85. See, e.g., the documents in ACDP-04-001-038/3 and ACDP-01-369-002/1. See also *Ehlers*, 30.07.1952; *EAK Vorstand*, 29.09.1952, p. 5, and 11.05.1953, all ACDP-04-001-002/2.

86. *Ehlers*, 30.07.1952; *EAK Vorstand*, 29.09.1952, p. 5, and 11.05.1953, all ACDP-04-001-002/2; *Bausch to Schröder*, 02.12.1955, ACDP-01-483-054/1. Ehlers became deputy party leader and a potential successor to Adenauer. His unexpected death in 1954 put a sudden end to his rise.

87. For example, *CDA leadership*, 15–16.03.1952, p. 3, ACDP-01-057-24/1.

88. *Kraske to Adenauer*, 24.07.1959, p. 24, 27, ACDP-01-157.

89. *Notes von Hassel*, 07.02.1962; *report Kraske to Adenauer*, 24.07.1959, pp. 23–24; *von Hassel to Fricke*, 23.09.1959, p. 2; "CDU-Reformen. Die Flickenteppich-Parte," *Der Spiegel*, 29.07.1959; *notes von Hassel on a confidential meeting with Adenauer*, 18.12.1961, pp. 2–3, all ACDP-01-157.

90. *Kraske to Adenauer*, 24.07.1959; "CDU-Reformen. Die Flickenteppich-Partei," *Der Spiegel*, 29.07.1959, all ACDP-01-157.

91. See Lois (2011) and Pollack and Pickel (2003).

92. "CDU-Mittelstandsvereinigung," *Industriekurier*, 12.11.1968, ACDP-04-004.

93. Pederson's volatility index for 1990–1994: 11.2 West, 31.8 East; 1994–1998: 12.8 West, 23.2 East (Conradt 2006, 18).

94. This does not mean that organizational questions played no role at all. The CDU faced a declining, aging, and predominantly male membership (Dilling 2017; Wiliarty 2013). In response, the party shifted toward a greater involvement of its members in selecting candidates (Turner 2013, 126). Organizational questions, however, were seen as less urgent than programmatic reform.

95. Merkel largely owed the party leadership to her influential op-ed, which made her the ideal candidate to send a signal of renewal. Her own Land branch of Mecklenburg Pomerania was the CDU's weakest branch, and the EAK, which she had briefly led in the 1990s, had lost too much in influence to serve as her base (see Clemens 2011).

96. For example, Laurenz Meyer, Eckhard von Klaeden, Peter Altmeier, Volker Kauder, and Norbert Röttgen.

97. "Enttäuschte CDU-Politiker gründen Wahlalternative," *Welt*, 04.10.2012, https://www.welt.de/politik/deutschland/article109606449/Enttaeuschte-CDU-Politiker-gruenden-Wahlalternative.html.

98. "Kardinal Meisners Helfer mischen die CDU auf," *Der Spiegel*, 25.12.2009, https://www.spiegel.de/politik/deutschland/kirchenstreit-in-der-union-kardinal-meisners-helfer-mischen-die-cdu-auf-a-667126.html; "Martin Lohmann tritt aus der CDU aus," Kath.net, 19.07.2013, http://www.kath.net/news/42929; "Konservativer Kritiker auf verlorenem Posten," Cicero, n.d., https://www.cicero.de/innenpolitik/konservativer-kritiker-auf-verlorenem-posten/42982.

99. "Ein konservatives Rebelliönchen," *Zeit*, 02.11.2012, http://www.zeit.de/politik/deutschland/2012-11/berliner-kreis-cdu-merkel-manifest.

100. "Konservative aus Union schließen sich zusammen," *Zeit*, 25.03.2017,: http://www.zeit.de/politik/deutschland/2017-03/cdu-csu-union-dachverband-freiheitlich-konservativ-auf bruch-alexander-mitsch.

101. "Was die Werteunion ist und was sie will," *ZDF*, 11.02.2020, https://www.zdf.de/nachrichten/politik/werteunion-cdu-100.html; "Werteunion: 'CDU vor Richtungsentscheidung,'" *ZDF*, 25.02.2020, https://www.zdf.de/nachrichten/politik/cdu-vorsitz-kanzlerkandidatur-100.html.

102. "Die junge CDU scharrt mit den Hufen," *Deutschlandfunk*, 07.12.2017, https://www.deutschlandfunk.de/konservativer-nachwuchs-die-junge-cdu-scharrt-mit-den-hufen.724.de

.html?dram:article_id=402570; "Keine Klüngel, klar konservativ: Wie Tilman Kuban die CDU neu denkt," *Focus*, 28.05.2021, https://www.focus.de/politik/deutschland/bundestagswahl/union -wie-tilman-kuban-die-cdu-neu-denkt_id_13338009.html.

103. "Das Spahn-Prinzip," *Frankfurter Allgemeine Zeitung*, 14.05.2017, https://www.faz .net/aktuell/wirtschaft/wirtschaftspolitik/cdu-hoffnungstraeger-im-portraet-das-spahn-prin zip-15014095.html; "Spahn verdrängt Minister Gröhe aus CDU-Präsidium," *Welt*, 09.12.2014, https://www.welt.de/politik/deutschland/article135199208/Spahn-verdraengt-Minister-Groehe -aus-CDU-Praesidium.html.

104. "CDU-Wahlkämpfer wenden sich von Merkel ab," *Der Spiegel*, 21.02.2016, https://www .spiegel.de/politik/deutschland/fluechtlingskrise-julia-kloeckner-wendet-sich-von-angela -merkel-ab-a-1078524.html; "Suche nach dem Anführer," *Der Spiegel*, 15.07.2007, https://www .spiegel.de/politik/suche-nach-dem-anfuehrer-a-25d39765-0002-0001-0000-000052263642.

105. "Der Sieg der Konservativen," *Frankfurter Allgemeine Zeitung*, 07.12.2016, https://www .faz.net/aktuell/politik/inland/cdu-kippt-doppelte-staatsbuergerschaft-sieg-der-konservativen -14563002.html.

106. "Die CDU hat Angst vor einer deutschen Tea-Party-Bewegung," *Der Spiegel*, 21.05.2021, https://www.spiegel.de/politik/deutschland/bundestagswahl-die-cdu-hat-angst-vor-einer -deutschen-tea-party-bewegung-a-e776665a-0002-0001-0000-000177604432; "Who Is Friedrich Merz, the New Head of Germany's CDU?," *Deutsche Welle*, 22.01.2022, https://www.dw.com/en /who-is-friedrich-merz-the-new-head-of-germanys-cdu/a-56247517.

Chapter Six

1. On centralization of power in the CDS, see Bruneau and MacLeod (1986, 81), Frain (1997, 86), Van Biezen (2003, 61, 75) and Matuschek (2008, 85); in the CDA, see Krouwel (1993, 71–74), Koole (1994, 286, 299), Duncan (2007, 73–74), and Wagner (2014, chap. 5.1); in the CSV, see Feltes (2008, 409–11, 420–21, 424, 441, 452), Grosbusch (2008, 333, 338–39, 349, 388), Kraemer (2008, 748, 750), and Schoentgen (2008, 261, 268, 316).

2. *Estutatos Partito do Centro Democrático Social*, Art. 84.

3. The Salazar-Caetano dictatorship had suppressed all political parties (Bruneau 1997, 1, 3). Only the Communist Party had existed clandestinely.

4. *Estutatos Partito do Centro Democrático Social*, Art. 84.

5. Magone (1999, 233) explains, "The cacique was the local boss . . . able, through his influence in the village, to offer a supply of votes . . . and to gain favors in return."

6. It is unclear whether PR had been used at some point before 1985. Matuschek (2008, 85) has been quite ambiguous regarding the precise format of the electoral system and the party statutes to which he is referring.

7. KVP, ARP, and CHU had previously benefited from the division of society into a network of social organizations, bound together by a common faith or ideology and of which political parties constituted the political expression (i.e., so-called pillarization; Bakvis 1981, 1–4, 35; Koole 1994, 278).

8. See Bardi and Morlino (1992, 473, 483), Koole and Van de Velde (1992, 631, 640), Müller (1992, 38, 46–47), and Poguntke and Boll (1992, 329, 332). When a minimum/maximum party membership is provided, I consistently use the maximum estimate.

9. See Bardi and Morlino (1992, 483, 493), Koole and Van de Velde (1992, 640, 651), and Müller (1992, 48, 58).

10. Luxembourg's division into four electoral districts (South, Central, North, and East) very likely inspired the CSV's structure at the subnational level.

11. *Statuten vun der Chrëschtlech-sozialer Volekspartei*, CSV. 1946, Art. 13.3.

12. *Statuten vun der Chrëschtlech-sozialer Volekspartei*, CSV. 1946, Art. 13.3.

13. Excluding the five members co-opted by the elected national executive.

Chapter Seven

1. Abbé Pierre, *Pour qu'une aube nouvelle*, 14.05.1950, p. 7, AN-457AP/166.

2. To recap, my framework requires that a political party has a formal organization that allows for internal competition and structures the selection process of the party leadership.

3. *Règlement du Parti*, 1905, Art. 30, 32–35, 39–42. http://sebastien-chochois.over-blog.com /pages/Les_statuts_du_Parti_socialiste_SFIO_en_1905-809394.html.

4. *Note sur les objectifs prochains*, 23.09.1946, AN-350AP/6; *Statuts Mouvement Républicain Populaire, 186 Rue de Rivoli*, 1944, Art. 40, 46, AN-681AP/10–1.

5. Similar to Italy, Austria and Germany, France's inter-war democracy had collapsed. It was replaced by a German occupation zone in the Northwest and the authoritarian Vichy regime in the Southeast.

6. *Assemblée constitutive*, 25.11.1944, pp. 27–28, 31–35, AN-350AP/12.

7. Called Comité Directeur (1944–50) and later Commission Exécutive. As the MRP's main leadership body, it met monthly and was assisted by two subcommittees, the Directory Office (Bureau Directeur) and the executive committee (Commission Exécutive Permanente).

8. The DC and CDU used a majority system for internal elections, while developing a high and moderate level of factionalism respectively.

9. *L'événement de la semaine*, AN-457AP/167; *Compte-rendu de la journée d'étude*, 20.01.1957, pp. 1–4, AN-350AP/10.

10. *Compte-rendu de la journée d'étude*, 20.01.1957, pp. 1–2, AN-350AP/10.

11. *La Voix du Militant. Organe de l'équipe d'étude et d'action pour un plus grand M.R.P.*, September 1957; *Rénovation Démocratique*, 01.10.1957, AN-457AP/167.

12. *Pierre-Marie Biarnès*, 25.09.1956; *Rénovation Démocratique*, 05.02.1958, p. 3, AN-350AP/10; *Brochure des Équipes d'étude et d'action pour la rénovation*, 1959; *Lettre ouverte de l'équipe de Rénovation Démocratique*, 05.05.1959, AN-457AP/168.

13. "L'opposition désamorcée," *Index quotidien de la presse*, 20.01.1958, AN-350AP/10.

14. Letter Simonnet; Georges Delfosse to Jean-Marie Daillet, 07.02.1958; Georges Delfosse to Pierre-Marie Biarnès, 07.02.1958, AN-350AP/10.

15. Teitgen to Simonnet, 04.03.1958; Biarnès to Daillet; Saint-Marc to Teitgen and Simonnet, both 15.03.1958; *Rapport sur la Rénovation Démocratique*, AN-350AP/10.

16. *Status*, 1944, Art. 15, 49–54, AN-681AP/10–1; *Statuto*, 1947, Art. 87, ASILS-DC Statuti.

17. *Status*, 1944, Art. 14, 39; *Statuto*, 1947, Art. 71; *Direzione Centrale della DC*, 08.03.1946, in Salvi (1959, 171).

18. *Status*, 1944, Art. 12, AN-681AP/10–1; *Statuto del Partito*, 1947, Art. 10, ASILS-DC Statuti.

19. *Status*, 1944, Art. 24–26, 32–35, AN-681AP/10–1. For example, 1726 delegates participated at the 1947 congress. *Évolution des effectifs*, AN-350AP/3.

20. The party in public office was the largest single group in the national executive (16 seats after the 1945 election) and would have still fallen short of a majority if it had won all twelve seats elected by the party council.

21. *L'Équipe d'Action dans l'organisation du secrétariat général*, AN-350AP/7; the directives in AN-350AP/9.

22. This unity should not be confused with similar political preferences. Bidault understood the MRP as a predominantly Catholic party, while Bacon and Menthon defended more left-wing positions. Robert Schuman (French Prime Minister from 1947 to 1948 and Foreign Minister between 1948 and 1953) advocated a more conservative party identity (Callot 1978, 274; Plaza 2008, 94).

23. *Situation du Mouvement en Septembre 1962*, AN-350AP/3.

24. *2ème Congrès National*, 13-16.12.1945, p. 50, AN-350AP/12.

25. *Tableau des Conseils Régionaux*, AN-681AP/10-1, Art. 40.

26. They received twelve and nine seats respectively in contrast to previously only four seats. The party in public office held fifteen seats. *Statuts*, 1945, Art. 40, 46, AN-350AP/5.

27. *Statuts*, 1945, Art. 40.

28. *Statuts*, 1945, Art. 20-29, 40.

29. *Statuts*, 1945, Art. 10.

30. *Congrès National*, 16.03.1947, pp. E/8-F/1, AN-350AP/15.

31. The old Comité Directeur had been abolished since it had become too large (i.e., around one hundred members) to remain an operable leadership body.

32. *Statuts*, 1949, Art. 32, 43, 44, 46, AN-350AP/5.

33. The national executive, in addition, included the MRP ministers, the party leader, party secretary, treasurer, and five co-opted members. If the MRP was not part of the government at the moment of the election, the parliamentary party chose five former ministers.

34. *Statuts*, 1949, Art. 35, AN-350AP/5.

35. *Neuville to Albert Gortais*, 25.07.1948; *Albert Gortais to Neuville*, 15.09.1948, AN-350AP/47; *Compte-rendu de la commission d'organisation*, 14.11.1956, AN-350AP/5.

36. *Statuts*, 1950, Art. 32, 35, AN-350AP/5.

37. *Lettre André Colin aux Fédérations*, 04.03.1952, AN-350AP/5.

38. *Maurice-René Simonnet aux membres du congrès extraordinaire*, 30.12.1958, AN-350AP/5; *Rapport sur le Mouvement*, 31.01-01.02.1959, pp. 12-19, AN-350AP/35.

39. "L'opposition désamorcée," *Index quotidien de la presse*, 20.01.1958, AN-350AP/10.

40. Only the seats for the Assemblée de l'Union Française had been abolished. *Status*, 1959, Art. 32, 34, 42, 44, AN-350AP/5.

41. *Status*, 1962, Art. 32. 42; *Lettre Georges Delfosse*, 27.04.1962; *Delfosse to Aumonier*, 11.07.1962; *Delfosse to Bidegain*, 24.09.1962; *Delfosse to Noddings*, 25.05.1962, AN-350AP/5.

42. *Statuts*, 1944, Art. 42, AN-681AP/10-1. For example, *Congrès National*, 24.05.1952; "Le MRP pose trois conditions à son maintien au gouvernement," *Combat*, 24.05.1952, AN-350AP/22.

43. *Congrès National*, 21.05.1955, p. F/2, AN-350AP/29.

44. It is unclear whether the MRP stayed with or without de Gaulle's approval. See Rioux (1987, 45-102), Callot (1978, 253-59), and Letamendia (1995, 80-85).

45. The accepted draft introduced a parliamentary system with a complex process of dissolution (Rioux 1987, 106; Letamendia 1995, 83).

46. *Liste des membres du Comité Directeur*, 24.01.1947, AN-350AP/46.

47. *Liste des membres du Comité Directeur*, 24.01.1947, AN-350AP/46.

48. *Election des membres de la commission exécutive*, 24.04.1947, AN-350AP/46.

49. *Congrès National*, 04.05.1951, pp. A/5-A/7; "De nombreux militants M.R.P. se font l'écho de l'indication de la classe ouvrière," *Humanité*, 05.05.1951, AN-350AP/21.

50. *Congrès National*, 18–21.05.1950, p.A2, AN-350AP/21.

51. The electoral system argument is further undermined by the Socialists being highly factionalized even though they competed under the same system (Campbell and Charlton 1978, 142).

52. Abbé Pierre, *Pour qu'une aube nouvelle*, 14.05.1950, p. 7, AN-457AP/166.

53. *Comité National provisoire du RFD*, 20.01.1959; "Ne Recommencez pas le M.R.P.," *France Observateur*, 05.02.1959; *Document préparatoire au débat sur la vie du Mouvement*; Compte-rendu de la réunion du RDF, 22–27.04.1959; *Simonnet*, 20.05.1959, AN-350AP/11; "Dans le vivier M.R.P.," *L'Aurore*, 08.05.1959; "Le XVIᵉ Congrès du M.R.P. a débattu de son élargissement," *La Croix*, 09.05.1959, AN-350AP/36.

54. *Commission de Coordination au 2ème Congrès National*, 1945, AN-350AP/13; *L'organisation du MRP*, AN-350AP/6.

55. *Commission Exécutive*, 03.12.1958; *Simonnet*, 30.12.1958, AN-350AP/5.

56. "Deux partis vont délibérer," *Lauren*, 27.05.1954, AN-350AP/28.

57. "Duel Pflimlin-de Menthon," *France-Soir*, 12.05.1956, AN-350AP/30.

58. *Congrès National*, 12.05.1956, p. G/6; "Conclusion du Congrès M.R.P.," *Le Figaro*, 14.05.1956, AN-350AP/30.

59. "Teitgen: 'Sur le plan des principes, comme sur celui des réalités, nous devons dire "oui" à la Fédération,'" *Forces Nouvelles*, 03.06.1965, AN-350AP/44.

60. *Congrès National*, 28.05.1965, pp. E1-J7, AN-350AP/43; "Lecanuet: 'Comment pourrions-nous dire "non" à nous-mêmes?'"; "Pflimlin: 'La Fédération n'est pas la bonne solution pour renforcer la Démocratie,'" *Forces Nouvelles*, 03.06.1965, AN-350AP/44.

61. One respondent mentioned the party merger, policy (dis)agreements, and general elections respectively.

62. K. Kühne, *Wahl der Vorsitzenden der CDU*, 17.12.2016, ACDP.

63. I focus on the Executive Council. The party president's role in selecting the heads of the LDP's influential "policy affairs research councils" (PARC) and other positions is discussed in the main text's next section.

64. Something acknowledged in Helmke and Levitsky's (2004) later work.

Conclusion

1. To reiterate, Seawright (2012, 9) has rightly emphasized that Kitschelt's concept of organizational entrenchment is more inclusive than Levitsky's (2003) focus on the de facto importance of rules and bureaucracies. To assess Levitsky's argument, in-depth qualitative work was conducted in chapters 3–7.

2. For example, Wiliarty (2010), Bloch Rubin (2017), and Bentancur, Rodríguez, and Rosenblatt (2020).

3. For example, Sartori (1976, 22), Katz (1980), Coppedge (1994), Boucek (2012), and Ceron (2012, 2015) on the negative effects of high factionalism.

4. Only the leader of the party's parliamentary group was an ex officio member of the national leadership.

5. Chapter 4 explained why the differences between Italy's open-list and Austria's flexible-list system did not fully explain the DC's and ÖVP's differences in factionalism.

6. For instance, Cross and Pilet (2014), Gauja (2016), Hazan and Rahat (2010), and the seminal volume by Scarrow et al. (2017).

7. Cadre, mass, catch-all, electoral-professional, and cartel party.

8. A similar statement can be made about Kitschelt's (1994) and Bolleyer's (2013) work on European parties and Coppedge (1994) and Levitsky's (2003) studies of Latin American parties.

9. With Hunter's (2010) study of Brazil's PT being among the few exceptions.

10. On political regimes, for example, Capoccia and Ziblatt (2010), Bernhard (2015), and Capoccia (2015). On public policy, Jacobs and Weaver (2015) and Béland, Rocco, and Waddan (2019). On political economy, Greif and Laitin (2004) and Greif (2006).

11. The first four analytical questions draw on Capoccia (2015, 167–71). The list of questions continues in the main text's next section.

12. The former could be seen as an example of layering and the latter as an example of displacement (see Mahoney and Thelen 2010, 15–16).

References

Ableitinger, Alfred. 1995. "Partei- und Organisationsstruktur." In *Volkspartei—Anspruch und Realität. Zur Geschichte der ÖVP seit 1945*, edited by Robert Kriechbaumer and Franz Schausberger, 137–61. Vienna: Böhlau.

Accetti, Carlo Invernizzi. 2019. *What Is Christian Democracy? Politics, Religion and Ideology.* Cambridge: Cambridge University Press.

Agosti, Aldo. 1999. *Storia del Partito comunista italiano.* Rome: Laterza.

Aldrich, John H. 1995. *Why Parties? The Origin and Transformation of Party Politics in America.* Chicago: University of Chicago Press.

Allern, Elin Haugsgjerd, and Tània Verge. 2017. "Still Connecting with Society?" In *Organising Political Parties: Representation, Participation, and Power*, edited by Susan E. Scarrow, Paul D. Webb, and Thomas Poguntke, 106–35. Oxford: Oxford University Press.

Ahmed, Amel. 2013. *Democracy and the Politics of Electoral System Choice: Engineering Electoral Dominance.* Cambridge: Cambridge University Press.

Ames, Barry. 1995. "Electoral Strategy under Open-List Proportional Representation." *American Journal of Political Science* 39 (2): 406–33.

Anria, Santiago. 2019. *When Movements Become Parties: The Bolivian MAS in Comparative Perspective.* Cambridge: Cambridge University Press.

Arian, Alan, and Samuel H. Barnes. 1974. "The Dominant Party System: A Neglected Model of Democratic Stability." *Journal of Politics* 36 (3): 592–614.

Armingeon, Klaus, Sarah Engler, and Lucas Leemann. 2022. Comparative Political Data Set 1960–2020. Zurich: Department of Political Science, University of Zurich.

Baerwald, Hans. 1986. *Party Politics in Japan.* London: Routledge.

Bakvis, Herman. 1981. *Catholic Power in the Netherlands.* Kingston, ON: McGill-Queen's University Press.

Bale, Tim. 2012. *The Conservatives since 1945: The Drivers of Party Change.* Oxford: Oxford University Press.

Bardi, Luciano, and Leonardo Morlino. 1992. "Italy." In *Party Organizations: A Data Handbook on Party Organizations in Western Democracies, 1960–90*, edited by Richard S. Katz and Peter Mair, 458–618. London: Sage.

———. 1994. "Italy: Tracing the Roots of the Great Transformation." In *How Parties Organize: Change and Adaptation in Party Organizations in Western Democracies*, edited by Richard S. Katz and Peter Mair, 242–77. London: Sage.

Barnea, Shlomit, and Gideon Rahat. 2007. "Reforming Candidate Selection Methods: A Three-Level Approach." *Party Politics* 13 (3): 375–94.

Barnes, Samuel H. 1967. *Party Democracy: Politics in an Italian Socialist Federation*. New Haven, CT: Yale University Press.

Barr, Robert R. 2005. "Bolivia. Another Uncompleted Revolution." *Latin American Politics and Society* 47 (3): 69–90.

Bazin, François. 1981. "Les députés MRP élus les 21 octobre 1945, 2 juin et 10 novembre 1946. Itinéraire politique d'une génération catholique." PhD diss., Institut d'Études politiques, Paris.

Béland, Daniel, Philip B. Rocco, and Alex Waddan. 2019. "Policy Feedback and the Politics of the Affordable Care Act." *Policy Studies Journal* 47 (2): 395–422.

Bell, David S., and Byron Criddle. 2014. "Party Organisation." In *Exceptional Socialists*, edited by David S. Bell and Byron Criddle, 33–57. London: Palgrave Macmillan.

Belloni, Frank P. 1978. "Factionalism, the Party System, and Italian Politics." In *Faction Politics: Political Parties and Factionalism in Comparative Perspective*, edited by Dennis C. Beller and Frank P. Belloni, 72–108. Santa Barbara, CA: ABC Clio.

Bentancur Pérez, Verónica, Rafael Piñeiro Rodríguez, and Fernando Rosenblatt. 2020. *How Party Activism Survives: Uruguay's Frente Amplio*. Cambridge: Cambridge University Press.

Bernhard, Michael. 2015. "Chronic Instability and the Limits of Path Dependence." *Perspectives on Politics* 13 (4): 976–91.

Besser, Christoph. 2008. *Die deutschen Vertriebenen in der Bundesrepublik Deutschland von 1939 bis 1990*. Version 1.0.0. GESIS Data Archive. Dataset.

Bettcher, Kim Eric. 2005. "Factions of Interest in Japan and Italy: The Organizational and Motivational Dimensions of Factionalism." *Party Politics* 11 (3): 339–58.

Bichet, Robert. 1980. *La Démocratie Chrétienne en France. Le Mouvement Républicain Populaire*. Besançon, France: Jacques et Demontrond.

Blenk, Gustav. 1966. *Leopold Kunschak und seine Zeit. Porträt eines christlichen Arbeiterführers*. Vienna: Europa-Verlag.

Bloch Rubin, Ruth. 2017. *Building the Bloc: Intraparty Organization in the U.S. Congress*. New York: Cambridge University Press.

Blum, Rachel. 2020. *How the Tea Party Captured the GOP: Insurgent Factions in American Politics*. Chicago: University of Chicago Press.

Boas, Taylor C. 2007. "Conceptualizing Continuity and Change: The Composite-Standard Model of Path Dependence." *Journal of Theoretical Politics* 19 (1): 33–54.

Bolleyer, Nicole. 2013. *New Parties in Old Party Systems: Persistence and Decline in Seventeen Democracies*. Oxford: Oxford University Press.

Bösch, Frank. 2001. *Die Adenauer-CDU. Gründung, Aufstieg und Krise einer Erfolgspartei 1945–1969*. Stuttgart: Deutsche Verlags-Anstalt.

———. 2002. *Macht und Machtverlust. Die Geschichte der CDU*. Stuttgart: Deutsche Verlags-Anstalt.

Borz, Gabriela. 2017. "Explaining Varieties of Factionalism: A Comparative European study." Paper presented at the Political Studies Association's Annual Conference, Glasgow.

Borz, Gabriela, and Carolina de Miguel. 2019. "Organizational and Ideological Strategies for Nationalization: Evidence from European Parties." *British Journal of Political Science* 49 (4): 1499–1526.

Bosmans, Jac. 2004. "The Primacy of Domestic Politics: Christian Democracy in the Nether-lands." In *Christian Democracy in Europe since 1945*, edited by Michael Gehler and Wolfram Kaiser, 54–66. London: Routledge.

Boucek, Françoise 2009. "Rethinking Factionalism: Typologies, Intra-Party Dynamics and Three Faces of Factionalism." *Party Politics* 15 (4): 455–85.

———. 2012. *Factional Politics. How Dominant Parties Implode or Stabilize*. London: Palgrave Macmillan.

Bouissou, Jean-Marie. 2001. "Party Factions and the Politics of Coalition: Japanese Politics Un-der the 'System of 1955.'" *Electoral Studies* 20 (4): 581–602.

Boyer, John W. 1981. *Political Radicalism in Late Imperial Vienna. Origins of the Christian Social Movement, 1848–1897*. Chicago: University of Chicago Press.

Boyer, John. W. 2010. *Karl Lueger (1844–1910). Christlichsoziale Politik als Beruf*. Vienna: Böhlau.

Braunthal, Gerard. 1994. *The German Social Democrats since 1969: A Party in Power and Opposi-tion*. Boulder, CO: Westview.

Bruckmüller, Ernst. 1995. "Die Ständische Tradition. ÖVP und Neokorporatismus." In *Volkspartei—Anspruch und Realität. Zur Geschichte der ÖVP seit 1945*, edited by Robert Kriechbaumer and Franz Schausberger, 281–316. Vienna: Böhlau.

Bruneau, Thomas. 1997. Introduction to *Political Parties and Democracy in Portugal: Organizations, Elections, and Public Opinion*, edited by Thomas C Bruneau, 1–22. Boulder, CO: Westview.

Bruneau, Thomas, and Alex MacLeod. 1986. *Politics in Contemporary Portugal: Parties and the Consolidation of Democracy*. Boulder, CO: Lynne Rienner.

Bufacchi, Vittorio, and Simon Burgess. 1998. *Italy since 1989: Events and Interpretations*. London: Macmillan.

Bundesagentur für Arbeit. 2023. *Arbeitslosigkeit im Zeitverlauf*. Nuremberg: Statistik der Bundesagentur für Arbeit.

Bundesanstalt Statistik Österreich. 1995. *Republik Österreich, 1945–1995*. Vienna: Österreichisches Statistisches Zentralamt.

———. 2017. *Ergebnisse der Volkszählung vom 21. März 1961*. Vienna: Österreichische Staatsdruckerei.

Bundeswahlleiter. 2016. Wahl zum 1. Deutschen Bundestag (August 14, 1949). Wiesbaden.

Burgess, Katrina, and Steven Levitsky. 2003. "Explaining Populist Party Adaption in Latin America: Environmental and Organizational Determinants of Party Change in Argentina, Mexico, Peru, and Venezuela." *Comparative Political Studies* 36 (8): 881–911.

Burrett, Tina. 2017. "Abe Road: Comparing Japanese Prime Minister Shinzo Abe's Leadership of his First and Second Governments." *Parliamentary Affairs* 70 (2): 400–429.

Callot, Émile-François. 1978. *Le Mouvement républicain populaire. Origine, structure, doctrine, programme et action politique*. Paris: Éditions Marcel Rivière et Cie.

———. 1986. *L'action et l'oeuvre politique du Mouvement républicain populaire*. Paris: Champion.

Campbell, Bruce A., and Sue Ellen M. Charlton. 1978. "The Ambiguity of Faction: Fragmen-tation and Bipolarization in France." In *Faction Politics: Political Parties and Factionalism in Comparative Perspective*, edited by Frank P. Belloni and Dennis C. Beller, 141–60. Santa Barbara, CA: ABC Clio.

Capoccia, Giovanni. 2005. *Defending Democracy. Reactions to Extremism in Interwar Europe*. Baltimore: Johns Hopkins University Press.

———. 2015. "Critical Junctures and Institutional Change." In *Advances in Comparative Histori-cal Analysis*, edited by James Mahoney and Kathleen Thelen, 147–79. Cambridge: Cam-bridge University Press.

Capoccia, Giovanni, and R. Daniel Kelemen. 2007. "The Study of Critical Junctures: Theory, Narrative, and Counterfactuals in Historical Institutionalism." *World Politics* 59 (3): 341–69.

Capoccia, Giovanni, and Daniel Ziblatt. 2010. "The Historical Turn in Democratization Studies: A New Research Agenda for Europe and Beyond." *Comparative Political Studies* 43 (8–9): 931–69.

Capperucci, Vera. 2009. "Alcide De Gasperi and the Problem of Reconstruction." *Modern Italy* 14 (4): 445–57.

———. 2010. *Il Partito dei cattolici. Dall' Italia degasperiana alle correnti democristiane.* Rome: Rubbettino.

Caramani, Daniele. 2000. *Elections in Western Europe since 1815: Electoral Results by Constituencies.* London: Macmillan.

Carey, John. 2007. "Competing Principles, Political Institutions, and Party Unity in Legislative Voting." *American Journal of Political Science* 51 (1): 92–107.

Carey, John M., and Matthew Soberg Shugart. 1995. "Incentives to Cultivate a Personal Vote: A Rank Ordering of Electoral Formulas." *Electoral Studies* 14 (4): 417–39.

Carty, R. Kenneth. 2010. "Dominance without Factions: The Liberal Party of Canada." In *Dominant Political Parties and Democracy: Concepts, Measures, Cases and Comparisons*, edited by Matthijs Bogaards and Françoise Boucek, 140–52. Abingdon: Routledge.

Cary, Noel. 1996. *The Path to Christian Democracy: German Catholics and the Party System from Windthorst to Adenauer.* Cambridge, MA: Harvard University Press.

Ceron, Andrea. 2012. "Bounded Oligarchy: How and When Factions Constrain Leaders in Party Position-Taking." *Electoral Studies* 31 (4): 689–701.

———. 2015. "The Politics of Fission: An Analysis of Faction Breakaways among Italian Parties (1946–2011)." *British Journal of Political Science* 45 (1): 121–39.

———. 2019. *Leaders, Factions, and the Game of Intra-party Politics.* New York: Routledge.

Chalmers, Douglas A. 1972. "Parties and Society in Latin America." *Studies in Comparative International Development* 7 (2): 102–28.

Chandra, Kanchan. 2004. *Why Ethnic Parties Succeed: Patronage and Ethnic Head Counts in India.* Cambridge: Cambridge University Press.

Chassériaud, Jean-Paul. 1965. *Le Parti Démocrate Chrétien en Italie.* Paris: Librairie Armand Colin.

Clemens, Clay. 2000. "The Last Hurrah: Helmut Kohl's CDU/CSU and the 1998 Election." In *Power Shift in Germany: The 1998 Election and the End of the Kohl Era*, edited by David P. Conradt, Gerald R. Kleinfeld, and Christian Søe, 38–58. New York: Berghahn.

———. 2005. "Hold the Champagne: Edmund Stoiber's CDU/CSU and Bundestagswahl 2002." In *Precarious Victory: The 2002 German Federal Election and Its Aftermath*, edited by David P. Conradt, Gerald R. Kleinfeld, and Christian Søe, 58–82. New York: Berghahn.

———. 2006. "From the Outside In: Angela Merkel as Opposition Leader, 2000–2005." In *Launching the Grand Coalition: The 2005 Bundestag Election and the Future of German Politics*, edited by Eric Langenbacher, 150–90. New York: Berghahn.

———. 2009. "Modernisation or Disorientation? Policy Change in Merkel's CDU." *German Politics* 18 (2): 121–39.

———. 2010. "Lose-Lose Proposition: Policy Change and Party Politics in the Grand Coalition." In *Between Left and Right: The 2009 Bundestag Elections and the Transformation of the Germany Party System*, edited by Eric Langenbacher, 24–47. New York: Berghahn.

———. 2011. "Explaining Merkel's Autonomy in the Grand Coalition: Personalisation or Party Organisation?" *German Politics* 20 (4): 469–85.

———. 2018. "The CDU/CSU's Ambivalent 2017 Campaign." In *Twilight of the Merkel Era: Power and Politics in Germany after the 2017 Bundestag Election*, edited by Eric Langenbacher, 140–60. New York: Berghahn.

Collier, Ruth Berins, and David Collier. 1991. *Shaping the Political Arena: Critical Junctures, the Labor Movement, and Regime Dynamics in Latin America*. Princeton, NJ: Princeton University Press.

Conradt, David P. 2006. "The Tipping Point: The 2005 Election and the Deconsolidation of the German Party System." In *Launching the Grand Coalition: The 2005 Bundestag Election and the Future of German Politics*, edited by Eric Langenbacher, 17–28. New York: Berghahn.

———. 2010. "The Shrining Elephants: The 2009 Election and the Changing Party System." In *Between Left and Right: The 2009 Bundestag Elections and the Transformation of the Germany Party System*, edited by Eric Langenbacher, 48–68. New York: Berghahn.

Conway, John. 1992. "The Political Role of German Protestantism, 1870–1990." *Journal of Church and State* 34 (4): 819–42.

Conway, Martin. 1996. Introduction to *Political Catholicism in Europe, 1918–1965*, edited by Tom Buchanan and Martin Conway, 1–33. Oxford: Clarendon Press.

———. 2001. "Catholic Politics or Christian Democracy? The Evolution of Inter-war Political Catholicism." In *Christdemokratie in Europa im 20. Jahrhundert*, edited by Michael Gehler, Wolfram Kaiser, and Helmut Wohnout, 294–309. Vienna: Böhlau.

———. 2022. *Western Europe's Democratic Age: 1945–1969*. Princeton, NJ: Princeton University Press.

Coppedge, Michael. 1994. *Strong Parties and Lame Ducks: Presidential Partyarchy and Factionalism in Venezuela*. Stanford, CA: Stanford University Press.

Corrales, Javier. 2002. *Presidents without Parties. Economic Reforms in Argentina and Venezuela in the 1990s*. University Park: Pennsylvania State University Press.

Cox, Gary W., and Frances McCall Rosenbluth. 1993. "The Electoral Fortunes of Legislative Factions in Japan." *American Political Science Review* 87 (3): 577–89.

Cox, Gary W., Frances McCall Rosenbluth, and Michael F. Thies. 1999. "Electoral Reform and the Fate of Factions: The Case of Japan's Liberal Democratic Party." *British Journal of Political Science* 29 (1): 33–56.

Crisp, Brian F. 1996. "The Rigidity of Democratic Institutions and the Current Legitimacy Crisis in Venezuela." *Latin American Perspectives* 23 (3): 30–49.

———. 2000. *Democratic Institutional Design: The Powers and Incentives of Venezuelan Politicians and Interest Groups*. Stanford, CA: Stanford University Press.

Cross, William, and André Blais. 2012. *Politics at the Centre: The Selection and Removal of Party Leaders in the Anglo Parliamentary Democracies*. Oxford: Oxford University Press.

Cross, William P., and Jean-Benoit Pilet. 2014. "The Selection of Party Leaders in Contemporary Parliamentary Democracies." In *The Selection of Political Party Leaders in Contemporary Parliamentary Democracies: A Comparative Study*, edited by Jean-Benoit Pilet and William P. Cross, 1–11. London: Routledge.

Cyr, Jennifer. 2017. *The Fates of Political Parties: Institutional Crisis, Continuity, and Change in Latin America*. Cambridge: Cambridge University Press.

D'Alimonte, Roberto. 2005. "Italy: A Case of Fragmented Bipolarism." In *The Politics of Electoral Systems*, edited by Michael Gallagher and Paul Mitchell, 253–76. Oxford: Oxford University Press.

Dalloz, Jacques. 1993. *Georges Bidault. Biographie politique*. Paris: Éditions L'Harmattan.

Dalton, Russell J. 2006. *Citizen Politics: Public Opinion and Political Parties in Advanced Industrial Democracies*. Washington, DC: CQ Press.

Damato, Francesco. 1979. *Dc contro Dc. Splendori e miserie di un partito di gomma*. Milan: Editoriale Nuova.

Decker, Frank. 2015. "Follow-Up to the Grand Coalition: The German Party System before and after the 2013 Federal Election." In *The Merkel Republic: An Appraisal*, edited by Eric Langenbacher, 26–47. New York: Berghahn.

Delbreil, Jean-Claude. 1990. *Centrisme et Démocratie-Chrétienne en France*. Paris: Publications de la Sorbonne.

Della Porta, Donatella, and Alberto Vannucci. 1994. *Corruzione politica e amministrazione pubblica. Risorse, mecanismi, attori*. Bologna: Il Mulino.

Diamanti, Ilvo. 1996. "The Northern League. From Regional Party to Party in Government." In *The New Italian Republic: From the Fall of the Berlin Wall to Berlusconi*, edited by Stephen Gundle and Simon Parker, 114–29. London: Routledge.

Dietzfelbinger, Eckart. 1984. *Die westdeutsche Friedensbewegung 1948 bis 1955. Die Protestaktionen gegen die Remilitarisierung der Bundesrepublik Deutschland*. Cologne: Pahl-Rugenstein.

Dilling, Matthias. 2014. "Geteilte Einheit. Faktionalismus in Christdemokratischen Parteien Westeuropas." *MIP Zeitschrift für Parteienwissenschaft* 20 (1): 79–88.

———. 2017. "Die CDU. Repräsentationsgarantien und -defizite einer Volkspartei." In *Parteien und soziale Ungleichheit*, edited by Elmar Wiesendahl, 89–121. Wiesbaden: Springer.

———. 2018. "Two of the Same Kind? The Rise of the AfD and Its Implications for the CDU/CSU." *German Politics and Society* 36 (1): 84–104.

———. 2022. "Denominational Conflicts and Party Breakthrough: The Negative Case of the All-German People's Party." *Social Science History* 46 (3): 505–29.

———. 2023. "Political Parties and Interest Incorporation: A New Typology of Intra-Party Groups." *Political Studies Review*, advance online publication, https://doi.org/10.1177/1478 9299231156556.

DiSalvo, Daniel. 2012. *Engines of Change: Party Factions in American Politics, 1868–2010*. Oxford: Oxford University Press.

Dittberner, Jürgen. 1984. "Die Freie Demokratische Partei." In *Parteien-Handbuch, Die Parteien der Bundesrepublik Deutschland 1945–1980, Bd. II: FDP bis WAV*, edited by Richard Stöss, 1311–81. Opladen: Westdeutscher Verlag.

———. 1987. *FDP, Partei der zweiten Wahl. Ein Beitrag zur Geschichte der liberalen Partei und ihrer Funktionen im Parteiensystem der Bundesrepublik*. Opladen: Westdeutscher Verlag.

———. 2010. *Die FDP. Geschichte, Personen, Organisation, Perspektiven*. Wiesbaden: VS Verlag.

Donovan, Mark. 1994. "Democrazia Cristiana. Party of Government." In *Christian Democracy in Europe: A Comparative Perspective*, edited by David Hanley, 71–85. London: Pinter.

Dümig, Kathrin, Matthias Trefs, and Reimut Zohlnhöfer. 2006. "Die Faktionen der CDU. Bändigung durch institutionalisierte Einbindung." In *Innerparteiliche Machtgruppen. Faktionalismus im Internationalen Vergleich*, edited by Matthias Basedau, Gero Erdmann, and Patrick Köllner, 99–129. Frankfurt: Campus.

Duncan, Fraser. 2006. "A Decade of Christian Democratic Decline: The Dilemmas of the CDU, ÖVP and CDA in the 1990s." *Government and Opposition* 41 (4): 469–90.

———. 2007. "Lately, Things Just Don't Seem the Same: External Shocks, Party Change and the Adaptation of the Dutch Christian Democrats during 'Purple Hague' 1994–8." *Party Politics* 13 (1): 69–87.

Duverger, Maurice. 1951. *Les parties politiques*. Paris: Librairie Armand Colin.

Eldersveld, Samuel. 1964. *Political Parties: A Behavioral Analysis*. Chicago: Rand McNally.

Elgie, Robert. 1995. *Political Leadership in Liberal Democracies*. London: Palgrave.

————. 2005. "France: Stacking the Deck." In *The Politics of Electoral Systems*, edited by Michael Gallagher and Paul Mitchell, 119–36. Oxford: Oxford University Press.

Ellinas, Antonis A. 2020. *Organizing against Democracy: The Local Organizational Development of Far Right Parties in Greece and Europe*. Cambridge: Cambridge University Press.

Endo, Masahisa, and Robert J. Pekkanen. 2016. "The LDP: Return to Dominance? Or a Golden Age Built on Sand?" in *Japan Decides 2014: The Japanese General Election*, edited by Robert J. Pekkanen, Steven R. Reed, and Ethan Scheiner, 41–54. New York: Palgrave.

Engelmann, Frederick C. 1962. "Haggling for the Equilibrium: The Renegotiation of the Austrian Coalition, 1959." *American Political Science Review* 56: 651–62.

Ennser-Jedenastik, Laurenz, and Anita Bodlos. 2019. "Liberal Parties in Austria." In *Liberal Parties in Europe*, edited by Emilie van Haute and Caroline Close, 129–45. London: Routledge.

Ennser-Jedenastik, Laurenz, and Wolfgang C. Müller. 2014. "The Selection of Party Leaders in Austria." In *The Selection of Political Party Leaders in Contemporary Parliamentary Democracies: A Comparative Study*, edited by Jean-Benoit Pilet and William P. Cross, 62–76. London: Routledge.

Enos, Ryan D., and Eitan D. Hersh. 2015. "Party Activists as Campaign Advertisers: The Ground Campaign as a Principal-Agent Problem." *American Political Science Review* 109 (2): 252–78.

Erk, Jan. 2004. "Austria: A Federation without Federalism." *Publius* 34 (1): 1–20.

Evans, Ellen Lovell. 1999. *The Cross and the Ballot: Catholic Political Parties in Germany, Switzerland, Austria, Belgium and the Netherlands, 1785–1985*. Boston: Humanities Press.

Fabre, Elodie. 2011. "Measuring Party Organization: The Vertical Dimension of the Multi-Level Organization of State-wide Parties in Spain and the UK." *Party Politics* 17 (3): 343–63.

Fallend, Franz. 1997. "Regierungsproporz in der Krise. Zur aktuellen politischen Debatte über die konkordanzdemokratische Regierungsform in Österreichs Bundesländern." *Österreichische Zeitschrift für Politikwissenschaft* 26 (1): 23–40.

————. 2005. "Die Österreichische Volkspartei (ÖVP): Erfolgreiche Wahlstrategie bei unmoderner Parteiorganisation." In *Zwischen Anarchie und Strategie. Der Erfolg von Parteiorganisationen*, edited by Josef Schmid and Udo Zolleis, 186–206. Wiesbaden: VS Verlag.

————. 2019. "Von Schwarz-Blau zu Türkis-Blau. Ursachen und Folgen der Koalitionsstrategien der ÖVP 1999/2000 und 2017." In *Die Schwarz-Blaue Wende in Österreich*, edited by Emmerich Tálos, 5–28. Vienna: LIT.

Fanti, Guido, and Gian Carlo Ferri. 2001. *Cronache dall'Emilia rossa. L'impossibile riformismo del PCI*. Bologna: Pendragon.

Faucher, Florence. 2015. "Leadership Elections: What Is at Stake for Parties? A Comparison of the British Labour Party and the Parti Socialiste." *Parliamentary Affairs* 68 (4): 794–820.

Fehlen, Fernand. 2008. "Die Wählerschaft von CSV und Rechtspartei im Lichte der empirischen Wahlforschung." In *Spiegelbild eines Landes und seiner Politik? Geschichte der Christlich-Sozialen Volkspartei Luxemburgs im 20. Jahrhundert*, edited by Gilbert Trausch, 461–501. Luxembourg: Saint Paul.

Feltes, Paul. 2008. "Modernisierung einer konservativen Volkspartei (1974/79–2004)." In *Spiegelbild eines Landes und seiner Politik? Geschichte der Christlich-Sozialen Volkspartei Luxemburgs im 20. Jahrhundert*, edited by Gilbert Trausch, 399–460. Luxembourg: Saint Paul.

Filippov, Mikhail, Peter C. Ordeshook, and Olga Shvetsova. 2004. *Designing Federalism: A Theory of Self-Sustainable Federal Institutions*. Cambridge: Cambridge University Press.

Foschepoth, Josef. 1986. "British Interest in the Division of Germany after the Second World War." *Journal of Contemporary History* 21 (3): 391–411.

Frain, Maritheresa. 1997. "The Right in Portugal: The PSD and CDS/PP." In *Political Parties and Democracy in Portugal: Organizations, Elections, and Public Opinion*, edited by Thomas Bruneau, 77–111. Boulder, CO: Westview Press.

Freidenberg, Flavia, and Steven Levitsky. 2006. "Informal Institutions and Party Organization in Latin America." In *Informal Institutions and Democracy: Lessons from Latin America*, edited by Gretchen Helmke and Steven Levitsky, 178–97. Baltimore: Johns Hopkins University Press.

Freire, André. 2006. "The Party System of Portugal." In *Die Parteiensysteme Westeuropas*, edited by Oskar Niedermayer, Richard Stöss and Melanie Haas, 373–96. Wiesbaden: VS Verlag.

Frey, Timotheos. 2009. *Die Christdemokratie in Westeuropa. Der schmale Grat zum Erfolg*. Baden-Baden: Nomos.

Fry, Earl H., and Gregory A. Raymond. 1980. *The Other Western Europe: A Political Analysis of the Smaller Democracies*. Santa Barbara, CA: Clio.

Furlong, Paul. 1996. "Political Catholicism and the Strange Death of the Christian Democrats." In *The New Italian Republic: From the Fall of the Berlin Wall to Berlusconi*, edited by Stephen Gundle and Simon Parker, 59–71. London: Routledge.

Galli, Giorgio. 1978. *Storia della Democrazia Cristiana*. Rome: Laterza.

Galli, Giorgio, and Paolo Facchi. 1962. *La sinistra democristiana. Storia e ideologia*. Milan: Feltrinelli.

Gamper, Anna, and Bernhard Koch. 2014. "Federalism and Legal Unification in Austria." In *Federalism and Legal Unification*, edited by Daniel Halberstam and Mathias Reimann, 103–19. Wiesbaden: Springer.

Gauja, Anika. 2016. *Party Reform: The Causes, Challenges, and Consequences of Organizational Change*. Oxford: Oxford University Press.

———. 2020. "The Challenge of Innovating Representative Democracy." In *Innovations, Reinvented Politics and Representative Democracy*, edited by Agnès Alexandre-Collier, Alexandra Goujon, and Guillaume Gourgues, 195–207. London: Routledge.

Gehler, Michael, and Wolfram Kaiser. 2004. *Christian Democracy in Europe since 1945*. London: Routledge.

Geiger, Tim. 2008. *Atlantiker gegen Gaullisten. Außenpolitischer Konflikt und innerparteilicher Machtkampf in der CDU/CSU 1958–1969*. Munich: Oldenbourg.

George Mulgan, Aurelia. 2002. *Japan's Failed Revolution. Koizumi and the Politics of Economic Reform*. Canberra: Asia Pacific Press.

———. 2018. *The Abe Administration and the Rise of the Prime Ministerial Executive*. London: Routledge.

Ginsborg, Paul. 1996. "Explaining Italy's Crisis." In *The New Italian Republic: From the Fall of the Berlin Wall to Berlusconi*, edited by Stephen Gundle and Simon Parker, 19–39. London: Routledge.

Giovagnoli, Agostino. 1996. *Il partito italiano. La Democrazia Cristiana dal 1942 al 1994*. Rome: Laterza.

Godechot, Thierry. 1964. *Le parti démocrate-chrétien italien*. Paris: Librairie Générale de Droit.

Golden, Miriam A., and Eric C. C. Chang. 2001. "Competitive Corruption, Factional Conflict and Political Malfeasance in Postwar Italian Christian Democracy." *World Politics* 53 (4): 588–622.

Gottweis, Herbert. 1983. "Zur Entwicklung der ÖVP. Zwischen Interessenpolitik und Massenintegration." In *Zwischen Koalition und Konkurrenz. Österreichs Parteien seit 1945*, edited by Peter Gerlich and Wolfgang C. Müller, 53–68. Vienna: Braumüller.

Grau, Andreas. 2011. "Goslar 1950. Vorbereitung, Konzeption und Ablauf des ersten Bundespar-
teitages der Christlich-Demokratischen Union Deutschlands." *Historisch-Politische Mitteilungen* 18 (1): 49–86.

Greene, Kenneth. 2007. *Why Dominant Parties Lose.* Cambridge: Cambridge University Press.

Greif, Avner. 2006. *Institutions and the Path to the Modern Economy: Lessons from Medieval
Trade.* New York: Cambridge University Press.

Greif, Avner, and David D. Laitin. 2004. "A Theory of Endogenous Institutional Change." *American Political Science Review* 98 (4): 633–52.

Grießler, Erich. 2007. "'Policy Learning' in der SPÖ. Innerparteiliche Dynamiken bei der Ents-
cheidungsfindung zur Fristenregelung." *Österreichische Zeitschrift für Politikwissenschaft* 36
(3): 267–83.

Gronchi, Giovanni. 1962. *Una politica sociale. Scritti e discorsi scelti (1948-1954).* Bologna: Il
Mulino.

Grosbusch, André. 2008. "Bewährung, Abnutzung und Erneuerung. Die CSV der sechziger
und siebziger Jahre." In *Spiegelbild eines Landes und seiner Politik? Geschichte der Christlich-
Sozialen Volkspartei Luxemburgs im 20. Jahrhundert,* edited by Gilbert Trausch, 329–98.
Luxembourg: Saint Paul.

Grzymala-Busse, Anna. 2002. *Redeeming the Communist Past: The Regeneration of Communist
Parties in East Central Europe.* Cambridge: Cambridge University Press.

Gundle, Stephen, and Simon Parker. 1996. *The New Italian Republic: From the Fall of the Berlin
Wall to Berlusconi.* London: Routledge.

Gurland, Arcadius R. 1980. *Die CDU/CSU. Ursprünge und Entwicklungen bis 1953.* Frankfurt:
Europäische Verlagsanstalt.

Haggard, Stephan, and Robert Kaufman. 2021. *Backsliding: Democratic Regress in the Contemporary World.* Cambridge: Cambridge University Press.

Hanley, David. 1994. "Introduction: Christian Democracy as a Political Phenomenon." In *Christian Democracy in Europe,* edited by David Hanley, 1–11. London: Pinter Publishers.

Harmel, Robert, Uk Heo, Alexander Tan, and Kenneth Janda. 1995. "Performance, Leadership,
Factions and Party Change. An Empirical Analysis." *West European Politics* 18 (1): 1–33.

Harmel, Robert, and Kenneth Janda. 1994. "An Integrated Theory of Party Goals and Party
Change." *Journal of Theoretical Politics* 6 (3): 259–87.

Haungs, Peter. 1983. "Die Christlich Demokratische Union Deutschlands (CDU) und die
Christlich Soziale Union in Bayern (CSU)." In *Schweiz, Niederlande, Belgien, Luxemburg,
Europäische Demokratische Union (EDU), Europäische Volkspartei (EVP),* edited by Hans-
Joachim Veen, 9–194. Vol. 5 of *Christlich-demokratische und konservative Parteien in Wes-
teuropa.* Paderborn: Schöningh.

———. 1986. "Kanzlerdemokratie in der Bundesrepublik Deutschland von Adenauer bis Kohl."
Zeitschrift für Politik 33 (1): 44–66.

———. 1995. "The CDU: Prototype of a People's Party." In *Political Parties in Democracy: Role and
Function of Political Parties in the Political System of the Federal Republic of Germany,* edited
by Josef Thesing and Wilhelm Hofmeister, 168–217. Sankt Augustin: Konrad-Adenauer-
Stiftung.

Hazan, Reuven Y., and Gideon Rahat. 2010. *Democracy within Parties: Candidate Selection Methods and Their Political Consequences.* Oxford: Oxford University Press.

Hehl, Ulrich von. 1999. "Konfessionelle Irritationen in der frühen Bundesrepublik." *Historisch-
Politische Mitteilungen* 6 (1): 167–87.

Heidenheimer, Arnold J. 1961. *Adenauer and the CDU: The Rise of the Leader and the Integration of the Party*. The Hague: Martinus Nijhoff.

Heimann, Siegfried. 1984. "Die Sozialdemokratische Partei Deutschlands." In *Parteien-Handbuch. Die Parteien in der Bundesrepublik Deutschland 1945–1980. NPD–WAV*, edited by Richard Stöss, 2025–2216. Opladen: Westdeutscher Verlag.

Hellmann, Olli. 2011. *Political Parties and Electoral Strategy: The Development of Party Organizations in East Asia*. London: Palgrave.

Helmke, Gretchen, and Steven Levitsky. 2004. "Informal Institutions and Comparative Politics: A Research Agenda." *Perspectives on Politics* 2 (4): 725–40.

Hijmans, Robert. 2015. "First-Level Administrative Divisions, Germany, 2015," University of California, Berkeley. http://purl.stanford.edu/nh891yz3147.

Hine, David. 1993. *Governing Italy: The Politics of Bargained Pluralism*. Oxford: Clarendon Press.

Höbelt, Lothar. 1999. *Von der vierten Partei zur dritten Kraft. Die Geschichte des VdU*. Graz: Stocker.

———. 2000. "The Prehistory of the Fourth Party Movement in Austria, 1947–1949." *Austrian History Yearbook* 31: 107–25.

Höhne, Roland. 2006. "Das Parteiensystem Frankreichs." In *Die Parteiensysteme Westeuropas*, edited by Oskar Niedermayer, Richard Stöss, and Melanie Haas, 161–87. Wiesbaden: VS Verlag.

Hoeth, Lutz. 2007. "Die Evangelische Kirche und die Wiederbewaffnung Deutschlands in den Jahren 1945–1958." PhD diss., Technische Universität Berlin.

Hornig, Eike-Christian. 2013. "The Genetic Origin of the CDU and Its Developmental Path to a Catch-All Party." *German Politics* 22 (1–2): 82–96.

Huneeus, Carlos. 2003. "A Highly Institutionalized Political Party: Christian Democracy in Chile." In *Christian Democracy in Latin America: Electoral Competition and Regime Conflicts*, edited by Scott Mainwaring and Timothy R. Scully, 121–61. Stanford, CA: Stanford University Press.

Hunter, Wendy. 2010. *The Transformation of the Workers' Party in Brazil, 1989–2009*. New York: Cambridge University Press.

Ignazi, Piero, and E. Spencer Wellhofer. 2012. "Votes and Votive Candles. Modernization, Secularization, Vatican II, and the Decline of Religious Voting in Italy: 1953–1992." *Comparative Political Studies* 46 (1): 31–62.

Irving, Ronald Eckford Mill. 1973. *Christian Democracy in France*. London: George Allen and Unwin.

Issar, Sukriti, and Matthias Dilling. 2022. "Analyzing Failed Institutional Change Attempts." *Political Research Quarterly* 75 (1): 203–15.

Jacobs, Alan M., and R. Kent Weaver. 2015. "When Policies Undo Themselves: Self-Undermining Feedback as a Source of Policy Change." *Governance* 28 (4): 441–57.

Janda, Kenneth. 1980. *Political Parties: A Cross-National Survey*. New York: Free Press.

Janssen, Siebo M. 2006. "Das Parteiensystem Luxemburgs." In *Die Parteiensysteme Westeuropas*, edited by Oskar Niedermayer, Richard Stöss, and Melanie Haas, 321–29. Wiesbaden: VS Verlag.

Jobke, Barbara. 1974. "Aufstieg und Verfall einer wertorientierten Bewegung: Dargestellt am Beispiel der Gesamtdeutschen Volkspartei." PhD diss., Eberhard Karls University of Tübingen.

Kaack, Heino. 1971. *Geschichte und Struktur des deutschen Parteiensystems*. Opladen: Leske+Budrich.

Kaiser, Wolfram. 2007. *Christian Democracy and the Origins of European Union*. Cambridge: Cambridge University Press.

Kalyvas, Stathis N. 1996. *The Rise of Christian Democracy in Europe*. Ithaca, NY: Cornell University Press.

Kalyvas, Stathis N., and Kees van Kersbergen. 2010. "Christian Democracy." *Annual Review of Political Science* 13: 183–209.

Katz, Richard S. 1980. *A Theory of Parties and Electoral Systems*. Baltimore: Johns Hopkins University Press.

———. 1986. "Intraparty Preference Voting." In *Electoral Laws and Their Political Consequences*, edited by Bernard Grofman and Arend Lijphart, 85–103. New York: Agathon.

———. 2002. "The Internal Life of Parties." In *Political Parties in the New Europe: Political and Analytical Challenges*, edited by Kurt R. Luther and Ferdinand Müller-Rommel, 87–118. Oxford: Oxford University Press.

Katz, Richard S., and Peter Mair. 1992. "Introduction: The Cross-National Study of Party Organizations." In *Party Organizations: A Data Handbook on Party Organizations in Western Democracies, 1960–90*, edited by Richard S. Katz and Peter Mair, 1–20. London: Sage.

———. 1993. "The Evolution of Party Organizations in Europe. The Three Faces of Party Organization." *American Review of Politics* 14 (4): 593–617.

———. 1995. "Changing Models of Party Organization and Party Democracy: The Emergence of the Cartel Party." *Party Politics* 1 (1): 5–28.

Key, Vladimer Orlando. 1949. *Southern Politics in State and Nation*. New York: Knopf.

Khol, Andreas. 1980. "Zwischen Technokratie und Demokratie. Die Parteireform der ÖVP 1979/80." In *Österreichisches Jahrbuch für Politik '79*, edited by Andreas Khol and Alfred Stirnemann, 435–68. Vienna: Oldenbourg.

Kirchheimer, Otto. 1966. "The Transformation of the Western European Party System." In *Political Parties and Political Development*, edited by Joseph La Palombara and Myron Weiner, 177–200. Princeton, NJ: Princeton University Press.

Kitschelt, Herbert. 1989a. "The Internal Politics of Parties: The Law of Curvilinear Disparity Revisited." *Political Studies* 37 (3): 400–421.

———. 1989b. *The Logics of Party Formation: Ecological Politics in Belgium and West Germany*. Ithaca, NY: Cornell University Press.

———. 1994. *The Transformation of European Social Democracy*. Cambridge: Cambridge University Press.

Kitschelt, Herbert, and Daniel Kselman. 2010. "The Organizational Foundations of Democratic Accountability: Organizational Form and the Choice of Electoral Linkage Strategy." Paper presented at the annual meeting of the American Political Science Association, Washington, DC.

Kitschelt, Herbert, Zdenka Mansfeldova, Radoslaw Markowski, and Gabor Tóka. 1999. *Post-Communist Party Systems: Competition, Representation, and Inter-Party Cooperation*. New York: Cambridge University Press.

Kitschelt, Herbert, and Steven Wilkinson. 2007. "Citizen-Politician Linkages: An Introduction." In *Patrons, Clients and Policies: Patterns of Democratic Accountability and Political Competition*, edited by Herbert Kitschelt and Steven Wilkinson, 1–49. Cambridge: Cambridge University Press.

Klein, Michael. 2005. *Westdeutscher Protestantismus und politische Parteien: Anti-Parteien-Mentalität und parteipolitisches Engagement von 1945 bis 1963*. Tübingen: Mohr Siebeck.

Kleinmann, Hans-Otto. 1993. *Geschichte der CDU, 1945–1982*. Stuttgart: Deutsche Verlags-Anstalt.

———. 1996. "Adenauer, Albers und die Anfänge der CDU-Sozialausschüsse. Unveröffentlichte Briefe." *Historisch-Politische Mitteilungen* 3 (1): 195–206.

———. 1997. "Die gesellschaftliche Basis der CDU/CSU." In *Christian Democracy in the European Union , 1945/1995*, edited by Emiel Lamberts, 123–36. Leuven: Leuven University Press.

Klotzbach, Kurt. 1982. *Der Weg zur Staatspartei. Programmatik, praktische Politik und Organisation der deutschen Sozialdemokratie 1945 bis 1965.* Berlin: Dietz.

Koch, Dieter. 1972. *Heinemann und die Deutschlandfrage.* Munich: Kaiser.

Koelble, Thomas A. 1992. "Recasting Social Democracy in Europe: A Nested Game Explanation of Strategic Adjustment in Political Parties." *Politics & Society* 20 (1): 51–70.

Kohno, Masaru. 1992. "Rational Foundations for the Organization of the Liberal Democratic Party in Japan." *World Politics* 44 (3): 369–97.

Kolinsky, Eva. 1989. Introduction to *The Greens in West Germany: Organisation and Policy Making*, edited by Eva Kolinsky, 1–8. Oxford: Berg.

Köllner, Patrick. 2004. "Factionalism in Japanese Political Parties Revisited or How do Factions in the LDP and the DPJ Differ?" *Japan Forum* 16 (1): 87–109.

———. 2006. "The Liberal Democratic Party at 50: Sources of Dominance and Changes in the Koizumi Era." *Social Science Japan Journal* 9 (2): 243–57.

Koole, Ruud A. 1994. "The Vulnerability of the Modern Cadre Party in the Netherlands." In *How Parties Organize: Chance and Adaptation in Party Organizations in Western Democracies*, edited by Richard S. Katz and Peter Mair, 278–303. London: Sage.

Koole, Ruud A., and H. Van de Velde. 1992. "The Netherlands." In *Party Organizations: A Data Handbook*, edited by Richard S. Katz and Peter Mair, 619–731. London: Sage.

Kraemer, Jean-Pierre. 2008. "Politische Kultur und Organisation der CSV." In *Spiegelbild eines Landes und seiner Politik? Geschichte der Christlich-Sozialen Volkspartei Luxemburgs im 20. Jahrhundert*, edited by Gilbert Trausch, 741–92. Luxembourg: Saint Paul.

Krauss, Ellis S., and Robert J. Pekkanen. 2011. *The Rise and Fall of Japan's LDP: Political Party Organizations as Historical Institutions.* Ithaca, NY: Cornell University Press.

Kreuzer, Marcus. 2000. "Electoral Mechanisms and Electioneering Incentives. Vote-Getting Strategies of Japanese, French, British, German and Austrian Conservatives." *Party Politics* 6 (4): 487–504.

———. 2001. *Institutions and Innovation: Voters, Parties, and Interest Groups in the Consolidation of Democracy, France and Germany, 1870–1939.* Ann Arbor: University of Michigan Press.

Kriechbaumer, Robert. 1985. *Von der Illegalität zur Legalität. Gründungsgeschichte der ÖVP.* Vienna: Multiplex Media Verlag.

———. 1995a. "Geschichte der ÖVP." In *Volkspartei—Anspruch und Realität. Zur Geschichte der ÖVP seit 1945*, edited by Robert Kriechbaumer and Franz Schausberger, 11–101. Vienna: Böhlau.

Kriesi, Hanspeter, and Swen Hutter. 2019. "Crises and the Transformation of the National Political Space in Europe." In *European Party Politics in Times of Crisis*, edited by Swen Hutter and Hanspeter Kriesi, 3–33. Cambridge: Cambridge University Press.

Krouwel, André. 1993. "Het CDA als catch-all partij." In *Geloven in macht, de christen democratie in Nederland*, edited by Kees van Kersbergen, Hans-Martien ten Napel, and Paul Lucardie, 61–77. Amsterdam: Spinhuis.

Kselman, Thomas, and Joseph A. Buttigieg. 2003. *European Christian Democracy: Historical Legacies and Comparative Perspectives.* Notre Dame, IN: University of Notre Dame Press.

Lane, Jan-Erik, and Svante O. Errson. 1994. *Politics and Society in Western Europe.* London: Sage.

Langenbacher, Eric 2015. "Introduction: Merkel's Nachsommermärchen?" In *The Merkel Republic: An Appraisal*, edited by Eric Langenbacher, 1–25. New York: Berghahn.

Langston, Joy. 2006. "The Birth and Transformation of the Dedazo in Mexico." In *Informal Institutions and Democracy: Lessons from Latin America*, edited by Gretchen Helmke and Steven Levitsky, 143–59. Baltimore: Johns Hopkins University Press.

Lawson, Kay. 1988. "When Linkage Fails." In *When Parties Fail: Emerging Alternative Organizations*, edited by Kay Lawson and Peter Merkl, 13–38. Princeton, NJ: Princeton University Press.

Lehmann, Pola, Simon Franzmann, Tobias Burst, Sven Regel, Felicia Riethmüller, Andrea Volkens, Bernhard Weßels, and Lisa Zehnter. 2023. *The Manifesto Data Collection: Manifesto Project (MRG/CMP/MARPOR)*. Version 2023a. Berlin: Wissenschaftszentrum Berlin für Sozialforschung and Göttingen: Institut für Demokratieforschung. https://doi.org/10.25522/manifesto.mpds.2023a.

Leonardi, Robert, and Paolo Alberti. 2004. "From Dominance to Doom? Christian Democracy in Italy." In *Christian Democratic Parties in Europe since the End of the Cold War*, edited by Steven van Hecke and Emmanuel Gerard, 105–31. Leuven: Leuven University Press.

Leonardi, Robert, and Douglas A. Wertman. 1989. *Italian Christian Democracy: The Politics of Dominance*. London: Macmillan.

Lepszy, Norbert, and Christian Koecke. 2000. "Der Niederländische Christlich-Demokratische Appell (CDA)." In *Schweiz, Niederlande, Belgien, Luxemburg, Europäische Demokratische Union (EDU), Europäische Volkspartei (EVP)*, edited by Hans-Joachim Veen, 119–260. Vol. 5 of *Christlich-demokratische und konservative Parteien in Westeuropa*. Paderborn: Schöningh.

Letamendia, Pierre. 1995. *Le Mouvement Républicain Populaire. Le MRP: Histoire d'un grand parti français*. Paris: Beauchesne.

Levi, Arrigo. 1984. *La DC nell'Italia che cambia*. Bari: Laterza.

Levitsky, Steven. 2001. "An 'Organized Disorganization': Informal Organization and the Persistence of Local Party Structures in Argentine Peronism." *Journal of Latin American Studies* 33 (1): 29–65.

———. 2003. *Transforming the Labor-Based Parties in Latin America: Argentine Peronism in Comparative Perspective*. Cambridge: Cambridge University Press.

———. 2005. "Crisis and Renovation: Institutional Weakness and the Transformation of Argentine Peronism, 1983–2003." In *Argentine Democracy: The Politics of Institutional Weakness*, edited by Steven Levitsky and Maria V. Murillo, 181–206. University Park, PA: Penn State University Press.

Levy, Daniel C., and Kathleen Bruhn. 2006. *Mexico: The Struggle for Democratic Development*. Berkeley: University of California Press.

Lieberman, Robert. 2002. "Ideas, Institutions, and Political Order: Explaining Political Change." *American Political Science Review* 96 (4): 697–712.

Loewenberg, Gerhard. 1971. "The Remaking of the German Party System." In *European Politics: A Reader*, edited by Mattei Dogan and Richard Rose, 259–80. Boston: Little Brown.

Lois, Daniel. 2011. "Church Membership and Church Attendance across Time: A Trend Analysis Considering Differences between East and West Germany." *Comparative Population Studies* 36 (1): 161–92.

Lucardie, Paul, and Hans-Martien ten Napel. 1994. "Between Confessionalism and Liberal Conservatism: The Christian Democratic Parties of Belgium and the Netherlands." In *Christian Democracy in Europe: A Comparative Perspective*, edited by David Hanley, 51–70. London: Pinter.

Lupu, Noam. 2016. *Party Brands in Crisis: Partisanship, Brand Dilution, and the Breakdown of Political Parties in Latin America*. New York: Cambridge University Press.

Luther, Kurt Richard. 1991. "Die Freiheitliche Partei Österreichs." In *Handbuch des Politischen Systems Österreichs*, edited by Herbert Dachs, Helmut Kramer, Wolfgang C. Müller, and Emmerich Tálos, 247–62. Vienna: Mansche Verlags- und Universitätsbuchhandlung.

———. 2003. "The FPÖ. From Populist Protest to Incumbency." In *Right-Wing Extremism in the Twenty-First Century*, edited by Peter Merkl and Leonard Weinberg, 185–211. London: Frank Cass.

———. 2009. "The Revival of the Radical Right: The Austrian Parliamentary Election of 2008." *West European Politics* 32 (5): 1049–61.

Macrae, Duncan, Jr. 1963. "Intraparty Divisions and Cabinet Coalitions in the Fourth French Republic." *Comparative Studies in Society and History* 5 (2): 164–211.

Madison, James. (1787) 1961. "Federalist No. 10: The Size and Variety of the Union as a Check on Faction." In *The Federalist*, edited by Alexander Hamilton, James Madison, and John Jay, 129–36. Cambridge, MA: Harvard University Press.

Magone, Jose M. 1999. "Portugal: Party System Installation and Consolidation." In *Changing Party Systems in Western Europe*, edited by David Broughton and Mark Donovan, 232–54. London: Pinter.

Magri, Francesco. 1954. *La Democrazia Cristiana in Italia, 1897–1949*. Milan: La Fiaccola.

Mahoney, James, and Kathleen Thelen. 2010. *Explaining Institutional Change: Ambiguity, Agency, and Power*. Cambridge: Cambridge University Press.

Mair, Peter. 1997. *Party System Change: Approaches and Interpretations*. Oxford: Clarendon Press.

Majerus, Jean-Marie. 2008. "Die Partei und die Bauernorganisation." In *Spiegelbild eines Landes und seiner Politik? Geschichte der Christlich-Sozialen Volkspartei Luxemburgs im 20. Jahrhundert*, edited by Gilbert Trausch, 627–73. Luxembourg: Saint Paul.

Mannewitz, Tom 2017. "Really 'Two Deeply Divided Electorates'? German Federal Elections 1990–2013." *German Politics* 26 (2): 219–34.

Mark, Craig. 2016. *The Abe Restoration: Contemporary Japanese Politics and Reformation*. Lanham, MD: Lexington.

Mattesini, Maria Chiara. 2012. *La Base. Un laboratorio di idee per la Democrazia Cristiana*. Rome: Studium.

Matuschek, Peter. 2008. *Erfolg und Misserfolg konservativer Parteien. Die spanische AP-PP und das portugiesische CDS-PP im Vergleich*. Wiesbaden: VS Verlag.

May, John D. 1973. "Opinion Structure of Political Parties: The Special Law of Curvilinear Disparity." *Political Studies* 21 (2): 135–51.

Mayeur, Jean-Marie. 1980. *Des partis catholiques à la Démocratie Chrétienne: XIXe–XXe siècles*. Paris: Colin.

McAllister, Ian. 1991. "Party Adaption and Factionalism within the Australian Party System." *American Journal of Political Science* 35 (1): 206–27.

McCloskey, Herbert, Paul Hoffman, and Rosemary O'Hara. 1960. "Issue Conflict and Consensus among Party Leaders and Followers." *American Political Science Review* 54: 406–27.

McDonnell, Duncan. 2013. "Silvio Berlusconi's Personal Parties: From Forza Italia to the Popolo Della Liberta." *Political Studies* 61 (1): 217–33.

Merkl, Peter H. 1978. "Factionalism: The Limits of the West German Party-State." In *Faction Politics: Political Parties and Factionalism in Comparative Perspective*, edited by Frank P. Belloni and Dennis C. Beller, 245–64. Santa Barbara, CA: ABC Clio.

Michels, Robert. (1911) 1959. *Political Parties: A Sociological Study of the Oligarchical Tendencies of Modern Democracy*. New York: Dover.

Misner, Paul. 2004. "Catholic Labor and Catholic Action: The Italian Context of 'Quadragesimo Anno.'" *Catholic Historical Review* 90 (4): 650–74.

Mitchell, Maria. 2012. *The Origins of Christian Democracy: Politics and Confession in Modern Germany*. Ann Arbor: University of Michigan Press.

Morgan, Jana. 2011. *Bankrupt Representation and Party System Collapse*. University Park, PA: Penn State University Press.

Morgenstern, Scott. 2001. "Organized Factions and Disorganized Parties: Electoral Incentives in Uruguay." *Party Politics* 7 (2): 235–56.

Mosley, Philip. 1950. "The Occupation of Germany: New Light on How the Zones Were Drawn." *Foreign Affairs* 28 (4): 580–604.

Mudde, Cas. 2007. *Populist Radical Right Parties in Europe*. Cambridge: Cambridge University Press.

———. 2019. *The Far Right Today*. Cambridge: Polity.

Müller, Jan-Werner. 2011. *Contesting Democracy. Political Ideas in Twentieth-Century Europe*. New Haven, CT: Yale University Press.

Müller, Josef. 1990. *Die Gesamtdeutsche Volkspartei. Entstehung und Politik unter dem Primat nationaler Wiedervereinigung, 1950–1957*. Düsseldorf: Droste.

Müller, Wolfgang C. 1984. "Direktwahl und Parteiensystem." In *Jahrbuch für Politik 1983*, edited by Andreas Khol and Alfred Stirnemann, 83–112. Vienna: Oldenbourg.

———. 1985. "Die Rolle der Parteien bei Entstehung und Entwicklung der Sozialpartnerschaft." In *Sozialpartnerschaft in der Krise. Leistungen und Grenzen des Neokorporatismus in Österreich*, edited by Peter Gerlich, Edgar Grande, and Wolfgang C. Müller, 135–224. Vienna: Böhlau.

———. 1989a. "Neuere Entwicklungen der Persönlichkeitswahl in Österreich." In *Österreichisches Jahrbuch für Politik 1988. Sonderdruck*, edited by Andreas Khol, Günther Ofner, and Alfred Stirnemann, 671–92. Vienna: Oldenbourg.

———. 1989b. "Party Patronage in Austria: Theoretical Considerations and Empirical Findings." In *The Austrian Party System*, edited by Anton Pelinka and Fritz Plasser, 327–56. Boulder, CO: Westview Press.

———. 1991. "Die Österreichische Volkspartei." In *Handbuch des Politischen Systems Österreichs*, edited by Herbert Dachs, Peter Gerlich, Horner Gottweis et al., 227–46. Vienna: Manzsche.

———. 1992. "Austria. 1945–1990." In *Party Organizations: A Data Handbook*, edited by Richard S. Katz and Peter Mair, 21–120. London: Sage.

———. 1994. "The Development of Austrian Party Organization in the Post-War Period." In *How Parties Organize: Change and Adaptation in Party Organizations in Western Democracies*, edited by Richard S. Katz and Peter Mair, 51–79. London: Sage.

———. 1996. "Die Organisation der SPÖ, 1945–1995." In *Die Organisation der österreichischen Sozialdemokratie*, edited by Wolfgang Maderthaner and Wolfgang C. Müller, 195–357. Vienna: Löcker.

———. 2000. "Patronage by National Governments." In *The Nature of Party Government: A Comparative European Perspective*, edited by Jean Blondel and Maurizio Cotta, 141–60. New York: Palgrave.

———. 2005. "Austria: A Complex Electoral System With Subtle Effects." In *The Politics of Electoral Systems*, edited by Michael Gallagher and Paul Mitchell, 398–416. Oxford: Oxford University Press.

Müller, Wolfgang C., and Delia Meth-Cohn. 1991. "The Selection of Party Chairmen in Austria: A Study in Intra-Party Decision-Making." *European Journal of Political Research* 20: 39–65.

Müller, Wolfgang C., Fritz Plasser, and Peter A. Ulram. 2004. "Party Responses to the Erosion
of Voter Loyalties in Austria: Weakness as an Advantage and Strength as a Handicap." In
Political Parties and Electoral Change: Party Responses to Electoral Markets, edited by Peter
Mair, Wolfgang C. Müller, and Fritz Plasser, 145–78. London: Sage.

Müller, Wolfgang C., and Barbara Steininger. 1994a. "Christian Democracy in Austria: The Austrian People's Party." In *Christian Democracy in Europe: A Comparative Perspective*, edited
by David Hanley, 87–100. London: Pinter.

———. 1994b. "Party Organisation and Party Competitiveness: The Case of the Austrian People's
Party, 1945–1992." *European Journal of Political Research* 26 (1): 1–29.

Müller, Wolfgang C., and Peter A. Ulram. 1995. "The Social and Demographic Structure of Austrian Parties, 1945–93." *Party Politics* 1 (1): 145–60.

Neumann, Arijana. 2012. *Die CDU auf Landesebene. Politische Strategien im Vergleich*. Wiesbaden: VS Verlag.

Nordsieck, Wolfram. 2021. *Parties and Elections: The Database about Parliamentary Elections
and Political Parties in Europe*. http://parties-and-elections.eu/.

Norris, Pippa. 1995. "May's Law of Curvilinear Disparity Revisited: Leaders, Officers, Members
and Voters in British Political Parties." *Party Politics* 1 (1): 29–47.

North, Douglas C. 1990. *Institutions, Institutional Change and Economic Performance*. Cambridge: Cambridge University Press.

Obinger, Herbert. 2005. "Austria. Strong Parties in a Weak Federal Polity." In *Federalism and the
Welfare State: New World and European Experiences*, edited by Herbert Obinger, Stephan
Leibfried, and Francis Castles, 181–221. Cambridge: Cambridge University Press.

Olson, Mancur. 1965. *The Logic of Collective Action: Public Goods and the Theory of Groups*.
Cambridge, MA: Harvard University Press.

Oppelland, Torsten. 1998. "Der Evangelische Arbeitskreis der CDU/CSU, 1952–1969." *Historisch-
Politische Mitteilungen* 5 (1): 105–43.

Orren, Karen, and Stephen Skowronek. 1996. "Institutions and Intercurrence: Theory Building
in the Fullness of Time." In *Nomos 38: Political Order*, edited by Ian Shapiro and Russell
Hardin, 111–46. New York: New York University Press.

Page, Scott. 2006. "Path Dependence." *Quarterly Journal of Political Science* 1 (1): 87–115.

Panebianco, Angelo. 1988. *Political Parties: Organization and Power*. Cambridge: Cambridge
University Press.

Pappas, Takis S. 2001. "In Search of the Center: Conservative Parties, Electoral Competition,
and Political Legitimacy in Southern Europe's New Democracies." In *Parties, Politics, and
Democracy in the New Southern Europe*, edited by P. Nikiforos Diamandouros, and Richard
Gunther, 224–67. Baltimore: Johns Hopkins University Press.

Parisella, Antonio. 1997. "La Base sociale della Democrazia cristiana. Elettorato, iscritti e or-
ganizzazione." In *Christian Democracy in the European Union, 1945/1995*, edited by Emiel
Lamberts, 189–209. Leuven: Leuven University Press.

Park, Cheol Hee. 2001. "Factional Dynamics in Japan's LDP since Political Reform: Continuity
and Change." *Asian Survey* 41 (3): 428–61.

Park, Gene. 2011. "The Politics of Scarcity: Fixing Japan's Public Finances." In *The Routledge
Handbook of Japanese Politics*, edited by Alisa Gaunder, 273–83. Milton Park: Routledge.

Pasquino, Gianfranco. 1972. "Le radici del frazionismo e il voto di preferenza." *Rivista italiana di
scienza politica* 2 (2): 353–68.

Patch, William. 2018. *Christian Democratic Workers and the Forging of German Democracy, 1920–1980*. Cambridge: Cambridge University Press.

Pearson, Benjamin. 2010. "The Pluralization of Protestant Politics: Public Responsibility, Rearmament, and Division at the 1950s Kirchentage." *Central European History* 43 (2): 270–300.

Pelinka, Anton. 2009. "Das politische System Österreichs." In *Die politischen Systeme Westeuropas*, edited by Wolfgang Ismayr, 607–41. Opladen: VS Verlag.

Pierson, Paul. 1993. "When Effect Becomes Cause: Policy Feedback and Political Change." *World Politics* 45 (4): 595–628.

———. 2000a. "Increasing Returns, Path Dependence, and the Study of Politics." *American Political Science Review* 94 (2): 251–67.

———. 2000b. "Not Just What, but When: Timing and Sequence in Political Processes." *Studies in American Political Development* 14 (1): 72–92.

Plasser, Fritz, Franz Sommer, and Peter Ulram. 1991. "Eine Kanzler- und Protestwahl. Wählerverhalten und Wahlmotive bei der Nationalratswahl 1990." In *Österreichisches Jahrbuch Für Politik 1990*, edited by Andreas Khol, Günther Ofner, and Alfred Stirnemann, 95–147. Munich: Oldenbourg.

Plaza, Arthur. 2008. "From Christian Militants to Republican Renovators: The Third Ralliement of Catholics in Postwar France, 1944–1965." PhD diss., New York University.

Poguntke, Thomas. 1994. "Parties in a Legalistic Culture: The Case of Germany." In *How Parties Organize: Change and Adaptation in Party Organizations in Western Democracies*, edited by Richard S. Katz and Peter Mair, 185–215. London: Sage.

———. 1998. "Party Organizations." In *Comparative Politics: The Problem of Equivalence*, edited by Jan Van Deth, 156–79. London: Routledge.

———. 2000. *Parteiorganisation im Wandel. Gesellschaftliche Verankerung und Organisatorische Anpassung im Europäischen Vergleich*. Wiesbaden: Westdeutscher Verlag.

———. 2002. "Parties without Firm Social Roots? Party Organisational Linkage." In *Political Parties in the New Europe: Political and Analytical Challenges*, edited by Kurt Richard Luther and Ferdinand Müller-Rommel, 43–62. Oxford: Oxford University Press.

———. 2006. "Political Parties and Other Organizations." In *Handbook of Party Politics*, edited by Richard S. Katz and William Crotty, 396–405. London: Sage.

Poguntke, Thomas, and Bernhard Boll. 1992. "Germany." In *Party Organizations: A Data Handbook*, edited by Richard S. Katz and Paul Mair, 317–88. London: Sage.

Poguntke, Thomas, Susan E. Scarrow, Paul D. Webb, Elin H. Allern, Nicholas Aylott, Ingrid van Biezen, Enrico Calossi, Marina Costa Lobo, William P Cross, Kris Deschouwer, Zsolt Enyedi, Elodie Fabre, David M Farrell, Anika Gauja, Eugenio Pizzimenti, Petr Kopecký, Ruud Koole, Wolfgang C. Müller, Karina Kosiara-Pedersen, Gideon Rahat, Aleks Szczerbiak, Emilie van Haute, and Tània Verge. 2016. "Party Rules, Party Resources and the Politics of Parliamentary Democracies: How Parties Organize in the 21st Century." *Party Politics* 22 (6): 661–78. https://doi.org/10.1177/1354068816662493.

Pollack, Detlef, and Gert Pickel. 2003. "Deinstitutionalisierung des Religiösen und religiöse Individualisierung in Ost- und Westdeutschland." *Kölner Zeitschrift für Soziologie und Sozialpsychologie* 55 (3): 447–74.

Pollock, James K. 1955. "The West German Electoral Law of 1953." *American Political Science Review* 49 (1): 107–30.

Pombeni, Paolo. 1976. *Le "Cronache sociali" di Dossetti, 1947–1951*. Florence: Vallecchi.

———. 1979. *Il gruppo dossettiano e la fondazione della democrazia cristiana (1938–1948)*. Bologna: Mulino.

Pridham, Geoffrey. 1977. *Christian Democracy in Western Germany: The CDU/CSU in Government and Opposition. 1945–1976*. London: Croom Helm.

———. 1979. "The Italian Christian Democrats after Moro: Crisis or Compromise." *West European Politics* 2 (1): 69–88.

Przeworski, Adam. 2019. *Crises of Democracy*. Cambridge: Cambridge University Press.

Przeworski, Adam, and John Sprague. 1986. *Paper Stones: A History of Electoral Socialism*. Chicago: University of Chicago Press.

Rae, Douglas. 1967. *The Political Consequences of Electoral Laws*. New Haven, CT: Yale University Press.

Rahat, Gideon, and Ofer Kenig. 2018. *From Party Politics to Personalized Politics? Party Change and Political Personalization in Democracies*. Oxford: Oxford University Press.

Rauchensteiner, Manfried. 1979. *Der Sonderfall. Die Besatzungszeit in Österreich 1945 bis 1955*. Graz: Styria.

———. 1987. *Die Zwei. Die große Koalition in Österreich 1945–1966*. Vienna: Österreichischer Bundesverlag.

Reed, Steven. 2011. "The Liberal Democratic Party: An Explanation of Its Success and Failures." In *The Routledge Handbook of Japanese Politics*, edited by Alisa Gaunder, 14–23. Milton Park: Routledge.

Reed, Steven, and Michael Thies. 2003. "The Causes of Electoral Reform in Japan." In *Mixed-Member Electoral Systems: The Best of Both Worlds*, edited by Matthew S. Shugart and Martin Wattenberg, 152–72. Oxford: Oxford University Press.

Reichhold, Ludwig. 1975. *Geschichte der ÖVP*. Graz: Styria.

Rémond, René. 1969. *The Right Wing in France: From 1815 to de Gaulle*. Philadelphia: University of Pennsylvania Press.

Rensmann, Lars. 2015. "The Reluctant Cosmopolitanization of European Party Politics: The Case of Germany." In *The Merkel Republic: An Appraisal*, edited by Eric Langenbacher, 136–61. New York: Berghahn.

Rioux, Jean-Pierre. 1987. *The Fourth Republic: 1944–1958*. Cambridge: Cambridge University Press.

Ritter, Gerhard A. 1990. "The Social Bases of the German Political Parties: 1867–1920." In *Elections, Parties and Political Traditions: Social Foundation of German Parties and Party Systems, 1867–1987*, edited by Karl Rohe, 27–52. Providence, RI: Berg Publishers.

Roberts, Kenneth. 1998. *Deepening Democracy? The Modern Left and Social Movements in Chile and Peru*. Stanford, CA: Stanford University Press.

Rogers, Daniel. 1995. *Politics after Hitler: The Western Allies and the German Party System*. Basingstoke, UK: Macmillan.

Rois, Christian. 2016. "Der Weg zum neuen ÖVP-Grundsatzprogramm und -Organisationsstatut. 'Evolution Volkspartei' aus der Perspektive der Organisationsentwicklung." In *Österreichisches Jahrbuch für Politik*, edited by Günther Ofner, Stefan Karner, and Dietmar Halper, 95–108. Vienna: Böhlau.

Rossi, Maurizio, and Ettore Scappini. 2012. "How Should Mass Attendance Be Measured? An Italian Case Study." *Quality and Quantity* 46 (6): 1897–1916.

Rossi-Doria, Anna. 1996. *Diventare cittadine. Il voto alle donne in Italia*. Florence: Giunti.

Rovan, Joseph. 1956. *Le Catholicisme politique en Allemagne*. Paris: Éditions du Seuil.

Sa'adah, Anne. 1987. "Le Mouvement républicain populaire et la reconstitution du système partisan français, 1944–1951." *Revue française de science politique* 37 (1): 33–58.

Sartori, Giovanni. 1966. "European Political Parties: The Case of Polarized Pluralism." In *Political Parties and Political Development*, edited by Joseph La Palombara and Myron Weiner, 137–76. Princeton, NJ: Princeton University Press.

———. 1971. "Proporzionalismo, frazionismo e crisi dei partiti." *Rivista italiana di scienza politica* 1 (3): 629–55.

———. 1976. *Parties and Party Systems: A Framework for Analysis*. Cambridge: Cambridge University Press.

Sauer, Thomas. 1999. *Westorientierung im deutschen Protestantismus? Vorstellungen und Tätigkeit des Kronberger Kreises*. Munich: Oldenbourg.

Scarrow, Susan. 2014. *Beyond Party Members: Changing Approaches to Partisan Mobilization*. Oxford: Oxford University Press.

Scarrow, Susan, Paul D. Webb, and Thomas Poguntke. 2017. *Organizing Political Parties*. Oxford: Oxford University Press.

Schattschneider, Elmer Eric. 1942. *Party Government*. New York: Farrar & Rinehart.

Schlesinger, Joseph A. 1984. "On the Theory of Party Organization." *Journal of Politics* 46 (2): 369–400.

Schmid, Josef. 1990. *Die CDU. Organisationsstrukturen, Politiken und Funktionsweisen einer Partei im Föderalismus*. Opladen: Leske+Budrich.

Schmitt, Hermann, and Andreas Wüst. 2006. "The Extraordinary Bundestag Election of 2005: The Interplay of Long-Term Trends and Short-Term Factors." In *Launching the Grand Coalition: The 2005 Bundestag Election and the Future of German Politics*, edited by Eric Langenbacher, 29–48. New York: Berghahn.

Schmitt-Beck, Rüdiger. 2014. "Euro-Kritik, Wirtschaftspessimismus und Einwanderungsskepsis. Hintergründe des Beinah-Wahlerfolges der Alternative für Deutschland (AfD) bei der Bundestagswahl 2013." *Zeitschrift für Parlamentsfragen* 45 (1): 94–112.

Schoentgen, Marc. 2008. "Von der Rechtspartei zur CSV. Gründung, Konsolidierung und Generationswechsel (1940–1959)." In *Spiegelbild eines Landes und seiner Politik? Geschichte der Christlich-Sozialen Volkspartei Luxemburgs im 20. Jahrhundert*, edited by Gilbert Trausch, 241–328. Luxembourg: Saint Paul.

Schönbohm, Wulf. 1985. *Die CDU wird moderne Volkspartei. Selbstverständnis, Mitglieder, Organisation und Apparat 1950–1980*. Stuttgart: Klett-Cotta.

Schroen, Michael. 2000. "Die Christlich-Soziale Volkspartei Luxemburgs." In *Schweiz, Niederlande, Belgien, Luxemburg, Europäische Demokratische Union (EDU), Europäische Volkspartei (EVP)*, edited by Hans-Joachim Veen, 337–404. Vol. 5 of *Christlich-demokratische und konservative Parteien in Westeuropa*. Paderborn: Schöningh.

Schwarz, Hans-Peter. 1995. *Konrad Adenauer: A German Politician and Statesman in a Period of War, Revolution and Reconstruction*, vol. 1, *From the German Empire to the Federal Republic, 1876–1952*. Oxford: Berghahn.

———. 2014. *Helmut Kohl. Eine politische Biographie*. Munich: Pantheon.

Scoppola, Pietro. 1963. *Dal Neoguelfismo alla Democrazia Cristiana*. Rome: Studium.

———. 1991. *La repubblica dei partiti. Profilo storico della democrazia in Italia (1945–1990)*. Bologna: Mulino.

Seawright, Jason. 2012. *Party System Collapse: The Roots of Crisis in Peru and Venezuela*. Stanford, CA: Stanford University Press.

Secher, Herbert. 1959. "The Socialist Party of Austria: Principles, Organization and Politics." *Midwest Journal of Political Science* 3 (3): 277–99.

Sharp, Tony. 1975. *The Wartime Alliance and the Zonal Division of Germany*. Oxford: Oxford University Press.

Shugart, Matthew S. 2005. "Comparative Electoral Systems Research: The Maturation of a Field and New Challenges Ahead." In *The Politics of Electoral Systems*, edited by Michael Gallagher and Paul Mitchell, 25–56. Oxford: Oxford University Press.

Skocpol, Theda, and Vanessa Williamson. 2012. *The Tea Party and the Remaking of Republican Conservatism*. New York: Oxford University Press.

Smith, Denis Mack. 1997. *Modern Italy. A Political History*. New Haven, CT: Yale University Press.

Spary, Peter, and Hans-Dieter Lehnen. 2000. Geschichte der Mittelstands- und Wirtschaftsvereinigung der CDU/CSU. http://www.mit-md.de/mediapool/136/1366541/data/Geschichte _der_MIT.pdf.

Stickler, Matthias. 2004. *Ostdeutsch heißt gesamtdeutsch. Organisation, Selbstverständnis und heimatpolitische Zielsetzungen der deutschen Vertriebenenverbände 1949–1972*. Düsseldorf: Droste.

Stirnemann, Alfred. 1980. "Innerparteiliche Demokratie in der ÖVP." In *Österreichisches Jahrbuch für Politik 1979*, edited by Alfred Stirnemann and Andreas Khol, 391–433. Vienna: Oldenbourg.

———. 1981. "Innerparteiliche Gruppenbildung am Beispiel der ÖVP." In *Österreichisches Jahrbuch für Politik 1980*, edited by Andreas Khol and Alfred Stirnemann, 415–48. Munich: Oldenbourg.

———. 1993. "Zwischen Zielgruppen- und Kommunikationsproblemen. Die Parteireform der ÖVP 1991." In *Österreichisches Jahrbuch für Politik 1992*, edited by Andreas Khol, Günther Ofner, and Alfred Stirnemann, 669–93. Munich: Oldenbourg.

Strauß, Franz Josef. 1989. *Die Erinnerungen*. Berlin: Siedler.

Streeck, Wolfgang, and Kathleen Thelen. 2005. *Beyond Continuity: Institutional Change in Advanced Political Economies*. Oxford: Oxford University Press.

Strickler, Matthias. 2004. *Organisation, Selbstverständnis und heimatpolitische Zielsetzungen der deutschen Vertriebenenverbände 1949–1972*. Düsseldorf: Droste.

Strøm, Kaare. 1990. "A Behavioral Theory of Competitive Political Parties." *American Journal of Political Science* 34 (2): 565–98.

Strøm, Kaare, and Wolfgang C. Müller. 1999. "Political Parties and Hard Choices." In *Policy, Office, or Votes? How Political Parties in Western Europe Make Hard Decisions*, edited by Wolfgang C. Müller and Kaare Strøm, 1–35. Cambridge: Cambridge University Press.

Sully, Melanie. 1991. "The Austrian Election of 1990." *Electoral Studies* 10 (1): 77–80.

———. 1995. "The Austrian Election of 1994." *Electoral Studies* 14 (2): 218–22.

Sveinsdóttir, Hulda Thora. 2004. "For Disharmony and Strength: Factionalism within the Conservative Parties in Japan, 1945–1964." PhD diss., University of Newcastle.

Tálos, Emmerich. 1985. "Sozialpartnerschaft. Zur Entwicklung und Entwicklungsdynamik kooperativkonzentrierter Politik in Österreich." In *Sozialpartnerschaft in der Krise. Leistungen und Grenzen des Neokorporatismus in Österreich*, edited by Peter Gerlich, Edgar Grande and Wolfgang C. Müller, 41–83. Vienna: Böhlau.

Tanaka, Martin. 2005. "Peru, 1980–2000: Chronicle of a Death Foretold? Determinism, Political Decisions, and Open Outcomes." In *The Third Wave of Democratization in Latin America:*

Advances and Setbacks, edited by Frances Hagopian and Scott Mainwaring, 261–88. New York: Cambridge University Press.

Thayer, Nathaniel. 1969. *How the Conservatives Rule Japan*. Princeton, NJ: Princeton University Press.

Thelen, Kathleen. 2004. *How Institutions Evolve: The Political Economy of Skills in Germany, Britain, the United States, and Japan*. New York: Cambridge University Press.

Turner, Ed. 2013. "The CDU and Party Organizational Change." *German Politics* 22 (1–2): 114–33.

Van Biezen, Ingrid. 2003. *Political Parties in New Democracies: Party Organization in Southern and East-Central Europe*. New York: Palgrave.

Van Hecke, Steven, and Emmanuel Gerard. 2004. *Christian Democratic Parties in Europe since the End of the Cold War*. Leuven: Leuven University Press.

Van Holsteyn, Joop J. M., Josje M. Den Ridder, and Ruud A. Koole. 2017. "From May's Laws to May's Legacy: On the Opinion Structure within Political Parties." *Party Politics* 23 (5): 471–86.

Van Kemseke, Peter. 2006. *Towards an Era of Development: The Globalization of Socialism and Christian Democracy*. Leuven: Leuven University Press.

Van Kersbergen, Kees. 1994. "The Distinctiveness of Christian Democracy." In *Christian Democracy in Europe: A Comparative Perspective*, edited by David Hanley, 31–47. London: Pinter.

———. 1995. *Social Capitalism: A Study of Christian Democracy and the Welfare State*. London: Routledge.

———. 1999. "Contemporary Christian Democracy and the Demise of the Politics of Mediation." In *Continuity and Change in Contemporary Capitalism*, edited by Herbert Kitschelt, Peter Lange, Gary Marks, and John D. Stephens, 346–70. Cambridge: Cambridge University Press.

———. 2008. "The Christian Democratic Phoenix and Modern Unsecular Politics." *Party Politics* 14 (3): 259–79.

Vaussard, Maurice. 1956. *Histoire de la Démocratie Chrétienne. France, Belgique, Italie*. Paris: Éditions du Seuil.

Vezzoni, Christiano, and Ferruccio Biolcati-Rinaldi. 2015. "Church Attendance and Religious Change in Italy, 1968–2010: A Multilevel Analysis of Pooled Datasets." *Journal for the Scientific Study of Religion* 54 (1): 100–18.

Vinen, Richard. 1995. *Bourgeois Politics in France*. Cambridge: Cambridge University Press.

Volkmann, Hans-Erich. 1988. "Adenauer und die deutschlandpolitischen Opponenten in CDU und CSU." In *Adenauer und die deutsche Frage*, edited by Josef Foschepoth, 183–206. Göttingen: Vandenhoeck & Ruprecht.

Von dem Berge, Benjamin, and Thomas Poguntke. 2017. "Varieties of Intra-Party Democracy: Conceptualization and Index Construction." In *Organizing Political Parties: Representation, Participation, and Power*, edited by Susan Scarrow, Paul Webb, and Thomas Poguntke, 136–57. Oxford: Oxford University Press.

Wagner, Andreas. 2014. *Wandel und Fortschritt in den Christdemokratien Europas. Christdemokratische Elegien angesichts fragiler volksparteilicher Symmetrien*. Wiesbaden: Springer.

Waldner, David. 2014. "What Makes Process Tracing Good? Causal Mechanisms, Causal Inference, and the Completeness Standard in Comparative Politics." In *Process Tracing: From Metaphor to Analytic Tool*, edited by Andrew Bennett and Jeffrey Checkel, 126–52. New York: Cambridge University Press.

Warner, Carolyn M. 1996. "The New Catholic Parties: The Popolari, Patto Segni and CCD." In *Italy: Politics and Policy*, edited by Robert Leonardi and Raffaella Y. Nanetti, 134–51. Aldershot: Dartmouth.

———. 2000. *Confessions of an Interest Group: The Catholic Church and Political Parties in Europe*. Princeton, NJ: Princeton University Press.

Wauters, Bram. 2014. "Democratising Party Leadership Selection in Belgium: Motivations and Decision Makers." *Political Studies* 62 (1): 61–80.

Webb, Paul, Thomas Poguntke, and Susan Scarrow. 2017. "Conclusion." In *Organizing Political Parties: Representation, Participation, and Power*, edited by Susan Scarrow, Paul Webb, and Thomas Poguntke, 307–19. Oxford: Oxford University Press.

Webster, Richard A. 1961. *Christian Democracy in Italy. 1860–1960*. London: Hollis and Carter.

Wertman, Douglas A. 1988. "Italy: Local Involvement, Central Control." In *Candidate Selection in Comparative Perspective: The Secret Garden of Politics*, edited by Michael Gallagher and Michael Marsh. 145–68. London: Sage.

———. 1995. "The Last Year of the Christian Democratic Party." In *Italian Politics: Ending the First Republic*, edited by Carol Mershon and Gianfranco Pasquino, 135–50. Boulder, CO: Westview.

Wiliarty, Sarah. 2010. *The CDU and the Politics of Gender in Germany: Bringing Women to the Party*. New York: Cambridge University Press.

———. 2013. "Gender as a Modernising Force in the German CDU." *German Politics* 22 (1–2): 172–90.

Wills-Otero, Laura. 2016. "The Electoral Performance of Latin American Traditional Parties, 1978–2006: Does the Internal Structure Matter?" *Party Politics* 22 (6): 758–72.

Wlezien, Christopher. 1995. "The Public as Thermostat. Dynamics of Preferences for Spending." *American Journal of Political Science* 39 (4): 981–1000.

Woloch, Isser. 2007. "Left, Right and Centre: The MRP and the Post-War Moment." *French History* 21 (1): 85–106.

Zariski, Raphael. 1962. "The Italian Socialist Party: A Case Study in Factional Conflict." *American Political Science Review* 56 (2): 372–90.

———. 1965. "Intra-Party Conflict in a Dominant Party: The Experience of Italian Christian Democracy." *Journal of Politics* 27 (1): 3–34.

———. 1978. "Party Factions and Comparative Politics: Some Empirical Findings." In *Faction Politics: Political Parties and Factionalism in Comparative Perspective*, edited by Dennis C. Beller and Frank P. Belloni, 19–38. Santa Barbara, CA: ABC Clio.

Ziblatt, Daniel. 2017. *Conservative Parties and the Birth of Democracy*. Cambridge: Cambridge University Press.

Zielonka, Jan. 2018. *Counter-Revolution: Liberal Europe in Retreat*. Oxford: Oxford University Press.

Zuckerman, Alan S. 1979. *The Politics of Faction: Christian Democratic Rule in Italy*. New Haven, CT: Yale University Press.

Index

www.ingramcontent.com/pod-product-compliance
Lightning Source LLC
Chambersburg PA
CBHW032118020426
42334CB00016B/992